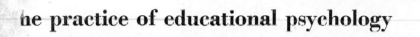

he practice of educational psychology

The practice of educational psychology

Maurice Chazan

Terence Moore

Phillip Williams

Jack Wright

with a chapter by *Muriel Walker*

LONGMAN

LONGMAN GROUP LIMITED
London
and LONGMAN INC.,
New York
Associated companies, branches and representatives
throughout the world

© Longman Group Limited 1974

First published 1974

ISBN 0582 50012 5
Library of Congress Catalog Card Number: 73-91457

Set in Monotype 11 on 12 pt Modern

and printed in Great Britain
by Western Printing Services Limited
Bristol

Contents

Acknowledgements

We are grateful to the following for permission to reproduce copyright material:
The Controller of Her Majesty's Stationery Office for data and graphs from *Ministry of Education Circular 347 of 1959, The Visually Handicapped*, Department of Education and Science 1973 and *Psychologists in Education Services*, Department of Education and Science 1968; also for Circular 3/74, Department of Education and Science 1974; Macmillan Publishing Company, Inc. of New York for 'Table of Types of Reliability Coefficients' from *Psychological Testing* 2nd edition by Anne Anastasi; David McKay Company, Inc. for a Table from *Statistics in Psychology and Education* by H. E. Garrett, copyright © 1966 by the David McKay Company, Inc. and published by them; the Open University for Data Collection from 'Practical Aspects of Data Collection' in Block 3 of *Educational Enquiry* by D. L. Nuttall and B. M. Moore (1973); the author for 2 tables from 'On Comparing Scores from Tests of Attainment with Scores from Tests of Ability to obtain Indices of Retardation by Differences or Ratios,' unpublished dissertation, Birmingham University 1961 by C. J. Phillips and the University of London Press for a figure from *Intelligence and Attainment Tests* by P. E. Vernon.

Foreword

The purpose of this book is to present an outline of the way in which educational psychology is applied in the work of school psychological services. Since the book is largely 'child-oriented' it might have been subtitled 'a handbook of psychological work with pupils and parents'. It has been prepared because the authors feel that texts of this kind will be needed to meet the demands of the increasing numbers of psychology graduates who train as educational and child psychologists. It will also be helpful in giving undergraduates who take honours courses in child and educational psychology some idea of the skills which will be used if they decide later to follow a career as psychologist in the education services. The gap between the theoretical work of the degree and the practical work of the applied psychologist is often a wide one. This book may help to make the gap easier to cross.

In order to appreciate the way in which the educational psychologist operates, the administrative framework in which he works, and which provides resources other than his own specialist skills for this purpose, must be understood. So Part One of this book discusses the organisation of educational and other services available for children who present the problems which are referred to the educational psychologist.

Part Two comments on the methods of investigation used by the educational psychologist. Part Three discusses the characteristics of the children with whom he largely works and the effectiveness of various educational and psychological treatment procedures. Part Four is concerned with the important question of communicating—not only with children and parents but also with teachers and other colleagues—and includes case material which illustrates this and other parts of the book. Finally, Part Five looks briefly at some of the ways in which the work of the educational psychologist will change and is now changing. In effect, it carries forward the contribution of the first chapter of Part One.

The book has been produced as a collaborative exercise between the four authors. Although each chapter can be mainly ascribed to the author named in the list of contents, all of us have helped in the preparation and development of the material. We have been jointly involved from the initial planning of the outline, through the discussions of the chapter drafts until the acceptance of the final typescript. The referencing has been done by Maurice Chazan, the indexing has been shared by Terence Moore and Jack Wright and the project has been coordinated by Phillip Williams.

Part One

Background

Part One consists of three chapters describing the setting in which the educational psychologist's work is carried out. The first chapter surveys briefly the school psychological service and the characteristics of the educational psychologists who work in it. This outline is taken up and developed later in the book. Some readers may find it helpful to go to Appendix 1 immediately after reading chapter 1, but this is not essential and is only advised for those who are not clear about the structure of the school psychological service as part of a child guidance service.

Chapter 2 discusses the ways in which special educational treatment is organised. The classes and groups which the education service provides for individual children with learning and behaviour problems—and which the educational psychologist himself often helps to establish—are essential methods of solving or at least easing some of the problems referred to the educational psychologist. While this second chapter describes some of the educational resources on which the psychologist draws heavily, chapter 3 ranges a little more widely. It outlines the sometimes bewildering range of organisations whose work impinges on that of the educational psychologist and with which he collaborates. These are mainly, but not entirely, different kinds of social work organisations.

1

The growth and scope of the school psychological service

The antecedents

During the late nineteenth century the great Education Acts which enforced compulsory school attendance for the child population of England and Wales brought into the schools children who previously would have roamed the streets. In the works of Warner's 1890 lectures on mental faculty, quoted by Burt (1957), the teaching profession had to deal with an 'aggregation of difficult children, urchins who could not be taught, ruffians who could not be controlled'. This situation was the spur which led to the development of arrangements for the special education of slow-learning children, not only in this country but also in the education systems of those other western European countries which were passing through similar phases.

The immediate problem, brought into sharp focus by the establishment of special schools and special classes, was the need to assess children's educational and intellectual development accurately and reliably, so that the special classes would be suitably used. Fortunately, in the work of men such as Galton, Binet, Pearson and others, the late nineteenth century and the first few years of the twentieth produced ideas which enabled this problem to be tackled. Although in the context of our present culture the idea of measuring intellectual development may not seem unduly revolutionary, nevertheless to the scholars and men of science of the Victorian era, imbued as this era was with the spirit of the physical sciences, the thought that qualities as intangible and 'insensible' as intelligence, personality, etc. could be accurately measured, was revolutionary indeed. It represented a major step forward in educational practice.

The first school psychological service

The conjunction of the need for special education and the means of mental measurement led to the establishment of services which could deal with these educational needs through the use of the appropriate psychological methods. In 1913 the London County Council appointed Cyril Burt, then a young man of thirty, to its service as a psychologist. Fortunately, Burt's terms of reference on his appointment were sufficiently wide to allow him to go beyond his immediate concern with the mentally defective children (in the terminology of that time) of the London area. The service which Cyril Burt founded, based in the Education Department and responsible for children with problems of learning and of behaviour, responsible also for research work in LCC schools and working closely with the medical and teaching professions, was the forerunner of the school psychological services which exist today and which deal with similar problems. The classic texts in educational psychology which Cyril Burt produced—*The Backward Child, The Young Delinquent, The Subnormal Mind, Mental and Scholastic Tests*—are based on data which he largely accumulated during his work with the LCC. In Chapter 14 we give some examples of the learning and behaviour problems which are referred to the educational psychologist today, as well as an illustration of a local research problem (see p. 310). Readers who are unfamiliar with the kind of problems with which educational psychologists deal should look quickly through a few of these cases at this point in order better to appreciate the material which follows.

Child Guidance Clinics

Burt's appointment was welcomed by the editor of the journal 'Child Study' in the following terms, 'This is excellent; other education authorities will please copy. Unfortunately Mr Burt is only to be a half-timer. There is work enough for several full-timers.' These suggestions were taken up quickly.

In the 1920s and 1930s other education authorities followed suit in establishing services similar to the one which the LCC had started. But during this period, the idea of a Child Guidance Clinic had also won much favour. The team approach to the guidance of children with problems had been initiated in 1899 by de Sanctis in Italy and in 1908 by Healy in the USA. This approach was fostered in the USA by the National Committee for Mental Hygiene and the Commonwealth Fund of America, which opened in 1920 a demonstration clinic 'to develop the psychiatric study of difficult predelinquent and delinquent children in schools and juvenile courts and to develop sound methods of treatment based on such study' (quoted in Department of Education and Science, 1968b).

In the late 1920s the Child Guidance movement spread to Britain with the opening of the East London Child Guidance Clinic in 1927 and of the Child Guidance Training Centre in 1929. By 1939 there were twenty-two Child Guidance Clinics in England and Wales. The clinics were staffed by three-man teams, consisting of a psychiatrist, a psychiatric social worker and an educational psychologist.

The war and the Blacker Report

During the war years problems of learning and behaviour in childhood emerged in sharper relief. No doubt the programme of evacuation and the disturbances of family life caused by national service for fathers and war work for mothers were partly responsible for this. Education in the schools often proceeded under great difficulties. The 1944 Education Act, with its creation of the concept of educational subnormality and its establishment of maladjustment as a category of handicap just as damaging as physical handicaps such as deafness or blindness, highlighted the need for a development of services concerned with the educational and psychological deviants in the school population. This, however, served to accentuate the differences between the alternative arrangements for dealing with this problem —the Child Guidance Clinics and the School Psychological Service. By this time, too, the clinics and the service had become identified to some extent with medical and educational approaches to these issues.

In 1948 Blacker produced his report on *Neurosis and the Mental Health Services* which looked at the sort of provision which should be made for children as well as for adults. The report proposed that the Education Authorities should establish Child Guidance Centres whose staff would include educational psychologists, whereas Child Guidance Clinics, staffed by the three-man teams mentioned above, should be established under medical auspices. The centres and the clinics would also be distinguished by function; thus the centres would deal primarily with diagnosis and the clinics would be concerned primarily with treatment.

Although the Blacker approach to the development of psychological services for children was administratively simple, it appeared impracticable to workers in the field, including educational psychologists. The separation of diagnosis from treatment was particularly disliked by the medical profession although the Ministry of Education issued a circular (No. 179) in which it suggested the establishment of Child Guidance Centres following the Blacker pattern. The proposals for Child Guidance Centres never developed in the way Blacker had expected, and the circular was later rescinded.

Postwar developments

One of the major effects of the 1944 Education Act was to lay on local education authorities obligations to provide appropriate education not only for the physically handicapped, but also for children with handicaps of maladjustment and educational subnormality. This gave impetus to the growth of demand for the services of educational psychologists. The needs of maladjusted children caused especial concern and resulted in the establishment of a National Committee whose report was published in 1955 (Ministry of Education, Underwood Report, 1955). This report saw the provision of adequate guidance facilities as one of the major needs of maladjusted children and drew attention, for the first time in an official Government publication, to the ways in which educational psychologists worked, to the need for an acceleration of their recruitment and to the deployment of educational psychologists by local education authorities.

In 1955 there were the equivalent of 140 full-time educational psychologists employed in England and Wales, serving a school population of approximately 6·5 million children. Some worked in School Psychological Services, some in Child Guidance Clinics, and some shared their time between the two. Underwood recommended that by 1965 the country should aim at a target of 250 educational psychologists, giving then a psychologist:pupil ratio of approximately 1:23,000. It is interesting to consider how far this falls below the ratios recommended by Unesco in Wall (1956) and those obtaining in the USA at the time and reported in Cutts (1955). The recommendation of the Summerfield Committee (see below) in 1968 suggested a minimum psychologist : pupil ratio of 1 : 10,000.

The Underwood Report made recommendations about the way in which the nation's services for helping handicapped children should be structured. In essence, the report proposed a comprehensive Child Guidance Service, in which the education and medical authorities worked as partners. The key to the partnership was the Child Guidance Clinic, which, in the Underwood pattern, would deal with the most serious problems of psychological and educational deviance. The clinic would be staffed by the orthodox child guidance team of psychiatrist (who could be the medical director), educational psychologists and psychiatric social workers, and would be based on premises provided by the School Health Service. But the educational psychologists would only spend half their time in the clinic. For the other half of their time they would work from the education department, operating a service for the schools (now semi-officially called a School Psychological Service) which would deal with a wider variety of problems than those seriously deviant children who were referred to the Child Guidance Clinic. The great advantage of this scheme (outlined diagrammatically in Fig. 1.1) lay in the integration between clinic and

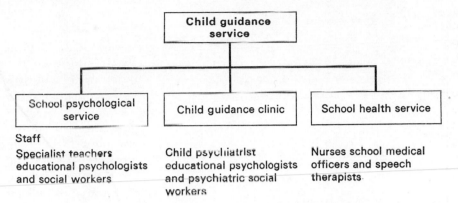

Fig. 1.1   A Child Guidance Service (based on Circular 347,
Ministry of Education, 1959)

school service provided by the education psychologist. The same educational psychologist worked in both settings. It is this kind of structure
which characterises the Child Guidance Service described in Appendix I of
this book (p. 348).

During the decade from 1955 to 1965 the profession of educational
psychology in England and Wales was under considerable pressure.
Services grew in response to demand, many new vacancies were created,
but the training centres were unable to attract sufficient recruits to fill the
vacancies. The rate at which the profession grew is shown in Fig. 1.2.
The interesting point about this growth is that it took place largely to
meet increased demands placed on the School Psychological Service.
The Child Guidance Clinic did not show the same degree of growth. By the
middle 1960s the situation had become serious. Not only had the demand
for educational psychologists considerably outstripped supply, but so
many educational psychologists were leaving the profession, largely for
posts in the expanding universities, the colleges of education and for senior
appointments in education, that between 1964 and 1965, as can be seen
from Fig. 1.2, the size of the profession actually dropped. This situation
led to the establishment in 1965 of a working party by the Department of
Education and Science, charged with considering 'the field of work of
educational psychologists employed by local educational authorities and
the qualifications and training necessary; to estimate the number of
psychologists required; and to make recommendations'. The report of this
working party, the Summerfield Report, was published in 1968 and provides a handbook to the practice of educational psychology in England
and Wales at present (Department of Education and Science, 1968b).
Most of the factual material presented in the rest of this chapter is based
on data provided by this report.

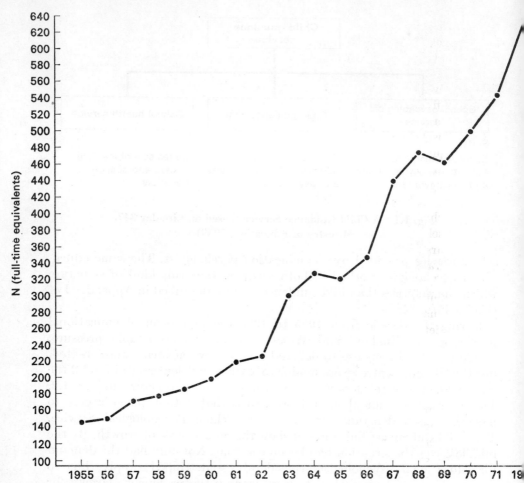

(The changes between (i) 1962/63 and (ii) 1968/69 are in part accounted for by changes in the system of recording personnel statistics)

Fig. 1.2   Educational psychologists in England and Wales 1955–72

The next few sections of this chapter concentrate on the educational psychologist and his work in the School Psychological Service. However the service is not solely the creation of educational psychologists. It is also staffed by colleagues from social work, from teaching and sometimes from other professions, the nature of whose work is not dealt with here.

The educational psychologist

The Summerfield working party conducted a survey of the background of the 326 educational psychologists who comprised the professional strength in England and Wales on 1 May 1965. At that time, the educational psychologist in England and Wales was a member of a young profession. Over half the members of the profession were under forty years of age. The profession was also mainly masculine, and becoming increasingly so. Over half the educational psychologists in service were men and in the first five years of the 1960s men entering the profession outnumbered women by three to one.

Almost without exception, educational psychologists held a university graduate qualification in psychology. In four out of five cases this qualification was an honours degree in psychology. A third of the profession held a higher degree in psychology or education.

In addition to holding psychological qualifications, two-thirds of educational psychologists were trained as teachers. Nearly all (nine-tenths) had taught in schools, and the median length of teaching experience was three to four years. About 60 per cent of the profession had also gained a postgraduate training in educational psychology. In short, the picture of the educational psychologist as an honours graduate in psychology, usually with a training for teaching, some years of teaching experience and then a postgraduate qualification in educational psychology (British Psychological Society, 1962b) was largely supported by the Summerfield survey.

Functions

The survey asked educational psychologists to estimate the proportion of their time spent in different functions each month. An approximate order of importance, based on the proportion of time spent in a given activity was then derived.

It is interesting to compare this order of importance, using 'time spent' as a criterion, with the order of importance given by the 560 USA school psychologists who ranked a number of functions for the benefit of the Thayer Conference (Cutts, 1955). This comparison is given in Table 1.1.

It would be wrong to draw firm conclusions from this table. The two surveys based their rankings on different criteria and in any case the nature of the work in both countries is changing rapidly. Nevertheless one cannot help noticing similarities between the work in both countries, once allowance is made for the slight changes in terminology—e.g. 'interview' (Cutts) for 'discussions' (Summerfield). Not only are the functions similar, but there is also a measure of agreement between the relative importance accorded them in both reports.

The objectives of the educational psychologist's work

These functions are all methods of working—means and not ends. It is not

Table 1.1   Comparison of the relative importance of different functions in the work of school psychologists (USA) and educational psychologists (England and Wales)

School psychologists (USA, 1955)	*Educational psychologists (England and Wales, 1965)*
1. Individual testing	1. Psychological assessment (mainly in schools)
2. Interviews (with pupils, parents, teachers, agencies)	2. Writing psychological reports
3. Special educational programmes	3. Treatment
4. Group testing	4. Discussions (with teachers and parents)
5. Clerical work	5. Organisation, administration and travelling
6. In-service training of school personnel	6. Informal talks and lectures to parents and teachers; attending professional gatherings
7. Public relations (speeches, parent education groups, professional organisations)	7. Formal training and lecturing— including supervision of trainee educational psychologists
8. Administration and supervision	8. Investigation and research
9. Remedial work	9. Case conferences
10. Educational programmes	10. Remedial work
11. Research	11. Visiting schools, hostels and hospitals
	12. Counselling parents
	13. Giving advice to other people and other departments
	14. Work connected with secondary school selection

easy to produce a concise definition of the educational psychologist's objectives. Perhaps the clearest analysis, although not one with which everyone would agree, is provided by Phillips (1971). He defines the central core of the educational psychologist's skills and responsibilities as 'the identification, diagnosis and treatment of individual children with learning and adjustment problems'. This approximates closely to the central theme of this book. Phillips argues that all the functions of an educational psychologist's work should be related to these aims. He divides activities which are not directly bearing on these aims into two categories:

(1) Those that follow intrinsically from the core skills, such as initiating forms of educational provision for particular kinds of childhood prob-

lems, and (2) those that are extrinsic, applications of psychology to the educational field which might be done by other people but which happen at a particular time in a particular locality to be part of the educational psychologist's duties, such as selection procedures.

It is an interesting exercise to go through the fourteen different functions of educational psychologists listed in Table 1.1 and categorise them according to Phillips's approach: basic skills, other skills (intrinsic), other skills (extrinsic).

Different approaches

Within the framework of skills that an educational psychologist possesses it is entirely possible to have different emphases, different psychological standpoints. Some educational psychologists stress the importance of family relationships in dealing with problems; others are more particularly aware of the role of learning theory in determining children's development and in modifying inappropriate behaviour. In an interesting paper, Barclay (1971) examined the characteristics of a group of ninety-nine American school psychologists. His analysis postulates a typology of three sorts of school psychologist, those whose psychological practices follow clinical procedures, those whose practices are behavioural, and those whose practices are based on self-concept theory. While most school psychologists followed an eclectic approach, Barclay was able to identify these approaches in his experimental population and to set up three groups, each of which reflected one particular orientation. There were interesting differences in approach between the three groups. Basically the emphasis of the clinical approach is on 'viewing specific problem behaviour in the classroom as the end product of distant dynamic causes'. The behaviourally oriented psychologist tends to 'look more at specific antecedents and consequences of behaviour and to focus more directly on such behavioural strategies that will alleviate the specific problem'. The essential point is that there are opportunities within the school psychological service for educational psychologists with widely different outlooks and theoretical persuasions.

It is possible to type the educational psychologist, not by theoretical inclinations, but by duties. Burt (1969) has proposed three sorts of educational psychologist, those who might be called child psychologists (dealing with diagnostic work with problem children), those who might be called remedial psychologists (dealing with children with learning difficulties and acting as a consultant to others) and an 'organisational' psychologist (dealing with administration and investigation in large LEAs). All these are ways in which the school psychological service is becoming more specialised in its central task of concern for children with difficulties of learning and adjustment. In the final chapter of this book we look at ways in which the service, and consequently the work of the educational psychologist, might develop in the future. We now turn to the organisation of those other services which are concerned both with the children who form the central core of the educational psychologist's responsibilities, and with their families.

2

The organisation of special educational treatment

In chapter 1 we saw how the work of the educational psychologist is intimately bound up with the education of children with problems of learning and adjustment. Children with severe learning or adjustment problems are regarded as 'handicapped pupils' as much in need of special educational treatment as children with physical handicaps. The purpose of this chapter is to examine the way in which the education service provides for children with different sorts of handicap. Some knowledge of the setting in which the educational psychologist's recommendations are likely to operate is essential if those recommendations are to be as effective and as helpful as possible. The field has been outlined by Gulliford (1971).

Historically, arrangements for the education of handicapped children have followed a fairly uniform pattern in most countries. While the rate at which these arrangements have developed has varied very much from country to country, the *sequence* of development has remained fairly consistent. Thus in most countries it has been children with physical handicaps who first had special provision made available for them. The blind and the deaf have usually been among the first groups of handicapped children to receive specialised education. In this country, it was in the last decade of the eighteenth century that the first schools for the blind and deaf were established (Pritchard, 1968). The special education of physically normal children with marked learning difficulties, children who are intellectually handicapped, has usually developed next. In Great Britain this began in earnest in the last decade of the nineteenth century, when the effect of the 1870 Education Act, which enabled all children to be educated, brought the problems of children with limited learning ability to the fore (e.g. Burt, 1957).

The special problems of the emotionally disturbed, the children who are known in Great Britain as the maladjusted, have usually been recognised last. With isolated exceptions it was not until the middle decades of the present century that education authorities began to establish special schools and classes for the maladjusted (Ministry of Education, 1955).

This sequence of educational provision for handicapped children has been accompanied by a change in the nature of the bodies providing education. Originally, special education was provided by interested individuals—for example Itard and Seguin are well known as pioneers in the education of children with marked learning difficulties (Pritchard, 1963). Later on, voluntary societies took over the work from individuals. As far as children with physical handicaps are concerned it was largely the work of bodies like the Royal National Institute for the Deaf and the Royal National Institute for the Blind which were responsible for developing schooling for children with these handicaps. The final stage in the sequence of provision comes when responsibility for providing special education begins to be accepted by local and national educational systems. The education of children with the three groups of handicaps which have so far been mentioned, physical handicaps, learning difficulties and maladjustment, has reached this final stage. But at the same time, as we shall discuss later, there are other groups of children whose need for special education is beginning to be recognised but for whom provision is not yet made by the state. Educational provision for these children is at one of the two earlier stages which have been described.

Prevalence of handicap

It is dangerous to try to specify the prevalence of these handicaps in the child population. Thus it is probable that the ascertainment of blind children is complete, and that all blind children in the UK have been identified. (Even so, one cannot be certain, since the definition of blindness as opposed to partial sightedness is not completely hard and fast.) But the same statement certainly cannot be made about the prevalence figures for handicaps such as maladjustment, for example, where widely differing estimates of prevalence have been made (see Chazan, 1968, for a review of findings). Table 2.1 (taken from Department of Education and Science, 1973) sets out the numbers of pupils assessed as requiring special educational treatment, by category of handicap. This information is an indication of the relative extent of provision which an educational psychologist might expect to find. But it should not be regarded as even a rough target for making provision. For example, in many cases more children are identified when more provision is made available. Note that Table 2.1 also gives an indication of the relative size of different *kinds* of provisions for

Table 2.1 Educational provision for handicapped pupils, 1972

	Blind	Partially sighted	Deaf	Partially hearing	Physically handicapped	Delicate	Maladjusted	Educationally sub-normal	Epileptic	Speech defect	Total
Assessment and placement during 1971											
Pupils newly assessed as requiring special educational treatment	160	371	356	624	1974	2186	3648	14311	341	147	24118
Pupils newly placed in special schools or boarding homes	143	304	321	545	1764	1964	2883	13236	169	111	21490
Handicapped pupils in January 1971[1]											
Attending special schools											
Maintained											
Day pupils	34	1225	1530	1086	6809	3983	2654	73157	244	351	91973
Boarding pupils	230	427	419	376	1224	1955	2639	7886	119	19	15294
Non-maintained											
Day-pupils	34	55	196	75	333	5	3	273	—	5	979
Boarding pupils	806	400	1263	466	1181	661	1020	1210	461	82	7550
Boarded in homes	1	—	4	1	10	90	669	50	1	—	326
Attending independent schools under arrangements made by Authorities	5	16	240	130	651	186	3257	1000	8	27	5320
Receiving education otherwise than at schools[2]	16	100	20	2610	1931	734	3966	1036	58	16	10487
Awaiting admission to special schools[3]											
Day pupils											
Age 5 and over	2	71	12	92	255	262	294	8623	3	23	9337
Under 5	6	15	43	57	233	26	3	808	2	13	1206
Boarding pupils											
Age 5 and over	52	111	42	73	194	549	1517	1778	43	71	4430
Under 5	67	19	30	15	51	1	8	19	1	3	214
All pupils	1253	2439	3799	4981	12872	8452	16030	95840	940	610	147216[1]
Awaiting admission for more than a year[4]	51	87	27	74	188	303	528	5049	17	43	6367

[1] Including pupils who prior to 1 April 1971 would have been deemed as unsuitable for education.

[2] In the form of home tuition, tuition whilst in hospitals and tuition in certain special classes and units not forming part of a special school. Certain other classes and units, mainly for the educationally subnormal, are not included.

[3] Including some pupils at present attending ordinary schools or receiving home tuition.

[4] These figures are included in those relating to pupils awaiting admission given above.

different handicaps. This is worth referring to when different kinds of provisions are discussed at later points in the chapter.

Table 2.2 (also taken from Department of Education and Science, 1973) gives information on the relative size of class to be found in schools for different kinds of handicap. Note how class sizes vary according to the kind of handicap and the different educational problems posed.

In the system which obtains at present in this country, there are ten legally established categories of handicap which are recognised by the education service. Under the general heading of children with physical handicaps occur the blind, the partially-sighted, the deaf, the partially-hearing, the 'physically handicapped' (including the orthopaedic and neurologically impaired), the epileptic, the delicate, and the speech defective. Under the heading of children with learning difficulties occur the educationally subnormal (often called slow-learners).

The third group of children are those who are emotionally disturbed and who are called maladjusted.

Before going on to discuss the provisions for different categories of handicap, there are some general points which need considering.

The widening concept of handicap

It is clear from the brief review of the history of special educational treatment, that the concept of 'handicap' for which special education is required has been considerably broadened over the last two hundred years. From the idea of physical conditions being handicapping we have moved to consider difficulty in learning as a handicap for which society needs to provide special education; more recently we have become sensitive to unusual behaviour as a handicapping condition for which again society needs to provide special help through its schools. It is difficult to speculate about the way in which the concept of handicap may become widened still further, but there are several other developmental conditions which could well be thought to need specialised education. Some of these conditions will be discussed at the end of the chapter.

Segregation or integration

One development in special educational provision has been a move away from the 'segregation' of children into communities of individuals with similar handicaps. Instead, policy has moved towards integrating handicapped children into a normal school community wherever possible. Unfortunately, the two words segregation and integration have acquired certain emotional overtones. It is easy to forget that each situation has its advantages, whether it be 'segregation', as in a day school for slow-learning children, or whether it be 'integration' as in an ordinary school providing

Table 2.2   Size of classes[1] in special schools[2]

January 1972

Category of class	Number of classes of the following size							All classes	Number of oversize classes[3]	Percentage of pupils in oversize classes
	1-5	6-10	11-15	16-20	21-25	26-30	31-35			
Blind	19	74	24	—	—	—	—	117	—	—
Partially sighted	—	38	94	13	1	—	—	146	14	13·0
Blind and partially sighted	—	—	5	—	—	—	—	5	—	—
Deaf	25	358	14	—	—	—	—	397	14	4·9
Partially hearing	11	148	20	1	—	—	—	180	21	16·2
Deaf and partially hearing	1	28	2	—	—	—	—	31	2	9·2
Physically handicapped	14	216	318	102	4	4	—	658	8	2·5
Delicate	—	24	76	80	44	17	—	241	—	—
Delicate and physically handicapped	—	16	50	53	16	2	—	137	—	5·3
Maladjusted	101	417	150	14	4	—	—	686	18	7·6
Educationally sub-normal	92	1068	1375	2067	223	20	15	5360	258	—
Epileptic	2	14	20	12	—	—	—	48	—	—
Speech defect	1	14	7	2	—	—	—	24	9	51·5
Other[4]	5	69	155	198	25	1	—	450	—	—
All classes	271	2484	2810	2542	317	44	15	8483	344	6·8

[1] The size of classes was determined by the number of full-time pupils only.

[2] Excluding hospital special schools.

[3] Classes where the number of pupils exceeded the maximum prescribed by Regulation 9 of the Handicapped Pupils and Special Schools Regulations, 1959. In the case of classes for the delicate and physically handicapped, the number 30 has been taken since the majority of the children were delicate.

[4] Classes (other than those included above) containing more than one category of handicapped pupil (not included in the calculation of oversize classes).

special education for a slow-learning child through the facilities which the school can itself offer. The decision as to which situation is better for a particular child must be made on educational rather than emotional grounds. And it must be remembered that psychological segregation can occur in a heterogeneous classroom.

The advantage of integration is basically a *social* advantage. Children will eventually leave school and take their places in a society which is not segregated. Consequently on social grounds the arrangement which the education system offers for their development should help them to live in a normal society. Equally the arrangement should help 'normal' members of society to develop an appropriate attitude towards handicap. If children meet a physically handicapped child as a member of their school community, then it can be argued that these children will develop tolerant and understanding attitudes towards the physically handicapped which will stay with them throughout their lives.

On the other hand the argument for segregation rests on the advantage which accrues when children can be given education which makes use of special techniques by specially trained teachers which the circumstances of the ordinary school cannot offer. For example, the special methods and materials which a teacher of a blind child uses to encourage learning will not normally be available in the ordinary classroom; nor will the classroom teacher have been trained in their use. Consequently, it is argued, a degree of specialisation implies a degree of segregation if children are to develop as effectively as they can within the limitation of their handicap.

This problem of segregation versus integration is encountered with almost every handicapped child. The educational psychologist often has a part to play in making the appropriate educational recommendation for handicapped children who are referred to him.[1]

Overlapping categories

Anyone who works with handicapped children will very soon realise that some children may easily be described as educationally subnormal, or maladjusted, or physically handicapped, simply because all three terms can be applied to them with equal accuracy. There is often a considerable overlap between categories of handicap and it can be argued that the categories are themselves administrative conveniences which are not always necessary. This point is being recognised in the training arrangements which are available for teachers of handicapped children. Often the qualification which is awarded at the end of the training course fits the teacher to work as a specialist in the education of handicapped children without necessarily specifying which particular type of handicap he is

[1] See Anderson, 1973, The Disabled School Child, for a good investigation of the issues posed by integration.

trained to encounter. All handicapped children, irrespective of their handicap, have some common problems of adjustment to a school situation in which they are inevitably at a loss, some common problems of adjustment to society and to life because of the very fact that they are handicapped and often some common problems of relationships within the family in which they are growing up. These problems are artificially separated if we categorise children's handicaps in the ways suggested by the legislation which sprang from the 1944 Education Act (Ministry of Education, 1945). For these reasons the approaches to teaching children with physical handicaps, children with learning handicaps and children with behavioural problems show a degree of overlap. As well as this common factor, there are some special skills needed for particular groups of children, most obviously for children with handicaps of vision and hearing. So, for teachers specialising in work with these particular groups, additional training is needed.

Although in the later part of this chapter broad groups of handicaps are discussed together, there is still overlap between these broad groups. For example a child with a degree of spasticity might be educated in a school for the physically handicapped; alternatively he might in some circumstances be educated in a school for the educationally subnormal. A partially hearing child may be placed in a unit for the partially hearing or in some circumstances he may be better placed in a class for the maladjusted. Educational psychologists working with handicapped children need to be aware of these overlaps, just as teachers of the handicapped need to be sensitive to some of the similarities in approach which occur throughout all schools for handicapped children.

Early ascertainment

Another general point of widespread relevance to special education is the need for early ascertainment of children with handicaps. This is a concept which has been to the fore in the education of children with hearing loss for a number of years. Teachers of the deaf and the partially hearing have long realised that the early years are critical for helping a child acquire language. For this reason children with hearing loss have been detected as early as possible and have often been placed in residential establishments as early as two or three years of age in order to give them the maximum advantage of special training in speech production. This early advantage has often been achieved at the risk of the adjustment problems associated with periods of separation from the parents and the home at an early age. As the importance of intervention in the early years of a child's life becomes increasingly realised (e.g. Bloom, 1964) this concept of early ascertainment, or detection, has spread across the other handicaps. For this reason most local authorities now have established a risk register (v. p. 67) which carries the names of children, in some cases from birth, who are suspected of being at risk. The child welfare clinic, which deals with problems of babies and young children, often has a section for handicapped babies at which special care can be provided and which may also be linked with social agencies of different sorts. In this way families with a handicapped child can receive specialist guidance. Some child welfare clinics run diagnostic clinics on the premises from which recommendations about children's needs for education for hearing loss, or education for severe subnormality may be made so that the earliest special education can be provided (see Segal, 1967).

Educational/medical provision

Special education is the education of handicapped children. Inevitably this means that it is a collaborative venture. No educational psychologist will be able to participate effectively in special education unless he is sensitive to and aware of the contributions made to the wellbeing of handicapped children by the medical staff of local authorities, and also by many other individuals. For example, the speech therapist is an obvious person with a role to play in the education of slow-learning children, so many of whom are children with speech problems. The consultants from the health service, too, are very intimately involved in the education of their child patients. For example the otolaryngologist from the local regional hospital will want to make a very clear and useful contribution to the educational problems of children with hearing loss. The social workers attached to the Department of Social Services will be able to give support to the family situation of many handicapped children (see Chapter 3). In short, the educational psychologist must never 'go it alone' in working with handicapped children. Although he is intimately concerned with the education provided for handicapped children, he does this best as a member of a team, whose composition varies according to the child concerned (Department of Education and Science, 1968b, p. 64). The educational arrangements which can be made are of course very important and the rest of this chapter will examine the educational provision made by the education service for three main groups of handicapped children, children with learning difficulties, children with physical handicaps and children with emotional handicaps, described below.

Children with learning difficulties

The only category of 'learning difficulty' which occurs in the legislation relating to handicapped children is educational subnormality. Since this term covers a wide range of problems it is convenient to divide the groups of children it covers into two, the severely handicapped, or ESN(s), and the moderately handicapped, ESN(m). Many education authorities also make provision for children with specific educational retardation, e.g. reading problems in children who are otherwise developing normally. Although these children are not necessarily educationally subnormal it is sensible to discuss the arrangements that can be made for them in this section. They are described in this text as educationally retarded.

Educationally subnormal (severe) children ESN(s)

Historically, these were children for whom responsibility had been transferred from the education authority to the health authority. They have in the past been called severely subnormal, or SSN. The ground for this transfer was usually the unsuitability of the children for education in ordinary schools. In practice this meant that the ESN(s) children were those whose level of development was effectively very limited and it was expected that children with intelligence quotients below the 50–55 level should be regarded as severely subnormal.

In the 1950s and early 1960s the twin pressures of research work (e.g. Tizard, 1964), indicating the extent to which children of even the most limited ability were educable, and parental pressure, resulting from the dissatisfaction which parents felt at the way their children were being denied the right of specialised education, led to a change in the arrangements for these children. From 1971 responsibility for their education was transferred from the Department of Health to the Department of Education and Science. As a result of this transfer, which led to an amendment of the legislation relating to handicapped children, their education became part of the responsibilities of the local education authorities and arrangements for their education were made by the LEAs in the same way as for other handicapped children. Circular 15/70 (Department of Education and Science, 1970b) deals with the consequences.

Broadly ESN(s) children, as the name suggests, are children with extreme learning difficulties. It might be thought that the intellectual level of the children would be uniformly low. In fact as a survey by the British Psychological Society (1966b) showed, the ability level of these children covers a wide range. A very few may have intelligence quotients over 100, although for most of these children the range of IQs falls between 50 and 30. The point of this observation is to indicate that ESN(s) children have been regarded as children with gross social inadequacy rather than as children with very limited intelligence. This has led to treatment difficulties.

ESN(s) children are mainly placed in two different establishments. Many children, particularly the more severely handicapped, are placed in hospitals or hostels for the subnormal. The reasons for placing a child in a hostel, in which he is residential, rather than a day school depend usually on the ability of the child's home and family circumstances to cope with the very severe problems which are posed by the presence in the home of a very limited child. Where the home can cope with the difficulties involved, and where the emotional relationships are sufficiently stable, severely subnormal children usually attend the day schools which the education authorities have established, usually based on the old training centres. Since 1971 children in both types of establishment have available to them the full range of educational services provided by local authorities. Indeed it can be argued that this section of the child population should have priority over other sections in receiving specialist attention. Yet at the time of the 1966 British Psychological Society Document only one-third of the educational psychologists who replied to the enquiry reported in the document had open access to training centres in their authorities. It is for reasons such as this, i.e. the need to ensure the wide availability of local authority services to severely subnormal children, that the transfer of responsibility occurred.

One of the problems in ensuring appropriate education for ESN(s) children, has been the inadequacy of the training which has been made available to the staffs of hospital schools and training centres. In 1959 the Scott Report (Ministry of Health, 1961) examined the qualifications of the staffs of training centres. At that time 66 per cent of the training centre staff held no qualifications, and in 1963 a training council was set up to authorise courses to prepare persons for work in training centres. Since then there has been a steady increase in the number of qualified staff. Not only have fulltime courses of training been instituted but many local authorities have established in-service courses of training to enable the staff to improve their level of competence.

Although the question of qualifications of staff has been a major problem in the arrangements for educating ESN(s) children another difficult problem has been the suitability of the buildings available. For example, the hospital placements of these children may occur in mixed wards of children and adults, largely because of the chronic overcrowding of subnormality hospitals. Similar problems existed, though on a somewhat lesser scale, in relation to severely subnormal children in training centres, where children were sometimes placed in buildings with middle-aged adults and where the facilities for special education of children were limited by the amenities available. The change in responsibility which occurred in 1971 should mark a new set of opportunities for the severely subnormal: the Department of Education and Science (1971b) has provided a helpful short survey of the situation at the time of the transfer of responsibility.

In 1959 the first three diagnostic or assessment units were established.

These units help in the assessment of children who at that time were known as children of borderline educability, children who could be placed either with the slow-learner or, today, in the special schools for the severely subnormal. The purpose of these diagnostic units is to make a careful assessment over a period of time of handicapped children who do not reveal their true educational needs in a normal assessment interview, but who need lengthy and careful observation for this purpose.

Since 1959 the number of diagnostic or assessment units has grown rapidly and there is now a sense in which many have become classes for young handicapped children, usually between two and seven years of age. They represent an additional facility for gaining more information on children with difficult problems, and are a valuable 'half-way house' for this end. More information about their operation is given in *Education Survey* no. 9 (Department of Education and Science, 1971a).

Educationally subnormal (moderate) children

The group of children known as the educationally subnormal have been recognised by the education systems, albeit under somewhat differing aliases, since the last decade of the nineteenth century. The current term, 'educationally subnormal' was introduced following the Education Act of 1944, when for the first time the children with marked educational difficulties were placed on the same footing as children with physical handicaps.

Educational subnormality is a descriptive category rather than a diagnosis, since the educationally subnormal group of children include all children whose educational development is markedly below that of other children of their age group. The phrase 'educationally subnormal' does not tell us *why* a child is having learning difficulties. The other categories of handicap which were noted on p. 16 are all explanatory categories. Thus a child may have learning difficulties because he is blind, or because he is partially hearing or because he is epileptic. But to say that a child has learning difficulties because he is educationally subnormal is tautologous. The same point can be made about the term 'slow learning' which in recent years has increasingly been used to replace the term educationally subnormal (moderate) and whose adoption the Plowden Report (Central Advisory Council for Education [England], 1967a) recommended. The ascertainment of a child as educationally subnormal or slow learning is no more than the first stage of a process of enquiry to determine the reasons for the learning problem. Otherwise, the term becomes, in the words of Denis Stott (1963a), a form of 'etiological dustbin'.

Just as there are at least two main sorts of provision for the ESN(s) so there are several different ways in which the education service accommodates the special needs of the educationally subnormal. Children can be placed in day and residential schools or they can be placed in special classes in ordinary schools. The relative efficiency of the different types of provision will be discussed in Chapter 9. At this point it is worth noting the procedures which have to be followed in order to place a child in a special school or class for the educationally subnormal. Although educational subnormality is a legally enshrined category of handicap, nevertheless there need be no formality about the arrangements under which a child is admitted to a special school for the educationally subnormal. Local authorities have a duty to find out which children require special educational treatment. Usually this duty is carried out by recourse to the formal procedure described in Section 34 of the 1944 Education Act. This stipulates the duties of the local authority in arranging medical examinations for children who may be ascertained as educationally subnormal, the obligations and rights of the parents of the children to be notified of the authority's decision and the parents' rights of appeal if they disagree with that decision.

However, there need be no formality about the offer of a place in a special school or a special class if the child needs it and if the parents accept an offer made by a local authority. It is essential, of course, to ensure that in the circumstances parents are aware of any ways in which a place in a special school may differ from that at an ordinary school. Apart from this, the keynote of the offer of special education to a child should be informality. Circular 11/61 of the Ministry of Education (1961) indicates the procedures to which educational psychologists need to pay attention in order to ensure that their local authorities are making arrangements for offering special education to slow learning children in as informal and as administratively simple a way as possible.

As with the two types of provision available for ESN(s) children, the decision whether a child should be placed in a residential school or in some form of day establishment rests mainly upon the child's needs, and the needs of his family, for some form of separation to take place. Usually, but not always, the social conditions of the home determine a child's needs for a residential placement for educationally subnormal children. It is probably for this reason that children in residential schools for the ESN(m) seem to have a higher proportion of behaviour problems than children in day schools for the ESN(m) (Chazan, 1964). The characteristics of educationally subnormal children will be discussed in Chapter 9, which includes a discussion of those 'below average' children for whom no special provision other than an appropriate curriculum in the ordinary classroom, is necessary. Meanwhile, however, it is worth noting that the decision whether a child is educationally subnormal rests solely on his educational attainments, not his ability.

Children who are educationally subnormal are ascertained through a variety of ways. For example, children may be nominated by their teachers as being in need of special help. Sometimes parents are concerned about their children's lack of progress and express their concern at a school medical examination or come directly to a child guidance clinic. Sometimes the school doctors suspect that children they examine may need special help because of learning difficulties and forward the names for a full examination by the local education authority. Often, however, it is one of the duties of the school psychological service to initiate surveys to determine the extent to which educational subnormality occurs in their schools. In this event the educational psychologist needs to be aware of the techniques of carrying out simple surveys to identify children with learning difficulties and P. Williams (1970) gives an indication of some of the points to be borne in mind in carrying out a survey to identify children with educational problems.

Many educationally subnormal children are taught in the ordinary school without recourse to any special education treatment. In taking decisions about the sort of placement which would be most appropriate to an educationally subnormal child, or indeed any handicapped child, the educational psychologist needs to think very carefully about the comparability of the different placements. For example, there is in some cases no need to recommend a change of school for an educationally subnormal child. It may be that he will be ideally placed remaining in his ordinary classroom, with the teacher being given some guidance about the type of work which it might be appropriate to expect the child to carry out. In another situation, the same child with the same problem may need the support of a special class of slow-learning children because the organisation of his ordinary class may not allow him to work as an individual. In yet another case the learning difficulties which he is showing may be associated with difficulties in the home and it may be that a residential school would be the best solution for a particular child's difficulty.[1] So, given a child with a specific learning problem, there is no rule-of-thumb solution. As with all problems referred to the educational psychologist, he must be aware of the assets in the child's present school situation which could be used to help him without a transfer; he must also be sensitive to the strength of the child's home situation which can be used to ease the learning problems he presents. Information from parents, the child's school, the school health service, or other social agencies which know the child and its family will all be important in reaching the appropriate recommendation.

The educationally subnormal are numerically the largest group of handicapped children for whom special education is provided. Table 29 (30),

[1] Brief details of schools for handicapped children in England and Wales are given in List 42 of the Department of Education and Science (1969b).

from the Department of Education and Science, Circular 15/70 (1970b, p. 64) gives the numbers of handicapped pupils at special schools over the twenty-year period 1950 to 1969. Since so many educationally subnormal children are being dealt with by the education system it is not unexpected to find that there are more courses for training teachers of slow-learning children than children of any other form of handicap. The large expansion in this advanced training has meant that the facilities now offered by special schools and classes for slow learning children are likely to be very satisfactory educationally if a child is placed in a special school or class for slow learners.

Educationally retarded children

Although educationally retarded children, that is children needing some form of remedial education, are not officially categorised as a separate group of handicapped children, nevertheless it is convenient to deal at this point with the administrative arrangements for their education. It is also worth noting that since these children do not fall into an official category, no returns are available about the incidence of children needing some form of remedial education. The term, too, is an elastic one. However, if we regard educationally retarded children as those whose problems are temporary, and who can reasonably be expected to need short-term help this indicates a point of distinction between these children and the educationally subnormal.

The classic case of remedial education is that of a child who has had considerable absence from school through illness and who on his return needs extra help, usually with the basic subjects of reading and number, in order adequately to take his place with his peer group. This of course is a simplification of the real situation since remedial classes do include many children whose learning difficulties occur for reasons other than absence from school. For example, some children whose learning problems are related to home conditions are placed in remedial classes. However, the range of abilities in such classes is markedly wider than that shown by children in schools and classes for the ESN, and remedial groups may well include children with quite high levels of ability.

The problem of ascertaining children for remedial education is an interesting one, and again the reader is referred to P. Williams (1970) for suggestions about problems and methods of survey in identifying children with specific educational problems. The report on *Children with Specific Reading Difficulties* (Department of Education and Science, 1972a) recommends a systematic screening of children at the age of 7–8 years in order to identify cases of specific reading disability.

Since remedial children are not a 'category of handicap' there are no formal procedures for offering children places in remedial classes. Nevertheless it is obviously essential that educational psychologists and others involved in these procedures should keep parents in the picture as far as offers of places in remedial classes are concerned.

The type of provision which is made available varies again from authority to authority. In general the following types of provisions are commonly found:

1. a peripatetic teacher visiting schools to see a small group of children for regular help.
2. a peripatetic teacher visiting schools to advise on methods of remedial education to be carried out by the school staff.
3. a full-time remedial teacher attached to the staff in order to carry out remedial teaching, usually in 'withdrawal groups' of perhaps six to eight children at a time. This type of provision is often characteristic of a large comprehensive school where one or two teachers may be employed for this purpose.
4. a remedial teaching centre, staffed by remedial teachers, and to which children travel for their remedial teaching. This is a type of provision which is characteristically set up in a large borough or conurbation where travelling to a local centre is fairly easily achieved.
5. a full-time remedial teacher attached to a child guidance service or child guidance clinic. Individual or small group remedial teaching can then be given to children who have been referred to a child guidance service, and for whom remedial teaching carried out in close consultation with clinic personnel is felt to be the best way of dealing with the difficulties presented.
6. individual remedial teaching by an educational psychologist is sometimes carried out, but this is usually done when the child's reading problem or arithmetic problem is such that it needs a careful psychological approach, perhaps through behaviour therapy, in order to modify the reading attitude, or reading success.

In Chapter 9 the results of investigations into the success and value of remedial education for educationally retarded children will be reported and discussed. At this stage it is worth commenting that there have been some enquiries which have looked at the relative value of different sorts of organisation for remedial teaching children. The classic investigation, in spite of some methodological weakness, is the one which Collins reported in 1961, in which he compared the progress of two groups of children who were taught (a) at a remedial teaching centre and (b) by a registered teacher, and (c) randomly selected controls who were given no special teaching at all. He measured the immediate scholastic improvement of the children after six months remedial teaching, and then the later improvement of the children $2\frac{1}{2}$ years after the end of the remedial teaching period itself.

He concluded that on the basis of six months treatment period the reading improvement of the children who were taught by a peripatetic teacher was better than that of the children who travelled to a centre for remedial teaching given there. Both showed more improvement than that shown by the control group. At the later stage, some $2\frac{1}{2}$ years after remedial teaching had finished, he found that there was no significant difference between the reading attainment of the three groups. He also reported findings for differences between the three groups for intelligence quotient, social maturity and emotional development at the later stage. As with reading attainment, he found no significant differences between the three groups in these other variables.

There are other enquiries into the relative efficiency of different remedial teaching organisations for children, but of course the difficulty is usually one of ensuring that important variables, such as the recalcitrance of the problems which the children exhibit and the quality of the teaching they get, are not confounded with the type of organisation being studied. It is for this reason that we urgently need careful enquiries which build on the early work reported by Collins in order to examine the relative value of different types of remedial teaching organisations for helping children's growth.

Physically handicapped children

It is convenient to describe the provision for educating physically handicapped children under three main headings: (a) blind and partially sighted, (b) deaf and partially hearing, (c) 'physically handicapped' and delicate. The general problems faced by educational psychologists when making recommendations about the educational future of physically handicapped children are not dealt with here: the reader will find a helpful discussion of this topic in Chapter 7 of a publication of the British Psychological Society (1966a).

Blind and partially sighted
These two groups of children are considered together, since they both have visual problems, although there is in practice a very clear tendency to try to separate the education of the blind from that of the partially sighted. The reason for this is fairly straightforward. With partially sighted children the emphasis is on using the limited vision of the children to the maximum possible extent, in other words modifying sighted methods of instruction so that the children make optimal use of their restricted vision; with blind children the emphasis is on developing special methods of instruction

which enable children to learn without having to rely on any sight at all. This distinction is not entirely clear, however, and a survey of blind and partially sighted children indicated that 59 of 817 children classified as blind and attending special schools for the blind, were being taught by sighted methods (Department of Education and Science, 1968a). In essence the teaching approach used will depend not only on the extent of the visual defect, but also on factors such as the personality characteristics of the child. Both groups of children are, however, similar, since both require specialised education and specialised materials, and usually the education of both groups has taken place in special schools in the past.

This is not the place to discuss in detail the education of children with visual handicaps, and readers wishing for a more detailed discussion can consult the publications produced by the Royal National Institute for the Blind (e.g., Royal National Institute for the Blind, 1965) and the report of the Vernon Committee (Department of Education and Science, 1972b).

The incidence figures show that the concentration of children with visual handicaps is unlikely to be sufficiently great to justify the provision of day special schooling, except in the largest conurbations. Nearly all of the arrangements for children with visual handicaps, have been boarding school arrangements with the larger authorities, or groups of authorities, providing residential schools for the blind and residential schools for the partially sighted. The smaller authorities have usually taken up places in these schools on a cooperative basis with the providing authority. Since there is no reason why blind children should necessarily be intellectually damaged there are arrangements for an academic education to be provided for blind children. The relatively small size of the schools has meant that the blind children who show academic promise are concentrated into a grammar-type stream at a particular residential school. At the same time some blind children and some partially sighted children do show a number of other handicaps, such as maladjustment and 'slow learning', and other physical handicaps. When this combination of problems arises the schools are faced with special challenges, and special establishments have been set up in order to cope with the particular problems of blind children with other handicaps.

Even in the schools for blind children, however, there is a high incidence of additional handicap. The survey just mentioned found that about 50 per cent of the survey sample of blind children had handicaps additional to blindness.

One of the more recent developments in the education of the partially sighted has been the establishment of day units for small groups of partially sighted children in large authorities which can attach these units to ordinary schools. This type of arrangement enables children to enjoy the benefits of integration into the normal community, and the advantages of living at home. But it is important that the specialised facilities available in these day units matches the level of facility provided in the special schools to which these children would otherwise go. There is a parallel here with the education of the partially hearing children, which we shall be discussing shortly.

One final point about the facilities available for visually handicapped children relates to the incidence of visual handicap in the population. On the whole the incidence is fairly steady, although occasional temporary bulges do occur. The often quoted example of variation in incidence is the high incidence of babies born with damaged sight during the years 1951 until 1955, approximately. The cause of the condition (known as retrolental fibroplasia, or RLF) was fairly soon associated with the oxygen concentration of the incubator atmosphere in which premature children were being placed, and, the cause having been established and appropriate measures taken, incidence levels of visual handicaps in children returned to normal levels.

It is unusual for an educational psychologist to come across a child whose visual handicap is so severe that special education is required, without that child having been identified beforehand. It is fairly common for an educational psychologist to be involved in the overall assessment of the abilities and adjustment of children with visual handicaps, so as to make a contribution to decisions which a local authority team will take about the best provision which can be made for that child's education. Psychological qualities such as these are just as important as the visual handicap itself in influencing the choice of education to which a child will best respond.

Finally, it is worth noting that an educational psychologist may come across in the ordinary schools children who are referred to him with learning problems, and who may have minor visual handicaps which contribute to the learning difficulties these children show. Such children have not been considered in this section, since very often a non-psychological decision such as the prescription of glasses will deal with their difficulties, but they are mentioned because the educational psychologist should be alert to the possibility of visual problems. If he suspects any form of handicap of this sort, obviously he should refer the child for medical examination.

The deaf and partially hearing
The incidence of deaf children has remained fairly stationary over the years. Some bulges, however, have occurred for reasons similar to those which have led to bulges in the incidence of visual defect. For example, when antibiotics were being used for the treatment of some childhood

diseases without full awareness of their side-effect, children's lives were sometimes saved at the expense of their hearing.

Since the incidence figures of children with deafness are higher than those of children with visual defects, educational provision includes both boarding schools and day schools. Unlike the provision and the policies underlying the treatment of children who are blind and partially sighted, there is a greater tendency for children who are deaf and children who are partially hearing to be educated together. There are also special arrangements for the education of academically gifted deaf and partially hearing children in schools which offer 'grammar-type' curricula, and from which children with hearing loss can move on to take higher level qualifications.

The partially hearing group of children appears to be growing steadily in size. It is likely that we are now identifying many more children whose hearing losses previously would probably have remained undetected. Admittedly the incidence of children with partial hearing depends on the criterion, but Kodman (1963) points out that irrespective of the criterion adopted, retarded children show three to four times the incidence of hearing loss which appears in normal children; this is one important reason why educational psychologists should be particularly sensitive to the possibility of hearing loss among the children with learning problems.

In the past, children with partial hearing have been educated in day schools, but more recently there has been a large growth in the provision of 'units', usually one or two special classes, attached to the ordinary schools. There are various reasons why this should be so. One of the most important of these reasons is the need for partially hearing children to enjoy a linguistically normal environment. Placing partially hearing children in special schools in which they mix either with each other or with deaf children restricts the quality of the speech environment in which they are placed, and is unlikely to help them to develop their own speech. Against this argument for integration can of course be set the special facilities which the special schools can offer for the education of partially hearing children, but with the advent of relatively cheap and better electronic equipment, the devices which have in the past been available in special schools can now be more readily installed in the units attached to the ordinary schools. In this way a partially hearing child has the dual advantage of the special electronic devices normally found in special schools, and also the linguistically normal environment of the ordinary schools. Finally there is the additional advantage experienced by children attached to units in the ordinary school, that they can live at home.

The Department of Education and Science (1967) conducted an educational survey of units for partially hearing children, and noted the very

rapid growth which took place in the first twenty years of the establishment of units. Units can vary in many ways, and the survey lists seven
different types of units which can be established by local authorities:

1. single class units in isolation from each other and from guidance;
2. single class units supported by a peripatetic service;
3. single class units directed by the school medical officer;
4. several single classes in one area but separate;
5. several single classes under the direction of the head of the local school
   for the deaf;
6. several single classes under the direction of a qualified and specially
   appointed organiser;
7. multiclass units.

The majority of units are placed in primary schools, and there is a
maximum number on roll of fifteen children per class, although the statutory maximum for the education for partially hearing children is ten per
class.

The type of unit established will depend on the resources and the
facilities which a given local authority is able to provide, but the important
points about the admission of children to partial hearing units, which is
an aspect of child guidance with which an educational psychologist is
likely to be involved, are that the children so admitted should be (a) partially hearing, (b) with a prospect of speaking naturally more by listening
than by lip reading, (c) with a prospect of acquiring language by natural
patterns and not by the imposed patterns of the profoundly deaf, and
(d) selected in consultation with the teacher.

The postwar developments in audiometry meant that a much larger
number of children whose hearing was not within the normal range, were
discovered. This resulted in the establishment of the partial hearing units
just described, and also led to the establishment of a new type of appointment, that of the peripatetic teacher of the children with impaired hearing.
The work of the peripatetic teacher has been surveyed by the Department
of Education and Science (1969a), and the pamphlet is well worth reading
by educational psychologists who are particularly involved with services
for partially hearing children.

Physically handicapped and delicate
Many authorities provide schools and classes for physically handicapped
children whose primary defect is not one of vision or hearing. These schools
very often contain a wide variety of handicaps. There are two main categories, those children whose handicaps are frankly orthopaedic, for example, a child who has a non-sensory physical impediment, such as a

crippled child or a child with damaged joints; and those with physical handicap which has associated neurological damage, for example, many children with cerebral palsy. Although the educational psychologist may well be concerned with the first of these groups of children, he is far more likely to be directly concerned with the second group, those who are likely to have particular learning difficulties associated with their physical damage. The characteristics and educational prognosis for these children are discussed in Chapter 10. From the point of view of the educational psychologist the provision which the local authority makes will hinge very largely on the incidence figures in a particular area. In many areas, too, voluntary societies make provision for the education of children suffering from physical handicaps. There is a sense in which the education of children with some of these physical conditions is at a stage which the education of children with visual and auditory defects had reached many years ago.

Perhaps the best example of a voluntary society which makes its own educational provision is the National Spastics Society, which provides a number of day and residential schools through the auspices of the Society itself. Consequently, when provision for special education of some types of physically handicapped children is being considered it is as well to bear in mind the resources of a voluntary society such as the National Spastics Society.

Spasticity is one of the three main types of cerebral palsy, for which there exist a number of specialist day units, day schools and boarding schools. But cerebral palsied children are often placed in schools which accept children with a wide variety of physical handicaps, and a recommendation as to which school is most appropriate for a particular child needs careful enquiry and thought. One of the important points to be borne in mind in considering possible placements is the incidence of educational subnormality among children with cerebral palsy. This has led to the establishment of special schools for children who suffer from both handicaps. For the academically capable child with cerebral palsy there is at the time of writing at least one grammar school.

A useful discussion of the educational progress of a sample of 343 children with cerebral palsy is given by the Department of Education and Science (1970a).

Another large group of physically handicapped children are those with spina bifida. In this condition the backbone fails to close on the spinal cord, which may be injured or infected at birth. This is a condition which deserves mentioning because of the increase in incidence, which at present is approximately 20 to 30 per 10,000 births. Mortality has been high but is now, because of medical advances, very much lower. If all spina bifida babies were to survive, this group of physically handicapped children would alone be the second largest category of handicapped children. Educational psychologists in the future may well see in the schools for physically handicapped children a very much larger number of children with spina bifida. This obviously suggests the need for further enquiries into the intellectual assets and deficits and personality characteristics of children with this particular form of handicap.

Finally, we need to consider delicate children. Like the other physically handicapped group of children, there is a sense in which delicate children do not need special education. If at all possible they should be retained in the ordinary schools, but where there are problems the delicate child may need placement in a special school or class (the characteristic situation with the physically handicapped is of course the chairbound child who cannot manage his ordinary school because of special problems of flights of stairs etc.).

Like the physically handicapped category, the delicate category covers a wide range of handicaps. Perhaps the characteristic delicate child is the child with the heart complaint who cannot stand the hurlyburly of the playground and the classroom of the ordinary school, and for whom the more sheltered arrangements of a special school may be needed. However, the facilities which delicate schools and classes offer often provide shelter for a variety of different conditions, notably maladjustment (Vincent and Wolff, 1970).

Obviously the question of the medical condition of the child is the essential factor in the placement of delicate children, but where a local authority has established classes for the delicate the extent to which children with behaviour problems are placed in those classes is equally a matter of interest to the educational psychologist. This last question— the issue of provision for children with behaviour problems—leads us on naturally to the last of our three groups of children needing special education.

Maladjusted children

In Tables 2.1 and 2.2 we are given information about the incidence of maladjustment. This provides a very misleading figure. It refers to the numbers of children who have actually been ascertained as maladjusted, and has little relation to the total incidence of maladjusted children in the schools. There are many children whose maladjustment is undetected. A discussion of the problem of screening for maladjustment and the criteria which might be used in deciding whether children are maladjusted or not is given in Williams (1972). The purpose of these introductory remarks is to indicate that the provisions available for maladjusted children are likely to need to grow rapidly in the next ten years, as the detection of maladjustment becomes more effective. For this reason maladjustment is a different type of handicap from physical handicaps where, with the possible exception of partial hearing, most of the children who fall in the handicapped group are detected at an early age.

It is convenient to divide the type of provision which is made for maladjusted children into two main groups, following the analysis made in the Underwood Report (Ministry of Education, 1955).

1. Day provision

(a) *Part-time special classes.* This type of provision is probably growing most rapidly. The children who attend part-time special classes usually remain in their own school for a portion of the week and spend the remainder of the school week in the part-time special classes which the authority provides for maladjusted children. Probably the major point at issue for educational psychologists who are concerned with helping to plan and establish provision of this sort is the decision as to where the class should be placed. There are of course some advantages in placing the part-time class on the curtilage of a school, since for some children this retains the link with the education system which they might otherwise miss. However, there are also advantages in placing some part-time special classes in accommodation which is very different from that which can be obtained on the school premises and where the atmosphere is entirely different from that which exists in school. Some authorities place part-time classes in old houses or, in some cases, in premises close to child guidance clinics. This has another advantage in that the facilities of the child guidance team are readily available and the teacher in charge of the class is himself in many cases part of the child guidance team.

(b) *Full-time classes.* A second approach is the establishment of full-time special classes. The big disadvantage about a full-time special class is the severance of any link which a child has had with his own class. However, there are children for whom a full-time special class is necessary, and while part-time and full-time classes have their advantages and disadvantages, clearly both are valuable in certain circumstances.

(c) *Day special schools.* This is an area in which there has been some growth recently. In 1955 there were three day schools in England and Wales but the number is now much greater (Department of Education and Science, 1969b). There are of course administrative advantages in concentrating a number of children into one school. Also the group of teachers working together feel much less isolated than when they are attached to the establishment of another school but yet are not part of it, as is the case with the part time or full-time day special class. But the advantages of administration and staff morale must be set against the segregation which the children may themselves feel.

(d) *Home tuition*. Some maladjusted children are unable to attend their ordinary school and may be in a situation where there are no special facilities in the area. In this case home tuition can sometimes be arranged. This is often something of a last resort except for unusual cases where home tuition may be a useful stage in a planned programme of recovery.

Maladjusted children are sometimes placed in special classes of slow-learning children or day open-air schools or other classes for delicate children. There are dangers in a deliberate policy of using classes and schools designed for other purposes in this way. Teachers who are pre-pared and ready to accept children with particular forms of handicap sometimes find it very hard to take into their groups a large number of maladjusted children, for whom they were not trained and who may well disrupt the learning processes and recovery of the other children in their classes. But in certain circumstances the placement of a single maladjusted child in other facilities for handicapped children can be justified and can indeed be valuable.

2. Residential facilities

(a) *Hostels*. Hostels for maladjusted children enable children to attend an ordinary school but to live in a situation where they can escape from the tensions of their normal home. Hostels are sometimes run by the Principal School Medical Officer or by the Social Service Department. They are usually small in size and in some cases, have a close association with their own special class on the premises or in a nearby school.

(b) *Foster homes*. It is sometimes possible for maladjusted children to be placed in foster homes through the auspices of the Social Service Depart-ment. This is not a common arrangement since parents of a maladjusted child usually accept a hostel placement more readily than a foster home placement, which might highlight any feelings of failure as parents they may have. However, there are certain circumstances in which this type of placement is useful.

(c) *Residential schools*. Where there are marked difficulties in the relation-ships in the family and the problems imply carefully thought out full-time treatment, a residential school is often recommended for maladjusted children. Residential schools vary enormously and where an educational psychologist is required to make a recommendation about a particular school for a maladjusted child it is well for him to make enquiries about the atmosphere and attitude of the school he has in mind. In this way he can help to ensure that the school is not only willing to take the child, but also has a definite contribution to make to rehabilitation. A conference with the school concerned and perhaps the local educational psychologist would be a useful step.

There is not a lot of evidence about the relative efficacy of different establishments in dealing with maladjusted children. There are a number of enquiries into the value of treatment procedures in general on disturbed children and H. J. Eysenck (1960c) and Levitt (1957) should be consulted on this. Roe (1965) has conducted an enquiry into the progress of maladjusted pupils with the Inner London Education Authority. Basically, she compared the progress of children who went to three different establishments for maladjusted children: (a) boarding school, (b) day special schools, and (c) tutorial (part-time) classes. She compared the progress of the children over a period of time on five variables, reading accuracy, reading comprehension, arithmetic, vocabulary, and social adjustment.

It is difficult to draw clear conclusions from this enquiry since the pupils were preselected for the groups which were compared on certain characteristics anyway; nor were the groups matched perfectly. However, as a general conclusion, it seems fair to say that in these particular circumstances children who attended the tutorial classes made more progress than children who attended the boarding schools, who in turn made more progress than children who attended the day schools. From the point of view of the educational psychologist perhaps the most important point to bear in mind is that this investigation by Roe is one of the very few enquiries which have attempted to compare the efficacy of different forms of treatment for maladjusted children. There is indeed a need for considerably more research in this field before we can justifiably make recommendations about the educational placement of children who are referred to educational psychologists for behavioural problems.

Children with other difficulties

Gifted children

There are those who believe that the gifted child is in a sense a handicapped child. He has to cope with education which is geared to children whose abilities are very different from his own. Therefore, it is argued, he needs some form of special treatment, and the organisation of special education should provide for gifted children.

Statements such as this do, of course, raise the immediate question of who are gifted children. Originally, in Terman's (1925) pioneering investigation, gifted children were defined as those with very high intelligence quotients. More recently the term has been extended to include children who display special talents, for example, a child with an outstanding musical talent or a child with an outstanding mathematical talent. These talented children have been included under the general description of gifted children. This type of approach can of course be extended so that we could regard as 'gifted' any child whose special interests and abilities pose problems for the classroom teacher which make him feel that he needs additional special resources to enable him to cope with that child's educational demands. However, irrespective of our view of the definition of giftedness, three different approaches have usually been used to cope with the educational problems that these children set.

The first of these approaches has been the use of special schools and classes along the lines of the main approach used for other sorts of handicapped children. A second approach has been through use of 'acceleration' in which the gifted child is placed with an older group of children so that his progress up the educational ladder is accelerated. The third approach is through the use of enrichment, in which the curriculum made available to the gifted child is enriched by introducing into it special areas of study which appeal to him.

In this country the first of these three approaches has rarely been used. With the exception of a few special establishments for the talented, such as the special schools for musically talented children, there have been very few instances of the segregation into special schools and classes which characterises education arrangements for some handicapped children. It has, however, been argued that there is a very small group of children who might be called the 'supergifted' with intelligence quotients of the order of five or more standard deviations above the average, for whom a special approach of this sort might be needed.

Acceleration has often been used for very able pupils, but as the organisation of the primary school sector changes so as to emphasise grouping by variables other than age, so the need for an accelerated child to move up to a group of children in which he alone would be out of the age group has diminished.

It might be argued that the third approach, enrichment, is the one most likely to be used by educational psychologists who have referred to them the problems of gifted children in the schools. This approach is used in, for example, the Brentwood experiment (Bridges, 1969). With the advent of educational technology enabling the classroom teacher to have available teaching resources and materials which can be used for children with very wide ranges of skills, it is probable that the third approach, the enrichment approach, is one which lends itself to modern ideas of education more readily than either of the other two. However, in spite of the need for studies on gifted children, little has been done in this country. For an educational viewpoint see Ogilvie (1973).

Deprived children
Another group whose needs began to be recognised during the 1960s, is that of children who can be regarded as socially deprived and in need of compensatory education. This recognition has developed from a realisation that children growing up in certain circumstances lack the normal stimula-

tion, interest, encouragement and environment which most children receive. These children, often growing up in the centres of large conurbations, can be regarded as likely to become educationally stunted. The meaning of deprivation and the compensatory education procedures which can be instituted to deal with this situation are discussed in Chazan (1973), which describes the range of compensatory education projects then operating in this country. There seems to be little doubt that educational psychologists will be concerned with projects to make use of the resources which are now available from government funds to deal with some of the problems posed by decaying areas and limited environments.

Conclusions

This chapter has not attempted to survey all the groups of children for whom some form of special education might be needed. Recently attention has been drawn to the particular stresses experienced by bereaved children and adopted children (Varma, 1973). And in an Appendix of this volume the work of the education service for the special language needs of immigrants is noted (see p. 352). There are also small specialist groups, for example children with severe language disorders, or with acute perceptual motor handicap, who do not fit readily in the framework of the major groups which have been discussed.

This raises the question of the need for categories at all. Traditionally, handicapped children in this country have been defined by nature of handicap. This has served a useful purpose in alerting the educational system, the teachers, the schools, the psychologists and medical officers, to the needs of particular groups of children. It has, as it were, aroused us so that we are aware of particular problems which otherwise we might have missed. But now that knowledge of educational handicap in children and the possible reasons for it is much more widely spread, it may be that this categorisation of children by type of handicap imposes an artificial pattern on a complicated situation, leading to some disadvantages as well as advantages. It may be that by thinking of a child as maladjusted we may lose sight of other problems, stemming perhaps from the deprivation which he experienced in the home in which he grew, or from some perceptual problems which he may also show. In other words because of the multiple nature of educational handicap, emphasising *one* of a number of handicaps may focus attention too narrowly. Ought the organisation of special education to be more concerned with the concept of handicap rather than with the particular category to which the major problem that the child shows can be allocated? It is with this notion of handicap as a unifying idea that the future of the organisation of special education may lie.

3

Allied social services

In his day-to-day work the educational psychologist cooperates with and consults not only the child's parents and the school staff but also many other agencies. He contributes on different occasions as a member of a variety of teams which may include teachers, doctors, medical auxiliaries, nurses and social workers. These are only some of the colleagues on the staffs of the social services of which the school psychological service is one part. For a general description of the whole range of the social services the reader is referred to one of the standard texts (e.g. Forder, 1969) but for the purpose of this chapter discussion is limited to those services which work directly with children and their families and, within those services, to those whose main function is social work, such as child care and probation, and those with another function that has a social work element in it, such as income maintenance.

These 'allied social services' are mainly statutory, and within the statutory framework most social work services are administered by the larger local authorities or, as is the case with the probation and after care service, by a local committee of magistrates. But voluntary organisations, too, are active in the field of social work and social service; examples of national bodies which have pioneered the residential care of deprived and delinquent children are Dr Barnardo's Homes, the National Children's Home and the churches, while the Invalid Children's Aid Association has long given social work help to handicapped children and their families. Another voluntary organisation has brought together parents and others concerned with the welfare of the mentally handicapped: the National Society for Mentally Handicapped Children, which in addition to giving advice and help to parents tries 'to influence the quality of provision and the structure of the social services available to the mentally handicapped'. The existence of statutory and voluntary provision in the same field gives variety and room for experiment, and there are many examples of a partnership between the two. In this summary, however, most of what is said applies to statutory provision, which on the whole is universalist.

The material is dealt with broadly in this order: firstly, those services with social work as their main object, mostly administered by local authorities; secondly, those services with social work as a minor part of another main function and finally some problems of referral. Classification is not easy since some services are rendered by local authorities, others by local offices of central government departments, and in one instance— hospitals—by regional boards with no apparent consistency. Fig. 3.1 may be helpful.

A useful introduction to the subject for the educational psychologist is the account in the Plowden Report (Central Advisory Council for Education |England|, 1967) of the three surveys of the social services and the primary schools, undertaken in three very different geographical and administrative areas of England. The research teams studied the nature and incidence of welfare problems arising among primary school children and the way they were brought to the attention of and dealt with by social workers. They also inquired into the degree of coordination, or lack of it, when several agencies or workers were involved. Their findings led the Plowden Committee to conclude that social problems were probably often unidentified, and, if recognised, were not always referred to the most suitable agencies. They felt that there was a need for teachers and social workers to learn more of each other's jobs and certainly much room for improvement in the relationship between teachers and the staff of the social services. The same conclusions were reached by the Gittins Committee (Central Advisory Council for Education [Wales], 1968) in Wales. It will be remembered also that the Newsom Committee (Ministry of Education, 1963) paid special attention to the problems of slum areas and favoured experiments in the joint training of teachers and social workers. The surveys carried out by the Plowden Committee covered virtually the same services as are dealt with in this chapter, and it is therefore of significance for the educational psychologist to know their shortcomings and achievements. Recent legislation and developments in training of both professions have gone some way towards coordination and understanding but gaps and some fragmentation are still expected.

The methods of work and skills used by the educational psychologist have been described elsewhere. Before an outline is given of the social work services, the first of the two types of services mentioned, it will be helpful to say something of the methods of social work. Social work was defined in 1959 by the Younghusband Committee (Ministry of Health, 1959, para. 15) as 'the process of helping people, with the aid of appropriate social services, to resolve or mitigate a wide range of personal and social problems which they are unable to meet successfully without such help'.

They pointed out that, of the three methods of social work, all of which require the professional skill and knowledge that come through training, only case work 'is at present systematically taught and practised in this country'. However, it should be noticed that the other two forms—group work and community work—have gradually and steadily gained ground both as methods and by inclusion in professional training. The educational psychologist has already met and worked with the psychiatric social worker in the child guidance team and, if he is fortunate, in the school psychological service also. This is one form of casework, and casework principles apply whatever the administrative setting.

The social caseworker helps individuals and families under stress mainly by a personal relationship, which may be long term or short term, using skills which demand a knowledge of personality development and social psychology. The help may be practical and material but is more often concerned with the delicate web of human relationships and indeed her own personality is a prime tool. The social worker may be of either sex, but for convenience here the pronoun used is that representing the majority in a particular occupation. In social work the majority are usually women. The relationship may be brief; it must never be superficial. Group work may be educational, recreational or therapeutic—possibly all three. A group worker or leader has a face-to-face relationship with a group, whatever its composition or activity, and takes a professional training which among other things gives an understanding of group dynamics and some competence in group work skills. Examples are recreational work in youth clubs and therapy in psychiatric hospitals. Community work and training for it were considered by a study group set up by the Gulbenkian Foundation. Their report, published in 1968, gave this definition:

> In general terms community work can be defined as a method of dealing with problems of social change; . . . and how to help people and the providers of services to bring about a more comfortable 'fit' between themselves and constant change, how to survive and grow as persons in relation with others. . . . The community work function is exercised by a few full-time professional or community workers, by others as a necessary part of their professional or administrative task and by local councillors and innumerable other voluntary workers.

Examples given of full-time posts were those of secretary to a council of social service or to a rural community council, warden of a residential settlement, a new town social development officer and others.

This perhaps oversimplified statement of the three methods of social work will serve the present purpose, but with a warning that the debate continues as to what exactly community work is, since it is very much in its infancy in Britain; and that with the bringing together of staff and specialisms changes are occurring in training for social work in general. There are, of course, many times when the social worker uses more than one method. The caseworker works with the individual within the family, which, after all, is a group. Neither the caseworker nor the group worker functions in a vacuum—in one way or another they both use community work skills from time to time.

From this brief description and the various official pronouncements we see that both social worker and educational psychologist share certain functions. The approach and emphasis may be different, but both are involved in processes of studying relationships, of investigation, diagnosis, treatment and follow-up, and above all in themselves establishing a relationship with children and parents, or substitute parents—in other words with families. Both are concerned with the social setting, whether of home, school or community. The administrative framework of the school psychological and child guidance services has been outlined earlier in this book. It suffices here to stress that the pattern varies from one local authority to another, and especially between rural and urban areas. It therefore rests with the educational psychologist to take the initiative in promoting the best possible cooperation and rapport with colleagues in other services *in the setting in which he is employed and with whatever resources are at his disposal*. Usually established posts in the school psychological service allow for one or more trained social workers, but his colleague may be untrained and inexperienced or the post unfilled. In the latter instance, he will himself be the one to make contact, if contact is necessary, with other services and social workers. We now turn to the social work services themselves.

The local authority social services departments

The proposed major reorganisation of local government into larger units, and of the National Health Service into unitary area health boards, to take effect in 1974, is bound to make a considerable impact on many of these services. However, we shall deal with the situation as it now is, and firstly, with the work of the local authority social services departments, which came into being on 1 April 1971, following the Local Authority Social Services Act of 1970. This, in itself a major reform within local government, carried into law the chief proposals of the Seebohm Report (Home Office, 1968a) and was timed to relate to other measures such as those introduced by the Children and Young Persons Act 1969, and the Chronically Sick and Disabled Persons Act 1970, both administered by the new Departments. The transfer on 1 April 1971 of the education of severely subnormal children to the LEAs, referred to in the previous chapter, was a related measure. By this rationalisation the training and education of children with all types of handicap, both mental and physical, now rests with the local education authority. When they grow up their care and training, especially if they are severely handicapped, lies with the local authority social services department; but that department will cooperate with the employment services in the rehabilitation of those capable of sheltered or open employment.

Figures 3.1 a and b show the position before and after 1 April 1971 and illustrate diagrammatically the chief aim of this reorganisation: to make

(a) Before 1 April. 1971

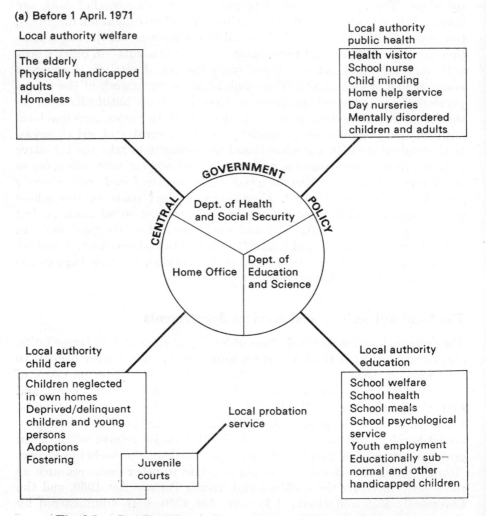

Local authority welfare

- The elderly
- Physically handicapped adults
- Homeless

Local authority public health

- Health visitor
- School nurse
- Child minding
- Home help service
- Day nurseries
- Mentally disordered children and adults

CENTRAL GOVERNMENT POLICY

Dept. of Health and Social Security

Home Office | Dept. of Education and Science

Local authority child care

- Children neglected in own homes
- Deprived/delinquent children and young persons
- Adoptions
- Fostering

Juvenile courts

Local probation service

Local authority education

- School welfare
- School health
- School meals
- School psychological service
- Youth employment
- Educationally sub− normal and other handicapped children

Fig. 3.1a   Social welfare work, including residential and day care, of county boroughs and county councils

(b) After 1 April. 1971

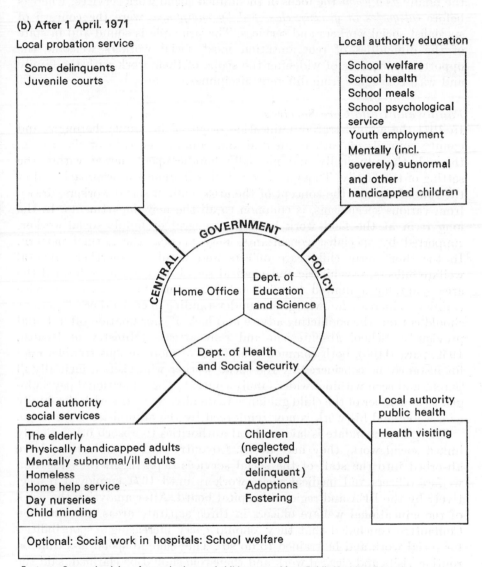

Local probation service

Some delinquents
Juvenile courts

Local authority education

School welfare
School health
School meals
School psychological
service
Youth employment
Mentally (incl.
severely) subnormal
and other
handicapped children

GOVERNMENT

CENTRAL   POLICY

Home Office   Dept. of
Education
and Science

Dept. of Health
and Social Security

Local authority
social services

The elderly
Physically handicapped adults
Mentally subnormal/ill adults
Homeless
Home help service
Day nurseries
Child minding

Children
(neglected
deprived
delinquent)
Adoptions
Fostering

Local authority
public health

Health visiting

Optional: Social work in hospitals: School welfare

Footnote: Care and training of severely abnormal children moved from Public Health to Education
Departments on 1 April 1971. From 1 April 1974 the new Counties supersede the County Boroughs and
present Counties, while most health functions of local authorities are transferred to new Area Health
Authorities (DHSS, 1972a).

Fig. 3.1b   Social welfare work, including residential and day care,
of county boroughs and county councils

the family *as a whole* the focus of the unified social work services, whereas before *categories* or *groups, classified by symptoms*, were the concern of specialist social workers and services. The principle is sound and in spite of the difficulties of reorganisation most social workers welcome the opportunity it gives of widening the scope of their work with the family and with colleagues from different disciplines.

Family and Child Care Services

In 1971 the administrative unification occurred in county boroughs and county councils of both residential and community care of the young, the old, the physically and mentally handicapped viewed within the setting of the family. Though there will be differences of approach and of the rate of change, the concept of the area team of social workers, drawn from various specialisms, is common to all the new departments. In the long term at the field work level the general or family social worker, supported by specialist consultants, may become the normal pattern. In the short term child care officers and family caseworkers, mental welfare officers, psychiatric and medical social workers, have formed the area team for a limited population. Close consultation and in-service training to increase knowledge and understanding of each other's functions should cut out the conflicting advice and lack of coordination often found previously. School absenteeism and rent arrears (Ministry of Health, 1959, para. 1100), both common symptoms of more serious trouble, may for instance, be considered by the social worker who visits a mentally ill parent and seen within a wider family context. The educational psychologist as a member of the child guidance team already works with the family as a whole and his work is now reinforced by the administrative change.

Though no mandate is laid on local authorities to absorb other closely linked social work, they may do so. Coventry and several others have absorbed into the staff of the social services department the education welfare officers and medical social workers until 1971 employed respectively by the LEA and regional hospital board. After analysing the work of the educational welfare officers in three separate areas, the Plowden Committee concluded that they 'should carry increasing responsibilities for social work and be trained to do so'. They should spend less time on routine visits and clerical work and their role should be clarified, said the Committee. There is some difference of opinion in the social work profession as to whether the new social services department provides a better base for the medical social worker than does the hospital, where she is one of the hospital team. However, it has appeared desirable in some areas to develop both these ideas by including both types of work in the new social work teams. One county has seconded a member of the social work team from the social services department to the school psychological service. These experiments are of particular importance to educational psychologists and they will be followed with interest.

The synthesis of the local authority personal social services has been explained at some length because it gives wider scope to the educational psychologist to use his initiative and expertise in his own work with children. He will now be able to count on the support of a *family* service, knowing that when he seeks its help any stress suffered by other members of the child's family will be taken into account. One of the most significant contributions he makes, either alone or as a member of the child guidance team, to helping children in trouble is at the diagnostic stage. One of the first things the Summerfield Committee did after it was set up in 1965 was to make a survey of the profession by sending a questionnaire to all chief education officers in England and Wales (Department of Education and Science, 1968b (Ch. 2.11 and App. 2B)). One item asked for frequency of contact in the educational psychologist's work between himself and other services concerned with children and their families. Figure 3.2(a) (reproduced from the Summerfield Report, p. 21) shows how the 330 educational psychologists who responded estimated their contacts with the specific services mentioned in the questionnaire. The Committee found that educational psychologists were more frequently in contact with the staff of the pre-1971 children's departments than with any of the other social services mentioned in their survey. 'Relationships with community mental health services were little mentioned.' The Summerfield questionnaire then invited the educational psychologists to volunteer information on contacts with any other services not listed. Figure 3.2(b), drawn to the same scale, is based on figures given in Table 2B: 19, Appendix 2B of the Report. The contrast between the two diagrams is marked. The health visitor, general practitioner and education welfare officer all have close contact with young children and their families and may be expected not only to recognise incipient behaviour difficulties and slow development but to refer parents to the educational psychologist or child guidance clinic. It is therefore to be regretted that of the 330 volunteering information only 12 per cent specified the health visitor, 6 per cent the general practitioner and a mere 3 per cent the education welfare officer; the highest percentage in this section being the 24 per cent who specified hospitals, including psychiatric units and special units. Perhaps this apparent failure in communication may be partly accounted for by staffing shortages in the social services; these figures may be taken tentatively rather than as absolute proof of a dearth of consultation, but we are assuming that consultation with allied social services is desirable, especially at an early stage.

To revert to past practice in children's departments, which is no doubt continuing in the new departments, professional consultation is commonly

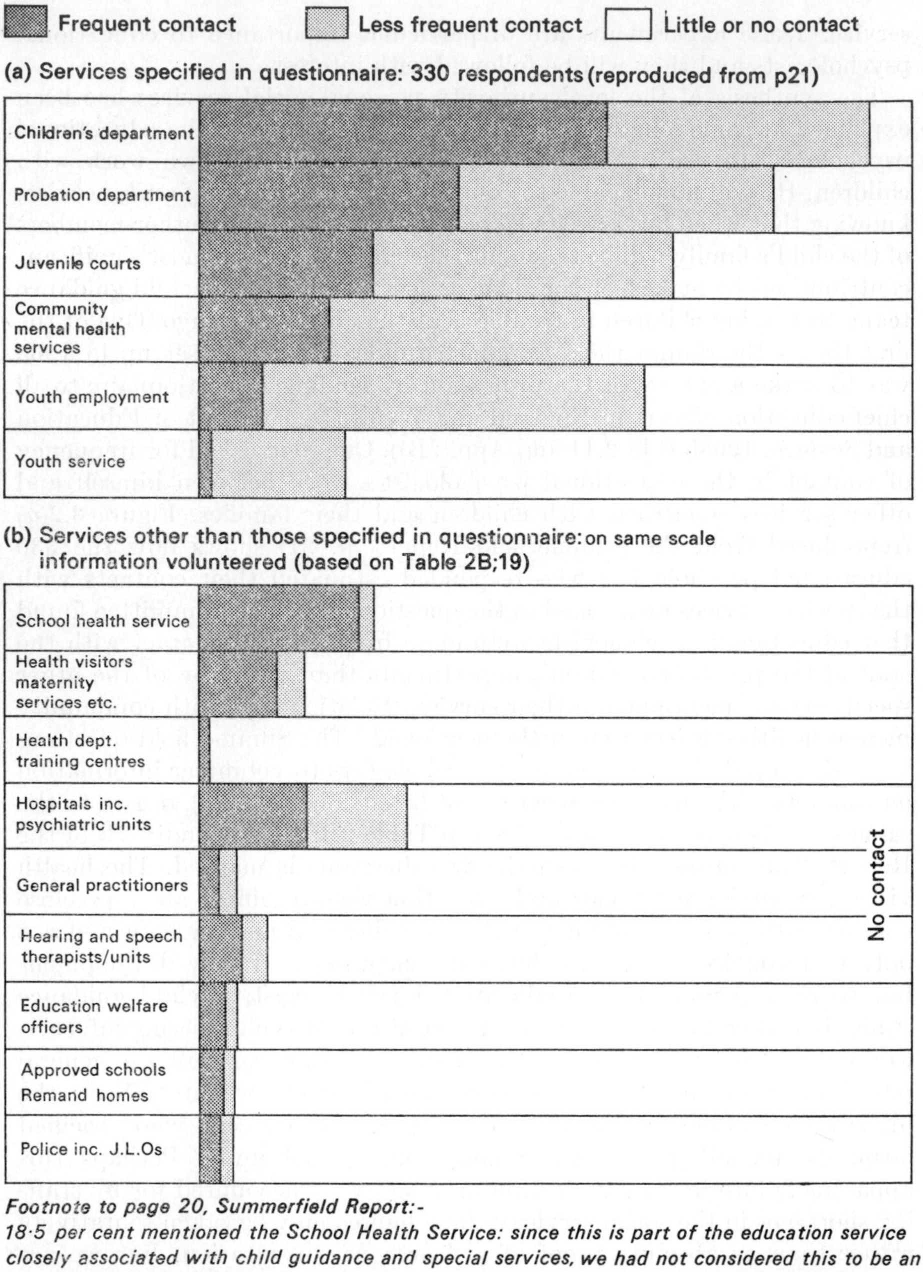

■ Frequent contact   ▒ Less frequent contact   □ Little or no contact

(a) Services specified in questionnaire: 330 respondents (reproduced from p21)

| Children's department |
| Probation department |
| Juvenile courts |
| Community mental health services |
| Youth employment |
| Youth service |

(b) Services other than those specified in questionnaire: on same scale information volunteered (based on Table 2B;19)

| School health service |
| Health visitors maternity services etc. |
| Health dept. training centres |
| Hospitals inc. psychiatric units |
| General practitioners |
| Hearing and speech therapists/units |
| Education welfare officers |
| Approved schools Remand homes |
| Police inc. J.L.Os |

No contact

Footnote to page 20, Summerfield Report:-
18·5 per cent mentioned the School Health Service: since this is part of the education service closely associated with child guidance and special services, we had not considered this to be an 'other' service. It seems to us possible that respondents who mentioned the School Health Service specifically may very well have had less contact with it than the majority who did not single it out.

Fig. 3.2 Psychologists in education services: 1968 (Summerfield)

achieved informally by regular case conferences, or by meetings of co-ordinating committees of colleagues *who are personally concerned with the child and his family*. It is important that residential staff should be invited together with other social workers, psychiatric, medical and educational staff, especially the educational psychologist. A joint plan of action is agreed and the responsibility for it is shared. The recommendation may be (*a*) to 'treat' the child within his own family; (*b*) to place him with foster parents with the aim of restoring him to his real parents as soon as possible; (*c*) to make a long-term foster placement where restoration is unlikely; or (*d*) to use residential facilities where fostering is unsuitable. Diagnosis is an essential preliminary both to preventive work and to care by the local authority. It is of interest to note that, though the total receptions into care in England and Wales increased from 1959 to 1966, from 1967 the number has continued to fall slightly so that in 1969 it represented 5·9 per thousand of the estimated population under the age of eighteen. Forty-seven per cent of these children came into care on account of a mother's confinement or of the short-term illness of a parent (Home Office Report, 1970). They remained for a few weeks only and were not in the wording of the Act 'deprived of a normal home life'.

Preventive work with families
A duty has been laid on local authorities since 1963 to give help in appro-priate cases to children neglected in their own homes and thus to try to forestall family breakdown and taking children into care. The pioneer work of the voluntary organisation, Family Service Units, in this field has drawn attention to a wide range of problems frequently found together in the same family and contributing to child neglect: mental subnormality and illness, a history of unstable family relationships and criminality are some of them (Philp and Timms, 1957). Advisory services and supportive projects of differing kinds have begun to develop. Full-time and part-time family advice centres are directly provided by the social services departments, run at health clinics or by voluntary bodies according to local preference. Some authorities have encouraged children's play groups and simultaneous group work activities with mothers, while others sponsor holiday schemes for mothers and children. A major responsibility of most child care officers has been advice on household budgeting, and some use rent guarantee schemes to prevent evictions. Reference as to the type and scale of preventive work may be made to Home Office Reports (1967 and 1970). As the social worker (previously child care officer) and home help organiser have since 1971 both become members of the staff of the same department, one may expect even closer cooperation here. In addition, recent legislation has not only strengthened the powers of the new unified social service department to protect and supervise children fostered

privately by their parents, but has transferred to it the administration of the
child minding regulations and the local authority day nurseries (not to be
confused with nursery schools), two forms of day care much needed by
working mothers and one-parent families. It is usual to maintain within
the department a register of 'families at risk' to ensure positive action
is taken, wherever possible, to try to resolve social problems at an early
stage. More will be said later about risk registers and the question of intervention in family life.

It will be appreciated from these comments that the whole trend of
present methods of child care and of recent legislation is to try to
strengthen family life, to deal with children in trouble according to individual need through social and educational means, and ultimately to
abolish criminal court procedure for all delinquent children (legally a child is
any person under fourteen years of age) except when a child has committed
homicide. The idea of punishment by a court is to be removed, and
although the juvenile court, sitting as a civil court, will remain, as far as
possible children and their parents will be dealt with outside the court by
social work methods and administrative procedures. This is the philosophy
underlying the Children and Young Persons Act 1969. Hence there is now
greater flexibility in child care and a greater variety of measures made
administratively possible by removing the somewhat artificial distinction
between neglected and delinquent children. Preventive work may continue with the family as a whole and may be aided, if the social worker
thinks fit, by short periods of foster care or residential care. Moreover,
there is no hard and fast division between community care and residence
in an institution; the criterion is the child's need. But some children are
unable to remain with their natural parents and provision must be made
for them either through a substitute family or in a community home.

The substitute family: adoption and fostering

It is often said that for a deprived child adoptive parents are the best
substitute for natural parents. Successful adoption, like successful fostering or placement in a residential institution, depends primarily on the
quality of the relationship between the child and the substitute parents or
adults who care for him. One form of care may be better suited than
another to an individual child, but the relationship calls for trust and
affection on both sides. The point about adoption is that it is permanent
and gives the child virtually the same legal rights as any biological offspring of the adopters. Important changes in 'the law, policy and procedure of the adoption of children' have recently been recommended by a
departmental committee (Home Office, 1972, the Houghton Report).
The report is at present under consideration and will doubtless lead to
legislation. There is space here only to touch on its more important pro-

posals, namely, that (1) there should be a comprehensive legal framework, supported by social work services for all adoptions; (2) the provision should become an integrated part of the general child care and family casework service; (3) local authorities and voluntary adoption societies should co-operate for this purpose; (4) it should be an offence for a person other than an adoption agency to place a child with a person who is not a relative for the purpose of adoption, and similarly an offence for a person who is not a relative to receive a child otherwise than through a registered adoption society. Thus the Committee unanimously recommend an end to third party adoptions, more clearly define the role of the guardian *ad litem* and of the social worker, and in general reflect changing social attitudes and the greater use of adoption as one form of helping deprived children. The educational psychologist is advised to read this important document, which is supported by a good deal of research evidence.

The Houghton Committee, having explicitly said that the welfare of the child should predominate in adoption policy, also considered cases where long-term fostering might lead to adoption. They made the suggestion that, when a child is received into care, and his needs are explained to his parents 'including the likelihood of his forming attachments with substitute parents which it might not be desirable to break', an explanatory leaflet, setting out the needs, rights and obligations of all concerned, be given to the parents.

Roughly half the children taken into care are boarded out with foster parents. Indeed the local authority has a duty to provide a foster home, when possible and desirable, for those children 'deprived of a normal home life', and successful fostering, as we have noticed, sometimes leads to adoption. Though there is no shortage of couples wishing to adopt, foster parents are in short supply. Great skill is required in finding and selecting foster parents suited to the needs of particular children, a growing proportion of whom appear to have some degree of handicap or maladjustment. The exacting role of foster parents and the shortage of placements for deprived and emotionally damaged children often involve repeated failures, frequent changes of foster home and an intensified sense of insecurity for the child. At the first sign of trouble early consultation between foster parents, social worker and educational psychologist may prevent or at least mitigate the worst effects of such a sequence. The ability to recognise symptoms, to understand each other's role and to work as a team must again be stressed.

Recently the question has been raised as to whether there should be professional foster parents, especially for difficult and maladjusted children. In the past foster parents have been selected as having qualities making them the best substitute for natural parents; though they receive a subsistence allowance for each foster child it is assumed they make no profit from the task. Professional foster parents, chosen for their special skills in handling difficult children, would in addition receive a salary. Long-term fostering, like adoption, is most promising with younger children. Those taken into care in their teens are often placed in lodgings or a hostel.

Residential care and the community

With the setting up of Children's Regional Planning Committees of groups of local authorities in 1970 greater flexibility and more effective use of a wider range of institutions and resources became possible in theory for the local authorities in each region. It will, of course, depend on the characteristics and resources of each region how quickly or otherwise this principle is applied. It hardly needs emphasising that the school psychological service is very deeply involved here, no less than in preventive work and fostering, and has a contribution to make to the many aspects of residential provision. The new name for residential institutions—community homes— implies that all resources, both statutory and voluntary, should be invoked in promoting this form of care. The educational psychologist helps diagnose and assess the child's needs on reception into care, advises on subsequent schooling and placement, and may be one of the psychiatric team which links the community home with the family. The new name applies to remand homes, approved schools, reception centres, residential nurseries, children's homes, hostels for working boys and girls, and family unit homes. Of all these, perhaps the family unit home most nearly achieves the ideal of integration with the community. This form of residential care most resembles a natural family for here not more than about ten children of both sexes and various ages are looked after by a married couple; the husband follows his usual occupation while the wife is the housemother. The members of this 'substitute family' visit neighbours, share schools and other facilities and, it is hoped, make friends with other families. Regional plans when complete had to be approved by the Home Secretary, and came into being on 1 April 1973.

The juvenile court and the Children and Young Persons Act, 1969

Enough has been said to show that the 1969 Act makes important and far-reaching changes in the care and treatment of neglected and delinquent children. The juvenile court eventually with regard to anyone legally defined as a child (under fourteen) will proceed only as a civil court; for young persons so defined (fourteen to seventeen) it will retain both civil and criminal functions, but its criminal function is more restricted. In the period immediately following the passage of the Act, the minimum age of criminal responsibility remained ten years, as it had been before.

Provision was made for it to be raised in due course to twelve, and at some later date first to thirteen and then to fourteen. At the same time as these measures divert the child from the court, the Act also extends the care of children so that social workers (child care officers) may through their greater administrative powers 'further the children's best interests and afford them opportunities for the proper development of their character and abilities' (Watson, 1970).

John Watson's words might equally be applied to the sphere of work of the educational psychologist: the connection between the two services is clear. If, however, the child is taken to court as being in need of care, one may expect the educational psychologist even more than in the past to contribute to the preliminary social inquiries made by the local authority and presented in court in a written report. We are reminded by John Watson that sound diagnosis leads to suitable treatment, while the reverse is true if the reports are superficial or inadequate. He is giving advice to the social worker, which could be taken to heart by some magistrates, too. It is again a question of good team work: sound diagnosis will be followed by suitable treatment only if all those involved—the social worker, the educational psychologist and the magistrate—have a clear and sympathetic understanding of each other's role. The reports, he points out, are not confidential in the usual sense, since the court must let the parents and child know the contents. The social worker is advised to handle them in such a way that the child or family is not hurt by inadvertently and tactlessly revealing that he is illegitimate or adopted, or that his parents are not married.

The Act introduces two new kinds of treatment, which may frequently call for consultation between social worker and educational psychologist. A supervision order replaces probation for all children under fourteen years, and for some young persons. Intermediate treatment, which is the responsibility of the Children's Regional Planning Committee, is a very flexible combination of literally any methods of care or training that the social worker, named as supervisor, deems suitable. It is not here possible to cover the complexity and detail of this important Act. The educational psychologist is advised to read the clear, concise and very practical guide to it written by John Watson. He will quickly realise how much is added to his own responsibilities by the legislation, and will appreciate the difficulties that have arisen for both social workers and magistrates in the early stages of implementation. (See also pp. 264 and 265.)

The probation and after care service

An outline of another kind of professional social work follows naturally from a discussion of social work with children and their families, for the two may overlap. A court may decide to put a teenager under the supervision of a probation officer, rather than of a child care officer, because the former is already supervising another member of the same family. The probation service, concurrently with the child care service, has undergone organisational changes. In 1963 it was renamed the 'Probation and After Care Service' when the staff were given the duty of after care of discharged prisoners, and when prison welfare officers were absorbed into the same service. This was another example of better integration of personnel and of greater flexibility. This measure, together with the Children and Young Persons Act 1969, has increased the probation officer's work with older people and diminished his work with children. Eventually all his work with children will pass to the social work staff of the new social service departments.

The probation officer's work may be described, as Parsloe (1967) says, as that of a social worker to the penal system, not merely to the courts. He is essentially a social caseworker, using the same methods as his colleagues in other settings—the interview, forming a relationship, supporting the family under stress, occasionally using group discussions or activities—but in some circumstances, not all, having the authority of the court or a court order behind him. We are here concerned with his functions in three ways. First mention has been made earlier of the preliminary social reports, which are a compulsory feature of the juvenile court. In some instances the probation officer may compile and present the report and in this may seek the help of the educational psychologist. Secondly, the probation officer may be named in a supervision or probation order as the officer who is to 'advise, assist and befriend' a boy or girl. Thirdly, parents of children known to the educational psychologist may themselves have been helped with regard to marital difficulties or may even have been on probation or in prison. Children's behaviour problems often stem from the parents' way of life. Over and above these official duties the probation officer may be approached from time to time informally by the parents of wayward youngsters. And those whose probation orders have expired may turn to him later in times of trouble. It will be seen from these illustrations that the probation officer's work has no very definite boundaries in the legal sense. It could be argued that the better his performance as a social worker, the more he will be approached and involved *unofficially*. But his duty is to the court as well as to his client.

A probation order is made for a definite period—not less than one, not more than three years—and clearly states the requirements laid down by the court, e.g. attendance at work or school; where the probationer is to live; it may require him to undergo medical or psychiatric treatment. The probationer promises to observe these requirements and if he fails to do so may be brought before the court again by the officer. But a requirement to submit to medical or psychiatric treatment may be beneficial when a youngster has become dependent on drugs, and a skilful probation officer can use the authority of the court in a positive way to encourage responsible behaviour. A supervision order is different; it may have certain requirements written into it or it may not; the intention is a more flexible instrument which leaves the *methods* of treatment to the supervisor's discretion, as the child's need changes. Furthermore, there is no legal enforcement of a supervision order, and John Watson, for a number of good reasons, expresses anxiety about this. As the staffs of the new social services departments expand, and as the probation and after care service becomes more adult-orientated, the probation officers will cease to have responsibility for supervision orders for *children*. Incidentally, although the probation officer works in a judicial setting and the child care officer in an administrative one, the latter has much greater power over a child's future, for she can in extreme circumstances remove him from his parents without recourse to the court.

Finally a growing trend in the probation and after care service is the use of volunteers, a practice more common in some other European countries, e.g. Holland. One of the best-known voluntary organisations with which the service collaborates is the National Association for the Care and Resettlement of Offenders (NACRO).

The social services of the local education authority

From consideration of the first group of social services, those employing professional social workers and having social work as their objective, attention now is turned to the second more heterogeneous group, which have other objectives but include to varying degrees an element of social work. First among these we deal with several services provided within the British educational system to complement and render more effective the pupils' education and the work of the teachers. Because the school psychological service is one of these services, the educational psychologist may see rather more of colleagues in them than he does of colleagues in services outside the education authority. Space does not permit a description of all the ancillaries, such as play centres, school camps and the school meals service, and three categories have been chosen as being especially relevant. They are: the school health service, social work with school children, and services for young people.

The school health service
In most county boroughs and county councils the principal school medical officer is also the medical officer of health. In some instances the school health service employs general practitioners part-time and in only two authorities, according to the Plowden Report, are the school and public

health services not integrated. Other features, which make for a more comprehensive family service, are that the health visitor, whose function is mainly health education, in the great majority of appointments serves also as school nurse and in some authorities is attached to general practice. Other auxiliary staff are speech therapists and physiotherapists. In those areas where the child guidance service comes under the aegis of the medical officer of health, the use of the title 'Family and Child Guidance Service' or 'Family and Child Psychiatric Clinic' reflects the trend towards treatment of the family as a unit. It is as well to remember then that the medical and nursing staff of the school health service are the same people who staff the local authority maternity and child health clinics; that health visitors visit every home where there is a new baby as well as the schools and probably have known not only the school children but the whole family over a number of years.

The previous chapter emphasised the role of the educational psychologist as a member of a team, working with the principal school medical officer and others in the early ascertainment and treatment of handicaps. If the Plowden Committee recommendation of holding medical and developmental assessments *before* entry to school is carried out, even closer association may be expected. Closer association would naturally follow from their further recommendation that, with higher standards of child care, selective and more intensive medical examinations should in later school life take the place of routine checks for all; a system that has been practised with success by some local education authorities.

Of all the supportive services within the educational system the school health service can most aptly be described as preventive. Since its introduction in 1907 it has made a substantial contribution to the general health of the nation. The advances made since World War II in the general physical condition of school children, in the removal of malnutrition, and in the provision of special schools owe a good deal to the earlier work of the school health service, as well as to other factors. But the Plowden Committee felt that better use could be made of scarce resources; they found great variations in standards of health between areas and felt that effort should be concentrated on 'those whose family and social circumstances give cause for concern'. In particular they wished the doctors and nurses in this service to increase their knowledge of social work, and wanted to see closer collaboration brought about between them and social workers by the exchange of relevant confidential information.

From 1 April 1974 the whole of the school health service and its staff was transferred from local education authorities to the new area health boards, and thus integrated into the National Health Service. It is assumed its functions will remain as outlined here (for a discussion of work with school medical officers, see p. 296).

Social work with school children
The effectiveness of social work with school children of all ages depends on the ability of the teacher to recognise, or prevent arising, any social problem, and on a social worker being at hand to help in any situation that the teacher cannot handle alone. Teachers will not necessarily recognise symptoms, or even advise parents to see a social worker. In a rural setting a farming couple, ignorant of child development, may blame the slow learning or dishonest habits of an adopted child on heredity and be unaware of their own mistakes in child rearing. A head of a primary school may advise a parent to ignore a child's tendency to enuresis in the hope that 'he will grow out of it', and be unaware of the parent's need for expert help. Conversely a family caseworker, involved with the family of a delinquent school child, may fail to consult a head, in whom the parents confide and with whom they have an excellent relationship. It is possible that the caseworker misses an opportunity for very effective professional cooperation.

Social workers attached to larger schools in the USA appear to be common. In Britain this form of social work, or a reorganisation that would mean existing social workers performed this function, has been advocated for some time, notably by the Plowden and Newsom Reports. Both drew attention to the pressing needs of slum areas, of immigrants and of what were afterwards designated educational priority areas. However, a little progress has been made. Pioneer work is being done by a few school-based teacher–social workers and some colleges of education prepare those in training for a dual role. Glasgow has for some years appointed full-time school-based social workers. London, with a system unique among local education authorities, has recruited and used volunteers since the early days of this century. The school counsellor, who is usually on the staff of a large secondary school, is becoming less rare. There is general agreement that with certain problems the teacher needs professional social work help. The evidence (Plowden Report, Vol. 1, ch. 7 and Vol. 2, App. 8) is that in these circumstances the head teacher most frequently turns to the education welfare officer, who visits children's homes and, as noticed earlier, is well placed to undertake preventive work. But the education welfare officer, previously known as the school attendance officer, spends on average 75 per cent of his time on attendance matters, administration and routine clerical work. The district assigned to him may cover several thousand families, and even if he is fitted by personal qualities and training (and few are trained) to be a social worker, shortage of time and a lack of definition of his duties prevent him from being one. In spite of these difficulties, there are some education welfare officers giving genuine social work support to the schools and to the school psychological service. After many attempts the Association of Education

Welfare Officers succeeded in gaining recognition for a Certificate in Education Welfare, but unfortunately preparation for it is by correspondence course or part-time study, and no substitute for full-time training in social work. Those education welfare officers who have been absorbed into the new social services departments, as in Coventry, will presumably have their role more clearly defined, and in the long term have social work training as well as the satisfaction of playing a much more positive part in family casework. But, until the education welfare officer is professionally trained and is allowed by a reorganisation and reallocation of duties to concentrate on welfare work, social work support for the head teacher is likely to remain inadequate. (See also p. 291.)

In Britain there appears to be very little difference between school social work and school counselling. School counsellors in this country were first trained at several university departments of education in the 1960s and courses were limited to trained teachers with some experience, mostly seconded by their local education authorities, who later employed them as teacher–counsellors or as full-time counsellors, mainly in large secondary schools. The function performed depends very much on where the counsellor was trained. There is some confusion about what counselling really is: the training certainly has something in common with social work but one course may emphasise this aspect, another educational and vocational guidance. The big difference between the education welfare officer and the school counsellor (apart from the obvious one of a different status and a full-time professional training for the latter) is that the school counsellor is school-based, forms a relationship with the children themselves and rarely visits their homes. If interviews with parents are arranged, they are most likely to occur on school premises. Both types of worker refer, as need arises, to other agencies, but the pattern varies a good deal. A clear description of how one *part-time* counsellor, with the strong support of the head (a *sine qua non*) introduced the work into a large girls' school has been written by Anne Jones (1970). The account is probably not typical but gives a good idea of the girls' emotional problems and adolescent questions and the delicate process of setting up counselling as a part of normal school life. (See also pp. 294 and 295.)

Services for young people
The Summerfield Committee found in their survey greater contact between youth employment officers and the school psychological service than between youth organisers and leaders and the school psychological service. There is, of course, room for much greater cooperation between all three services. Too often the youth service and the youth employment service, the one concerned with the leisure, the other with the working lives of the same young people, operate in isolation from each other. The former is

part of the provision of further education, formal and informal, which is a duty of local education authorities. The latter service is delegated to them by the Department of Employment, and the majority, especially in more populous areas, do exercise this power. In a few mainly rural areas the authorities have not chosen to provide a youth employment service and the Department of Employment provides it. Now the minimum school leaving age has been raised the upper limit of the youth employment service will probably be raised to twenty-one or twenty-two; until that happens the range covered is sixteen to eighteen years or older if the young people are in full time education. The organisation of the Youth Employment Service is under review.

The youth service is a partnership between the state and many voluntary organisations to meet the recreational needs of the fourteen to twenty-one year olds. The local education authority appoints a youth committee representing the various interests and a youth officer whose duties are largely administrative. Among other activities he tries to promote a service which meets the local needs of youth, advises club leaders, deals with applications for grant in aid from voluntary bodies and sponsors courses for the training of youth leaders. But at the grass roots level it is the youth leader whom the club members know; he or she may be full-time and professionally trained in group work and other skills, but this is a service sustained by a large number of part-time leaders or instructors; and of the part-timers many give unpaid service because of a genuine interest in young people. Latterly there have been developments in youth work with unattached youngsters and a move from traditional methods of running clubs. It appears that the personnel of the youth service and the school psychological service have little contact, but there may be an occasion when the educational psychologist wishes to enlist the help of a youth leader as a part of treatment for a teenager. Apart from mutual referrals, both might undertake educational work on mental health through informal discussions with interested young people, rather like that done by the National Association for Mental Health in the community generally.

The careers officer (or youth employment officer as he is sometimes called) has both educational and industrial interests. His chief function is to serve as a link between young people, their parents and teachers on the one hand and the world of work on the other. He differs from the youth leader in that he deals with boys and girls individually, using the interview as the culmination of the programme in school. It is true the social caseworker, too, uses the interview as a main tool but she has a closer relationship: a careers officer normally interviews up to 500 school leavers per annum, apart from young workers, whereas the social worker's caseload may vary from fifteen to fifty families at a time. However, the two relationships have something in common: the careers officer by supplying information, advice and guidance helps the youngster to arrive at his own decision about a career. He sees nearly all those who leave school at the minimum leaving age, and many who go on to full-time higher education: in some ways educational and vocational guidance are inseparable, and in principle the process is continuous. Unfortunately, in the existing framework of the service, continuity is limited.

Whether careers officers are employed by local education authorities or by the Department of Employment their functions are the same. Like the school counsellors, they depend on cooperation with the heads of secondary schools and work closely with them and with careers masters and mistresses. Parents are invited to interviews and to careers talks and meetings in schools to familiarise them with job requirements and the choice of occupations available. The work has three stages: the first is a programme linking with the school syllabus a knowledge and discussion of working life, of occupations and what they demand in personal qualities and qualifications or training; this programme at its best extends over one or two years and makes use of any method suited to local conditions—radio, television, visits to places of work, speakers and films. The second stage is of one or more individual guidance interviews, held in the school with the careers officer, before which the head supplies a confidential report on the boy's or girl's general ability and attainments and information from the cumulative school record which is relevant to employment and which will be helpful to the careers officer in giving advice. An important part of the confidential report is the school medical officer's recommendation as to any type of work to be avoided, where health risks are indicated. After the interview follows the third stage of job placement and follow-up. Not all school leavers need the help of the service in finding employment; rather fewer than half obtain their first jobs in this way. The service has among its duties that of trying to place any young people who are unemployed and need help on leaving school, and to keep in touch with them during the first years of working life. The last injunction is a gospel of perfection and it is here, when the onus passes to the youngster to make the contact with the service, that the continuity of vocational guidance breaks down. The satisfied customer will see no reason to return, and only some of the unhappy, timid or rebellious unemployed youngsters will do so. Those who are discouraged from coming may be the ones most in need of a social worker's help.

The career officer's industrial interests complement his work with schools and school leavers. If they get crowded out by pressure of other work, the quality of vocational guidance will suffer. He visits places of employment to study occupations, and to maintain good relations with employers, whom he sometimes advises on recruitment and training. He maintains a register of current vacancies and builds up records of job analyses and industrial surveys, which is meant to cover the whole changing field of employment of young people. This is no easy task.

Happily the majority of school leavers do not present social problems, but for the few consultations with or referral to other specialists or agencies is necessary. One of these is the educational psychologist. Inevitably the careers officer sees a few children who were earlier brought to the attention of the educational psychologist, and of these some need continuing help and oversight. They may be at risk during adolescence anyway, but there may be special factors affecting a choice of employment or vocational training. Alternatively a school leaver from a private school may come to the careers officer and appear to be in need of psychological help of a kind that would have been available earlier in his school life had he been in a state school. Like the health visitor and the education welfare officer, the careers officer is well placed to refer to the school psychological service, the child guidance clinic or any other suitable agency. A more accurate assessment than the average school leaving record, passed to the youth employment service, is needed for an educationally subnormal leaver educated at a small private school especially if the parents are unwilling to accept their child's subnormality. The special considerations needed for tactful communication with parents are discussed in Chapter 8. Aptitude and interest tests may suggest that a physically handicapped boy or girl has potential that the school leaving report has not revealed. Both have implications for vocational guidance and job placement. What has been said clearly calls for systematic consultation, interchange, with proper safeguards, of confidential information and very good teamwork over a fairly long period in the interests of all school leavers, whether handicapped or not.

This is even more essential when handicapped pupils are about to leave school or to pass into vocational training. Mention was made in the last chapter of the substantial amount of work the educational psychologist does in this field with the principal school medical officer and his staff. Handicapped children will in every way be less *socially* handicapped later as adults if they manage to achieve a measure of economic independence and the many social satisfactions that go with it. The careers officer, in all his work with the handicapped, has access to the disablement resettlement officer and the rehabilitation services of the Department of Employment, provided under the Disabled Persons (Employment) Acts. In addition, there are the community services provided for the chronically sick and disabled, geared more, but not exclusively, to the homebound and those unable to follow paid employment; these were mentioned earlier as part of the family service of the new social services departments. But it is during the child's school life that the process of planning for his future begins with any assistance these other agencies can give. The cooperation of careers officer, educational psychologist and school medical officer is vital in assessment, guidance and after care in this transition from school to work. Besides having the best possible assessment of his educational and vocational potential, the handicapped youngster should surely have full-time vocational training whenever he is able to profit from it. Fortunately, teamwork is institutionalised in relation to many special schools and could be so organised for all. But some of the handicapped school leavers are in schools for the normal, and a small number (Home Office, 1967) will be found in residential community homes (previously approved schools or children's homes). The latter present a double challenge and should not be overlooked, since a history of deprivation or delinquency is added to the handicap and parental support may be lacking. Those in the day schools for normal children and in the community homes are perhaps most likely to slip through the net and drift into unsuitable work, unemployment and delinquency. A hazard for the school leaver from the residential special school in the past was that he could have been trained for an occupation that did not exist in his home area. With greater cooperation between schools and the youth employment service, and between careers officers of different areas, this is unlikely to happen today. But it does point to the need for careers officers to be brought into consultation at an early stage by the school.

Finally a word should be said about the rehabilitation services of the Department of Employment. A handicapped boy or girl, whether leaving school or later, may be assessed at one of the industrial rehabilitation units over a period of anything from a few days to twelve weeks, may apply for full-time vocational training and receive free tuition and a subsistence allowance during the training, and may apply to be included in the Disabled Persons' Register. Registration is intended to give a certain priority and a degree of protection to disabled people in the open labour market; the Acts require larger firms to employ a certain quota who are disabled. The system of rehabilitation depends for success on a high degree of coordination between statutory and voluntary bodies, and there are severely handicapped people who have benefited greatly from it. But, however good the provision and however kindly and interested the careers officer, the fact remains that there is nothing like enough vocational training for the handicapped. Much of it is still left to the initiative of voluntary bodies. The other defect of services for handicapped young people in this vital period of transition is the lack of a continuing relationship with a social worker or of a proper system of after care, as some research has shown (Ferguson and Kerr, 1960).

Apart from cooperation with regard to handicapped school leavers, an educational psychologist whose interest lies in the links between educational and vocational guidance may be invaluable in a number of ways: in promoting psychological tests for vocational assessment, in research projects for evaluating the service, in job analyses and by participating in in-service training of careers officers.

The National Health Service

Since its inception in 1948 the National Health Service has had a three-pronged administration; the family doctor services; the local authority personal health services and the hospital services. Proposals for reorganisation have been published and were scheduled to occur in April 1974 (at the same time as reforms in local government). They have changed this hitherto tripartite structure into a unitary administration by area health boards, the boundaries of which correspond with those of the new county councils. Reference has twice been made to the local authority personal health services—within this second heterogeneous group—in connection with the new social services departments and with the school health service. Some clarification is needed of the social work aspects of the other two 'prongs'.

The general practitioner can now be added to the three colleagues previously said to be in a strategic position to give early warning of social problems and to take preventive action by suitable referral to other agencies. He can do this because he visits and gives a service to the whole family and often knows its members very well from birth. It has been remarked that in some instances health visitors have been attached to general practice. In addition two promising experiments of attachment of social workers were mentioned by the Seebohm Committee, who regarded 'team work between general practice and the social services as vital', pointing out that health centres and group practice provided the proper base for it, though provision of health centres falls short of this ideal (Home Office, 1968a, paras. 690–700). The same Committee strongly emphasised the need for better communication between the two professions for they share responsibility in a range of situations that relate to the emotional aspects of illness. They summed up: 'The general practitioner is in touch with a higher proportion of those who are in difficulties than any other of the social services and he needs the full support of them all.'

The other settings of social work in the National Health Service are in the hospitals. The medico-social worker (previously called the almoner) may be attached to one hospital or a group. She, for the post is generally filled by a woman, is concerned with the social care of patients and their families, and is therefore one of the hospital team and advises the medical and nursing staff about any personal and social circumstances that might help or hinder a patient's recovery. She also has close contacts in the community with the social services department, the health visitor, the disablement resettlement officer and voluntary organisations.

The psychiatric hospital or the psychiatric unit of a general hospital employs a psychiatric social worker who performs a similar task in the care of the mentally ill. The same worker may be a member of the child guidance team and work in both settings. Much of this work is with families in the community, some of whom will very possibly be known to the educational psychologist as a member of the same team. The reduction in length of stay and of numbers of patients in mental hospitals followed from the implementation of the Mental Health Act 1959, with its emphasis on community care. Community care, as we saw earlier, is now the duty of the new social service departments, so there is necessarily a close link between them and the psychiatric hospitals and units in the pre-care and after-care of patients. There are different ways of organising this very demanding kind of social work as between local authorities and area health boards. Some areas have extremely well integrated schemes of mental health services to which the school psychological service makes its contribution. It is advisable for the educational psychologist to find out in his own area exactly where responsibilities lie.

Social security

Material aid in the form of cash payments to meet a variety of hazards to income is the responsibility of the central government administered through the local officers of the Department of Health and Social Security. It is of two kinds: (*a*) insurance benefits obtainable as a result of fulfilling contribution conditions, both being paid to a certain extent on an earnings related basis; (*b*) supplementary benefits which anyone over sixteen years of age is entitled to claim on proof of need. Claimants to the latter may receive also a rent allowance or help towards mortgage repayments.

This is one of the services where personal help and the duty to care for the welfare of clients is combined with a uniform standard of administration according to stated regulations. There are, however, discretionary payments of supplementary benefits again on proof of need. Whereas a social worker may have a caseload of forty or fifty individuals or families, a supplementary benefits officer may have a caseload of up to a thousand. In the spring of 1971 the Department launched a campaign to seek out those in need and to try to ensure that all citizens, especially members of families with children, had all the benefits to which they were entitled. This was a prelude to introducing in August of that year the newly devised Family Income Supplement. This is payable to families living on very low wages on proof of need and up to a certain maximum. The parents or parent (the supplement is payable to single-parent families) must be in paid employment.

There are probably few children in contact with the school psychological service whose parents are in receipt of supplementary benefits, but the claims are likely to be heavier in educational priority and poorer urban areas. Attention has been drawn to the greater prevalence of social problems in families of children with low intelligence and in remedial classes, and poverty is a fairly common occurrence in this group. Though the cases may be few the educational psychologist needs to know in general the statutory provision for income maintenance, while it rests with the social worker to ensure that the parents are aware of their full entitlement. For instance, a parent with dependent children claiming supplementary benefit is automatically entitled to a range of other means tested benefits, free school meals being one of them. The supplementary benefits officer is normally a member of the case conference or local coordinating committee, previously mentioned, and it is here that the educational psychologist, mental welfare officer and others concerned with different facets of the same problem in the same family will meet him.

Housing

It was noted earlier that rent arrears, like absenteeism, may be a symptom of an incipient social problem or of deeper trouble. Moreover, just as chronic poverty or the repercussions of an unexpected financial crisis in the family may accentuate maladjustment or learning difficulties, so may bad housing. Even when the family income is adequate, in parts of the country where there is overcrowding and a severe housing shortage a family may suffer ill-health or a child be deprived of space to play or to do homework through bad housing. It is often an associated factor in mental illness though appropriate action may be left to a social worker or referred to the social services department.

Unlike that of health and education, housing provision is not universal and comprehensive. Roughly half the houses in England and Wales are provided by the smaller local authorities, now district councils, the other half by private enterprise. The staff of the social services department usually cooperate closely in family casework with the housing authority, and may prevent family breakdown where eviction is threatened. Early warning is, of course, less easy where the family is in privately rented accommodation. In local government the housing authority is not the same as the social services authority. Unfortunately from 1 April 1974 the two services are still administered at different levels, social services by the county and housing by the district. There are, however, indications that the government is committing itself to greater responsibility through housing advisory centres and a fair rents policy, to be applied in both public and private sectors.

Voluntary bodies and voluntary assistance

There have been references in this chapter to provision by voluntary organisations for deprived and delinquent children, for problem families, and of unpaid voluntary service given by individuals of goodwill to the youth service, to the after care of ex-prisoners, and to London school children and their families. These are a few of the many voluntary bodies and forms of voluntary service that proliferate in Britain. Most of our statutory social services depend greatly on them and the educational psychologist meets them in connection with all the social services so far discussed: a few of their distinctive features and functions may usefully be summarised. In general voluntary organisations pioneer and experiment, complement or supplement statutory services, raise money, co-ordinate a particular kind of provision, e.g. for the disabled, or all the services in a town, e.g. a council of social service, draw attention to new needs or to gaps in the services by forming pressure groups and in many other ways constitute an important segment of social provision. A few illustrations only are given.

The Royal National Institute for the Blind provides some of the special education establishments mentioned in Chapter 2, Worcester and Chorley-wood Colleges, residential grammar schools for blind boys and girls, and residential education for blind pupils with multiple handicaps at Condover Hall. At the invitation of the Department of Education and Science, since 1956 it has also provided a residential course (which includes vocational assessment) at Hethersett, to bridge the gap between school and employment. The Spastics Society plays a similar part in provision for spastic children and adults. Both organisations, in addition to residential institutions, offer social work and employment advisory services. Over two-thirds of existing approved schools (community homes) were established by philanthropic or voluntary bodies. Another important function of some voluntary organisations is to offer a personal service to help support handicapped people and their families in the community. At the national level the coordinating function is usually combined with consultation with government departments on policy.

There are many other kinds of voluntary action which also might interest the educational psychologist. In a special category are local branches of the Association for the Welfare of Children in Hospital, and of the Association for the Advancement of State Education. Both of these may be sensitive to certain needs in the community and be able to alert official committees to them. A good example of unpaid service by a volunteer is mentioned in *Half our Future* (Ministry of Education, 1963, para. 232), the volunteer acting as informal counsellor to pupils leaving a senior girls' school. It is evident that, if statutory provision is lacking in time of need, the educational psychologist may be able to explore other resources of a voluntary nature.

Problems of referral and of risk registers

Questions of whether to maintain registers of children or families 'at risk', when to intervene in family life and of the transfer of confidential personal data between professions or even between those in the social work profession pose some difficult considerations of professional ethics. An attempt is made here to suggest a few guiding principles, but within these each case may be decided on its merits.

The argument for maintaining a register of those at risk (whether of handicapped children by the school medical officer; of problem families by the director of social services; or of 'disadvantaged' youths by the careers officer) is the laudable one of doing it in the client's interest, of using it to take early action in preventing a more serious problem. It is no use having a risk register unless the professional worker assumes the 'right to intervene'. But if the parent is not breaking the law in the way he treats his child, who has the right to intervene and on what grounds? Whose standards are to prevail? Further, the maintenance of *separate* risk registers appears to conflict with genuine cooperation and coordination. Therefore, it is argued by the Plowden Committee and others that the confidential information should be shared. But who is to agree to the sharing and as to what information is relevant for what purpose?

There are certain principles well recognised by professional social workers and applied in the interests of their clients. (If the 'client' is a child, one assumes the parent acts for him until he is sufficiently mature to make his own decisions.) The social worker tries to build up a relationship of mutual trust between herself and the client; any confidence given within this relationship is only divulged to a colleague with the client's permission and when necessary in the interest of the client or the community. She also refrains from standing in judgment over her client and, consequently, respects his right to self-determination. For an elaboration of these and other principles reference may be made to any textbook on social casework, but it is an oversimplification to expect it to resolve all the difficulties of confidentiality and of the code of ethics observed by the social worker. Useful discussion papers on the problems of confidentiality and a code of ethics have been published by the British Association of Social Workers (1970).

Two main points can be made here. The codes of ethics of the social worker and of the educational psychologist, which are probably very similar in kind and in application, are matters of concern to their professional organisations. The organisation of risk registers at local level is a question of mutual consultation and agreement between the chief officers and staff of the departments concerned, and especially of local authority social services, education and health departments, in the light of guidance which professional associations and central government departments may give. The devising and maintenance of confidential record cards and files, as well as cumulative school records, are an essential adjunct to the procedure adopted.

Conclusion

An attempt has been made in this chapter to put the work of the school psychological service in perspective in relation to those other social services with which it may be expected to collaborate. It has been possible to sketch only a short outline, and one biased towards interaction with the school psychological service, of those services that touch on the welfare of the family. The constant factor is the presumed existence of a desire by all the professional people concerned to engage in team work at any point if it will enable a service to function more effectively. The chief variables are the type of worker—from unpaid amateur to professional social worker or civil servant; and the administrative framework—varying from small voluntary body to a nationwide network of local offices of a large government department. It seemed unwise to burden the reader with too much detail of legislation, since Acts are constantly changing and reference can be made, as need arises, to those who administer them or to one of the useful explanatory booklets. It will not be surprising, however, if the educational psychologist's impression of the allied social services is one of great complexity and some confusion; but it may be reassuring to reflect that harassed parents and children have others on whom to lean and that the burden is not his alone.

Part Two

Diagnostic procedures

Child assessment is one of the first stages in the educational psychologist's operations. His assessment techniques are varied and range from the relative precision of a well-designed psychometric instrument to the intuitive skills which may be involved in a clinical interview. The educational psychologist needs a wide range of techniques if he is to deal adequately with the varied problems that he has to tackle. Thus he may be called upon to conduct a survey of a large county in order to determine the incidence of reading disability in a primary school age group, or he may be asked to investigate the difficulties of a child of twelve who is showing signs of school refusal.

The purpose in Part Two is to discuss the usefulness of the numerous tests and techniques now available to the educational psychologist and to consider aspects of their application. A scheme of classification is necessary, and the scheme proposed by the British Psychological Society (1965) will be adopted. The Society suggests a threefold classification:

1. Tests of attainment in e.g., number, comprehension, fluency, etc.

2. Psychological tests of cognitive abilities, special aptitudes, interests, or orectic functions. They include: (a) group tests, normally employing pencil and paper; and (b) tests designed to be administered individually, which may employ apparatus.

3. Clinical instruments or quasitest devices, which permit a diagnostic assessment of individual performance, but do not yield an objective score.

Part Two contains five chapters. Chapter 4 deals with theoretical issues in using the standardised techniques discussed in chapters 5 and 6; chapter 5 is concerned with parts 1 and 2(a) of the Society's classification and chapters 6 and 7 are concerned with parts 2(b) and 3 of the society's classification; chapter 6 deals with the handling of diagnostic situations with children. Chapter 8 deals generally with the handling of diagnostic situations with parents.

4

Theoretical considerations

In almost every task in which he is engaged, the educational psychologist relies on data collected by a variety of means. When he is engaged in the problems of individual children, as in chapter 6, he often has to investigate hypotheses by means of data gathered by a variety of methods (test procedures, interviews, etc.) about a variety of conditions (intellectual qualities of the child, relationships at home, etc.). When he is carrying out a survey to answer a local research question his data are usually collected more simply, through standardised procedures such as questionnaires or attainment tests.

But irrespective of the methods used for data collection there are some basic considerations which apply to data of all kinds. The quality of the data obtained by the educational psychologist depends in no small measure on the quality of the methods he uses to collect it. The quality of the methods can be assessed against a number of considerations and in this chapter we examine some of them in relation to norm-referenced tests.

The principles discussed apply to any method of data collection. 'How reliable are my data?' is a question which can and should be raised in relation to information collected through an interview as well as to a set of scores obtained from a reading test. But since the greatest concern for quality of data has been shown by the norm-referenced test, it is this method of data collection that we use in this chapter to illustrate these principles. The reader is invited to generalise the application of the principles of evaluating methods of data collection discussed below to the other techniques of data collection used, which are discussed in later chapters in this Part. He is also strongly advised to read Levy (in press).

Evaluating educational and psychological tests

In choosing an attainment test or a group test of ability the educational psychologist usually has to decide between various possibilities. The evaluation of test material is a task which demands some knowledge of a number of elementary principles of measurement in psychology and education. There are obvious practical considerations to be taken into account, most notably the expense of a test and the time it takes to administer. These are not discussed, but their importance can rarely be neglected.

Construction

The test manual should give details of the construction procedure. Test construction is a specialised activity and it is not usually necessary for the educational psychologist to be an expert in it. But he should have an acquaintance with the techniques used to construct his tools and he should be able to distinguish the well-constructed test from the poorly constructed one. Among the questions that can be asked are the following:

(a) What principles were followed in deciding the test content?

Consider an eighty-item test of numeracy among ten-year-olds. One test constructor may have decided to include twenty items on each of the four rules of number. Another constructor may wish to allocate twenty items to reasoning problems and include ten on knowledge of time and ten on knowledge of length, leaving forty items for the four rules of number. A third constructor may wish to include some items dealing with capacity. But whatever the content its composition should be stated in the manual and the rationale given.

(b) What determined the type(s) of item used in the test?

The range of item types commonly incorporated in standardised tests is documented in many texts (e.g. Wood, 1960), and includes true–false items, multiple choice items, matching items, completion items, etc. There are certain problems associated with the use of the different item types and a good test constructor chooses item types with care. As an example of the sort of point which needs watching, consider tests of verbal ability at the primary school level. Such tests often use multiple-choice items, e.g.

Black is to *coal* as *white* is to   fire snow grey bright

In a test of a hundred items, each of which requires a choice to be made from four possibilities, a score of twenty-five can be obtained through chance alone, if a child guesses at random. This situation can be dealt with, at slight inconvenience to the scorer, by using a correction for guessing. The appropriate formula is

$$S = \frac{R - W}{n - 1}$$

S is the score to be used in assessing the child's performance,

R is the number of right answers (25)

W is the number of wrong answers (75)

n is the number of choices per item (4)

So in this case $S = 25 - (75)/(4-1 = 0)$, which is a much better evaluation of the guesser's performance than 25.

But children rarely guess and the guessing correction is not always incorporated in the multiple-choice verbal ability tests which are available.[1] Those few children who do guess, however, are usually the children who are quite unable to tackle the easiest item—perhaps they even cannot read—and these are usually the children in whom the educational psychologist is most interested. Consequently, where an educational psychologist is using a test to identify low ability children, the usual multiple choice type of test, without guessing correction, can lead to errors, admirable though it may be for other purposes.

(c) *What item analysis techniques were used?*

Test constructors usually create about three or four times the number of items they will use in the final version of the test. The items are tried out in order to choose those most suitable for incorporation in the final version. In order to choose well, test constructors calculate two characteristics of each item, its difficulty and its discriminating power.

Difficulty refers to the proportion of the try-out population who pass the item. An item which is so hard that it is passed by none of the population is said to have a facility index of 0. An item which is so easy that it is passed by all (100 per cent) of the population is said to have a facility index of 100. An item of intermediate difficulty which is passed by, say, 40 per cent of the population is said to have a facility index of 40.

Discriminating power is a measure of the extent to which an item distinguishes the good performers from the poor performers. Good and poor performers can be defined in a number of ways. Let us, for the sake of illustration, take a definition which test constructors occasionally employ and regard all children who score at or above the median, when their performance on *all* the items is totalled, as good performers. Children who score below the median are then regarded as poor performers.

Now let us consider two items, both of which are passed by 40 per cent of the try-out population. (Facility index in both cases is 40.) In the case of the first item the 40 per cent who are successful may come entirely from the good performers (the top half), while the poor performers (the lower half), all fail.

In the case of the second item the successful 40 per cent could conceivably be equally distributed between the top half and the bottom half.

---

[1] The fact that they are 'power' tests, rather than 'speed' tests, makes its incorporation less necessary. See Wood (1960), p. 39.

Although both items are of equal difficulty, the first is clearly a perfect discriminator, whereas the second is of zero discriminating power. A clear discussion of the simple discrimination model is given in Nuttall (1973).

Many item analysis procedures have been developed, most of which are much more complex than the example given.[1] The characteristics of the items which are accepted will determine the characteristics of the test itself. For example, a test may be needed as part of a programme of educational guidance designed to select the lowest 10 per cent of the population in reading ability, so that further enquiries, followed by recommendations, can be made. A test whose items have been chosen so that high reliability is obtained in the region of the tenth percentile is clearly valuable here, so that selection errors are minimised. A test should therefore give information about its rationale for item analysis and for item choice, so that its suitability for a particular task can be more easily assessed.

(d) *Are the instructions clear and unambiguous?*

(e) *Is the presentation and format attractive?*
These seem obvious questions to ask but often they assume considerable importance in choosing a test for a specific purpose. There are tests of reading readiness, for example, which are quite appropriate for use in the ordinary infant school. But in schools and classes for slow-learning children, containing a proportion of children with perceptual problems, the spacing between items needs to be much more generous to allow the instructions to be followed properly.

Standardisation
When the items have been chosen, the format decided and the instructions composed, the test is standardised. Some of the more important questions to ask about the standardisation procedure are suggested below.

(a) *What are the characteristics of the standardisation population?*
Tests are standardised on specified populations and details of the standardisation population should be given in the manual. The age range is the most obvious characteristic. It cannot be assumed that a test is standardised on children of the age range of the conversion table in the manual. Test constructors sometimes extrapolate their standardisation findings so that the commercially available test covers a wider age range than that of the standardisation population.

Given certain conditions, this is a justifiable procedure, but the manual should indicate the extent (if any) to which extrapolation has taken place.

[1] For a discussion on various techniques of item analysis see Gulliksen (1950) or Anstey (1966). A useful comparison of a number of item analysis methods is given in R. Evans (1968).

Different parts of the United Kingdom exhibit different overall attainment standards. See, for example, Horton (1973) for a survey of reading standards in Wales.

The social class breakdown of families of the standardisation population is increasingly becoming regarded as an essential piece of information. It is important that this breakdown should refer to the actual children of the standardisation population, and not to the area in which the standardisation took place. Usually standardisation is carried out in state schools, not private schools. Different parts of the country vary significantly in the percentage of children attending private schools. If a test has been standardised in an area where this percentage is high, then the social class breakdown of the area would give a distorted picture of the standardisation population.

The date of standardisation is extremely important, especially for tests of attainment. The Newsom Report (Ministry of Education, 1963) showed how, in a period of nine years, the average reading standard of secondary school children improved by twenty months. The Plowden Report (Central Advisory Council for Education [England], 1967) gave information of the marked changes in reading standards in primary schools. The norms provided for reading tests standardised in the early 1950s (or before), are clearly seriously inaccurate for children today. This type of discrepancy is known as 'zero error', and underlines the importance of knowing the date of standardisation.

(b) What data are given on reliability?
Every test should be accompanied by data on the reliability of scores obtained from it. Reliability is an indication of the accuracy with which we can treat the score which children obtain on the test, and there are a number of different approaches to the measurement of reliability, each of which expresses its estimate of reliability in the form of a correlation coefficient. These different approaches each tap different sources of inaccuracy in test scores and consequently reliability coefficients calculated by these different methods for the same test will vary.

The five main types of reliability coefficient are given in Table 4.1, which is taken from Anastasi (1961).

Reliabilities calculated by the first two procedures are usually lower than those calculated in other ways since individual fluctuation across a period of time enters. Clearly the size of these two coefficients will depend, among other things, on the time which elapses between test and retest, and where stability coefficients are quoted this information should always be given.

The split-half method usually produces the highest type of reliability, and coefficients calculated through Kuder-Richardson formulae usually

Table 4.1   Types of reliability coefficients

Procedure	Conventional designation	Error variance
Retest with same form on different occasion	Coefficient of stability	Temporal fluctuation
Retest with parallel form on different occasion	Coefficient of stability and equivalence	Temporal fluctuation and item specificity
Retest with parallel form on same occasion	Coefficient of equivalence	Item specificity
Split-half (odd–even or other parallel splits)	Coefficient of internal consistency	Item specificity
Kuder-Richardson (and other measures of inter-item consistency)	Coefficient of internal consistency	Item specificity and heterogeneity

the next highest. Kuder-Richardson formula 20 is reasonably easy to compute and gives a coefficient which is equal to the average of all possible split-half coefficients. It is very often used when coefficients of internal consistency are quoted for group tests of attainment. These are usually very high. Its relationship to Cronbach's coefficient a is discussed in Willmott (1973).

The interpretation of the reliability coefficient(s) given in the test manual will thus depend on the *sort* of reliability coefficient that the test constructor offers and its relationship to the task for which the test is being chosen. Other things being equal, it may seem that the higher the coefficient the better the test. But there are other factors which affect the size of the coefficient, apart from those factors already mentioned.

One factor is the length of the test—a short test will tend to have a lower reliability coefficient than a long test. The effect of doubling a test's length on its reliability is given by the Spearman-Brown prophecy formula

$$r = \frac{2r'}{1+r'}$$

where r is the reliability expected for the doubled test and r' is the reliability of the test. Thus if a test has a quoted reliability of 0·70 one effect of doubling the length of the test will be to increase the reliability to 0·82 $[(2 \times 0\cdot70)/(1+0\cdot70)]$.[1]

The reliability given for a test will also depend on the characteristics of the group on which it was calculated. Many tests do not use the full

---

[1] For a detailed discussion of the effect of increasing test length Gulliksen (1950) should be consulted.

standardisation sample for reliability calculation and draw a special sample of children for this purpose. If this special sample is more homogeneous than the standardisation sample then a lower reliability will result than if the full range had been used. Thus if the reliability is calculated from a sample of eight-year-old children it will be lower than the reliability calculated from a sample of children from, say, the eight-, nine- and ten-year-old groups taken together.

Some tests quote several different reliability coefficients, obtained on age groups of different range and this practice is helpful in choosing a test for a particular purpose.

The same principle, that restricting the range of the population diminishes the size of the reliability coefficient calculated from it, applies to a restriction in ability—or indeed to a restriction in any quality which is positively correlated with the test. If this point is not understood, consider a test of a simple physical skill, speed of running. Imagine twenty children, one from each age group 0 to 19 years inclusive. There would be a wide variation in speeds between the children and the correlation between age and speed would be positive and very high. Now imagine that we had taken twenty children who were all within a week or two of each other in age, tested their running speeds, and worked out this correlation between age and speed. Many other variables, such as natural talent, drive, etc., now affect the situation to a much greater extent than they could previously and the oldest children in this second group of twenty are only marginally likely to be the fastest runners. The correlation between age and speed will now appear low (though still probably positive). One effect of restricting the range of the population has been to diminish the correlation. This is the effect which applies to the calculation of reliability coefficients on populations whose range is restricted.

An example of this effect is shown in the manual for the first version of the Illinois Test of Psycholinguistic Abilities (McCarthy and Kirk, 1963). The split-half reliability coefficients of six-month age groups between the ages of 2 years 6 months and 9 years range between a maximum of | 0·94 and a minimum of +0·85. But the overall split-half reliability coefficient for the whole age range (2 years 6 months to 9 years) is +0·99.

All these points need consideration in evaluating the quoted reliability of a test.

(c) How valid is the test?

Every test should give information on validity, i.e. how well it fulfils the purpose for which it was constructed. The distinction between reliability and validity is easily appreciated by considering a test of children's height measured by means of a ruler. This would be a highly *reliable* test, but if the purpose of the exercise is to predict the performance of the children in academic subjects in a year's time then the test is virtually useless—i.e. its *validity* for this purpose is negligible. As a predictor of the children's height in a year's time it would of course have a good validity. There are four main types of validity which test constructors have accepted.

(i) *Construct validity.* Tests are usually intended to measure abstract qualities or 'constructs' such as intelligence, reading skills, etc. The extent to which a test measures the quality specified is an indication of its construct validity. The existence of these psychological and educational constructs has been demonstrated through statistical procedures such as factor analysis and these are the procedures which are usually used to determine how well a test meets its measurement objectives. Thus a test of so-called 'general intelligence' may be tried out in a battery of other tests and a factor analysis performed on the resulting scores in order to see the extent to which the test of general intelligence is really loaded with 'g', the general intelligence factor. The greater the g loading of the test, the greater is its construct validity. Construct validity is perhaps the most satisfactory theoretical approach to the problem of validity. Thus factor analytic studies of the Terman-Merrill scales (reported in Anastasi, 1961, pp. 204–5), indicate clearly that in the higher age ranges this test is measuring a verbal ability factor.

(ii) *Predictive validity.* Sometimes the theoretical content of a test in terms of factor loadings is not as important as the extent to which a test predicts behaviour in a certain situation. Thus a test designed to help in selecting children who will respond quickly to remedial education is fulfilling the purpose for which it was constructed if the children it identifies do respond quickly, regardless of the factor loadings of the test. This approach to validity is known as predictive validity, and is particularly applicable to tests used in educational and vocational guidance, where findings on predictive validity should be quoted in the test manual. The validity of tests used in the 11+ examination was measured by checking on the extent to which they predicted success in GCE examinations in the secondary schools (see, for example, Vernon, 1957, ch. 5).

(iii) *Concurrent validity.* Some tests are used to provide speedy and trustworthy measures of qualities which would otherwise require less economical assessment. Thus a test may be developed with the intention of measuring emotional instability in children, a quality which had hitherto been assessed through psychiatric interview. One way of checking on how well the test fulfils this aim would be to correlate test scores with the psychiatric assessments, obtained concurrently. This is known as concurrent validity.

Concurrent validity is sometimes shown by correlations between the test and other, established tests in the same field. But unless the new test has virtues which are absent in the old test (e.g. economy) a very high concurrent validity of this type may make one wonder why the new test was constructed at all.

(iv) *Content validity.* In this approach to validity the test content is carefully scrutinised in order to see how well it covers the particular field the test is measuring. Thus if a test of word recognition consists of a set of words which children are asked to recognise and the set chosen is a reasonable sample of the population of words which one can expect children to recognise then the test is indeed valid. It has content validity, regardless of whatever other information other approaches to validity may provide. This approach to validity is perhaps less satisfactory than the other approaches, but it is used with tests in some areas of educational attainment.

Well standardised tests provide information in some or all of these areas of validity. In choosing tests the user needs to be aware of the different rationales behind these different approaches and to evaluate the tests in relation to the purpose for which he intends to use them.[1]

Interpreting scores

Single scores

A score on a standardised test will give information on how well a child has performed in relation to others of his age. There are a number of different scales in use which give this information, the most common being percentiles, standard deviation scores (z-scores), deviation quotients, t-scores and stanines. The relationship between the more important of them is shown in Fig. 4.1, from which it can be seen that a deviation quotient of 115 (where $\sigma = 15$), a percentile score of 84, and a z-score of $+1\cdot0$ are all equivalent scores.

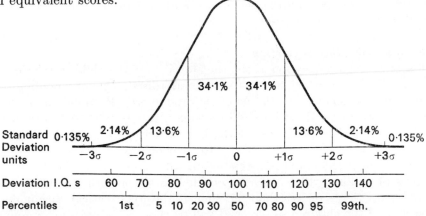

Source Vernon (1960)

Fig. 4.1   The relation between the normal distribution, deviation IQs and percentiles

[1] Unfortunately few published tests use the multi-trait multi-method matrix approach to validity. See Campbell and Fisk, 1959, Psychol. Bull. vol. 56, (2) 81–106.

Some tests, especially attainment tests, give scores in terms of attainment ages. In this case the score obtained does not give information about a child's standing in relation to his own age group, but in relation to average performances of other age-groups. This is an easily grasped way of presenting results, perhaps particularly for educationalists, used to thinking in terms of age groups, but it is associated with difficulties of interpretation. Thus units of attainment age are likely to have different sizes at different points in the scale. The meaning of a one-year increment in reading age between reading ages six and seven will be quite distinct from the increment in reading age between reading ages thirteen and fourteen, a situation which has implications for the interpretation of remedial reading results, for example. This point is discussed in Davies and Williams (1974).

Older tests used to furnish an attainment quotient which was calculated by multiplying the ratio of attainment age to chronological age by 100, i.e. AQ = (Att. age)/(Chron. age) ×100. This type of attainment quotient cannot be interpreted in the same way as a deviation quotient and is fast disappearing.

The meaning which can be attached to a single score depends upon a number of factors, some of the more important of which are given below.

The administration

It is useless to attach meaning to scores if the test has not been administered in accordance with the instructions of the constructor. For example it is sometimes tempting to use a group test as an individual test. But this is of no value; the tables of norms will have been constructed on the performance of groups, and the performance of an individual may represent an entirely different situation.

The standardisation population

All scores give information about the standing of the child in relation to the population on which the test was standardised. Thus if a reading test was standardised on a population of children in, say, Birmingham in 1970, then the scores obtained by children today, in any part of the country, will represent their reading standing in relation to the 1970 Birmingham children of their age group, and not to their own peer group.

This is of considerable importance in taking decisions about deviant groups of children. If it has been decided to screen off all children with reading quotients of less than 85, then if the hypothetical Birmingham test is used the children so screened will be those whose reading standard is lower than that of the 1970 Birmingham children with scores of 85. The contemporary group of poor readers may be very different in size from the 15 per cent that might have been expected (see Fig. 4.1) since standards of reading will vary between areas and across time. In situations of this nature the educational psychologist will be wise to follow Vernon's advice (1960, p. 92) and produce his own local norms. This approach is likely to be particularly valuable for attainment tests where variations between areas and across time (zero error) may be high. (It is almost essential if comparisons between scores on different tests are to be meaningful.)

A particular problem of interpretation arises in the case of handicapped children. Should the raw score of a spastic child on an intelligence test be evaluated in comparison with a 'normal' population, through the test's ordinary conversion table, or should the score be evaluated in comparison with the scores of a population of spastic children, which the test itself may provide, or which may be available in the journals?

The short answer is that both types of evaluation should be readily available and both should be used. In the final analysis the reason for the assessment will decide to which of the two evaluations should the greater weight be attached. Thus if the child has been seen with a view to his suitability for transfer to a school for spastic children then his development in relation to that handicapped population will be the more important information. But if the child has been seen for vocational guidance it may be more important to know his standing in relation to the ordinary population.

The reliability of the test

Each score obtained on a test is a score which is likely to vary on retest. The reliability of the test gives the extent to which variation is likely to occur for the population on which the reliability figures were obtained. No test is perfectly accurate and each score represents a measurement taken from a band of inaccuracy around a hypothetical true score. The greater the reliability the narrower the band of inaccuracy.

The statistic which determines the range of this band of inaccuracy is the standard error of measurement (SEm), which depends on the reliability of the test and the standard deviation of the test scores. A low reliability will increase the band of inaccuracy: the larger the spread of scores that a test gives the broader will be the band of inaccuracy associated with a single score. The formula for the standard error of measurement is

$$\text{SEm} = \sigma\sqrt{1-r}$$

Take a test with a reliability of 0·89 and a standard deviation of 15 points.

$$\text{SEm} = 15\sqrt{1-0·89} = 5 \text{ points.}$$

This figure of 5 points is our best estimate of the standard deviation of the distribution of scores which would be found if a child could be given this test a large number of times. The single score which we obtain for a child from our one administration of the test is taken from this distribution of test scores and our best guess of its position in the distribution is that it lies at the mean (the hypothetical 'true' score). So if a child obtains a score of 94 on a test with a standard error of measurement of 5 points we assume his retest scores will be normally distributed with a σ of 5 points about a mean of 94. This enables us to use our knowledge of the normal curve (see Fig. 4.1) and say that there are about two chances in three that a retest score of a child who scores 94 will lie between 89 and 99 (94 $\pm$ 1 σ, i.e. 94 $\pm$ 5). If we want to increase the accuracy of our prediction of retest performance we have to extend our boundaries.

A probability of occurrence of one in 20 (the 0·05 level) is frequently valuable to calculate. The boundaries of the score range set by this level of probability are obtained by calculating the scores which lie $\pm$ 1·96 σ from the mean. So we can assume that there is one chance in 20 that a retest score of a child who scores 94 on this test will lie outside the range 84 − 104 (94 $\pm$ 1·96 σ, i.e. 94 $\pm$ 10, to the nearest whole number). Conversely we can say that there are 19 chances in 20 that a retest score of a child who scores 94 will lie between 84 and 104. Confidence bands appropriate to other probabilities can be derived from Table 4.2.

Table 4.2

Fractional parts of the total area (taken as 10,000) under the normal probability curve, corresponding to distances on the baseline between the mean and successive points laid off from the mean in units of standard deviation. Example: between the mean and a point 1·38σ ($x/\sigma = 1·38$) are found 41·62 per cent of the entire area under the curve.

x/σ	0·00	0·01	0·02	0·03	0·04	0·05	0·06	0·07	0·08	0·09
0·0	0000	0040	0080	0120	0160	0199	0239	0279	0319	0359
0·1	0398	0438	0478	0517	0557	0596	0636	0675	0714	0753
0·2	0793	0832	0871	0910	0948	0987	1026	1064	1103	1141
0·3	1179	1217	1255	1293	1331	1368	1406	1443	1480	1517
0·4	1554	1591	1628	1664	1700	1736	1772	1808	1844	1879
0·5	1915	1950	1985	2019	2054	2088	2123	2157	2190	2224
0·6	2257	2291	2324	2357	2389	2422	2454	2486	2517	2549
0·7	2580	2611	2642	2673	2704	2734	2764	2794	2823	2852
0·8	2881	2910	2939	2967	2995	3023	3051	3078	3106	3133
0·9	3159	3186	3212	3238	3264	3290	3315	3340	3365	3389
1·0	3413	3438	3461	3485	3508	3531	3554	3577	3599	3621
1·1	3643	3665	3686	3708	3729	3749	3770	3790	3810	3830
1·2	3849	3869	3888	3907	3925	3944	3962	3980	3997	4015
1·3	4032	4049	4066	4082	4099	4115	4131	4147	4162	4177
1·4	4192	4207	4222	4236	4251	4265	4279	4292	4306	4319

Table 1.2—*contd.*

1·5	4332	4345	4357	4370	4383	4394	4406	4418	4429	4441
1·6	4452	4463	4474	4484	4495	4505	4515	4525	4535	4545
1·7	4554	4564	4573	4582	4591	4599	4608	4616	4625	4633
1·8	4641	4649	4656	4664	4671	4678	4686	4693	4699	4706
1·9	4713	4719	4726	4732	4738	4744	4750	4756	4761	4767
2·0	4772	4778	4783	4788	4793	4798	4803	4808	4812	4817
2·1	4821	4826	4830	4834	4838	4842	4846	4850	4854	4857
2·2	4861	4864	4868	4871	4875	4878	4881	4884	4887	4890
2·3	4893	4896	4898	4901	4904	4906	4909	4911	4913	4916
2·4	4918	4920	4922	4925	4927	4929	4931	4932	4934	4936
2·5	4938	4940	4941	4943	4945	4946	4948	4949	4951	4952
2·6	4953	4955	4956	4957	4959	4960	4961	4962	4963	4964
2·7	4965	4966	4967	4968	4969	4970	4971	4972	4973	4974
2·8	4974	4975	4976	4977	4977	4978	4979	4979	4980	4981
2·9	4981	4982	4982	4983	4984	4984	4985	4985	4986	4986
3·0	4986·5	4986·9	4987·4	4987·8	4988·2	4988·6	4988·9	4989·3	4989·7	4990·0
3·1	4990·3	4990·6	4991·0	4991·3	4991·6	4991·8	4992·1	4992·4	4992·6	4992·9

Source: Garret (1953)

Suppose we wish to establish the range of scores within which we can be 90 per cent certain that a child with a score of 103 will fall on retest. Table 4.2 shows that the distance between the mean and the demarcation point for 45 per cent of the scores is 1·645. Therefore 90 per cent of the scores on retest will lie within the range $103 \pm 1 \cdot 645 \times 5$, i.e. within the range 95 to 111. (For work with individual children this particular probability level is useful.)

Effect of score value on interpretation

In the preceding discussion it has been assumed that the child's obtained score is the mean of the distribution of scores which would result from repeated testing. This assumption is reasonable if the score which was obtained lies at or close to the test mean. If the score is well above average the chances that it might have been one of the higher scores in this distribution are increased. Conversely the lower the score the greater the likelihood that it might have been one of the lower scores in this distribution. Either way our estimate of the band within which retest scores are likely to fall will be altered. This altered estimate is easily obtained.

First, estimate the mean of the distribution of retest scores. If a child obtains a score of 120 on the test mentioned above (with a reliability of

0·91) then the mean of the distribution of retest scores is $100 + 20 \times 0·91 = 118$.

Proceeding as before, we can be 90 per cent certain that a retest score will lie between 110 and 126 (118 ± 8).

If at the age of eight a child obtains a full-scale IQ of 80 on the Wechsler Intelligence Scale for Children (Wechsler, 1949), then we can be 90 per cent certain that a retest score should lie between 75 and 89. (From the WISC manual $r = +0·92$ and SEm $= 4·25$ at $7\frac{1}{2}$ years of age.)

The interpretation of score differences, as opposed to single scores, is an important but somewhat more technical part of the educational psychologist's skill, and dealt with in Appendix 2, to which the following tables refer.

Table 4.3   The reliability of a difference: standard error in two tests having standard deviations of 15

r_m	1%	5%	10%		1%	5%	10%
0·99	5·46	4·16	3·49	0·81	23·82	18·12	15·21
0·98	7·73	5·88	4·94	0·80	24·44	18·59	15·61
0·97	9·46	7·20	6·04	0·79	25·04	19·05	15·99
0·96	10·93	8·31	6·98	0·78	25·63	19·50	16·37
0·95	12·22	9·30	7·80	0·77	26·21	19·94	16·74
0·94	13·38	10·18	8·55	0·76	26·77	20·37	17·10
0·93	14·46	11·00	9·23	0·75	27·32	20·79	17·45
0·92	15·46	11·76	9·87	0·74	27·86	21·20	17·79
0·91	16·39	12·47	10·47	0·73	28·39	21·61	18·13
0·90	17·28	13·15	11·04	0·72	28·92	22·00	18·47
0·89	18·12	13·79	11·57	0·71	29·43	22·39	18·79
0·88	18·93	14·40	12·09	0·70	29·93	22·77	19·11
0·87	19·70	14·99	12·58	0·69	30·43	23·15	19·43
0·86	20·45	15·56	13·06	0·68	30·91	23·52	19·74
0·85	21·16	16·10	13·51	0·67	31·39	23·88	20·05
0·84	21·86	16·63	13·96	0·66	31·86	24·24	20·35
0·83	22·53	17·14	14·39	0·65	32·33	24·60	20·64
0·82	23·18	17·64	14·80	0·64	32·79	24·95	20·94

r_m is the average of r_{xx} and r_{yy}.

Source: Phillips (1961).

Table 4.4   Significant deviations from expectation

For standard scores of mean 100 and standard deviations 15, with Tests X and Y, the table shows difference values which are significant at 5 per cent and 1 per cent levels of probability.

$r_{xy}=$ Y	0·50	0·55	0·60	0·65	0·70	0·75
70	$\frac{6}{15}$	$\frac{7}{16}$	$\frac{8}{16}$	$\frac{8}{16}$	$\frac{0}{16}$	$\frac{9}{16}$
80	$\frac{11}{20}$	$\frac{12}{20}$	$\frac{12}{20}$	$\frac{12}{20}$	$\frac{12}{19}$	$\frac{11}{18}$
90	$\frac{16}{25}$	$\frac{16}{25}$	$\frac{16}{24}$	$\frac{15}{23}$	$\frac{15}{22}$	$\frac{14}{21}$
100	$\frac{21}{30}$	$\frac{21}{29}$	$\frac{20}{28}$	$\frac{19}{26}$	$\frac{18}{25}$	$\frac{16}{23}$
110	$\frac{26}{35}$	$\frac{25}{34}$	$\frac{24}{32}$	$\frac{22}{30}$	$\frac{21}{28}$	$\frac{19}{26}$
120	$\frac{31}{40}$	$\frac{30}{38}$	$\frac{28}{36}$	$\frac{26}{33}$	$\frac{24}{31}$	$\frac{21}{28}$
130	$\frac{36}{45}$	$\frac{34}{43}$	$\frac{32}{40}$	$\frac{29}{37}$	$\frac{27}{34}$	$\frac{24}{31}$

Note: There are two variables: the correlation between X and Y, and the value of Y. The body of the table contains the values of $(Y - X)$. In each cell the upper figure is the 5 per cent value and the lower figure the 1 per cent value.

Source: Phillips (1961).

5

Assessment procedures in schools

Purpose

Since there is a wide range of assessment procedures used in schools, varying from the simplest of unstandardised classroom tests, through carefully produced and nationally normed measures of attainment to sophisticated operations for assessing personality, it is clearly not possible in the space of this chapter to cover the whole of this range. The purpose here is to discuss some of the principles which lie behind the use by educational psychologists of assessment procedures in schools and to discuss some of the current tendencies in the practice of educational psychology in this area.

For a discussion of the general principles of assessment procedures and methods of testing, one of the standard textbooks such as Cronbach (1966) or Anastasi (1961) will be needed. Mittler (1970b) is particularly useful as a guide to practice in this country. Buros (1972) is the recognised sourcebook for lists and reviews of psychological and educational tests, and details of all instruments but the most recent are included in his very wide coverage. A much less technical book which focuses on some of the field of interest of the educational psychologist is S. Jackson (1968). This gives brief basic data about a number of tests which are currently in use in British schools, and is a useful volume for the educational psychologist to have on his shelves.

Another useful handbook is O. G. Johnson and Bommarito (1971). This covers over 300 measures of child development which are not commercially available, but have been reported, usually in journal articles. Those surveyed can be used within the age range from birth to thirteen years. Many of them are easy to use as they stand, or with a little development by the educational psychologist.

Finally, no educational psychologist should be without the various catalogues of the National Foundation for Educational Research.

How the educational psychologist is involved

In many areas the educational psychologist is still seen as the person on the local authority staff who is the expert in the field of assessment in schools. Even where local authorities employ their own personnel, often with specialist qualifications relating to this particular field, the educational psychologist still has a part to play in the instruments which are used in schools, if only because to some extent they impinge on his own work. Reports on children sent to him by schools will contain information about assessments made by the schools. Hence the instruments used are of importance and interest to the school psychological service.

The educational psychologist is involved in assessment work in school in different ways. First, he is involved *indirectly* since he is often called upon to advise his local authority over their assessment procedures. This advisory work might involve dealing with a question from a teacher about an appropriate reading test to be used with eight-year-old children. It might also involve an educational psychologist with a particular interest in this field setting up a test advisory service which can be widely used by schools and other institutions in his area for help and guidance over the assessment procedures they use.

This indirect advisory role can work out in practice in various different ways. For example, the school psychological service might run a small test library on its premises, where teachers can consult examples of different tests. The school psychological service can also, often in conjunction with the local area training organisation,[1] conduct courses to help with increasing the expertise of interested teachers and others. In carrying out work of this kind it is important to be sensitive to the professional problems which arise in ensuring that tests are used carefully and judiciously. For example, the National Foundation for Educational Research, which through its test service is the largest supplier of tests in this country, has a carefully designed system for grading tests (NFER, undated) to ensure that appropriate instruments are not placed in the hands of individuals who, without appropriate training, might make incorrect inferences and take damaging action as a result of this. The British Psychological Society, through its Test Standards Committee, has published documents (1965, 1969) which indicate ways in which tests can be described and courses classified. These are useful, and all psychologists should read them.

[1] The Area Training Organisation (ATO) is a consortium of parties interested in training arrangements for teachers. The members are usually colleges of education and other institutions of higher education, teacher associations and local education authorities. The ATO is normally closely linked with an institute of education and its influence is limited to the area of operation of the institute concerned. Following the publication of the White Paper on Education (Department of Education and Science, 1972c) the future of ATOs may be in doubt.

Secondly, the educational psychologist is also involved *directly* in using instruments of this sort. For example, he may be required to carry out surveys of different sorts on the school population. Thus he may be required to conduct a survey for identifying children in need of remedial teaching. He may also be required to collaborate with the schools in assessing the need which the local authority has for providing classes for children with severe behaviour problems. In both these cases it is likely that some form of assessment work in schools will be needed, including measures of children's attainment and possibly questionnaire assessments of children's behaviour. So the psychologist needs to be proficient in survey work of this sort. He may also be required by his local authority to conduct small scale research. Even if he is not involved personally in conducting the research (see Department of Education and Science, 1968b), he may well be involved in helping over the planning of the local research project which will again involve being able to give correct guidance over the use of the assessment measures which the project will involve.

Kinds of procedures used

So far the discussion has suggested that the educational psychologist's use of assessment procedures in school is related to advisory work and work of a survey/research kind. But the educational psychologist also works with schools over the development and progress of children who have been referred to him as individuals and whom he will have himself assessed, using the approaches to be discussed in chapters 6 and 7.

Chapters 6 and 7 deal with the psychologist's work with the individual child. Since procedures used in schools and those used with individual children overlap, the difference between this chapter and the following two is not one of kind but of emphasis. In the direct and indirect work with schools discussed in this chapter the psychologist is unlikely to use the specialised individual procedures of the diagnostic interview discussed later. He will, however, use procedures which can be classified into four main areas:

(*a*) *Measures of school progress.* Attainment measures, both individual and group, are widely used in schools. They range from simple measures of reading performance to more sophisticated measures of the extent to which the objectives of a particular curriculum have been met.

(*b*) *Group tests of cognitive skills.* The individual tests of intelligence and intellectual development are related to the work discussed in the next two chapters. But survey work, for example, sometimes uses group tests of cognitive skills. The single-score intelligence test has fallen into disfavour,

but measures of children's thinking processes—for example verbal reasoning, or fluency, or conservation are widely used.

(c) *Group tests of personality and adjustment.* The advent of the counsellors
(Hamblin, 1972) has led to a considerable increase in the use of techniques
such as 'problem inventories' with older pupils. Survey work for identifying maladjustment has led to widespread use of teacher-completed check-
lists and schedules with younger children. At the same time increasing
sophistication in the development of factorially validated instruments,
has led to a growing appreciation of the use of Eysenckian and Cattellian
tests in particular circumstances.

(d) *Non-standardised techniques.* The assessment procedures so far described all have associated norms, even if these are crude in some cases
(e.g. maladjustment schedules). But there are a number of non-standardised procedures which are of great use in schools. One example is sociometry
(K. M. Evans, 1962, is an easy introduction to the application of sociometry
to education). This technique gives speedy and useful information on
group social structure. Another is interaction analysis (Flanders, 1970)
which gives teacher and educational psychologist insight into the nature of
the environment of classroom relationships.

   In the rest of this chapter we shall concentrate on questions which apply
to the educational psychologist's use of some or all of these four kinds of
procedures.

Preliminary considerations

Every time a child is seen in school, he suffers some break in his ordinary
routine. This, as is discussed in chapter 6, can be disturbing to him. At the
same time any assessment work in school also involves a disruption of the
school routine. Fitting the work into the pattern of school events is therefore not only a matter of courtesy on the part of the educational psychologist, it is also a procedure which is most likely to produce undistorted
results. Thus an assessment procedure which can be completed within the
confines of a normal school period has considerable advantages. On a
large scale, survey work involving large groups of children, particularly at
secondary school, is conveniently carried out at particular times of the year
only. The summer term is particularly difficult because of external
examinations, and half-terms and beginnings and end of terms have to be
avoided. Many primary schools, too, find that they are at their busiest
for the month or so before Christmas, so in planning large-scale work with
schools it is important to bear the time of year in mind.

Another way to avoid widespread inconvenience is through the judicious use of sampling procedures in connection with survey work. Too often psychologists have carried out surveys which measure the attainment of every child in an age group, when for the purposes of the survey a sample of perhaps 25 per cent or so would have been quite as effective (see P. Williams, 1970). If it is necessary to obtain an assessment of every member of, for example, a particular cohort, it may still not be necessary to test every child. For example it may be quite as useful and much less time-consuming and costly to obtain teacher's opinions on all children, followed by assessment procedures on an indicated proportion. These are points which should be considered during the planning of the assessment work, to which we return later. The important point to stress here is the need for thought in ensuring that the assessment work the psychologist does is as little disturbing to the routine of the children and the schools as possible.

Another important point is the choice of instrument. The way in which instruments can be evaluated has been discussed in chapter 4, since this applies both to work in schools and to psychological work with individual children. But, particularly in relation to work in schools, the psychologist may sometimes need to design instruments of his own. For example, he may need to prepare a questionnaire which samples teachers' opinions about the incidence of particular behaviour in schools. Or he may need to prepare a more elaborate set of questions which children will themselves be required to answer in order to identify individuals with particular problems. Examples of good and bad questionnaires are given in Oppenheim (1966).

The need to pretest the assessment procedures, whether the psychologist is conducting a survey or carrying out research work, can easily be overlooked. The value of pilot work can never be overemphasised, even if it involves nothing more than a try-out of a test which is new to the educational psychologist. Unforeseen questions are almost sure to arise, they must be dealt with before any survey or investigation is launched.

Most of these preliminary issues are matters of courtesy and commonsense. Careful planning and forethought will deal with many of them. Table 5.1 is a checklist prepared from the point of view of the research

Table 5.1   Data collection: a brief checklist

PLANNING

Scale	Is the number of research variables compatible with the research design?
	Is there a risk of collecting more data than is needed?
	Is the sample of really manageable proportions?

Table 5.1—*contd.*

	Is the sample manageable geographically? Has approval/support of LEAs, Heads etc. been obtained? Has a pilot study been allowed for?
Instruments	Are the test instruments entirely relevant to the design? Are questionnaires sufficiently to the point? Has a coding frame been prepared? Will the instruments be available when needed? Are the tests of a reputable standard of construction? Is pretesting necessary? Is individual testing necessary? Is there back-up support for interpreting test results?
Timing	Has allowance been made for the possible intrusion of holidays? examinations? medical inspections? extramural courses? early leaving?
FIELDWORK	Are school staff properly in the picture? Can the researchers administer the test instruments themselves? Is test administration easily standardised? Have administration procedures been 'rehearsed'? Are there likely to be any problems of rapport? Has allowance been made for extra copies of test instruments? Is a stopwatch necessary? Are seating arrangements adequate? Is school/staff/pupil anonymity safeguarded?
DATA PREPARATION AND PROCESSING	
General	Are there proper arrangements for scoring/coding and the checking of scoring/coding? Is your raw data retained in a safe place?
Machine analysis	Before card punching, have all coding ambiguities been removed? If for document reader, are the answer sheets entirely 'clean'?

Source: Nuttall and Moore (1973).

worker. The educational psychologist is in a somewhat different position, since, unlike the research worker, he is employed by the education authority and so questions of access to school, for example, are likely to be more easily resolved. But the checklist is still of use as a reminder of steps which should be considered in planning.

Group tests and the psychologist

Many of the instruments which the psychologist uses in educational work are group tests. These differ from individual tests and procedures in a number of ways.

In group testing the psychologist has hardly any opportunity for making an assessment of the child's personality through observation of the way he tackles the task. There is no face-to-face contact of the sort which can prove so informative in individual work and which is discussed in the following chapters. It is difficult to assess any unusual approach or reaction if there is no personal contact. For the same reason the educational psychologist has less chance of assessing the extent to which a child is cooperating in the procedure. There are a number of social and emotional reasons why performance in tests may vary, and where a psychologist has no opportunity of observing carefully a child's performance he is less able to deduce the extent to which a child is collaborating. In other words, although the test used may possess satisfactory reliability and validity data, for some children inappropriate estimates are bound to be obtained.

Another aspect of the same problem is the possibility of chance errors. For example, children may turn over two pages of a booklet at once. While this is not an inherent weakness in group testing itself, it does underline the importance of adequate supervision in the testing situation in order to minimise the occurrence of this kind of event.

Group testing is of little use for work with handicapped children. Nearly all group tests are designed specifically for children without physical or personality problems and this to some extent limits their use in the educational psychologist's practice. Group tests are usually designed to discriminate in the middle ranges of children's performance. Many of the earlier group tests of ability and attainment were designed to be of use for children in the ten- to eleven-year-old age range, so that schools could use them in their preparation for the eleven-plus procedure. Discrimination would then be at its best in the high-normal range so that the eleven-plus procedure could be at its most informative. For that particular purpose, this was admirable, but for psychologists working with children of limited attainment such group tests, though still very much in use, are not very effective.

Group tests are rarely designed to be used with young children. It used to be felt that children below the age of six years or so could not participate in the group testing situation and that this view applied to some extent to children as old as eight. There is evidence that this may have been something of an oversimplification (R. Evans, unpublished) but nevertheless any educational psychologist wanting to use group tests with young children must be aware of the special problems which this age group poses

Learning problems

Children with learning problems are discussed in Part Three. There the point is made that learning problems and behaviour problems are closely related. This means that in investigating learning problems, an educational psychologist may well draw on any or all of the kinds of assessment procedures mentioned on p. 88. But he will probably lean more heavily on measures of attainment and cognitive skills for identifying children with learning problems and for assessing the effectiveness of the changes he recommends.

Measures of attainment and cognitive skills have a long history of use in education. A fairly full, but not comprehensive list is published in the annual catalogue produced by the National Foundation for Educational Research. There are also a number of specialised texts which discuss particular sub-areas (e.g. J. D. Williams, 1970).

In choosing which attainment tests to use or to advise, attention must of course be paid to the special points for evaluating measuring instruments discussed in chapter 4. At the same time there are a number of specific points which need to be made.

Curriculum variety

One of the interesting features of education in the last decade or so has been the dramatic increase in the variety of curricula in schools. This change has considerable implications for the psychologist's work in schools. Thus it is of little use any educational psychologist picking up a test of mathematics, for example, and looking at the data about validity in order to check that the test will be appropriate. Nor is it much use his looking through the content as an additional safeguard, if his only criterion is the mathematics which he himself was taught at school. The curriculum in many schools is changing very rapidly. One school may be involved with Nuffield mathematics. Another less than a mile away may be involved with an entirely different mathematics project with an entirely different set of objectives. It is idle to think that one can use tests of attainment without knowing in considerable detail what the objectives of a school, or even class, are likely to be in a particular curriculum area.

One implication of this rapid curriculum change is the need for educational psychologists themselves to help in devising appropriate criterion-referenced tests. A clear discussion of the difference between criterion-referenced and norm-referenced tests is given in Nuttall (1973).

Curricular change

Not only have traditional subject areas such as mathematics spawned a range of new curricula. New areas have been introduced into the curriculum. Thus the current growth of emphasis on language teaching represents a new area of interest and work for the school psychological service. There is now a large psychological literature on languages skills and their development. Important though this area is, its recognition as an important sphere of activity in the early school years in particular, has been slow to be achieved. From the point of view of this chapter it is unfortunate that many of the skills used to assess the quality of the language achievement of children are again, buried in the research literature. There are notable exceptions, particularly the pioneer work of the ITPA (Kirk *et al.*, 1968), mentioned on p. 122, and the Reynell test (Reynell, 1969). But both of these are individual scales and are not appropriate to survey work. There is a considerable need for simple group tests which can be used to survey the language skills of children without requiring the labour entailed in a detailed analysis of the linguistic structures involved.

Another example of curricular change is the spread of interest from the teaching of early reading skills to the teaching of intermediate reading skills. The nature and development of these skills have been discussed by Merritt (1970). As we become aware of the different kinds of reading skills, so the various ways in which children's progress can be assessed, and then facilitated, become apparent. Specialist work in this area is the province of the remedial teaching service, but all psychologists will need to be aware of developments which can rapidly outdate their assessment procedure, and the publications of bodies such as the Schools Council should be studied carefully.

Non-cognitive variables

The developments in the assessment of cognitive skills in school have been great. But it can be argued that developments in other areas have been at least as rapid. The strong relationship between personality variables and classroom attainment has been demonstrated and explored. Much of this has been built upon the body of work accomplished, in particular by Warburton (1968). Studies such as that of Cattell *et al.* (1966) in which a high proportion of the variance in attainment in primary school children was ascribed to variations in personality characteristics have indicated the increasing importance that assessment of personality characteristics of children is likely to have for the educational psychologist. The scales which are currently used to measure these variables rest mainly on one of the two main theoretical approaches to personality assessment, that of Eysenck on one hand and that of Cattell on the other. Useful though these scales are for research purposes the strong grounding they have in psychological theory may make them at the moment a little too remote for easy direct application to children's classroom learning problems.

Motivation questionnaires

Another approach which is more immediately relevant is that of the motivation questionnaire. Here scales have been developed by Entwistle (1968) and Summer and Warburton (1972), for example, which should have direct application to the work of educational psychologists interested in screening groups of children to identify those with poor motivation. Linked with motivation is the idea of reward-preferences. Scales such as those described by Dunn Rankin et al. (1969) have value in giving psychologists and teachers insights into the kinds of rewards children prefer.

Motivation for work and attitude to school are two concepts which are closely entwined, and psychological work on attitudes and their measurement is likely to have an increasing impact on the work of the educational psychologist in school. It is rarely that one finds an attitude scale particularly suitable to an enquiry which one wishes to make. For this reason school psychological services may want to construct simple attitude scales for screening the attitude of pupils to particular questions. Guidance on doing this is readily to be found in A. N. Oppenheim (1966) and classroom problems and children with difficulties may well be the more easily solved and handled with a knowledge of the nature of the attitudes of the groups and individuals concerned.

Behaviour problems

Children with behaviour problems are discussed in Part Four. Nowadays, screening for maladjustment and behaviour problems is a growing part of the psychologist's preventive work in schools. The kinds of measures that are likely to be used by the educational psychologist in connection with behaviour problems will mainly be drawn from group tests of personality and adjustment among and from non-standardised techniques.

Measures of personality and adjustment have a much shorter history than measures of attainment and intellect. Indeed, it can be argued (see chapter 2) that the much slower development of special provision for children with behaviour problems is a function of the relatively short time that acceptable measures of behaviour and adjustment have been available. Useful reference material is given in P. E. Vernon (1964), Chazan

(1970) and P. Williams (1974). At the same time, the following additional points regarding variety of assessment need to be made.

Maladjustment is very 'situation-specific', i.e. deviant behaviour may appear in one environment but not in another. It is also a variable condition: the behaviour can disappear and reappear. For these reasons the investigation of maladjustment and of behaviour problems demands a variety of approaches. This is why the techniques of Bower (1969) are useful. Many school psychological services will want to develop their own patterns of assessment for screening for maladjustment and behaviour problems, and the Eli Bower technique is a very useful point of departure for this. The three-pronged weapon that Bower recommends—assessment by peers, by adults and self-assessment—can be modified or extended to suit particular purposes and particular age groups. For example, with younger children the educational psychologist would want to rely more on assessment by adults and use a modification of the peer-assessment technique to which young children can respond validly.

General points

There are a number of general issues connected with assessment procedures in schools, irrespective of whether the educational psychologist is concerned primarily with learning problems or behaviour problems:

Early identification
Recently, (see p. 19), early identification of handicapped children has been increasingly recommended. There has been a proliferation of scales designed for this purpose. Most of these scales are American in origin, most are short, but many lack accurate validation. A useful survey has been prepared by Ferguson (1972).

Most of these approaches have been concerned with children who are in the first stages of schooling. One of the newer procedures, which has been produced in this country, is the Swansea Evaluation Profile (School Entrants) which has emerged as a result of the Schools Council Research and Development Project in Compensatory Education. This is designed for use with children in the first term of their infant or first school. It combines information about the child's development with information about his adjustment to school and information about his home background. The purpose of the scale is not only to identify children who are likely to have difficulties in school, but to try to indicate which particular difficulty a child is most likely to experience. The profiles themselves (R. Evans *et al.*, to be published) are new, and the information about their performance is awaited. The technical manual (R. Evans, unpublished) gives information about their construction and technical characteristics.

But early identification does not stop at entry to school. One of the most interesting areas of enquiry and development has been the production of 'risk registers' which local authorities have designed on the basis of information compiled about children from birth onwards. One of the purposes of risk registers has been to ensure that the education services are alerted to the entry into school of a child about whose development there may have been some question or query during the years when the Health and Welfare Services had been concerned (v. p. 67). In the past this has largely meant the identification of individual children with severe learning or behaviour problems, or problems of adjustment associated with physical handicap. These are the children whom education psychologists generally have referred as individual cases. But research such as that of the National Child Development Study (Davie *et al.*, 1972) suggests that the identification procedures which relate at the moment to children of school age may be carried downwards into earlier age groups. We may then be able to screen for children with milder learning problems much earlier than is at present the case.

Measurement of the environment

Much of this chapter has focused on assessing various characteristics of the child in school. But learning and behaviour problems need to be seen in their environment if they are to be adequately described and understood. The assessment of home background and parental attitudes, which are so influential on children's school progress (e.g. Peaker, 1967, 1971) is almost invariably done through the more clinical approach of the parental interview, discussed in chapter 8. Usually, too, this forms a part of the educational psychologist's work with individual referrals which is mainly outside the scope of this chapter. But there is still the school environment itself, information on which is important to the educational psychologist in a number of ways, and which is usually assessed in the non-standardised techniques outlined earlier.

The material circumstances of the school may not be directly influential in school progress. But they do have an effect on questions such as teacher recruitment and teacher morale. These circumstances can easily be assessed by a simple purpose-designed rating scale. Most psychologists will feel they know the schools they visit sufficiently well not to need quasi-objective measures of this variable. But where a local research study tries to answer questions concerned with, for example, the relationship between school facilities and educational success, a scale such as the Infant School Amenities Index (Laing, 1971) is a useful model for the educational psychologist to develop.

More important to individual children with learning disabilities is the psychological atmosphere of the classroom and more particularly the quality and nature of the interchange which goes on between pupil and teacher. Assessment of this relationship is complementary to the behaviour modification techniques which educational psychologists are helping to introduce into the classroom (e.g. Ward, 1971). As an introduction Flanders (1970) is well worth reading. A good description of interaction analysis and a teaching exercise based on it is given by Moseley (1972a). It is a valuable technique for giving teachers and psychologists insight into the classroom setting in which learning and behaviour problems arise.

Sensory handicaps

The presence of sensory handicaps is one of the first possibilities an educational psychologist wishes to exclude when he examines a child. Because of the damage that even mild sensory impairment can cause, screening for children with hearing loss or visual defects is now a regular practice in many local authorities. This is very much the province of school medical officers, and psychologists interested in this side of their work will need to gain specialist training at, for example, some of the short courses run by the British Psychological Society. A useful discussion of methods used in screening for hearing impairment is given in Dale (1962) and there is a helpful chapter by Reed in Mittler (1970b). Much of the educational psychologist's work in this field will be with individual children, which is the theme of the next chapter.

6

The educational psychologist and the individual child

Approaching the problem

Individual children are referred to an educational psychologist by adults who are concerned about their mental or personal development, behaviour and adjustment or progress at school, or when an educational or vocational choice has to be made. The adult may be the child's parent or another relative, his head teacher, a doctor or psychiatrist, or a member of some other profession concerned with children. His relationship to the child and family will to some extent colour his perception of the problem and determine the relative emphasis he places on its various aspects.

Implicit in each referral are one or more underlying questions: Why is the child behaving like this? Could his work/behaviour/happiness be improved? How could this best be effected? Often, however, the actual questions asked are much more specific, focused on worrying symptoms and their removal rather than on the situation as a whole, and it may fall to the psychologist to introduce a wider perspective.

While educational psychologists vary widely in their personalities and theoretical bias, their approach to problems will have a common element due to their training and experience, distinct from that of other professionals with whom they collaborate. The ways in which different professional contributions can complement one another are discussed in detail in chapter 13; here we are concerned with one aspect of the psychological approach—the application of scientific method to the study of individuals.

His training in experimental design will have predisposed the psychologist to tackle any problem systematically, formulating, checking and modifying hypotheses at each stage, controlling variables that may contaminate results, estimating the error of his measurements, often presenting only tentative conclusions. At the same time experience in life situations (especially perhaps in schools) will have made him well aware of the difficulties of applying these strict canons in investigating the problems of individuals, especially those urgently seeking his help. Still the guiding principles remain. Their use in clinical situations is sensitively discussed by Gwynne Jones (1970) and Shapiro (1970). Wedell (1972) proposes a general diagnostic strategy for the investigation of learning difficulties. In this chapter we shall consider how these principles work out in practical situations commonly encountered by educational psychologists.

When an educational psychologist is asked to give an opinion about a particular child his first need is to be clear about the real purpose of the referral. This will determine the questions he asks himself, the choice of tests to be given, the behaviour to be specially noted and the form of his final report. It may also prompt him to seek certain information before he sees the child, in order to focus effectively on what still needs to be discovered. Let us take a few typical examples.

Example A
John, a boy of eleven, is referred by the head teacher of his junior school for disruptive and immature behaviour and inability to cope with work. He can scarcely read or write and spends most of his time out of his seat distracting other children. The practical issue underlying this referral is whether the situation can be remedied if John stays in his present class, whether his needs would be better served by a small remedial or tutorial class, or whether he should be transferred to a school for educationally subnormal or for maladjusted children. To answer this question the psychologist must make a full and detailed individual assessment of the boy's abilities, discover how far his retardation is due to low intelligence, how far to specific weaknesses in visual, auditory, motor or linguistic functions, how far to social and cultural impoverishment, and how far to emotional disturbance. He must also consider whether the boy's restlessness is likely to have a neurological basis, whether it may relate to a disturbed family life, or whether it is primarily due to boredom with a school situation he cannot understand. John's performance and behaviour in the various parts of the intelligence test will give clues which can be followed up by supplementary tests, observations and enquiries as needed. Light may be thrown on the problem by getting John to discuss his life outside school, by the use of a scale of social competence (checked with information from adults) and possibly one or two personality tests selected in the light of information already gathered. John's attitude to his learning difficulties is important, and so is his response to a sympathetic adult who tackles him about them: both may affect his readiness to learn in favourable conditions. These and other relevant facts cannot be measured but can be noted from clues in his behaviour and conversation.

Before even seeing the child the psychologist will need some information from the school. Why has the problem not been referred before? Perhaps the boy has only recently come to this school; if so, are there records from his previous schools? If he came from another area he may already have been examined psychologically, in which case a copy of the previous report could save duplication of effort if recent, or if less recent could afford the basis for valuable assessment of progress over time. Has the child missed much schooling or had many changes of teacher, especially in the critical years for learning the basic skills between six and eight? Has he been given any special help individually or in a small group; how much, and how did he respond? What is known about his home background and the attitudes of his parents to him and to his progress? What abilities and interests does he show, if any? How does he behave to adults and children in situations that do not involve learning?

To go into these questions satisfactorily will involve discussion with both the head and the class teacher. Such discussion is essential in any case where the child shows problems of learning or behaviour in school. Some time spent in the classroom observing John's behaviour and associated events will add a further dimension to the psychologist's understanding. If the referral comes from elsewhere, the approach to the school will have to be made, with parents' permission, either before or after the child has been seen.

Example B

Lucy, aged seven, is brought by her parents on their doctor's recommendation because she hates going to school and frequently has bilious attacks or other minor ailments on school mornings, which generally clear up if she is allowed to stay at home. When arranging the appointment, the psychologist asks the parents whether he may contact Lucy's school to learn how she adjusts when she is there, but the mother demurs, saying that the teacher has no time for psychological theories and might take it out on the child if she heard of the consultation. The psychologist notes this observation without prejudice: it may or may not be correct, but does indicate an area of disagreement between mother and teacher. Here the implicit questions are whether the child should be moved to a different school or a different class and/or whether her difficulty lies really in leaving the mother's side.

Since school reports brought by the mother show Lucy to be doing excellent work at school, a detailed assessment of her intellectual abilities is not required, but observation of her approach to tasks she finds difficult will still be valuable, and for this purpose the psychologist may well select certain subtests from an intelligence scale. The initial situation in which the child is asked to leave her mother for the test will itself be revealing about the behaviour of both parties. Should the child be too distressed to comply, the mother may be allowed to accompany her and sit in the testing room for the first ten or fifteen minutes while she settles down and adapts to the new person and situation. During this time Lucy may be asked to draw, to display her known accomplishments in reading, to do a simple puzzle or other buffer task to instil confidence, while note is taken of how far the mother can allow her to make her own adjustment or whether she feels impelled to offer help, encouragement, chiding or criticism, to answer questions intended for the child, or otherwise to usurp the psychologist's attention for herself. In any case she will be asked to withdraw as soon as the child seems able to cope on her own and any change in Lucy's behaviour in her mother's absence will be noted. Her perceptions and feelings about life both at school and at home need to be explored. The exploration may start on a factual basis by asking her the names and ages of her siblings and other playmates, and then proceeding through an ordinary day asking in detail about the daily routines, how much she does for herself and who does things for her; selected questions of this kind will yield a score for social competence which can be related to that of the average child of her age. Tests may be selected which will throw light on her feelings about family relationships and the roles of parents and children. Strangely, no similar tests seem to have been devised in relation to school life. Here the psychologist may put a few tactful questions, encouraging the child to talk and perhaps at the same time to draw a scene or two of her school and the people in it; or he may explore the child's personal constructs in this area, adapting the simplified repertory grid technique developed by Ravenette (1968); or he may devise an *ad hoc* projective procedure such as starting a story about school and asking the child to continue it, either in words or in play with dolls—always bearing in mind the distinction between fantasy and fact.

But clearly it is important to know the teacher's point of view, and either the psychologist or a social worker, if one is available, will have to discuss with Lucy's mother her feelings on the subject until she is able to see the necessity of contacting the school and seeking cooperation.

Management of the situation

Example B shows how the first meeting with a child may have to be discreetly managed so as to gain his confidence and enable him to do himself justice. Procedures must be flexible enough to allow of variation to meet the individual case, as well as adaptation to external circumstances which may be far from ideal.

Educational psychologists usually see children either in their schools or in an office which may or may not be situated in a child guidance centre.

The setting can make an important difference to the child's approach to the meeting, as can the way in which he is prepared for it. In a school the choice, if any, may lie between the medical room, the staff room, an empty classroom and the head teacher's office. The first and last of these may have frightening associations for the child; any of them is subject to invasion without warning; while bells, the noise of children going to play and the general bustle of school life make the situation such that many psychologists will attempt no more than a preliminary chat with the child, or at most a few brief screening tests. In spite of all these difficulties, by doing some of the work in the school, the psychologist gets to know the staff and something of the school environment. This is invaluable to the psychologist and helpful to the school staff. Modern school buildings are increasingly making reasonable accommodation available.

There is also the point that a child called out of his group to meet a special visitor is placed in the full glare of his classmates' curiosity. Most head teachers nowadays are concerned for their children as persons, and it is rarer than it used to be for a headmaster to walk into the classroom and announce to the teacher, 'The psychologist has come to see Tommy Jones', adding to the child, 'Come along, boy, this gentleman is going to ask you some questions'. Some heads will even take over the class while the psychologist has a few words with the teacher about Tommy's problems. He can then ask the teacher on their return to point out Tommy unobtrusively and to allow him to watch the rest of the lesson from a vantage point where he can see Tommy's responses, after which it may be possible to take the boy aside less publicly in the course of a break.

If full investigation is required, the parents are generally asked to bring the child to the psychologist's office. This may be less frightening to the child (unless it is in a medical setting which may reactivate memories of painful experiences) than it is to the parents. Their feelings will be conveyed to the child in the explanation they offer him of the purpose of the visit. It may be presented in terms of help, of punishment, of searching enquiry, or left as a complete mystery, just as the problem itself may take on many shades of meaning depending on the parents' emotional attitude towards it. There is no universally appropriate formula that can be offered to parents for preparing their child; and as their own attitudes to the consultation are as important as his, a preliminary contact with them to discuss the reason for referral, the procedures and the question of preparation is always helpful when it can be arranged. This is particularly true since some psychological procedures appear to the uninitiated to have little or no relevance to the problem.

Example C
Billy, aged nine, was referred by the school medical officer to the child

guidance clinic for nocturnal enuresis. As was customary the parents were offered two appointments: on the first visit a psychiatric social worker would take the social history while the psychologist saw the child; on the second, the psychiatrist, armed with reports from both, would interview the child and the parents, after which a case conference would be held and a joint decision reached as to the best course of action.

Since the medical officer's report indicated some learning difficulties, especially in arithmetic (and since enuresis is sometimes, though by no means always, associated with retarded development), the psychologist embarked on a full assessment of intelligence and attainments, postponing any assessment of personality until a later occasion. Billy was very tense and restless. He never really settled down to the test and only seemed to be giving it half his attention. The inexperienced psychologist did all he could to put him at ease and twice asked rather nervously whether he wanted to visit the toilet. Each time Billy looked down and shook his head in obvious embarrassment. The psychologist felt obliged to report that the boy seemed too anxious to do himself justice on the tests and that the results probably underestimated his ability to an unknown extent. On the second visit the reason became clear. The mother told the social worker: 'He felt so let down after last time. We had told him he was going to see a gentleman who would help him to stop wetting his bed. He expected to be examined physically and to have some kind of treatment, I don't know what. Instead all he got was questions and sums and things. He was so worried he couldn't think.'

What should the psychologist have said to the boy to explain the purpose of the tests? Should he have asked Billy why he thought he had come? To embark on a discussion of his problem might have loosed a flood of confidences that would have anticipated and might have stultified the psychiatric interview, yet to avoid the subject altogether did in fact stultify the test. It is generally best to discover why a child believes he has come. He can then be promised that the problems preoccupying him will be discussed in full, and that everyone is trying to find a solution. If he is bursting to talk about them he should be allowed to do so for a little, the psychologist remaining noncommittal and merely noting what the child says. He can then explain that the tests help the people concerned to understand more about him so that they will be able to help him better. Even though this does not explain everything a child will probably consent to go through with them having ventilated his immediate anxiety and obtained assurance that his problems will not be overlooked. Where the problem is one with which the psychologist himself proposes to deal, or is any kind of learning difficulty, he can of course discuss it more freely at whatever stage seems most appropriate.

In any case the psychologist's whole approach must make it quite clear that he is sympathetic and interested in understanding the child's views. Whether the referral problem is discussed or not, it will be well worthwhile to get the child to talk a little about whatever interests him most. One may ask, for example: What is the thing you like doing best of all? Do you collect anything? Have you any pets? What do you do on your holidays? What is the best time you ever remember having? Any of these questions may lead on to an informative account of some segment of the child's life and these can be pieced together as time permits.

While a good working relationship can often be established with a confident child through this kind of general conversation, shy children may find talking to a stranger an ordeal in itself. They would much prefer to be given something to do straight away, as would most young children whether shy or not. But it would be a mistake to plunge into a scorcable test forthwith; some of the child's attention in the first few minutes will certainly be directed to taking in his surroundings and the new person he must deal with. During this phase he may be offered a task which is satisfying in itself without demanding maximum effort. He may be given paper and colours and asked to draw anything he likes; much can be inferred from his choice of subject and execution of it. Some children, however, spend longer on a drawing than is expedient and dislike being interrupted. A dozen or so variously shaped blocks (such as Lowenfeld's 'Kaleidoblocs') can be offered for three-dimensional construction; if found too attractive to be easily relinquished they can be used as a bait for the next visit. Or a simple puzzle can be tried; should the child be unable to complete it in a short time the psychologist can finish it with him, introducing an element of collaboration.

Once the test proper begins the child will of course have to work without any help at all, and his ability to do this effectively will be as important for the diagnosis of his potential as will the test results. The psychologist's objective will be to maintain the child's morale and motivation at the optimal level so that he displays his ability to best advantage. The test score will then be an estimate of the highest standard he can attain in favourable circumstances; that he may frequently fall somewhat short of this is to be expected since conditions in everyday life are seldom optimal— a point to be borne in mind in reporting the results. But children vary in the conditions they require to elicit their best efforts, and it is here that the psychologist's art comes in. He must be quick to take his cue from the child as to how much praise, reassurance, encouragement, challenge or friendly banter is needed; when to take 'I don't know' at its face value and when to insist on further effort; when to follow up a self-evident failure with an easier test although it may be out of the usual sequence; and when to stop testing altogether for a time and to introduce some more rewarding activity. Most children respond well to a good measure of praise, but praise quickly loses its value if it is seen to be indiscriminate. A trainee psychologist was testing an intelligent child of eight. 'If I cut an apple in half how many pieces would I have?' he asked. 'Two,' replied the child. Eyes on the manual, mind probably on the scoring of some previous response, the trainee murmured, 'Very good! That's very good indeed!' How startled he would have been had he glanced up and caught the look of withering scorn on the child's face! Praise should be given not for success but for what, for *this* child, constitutes a good effort.

Most individual intelligence tests, or the subtests of which they are composed, proceed from easy to difficult items, and one has to continue until a child has failed a specified number of times, in order to find his ceiling of ability. In verbal tests the questions simply become too difficult, but most children are used to being asked questions to which they do not know the answers and will readily accept from the adult a face-saving remark such as 'Those last few are really meant for older people'. Some ask repeatedly whether their answers are correct. To tell them would be to produce anxiety when they were not, with a cumulative sense of discouragement or perhaps a compulsive puzzling over the unknown answers which could deflect their attention from subsequent questions. It is better therefore to tell such a child frankly that it is 'against the rules' to tell them whether their answers are right or wrong (in a school situation one can add with truth 'because you might tell other children the answers'), consoling him at several suitable points in the test with some such remark as 'You did that one jolly well!' 'You are really rather good at this, aren't you!' or whatever comes naturally.

Certain of the non-verbal performance tests are in the nature of puzzles in which failure is self-evident. This is where the perfectionist may have to be comforted, the defeatist encouraged. Success is so important to some children that they will struggle on long past the time limit. It is both kind and revealing, where time permits, to allow such a child to continue, at least with one or two items, until he either succeeds (he need not know that delayed success cannot be credited in the score) or gives up of his own accord. Those who give up prematurely, on the other hand, either from passivity or because it is too painful to try and to fail, can be urged to 'see if you can do some of it' and praised for any partial success.

Timing of tests, where necessary, should be done unobtrusively. A sharp child will nevertheless detect a stopwatch, however silent and carefully hidden. The present writer finds it best, if the child seems intrigued or bothered by it, to satisfy his curiosity by showing him the watch and letting him start and stop it a few times; but it should always be out of sight while he works on the test.

Occasionally (much more rarely than many teachers would suppose) one comes across a child who will not bother to exert himself. He is usually up against authority and resents the whole procedure. This is a rather common attitude among youngsters sent for psychological examination after committing some delinquent act. The only thing to be done is to talk to the child in such a way as to convince him that one is not a punishing authority but somebody interested in him as a person and receptive to his point of view. On occasion the whole first session may have to be devoted to establishing rapport, in the course of which one may learn a good deal about the boy's (or girl's) life and outlook. It should then be possible to persuade the youngster that it is in his interests to show you what he can do of your test. He may even take it as a challenge. The result will be far more valid than any that might be obtained from sulky responses given in a spirit of antagonism.

Observations during the interview

As already suggested, the observations that can be made from a child's behaviour during the interview are often quite as important as the test results. It is convenient to have in mind, if not on paper, a number of headings under which notes can be jotted down for the linked purposes of summarising one's impressions of the child, gathering clues to his problem, writing reports and recollecting the child's individuality at a later date. One possible list of headings would be as follows:

Appearance and physical condition
General behaviour and emotional state
Interpersonal responses
Spontaneous conversation
Response to test demands
Language
Movement

Let us look at these in turn.

Appearance and physical condition
If one saw only a hundred children in a year—and most psychologists see far more than that—it would scarcely be possible to recall every child without some written aids to memory. In the absence of a photograph the most useful notes for this purpose consist of a few words of description of the child's physique, features, colouring and dress, voice and mannerisms, supplemented by a few remarks recorded verbatim. Such a description is also relevant to the child's persona, the impression he makes on others and the reactions he is likely to elicit in consequence. A tall child is often thought to be older than he is and expectations are raised accordingly. A physically and socially attractive child can get away with behaviour

that would not be tolerated in one less favoured. Any physical deformity or peculiarity (unless so marked as to amount to a recognised handicap, which may be sympathetically accepted) can call up primitive aversion which will spread through the peer group and make the child unpopular; or it can cause an Adlerian sense of inferiority, distorting behaviour and relationships from the child's own side. Clothing that is ill-fitting or un-fashionable in the child's own group can produce similar effects, as can dirty nails, skin or hair in a circle that values cleanliness. These and the opposite conditions also give important clues to parental standards and sometimes, as in the case of an effeminately dressed boy, to the role played by the child in the family.

The child's state of health and any signs of fatigue and listlessness are obviously important in deciding whether he is in a condition to do himself justice on the tests.

General behaviour and emotional state
Even more revealing of personality than appearance is the individual's style of behaviour. Posture, gait, facial expression; tics and nervous fidgety habits; constriction or expansiveness of movements; interest in surroundings; the degree and manner in which feelings are expressed—any characteristic that distinguishes this child from others is worth noting. The first interview is bound to be a novel situation for him, and his manner of coping with it may give valuable insight into his powers of adaptation. If the referral has been built up for him into a highly charged event, his ability to accept reassurance and to recover from initial anxiety or, alterna-tively, continuing tension, suspicion and hostility are all important to an understanding of the problem. An unresolved state of emotional distur-bance can vitiate test responses more than might appear to an inexperi-enced observer. It is particularly likely to affect those tests that require clear and precise thinking, as in mathematical operations; speed of response, as for example in coding tasks; and the flexibility needed for rearranging mentally the elements of a situation. The anxious person may also be unable to recall what he knows. If a child is too emotionally upset to function properly, it is best to devote the first meeting to conversation and to creative activities such as drawing, mosaic construction or play, from all of which a good deal can be learnt. It is astonishing how often a child untestable on the first occasion will return relaxed and cooperative on the second visit if once he is convinced that the psychologist is a person who can be trusted not to force him beyond his power to cope. It also helps if the parent who brings him has been similarly convinced.

Interpersonal responses
The child's manner of leaving and rejoining his parents is always worth

noting. With children under school age, and with many in the early school years, a certain degree of dependence in a strange situation is normal; indeed, where a child under five goes straight to a strange adult without a backward look, or ignores his parents on return, one should be alert to the possibility that the bonds of mutual affection are underdeveloped. More common are mother–child pairs who cannot be separated. One may then have to accept the mother's presence in the testing room, at least for a time, and glean what one can about the relationship as discussed in example B. Some children will relate happily to the psychologist as long as their mother is in the room; others respond better when she has left. The manner of making the new relationship can reveal the degree of confidence the child feels both in himself and in other people, his need to put them into a parental role, to test out their authority, to demand praise, reassurance, affection, or to enter into a relationship on equal terms with more or less friendliness, reserve or self-assertion.

Spontaneous conversation
Once a relationship is formed, it is well for the psychologist to remain silent occasionally, allowing the child to talk if he will on his own initiative. It is worth noting the gist of any spontaneous conversation (unless it is too copious to record!), how readily it is offered and its relevance or otherwise to the matter in hand.

Response to test demands
Since the educational psychologist's approach to the child differs from that of a psychiatrist in making specific demands in the form of tests, it is important to note his response to these demands. Children are expected to conform to adults' requirements for a great part of the time and their attitudes in this type of situation are correspondingly important as reflecting a large segment of real life. This is not altered by the fact that the session should be made as pleasant an experience as possible; it is still a situation structured and imposed by the adult. Some of the dimensions on which the child's response can be assessed have already been pointed out. The most important can be listed as follows:

Cooperation *versus* resistance
Interest *v.* boredom
Concentration *v.* distractibility
Stamina *v.* fatigue
Persistence *v.* defeatism
Attitudes to success and to failure
Self-satisfaction *v.* self-criticism.

Although any of these may vary from one part of the interview to another it is possible for those who favour quantification to use five point rating scales for the above or similar variables. Stutsman (1931) in her book on the Merrill-Palmer Scale proposes a series of such scales. Others will prefer to write freer comments. It cannot of course be assumed that the child's behaviour in this unique situation, when confronted for an hour with the exclusive attention of a strange adult, is likely to reproduce his behaviour anywhere else; but it can be compared with the behaviour of many other children in exactly the same situation and this is where individuality shows up. The child shows himself *capable* of good concentration, *liable* to tire easily, *prone* to give up more rapidly than most, *clearly in need* of a boost to his self-confidence, or as the case may be. These are qualities that may seldom be shown or noticed in a large class at school, while their significance may be lost on parents for lack of an objective standard of comparison. Yet they are crucial to the use a child makes of his abilities, and can thus affect the whole course of his life.

Language
Although the standard intelligence tests require some mastery of verbal concepts and include a measure of vocabulary in terms of the range of words of which the subject understands the meanings, they avoid evaluating his actual use of language, since this is so largely determined by culture and social class. There are specific tests of language usage when a measure of this is required, but while such tests show us the resources an individual can muster when challenged, they do not reveal the level at which he habitually communicates. As Bernstein (1971) has shown, this level is fundamental to a person's orientation to his environment, as well as to the understanding of him that others can reach. It is therefore worth noting down verbatim some of the subject's remarks, especially those made in free conversation. A sample of these, selected to include one or two of the most effective sentences as well as a few examples of communication failure, plus any recurrent turns of phrase or verbal mannerisms, can be examined later for characteristics of the linguistic code that the subject employs when talking to an unfamiliar adult. Of course this is likely to be quite different from the code he employs with his peers or with his parents, but it is of interest none the less. With children up to five or six the actual length of sentences is a useful guide to linguistic maturity; while at any age the number of ideas combined in a single statement, the complexity of logical relationships shown in the use of subordinate clauses, and the appropriate matching of words and sentence structure to the meaning to be conveyed are indications of the intelligent use of language. This will be modified both by the subject's social background and by his personality: either may for example favour terseness or pithy expressiveness over elaborate formulation of ideas, but quality will be apparent through

these local and personal variations. Similarly with correctness and clarity of pronunciation. The psychologist should at the same time be on the lookout for defects which may be a handicap to the subject in conveying his meaning. These can include difficulty in the production of certain speech sounds, a tendency to stammer or stutter or 'trip over the tongue', undue hesitancy and inability to think of the right word or to formulate a sentence to the child's own satisfaction, frequent recourse to makeshift expressions such as 'you know', 'what do you call it' or vague terms such as 'thing'. Some of these are characteristic of children at certain stages of development where their thinking outruns their verbal facility, while at older ages they may be due either to social and educational impoverishment or to a specific language handicap.

Comprehension of language is probably easier to assess from the responses to verbal test items, but incidental observations are again relevant. For example, where a subject repeatedly asks for repetition of questions one must consider whether his attention is elsewhere, whether his hearing may be at fault or whether he has difficulty in taking in ideas expressed in words. Partial deafness should be suspected where the subject watches the speaker's lips or where his own speech lacks (for example) high frequency consonant sounds; this suspicion can be checked with an easy screening test such as the Reed (n.d.) Hearing Test cards, mentioned in the previous chapter. Where hearing is intact, difficulty in comprehending questions and instructions may be due to a poor cultural background, a non English speaking home, or a tendency to receptive aphasia

Movement

Another set of characteristics worth noting is the amount, quality and coordination of the subject's movements. Is he a child who simply cannot sit still even when absorbed in what he is doing? Or at the other extreme, does he seem to find it an effort even to get up from his chair? Are his movements unusually quick or slow? Notice his gait as he walks, his posture when standing and sitting and the coordination of large muscles: the use he makes of his body can reveal a good deal about his attitude to life and his physical effectiveness. Then notice his finer movements, especially of the hands in writing or drawing and in handling material in performance tests—are they deft or clumsy, relaxed or tense, fluent or jerky? The handling of writing implements is a skill so constantly called upon in education that even a slight handicap can put a person at a serious disadvantage. In the early stages of learning to use a pencil, therefore, it is worth calling the attention of a teacher or parent to an awkward or overtense grip before it becomes a habit too ingrained to alter.

Lateral dominance—the degree of right- or left-handedness and the dominant or focusing eye—should also be noted where there is either manual incoordination or poor spatial organisation, e.g. frequent reversals in reading or writing. Natural handedness, which is controlled by the dominant cerebral hemisphere, cannot be judged from the use of a pencil as this is subject to training. Observation may be made of the hand spontaneously preferred for tasks requiring fine coordination, such as the balancing of bricks on a high tower, provided the bricks are placed so as to be equally accessible to either hand. For more detailed assessment a selection can be made from the tests proposed by A. J. Harris (1947).

Involuntary movements are also worth noting, whether they are merely clumsy or suggestive of nervous tension. An overflow of energy in the form of fidgets and fiddling is natural enough in a child obliged to sit still for an hour, but tics, tremors, mouthing, hair-twiddling and the like are commonly signs of anxiety.

Principles of test administration

This chapter so far has emphasised the less formal aspects of the psychologist's task: choosing a strategy of investigation, managing the situation so as to ensure good cooperation, collecting incidental clues to the child's individuality. In considering test administration we now come up against the limits beyond which informality cannot usefully go. One of the ways in which a psychologist's approach to diagnosis differs from that of a psychiatrist is in the application of objective standards of comparison. The psychologist functions on two levels at once. Like the psychiatrist, he sees the subject as a unique individual with his own pattern of strengths, weaknesses and coping styles; in addition he must see him quite objectively, usually in relation to other subjects of the same age. It is to the latter end that he uses tests. In so doing his aim should be to get not a favourable but a true picture of the subject's abilities and personality. It is as important in the subject's own interest to know his effective limitations as to gauge his potential assets; the former may be the core of the problem for which the psychologist's help is being sought.

It follows that tests should always be administered strictly in accordance with the intentions of their authors. Educational psychologists, who have usually been teachers and who tend through sympathy to identify with children they test, may at first feel a desire for the child to succeed and be tempted to give him 'the benefit of the doubt', or to lead him through supplementary questioning to an answer he could not have achieved unaided. In resisting this temptation one may remind oneself that the child has to compete with others, most of the time without special assistance: his ability to do this is what one is trying to estimate. An assessment of his response to individual teaching would be a different objective requiring an experimental programme, one which a psychologist might legitimately undertake with the help of a remedial teacher, but which must not be confused with diagnostic testing.

The basic rule in testing is that the standard instructions for every item must be followed, since to do otherwise alters the difficulty of the item to an unknown extent and this nullifies its validity as a basis of comparison with the standardisation sample. When using a test for the first few times it is best to read the directions to the subject from the manual (having first studied them oneself); even when committed to memory, which makes for better rapport and closer observation, one should recheck with the manual at fairly frequent intervals, since modifications tend to creep in unawares.

There is an art in giving test directions in such a way as to capture the subject's interest and ensure that he takes in the elements of the task to the best of his ability. This is a matter of tempo, clarity, phrasing and emphasis, all of which the experienced psychologist quickly adapts to the needs of each individual testee. The directions prescribed by some test authors in an effort to forestall misunderstandings are so long-winded that they can easily cause confusion to subjects whose verbal decoding ability is limited. For such subjects, including all young children, the instructions must be broken up into short phrases. For all subjects it helps to emphasise the few key words, and this can be done in such a way as to produce a conversational, not a stilted effect.

There are certain occasions for deviation from the rule about strict adherence to the standard wording. The special problems of testing the very young, the handicapped and the hyperkinetic will be discussed later. Apart from these there are the problems of communicating with people from cultures or subcultures where the words do not have the meanings that the test assumes. The British Psychological Society has approved certain changes in the instructions of the Binet and Wechsler Scales for use in Britain, and these are now incorporated in manuals on sale in this country. It is occasionally necessary to alter a word to make an item intelligible in a local idiom, but the aim should always be to preserve the original level of difficulty: to check on this it is worthwhile keeping a record of the percentage of children passing the reworded item. Where the discrepancy between the language of the test and of the testee exceeds isolated words or expressions, however, verbal ability cannot be assessed from the test norms. To translate questions into a completely different language, for example, is to take no account of the frequency, difficulty or connotation of words that may approximate only roughly to their English equivalents. In such cases one can only estimate ability within a rather broad range.

The tendency today is to rely less on global estimates of intelligence and more on profiles describing an individual's strengths and weaknesses. This process can be carried beyond the simple reporting of subtest scores, to take account of the quality of responses whether successful or not. In choosing one's marking symbols (which should preferably be unintelligible to the child) it is useful to adopt signs for a near miss, a good quality response, a bare pass etc. although these do not of course modify the score. Abbreviations such as *dk* (don't know), *nr* (no response), are useful to describe the subject's behaviour in failure. Any interesting reply should be recorded verbatim to round out the picture of the subject's thinking. This may be further investigated if time permits by supplementary questioning to certain test items, but this should always be done after the end of the test, never in the middle as it can easily modify subsequent responses. This refers to questioning that goes beyond the normal scope of the test, not to ordinary supplementary questions which may be necessary to establish the scoring of a response.

While most test manuals give instructions, which should be carefully studied, concerning the administration and scoring of the tests, they cannot be expected to cover all contingencies. There will be occasions when scoring is genuinely in doubt; when one or more items have been spoiled through an examiner's error, an interruption or other accident; or when the test could not be completed in the time available. In such cases the best course is to calculate a minimum and a maximum result, counting all the spoilt or omitted items (within reasonable limits) first as failed and then as passed, and thus to report the range of possible score. To this one may add one's clinical impression that the testee is likely to be nearer the top or nearer the bottom of the range. Such a report is likely to be truer and more useful for most purposes than a precise figure estimated on inadequate grounds. Exact figures when obtained should in any case be qualified with a margin of error wherever anxiety, communication difficulty or any other factor throws the slightest doubt on their validity, or where there are grounds for supposing that the quotient may rise or fall in the future.

The scoring of tests nearly always involves clerical work, usually including arithmetic and the reading of tables. This should always be checked, especially when it has been done quickly in order to discuss the test result immediately afterwards, or when a decision affecting the child's education or career depends on it. If children have to be seen in succession it is very advisable to allow ten or fifteen minutes between tests to ensure that all responses have been fully recorded, incidental jottings made intelligible for future reference, and identifying data entered on all test forms and loose sheets. A young child's date of birth and age should always be checked against records or confirmed by the parent. Note that some tests require age in years and *completed* months; others to the *nearest* month. Finally, after each test the material should always be replaced in its proper boxes and cards in numbered sequence ready for the next occasion. A moderate obsession with tidiness is a distinct advantage in carrying out a standardised procedure.

7

Techniques of individual assessment

No attempt can be made here to discuss particular tests in detail or to give a comprehensive list of the tests available. There are far too many, and there is an extensive literature on each of the most widely used scales. Every psychologist should have access to the Mental Measurements Year Book edited by Buros (1972), in which are assembled critical articles on tests of all kinds—an invaluable help in selecting new tests and keeping up to date concerning older ones. Here we shall discuss mainly the types of instrument available for various purposes, mentioning briefly the better known of each type. In Britain, NFER and Psychological Test Publications will advise on the selection of tests and can supply those of many publishers, including some from overseas.

Intelligence tests

The individual test of intelligence, providing as it does a reasonably reliable estimate of general ability sampled through a wide range of tasks, has always been the educational psychologist's main tool—so much so that many people seem to regard the administration of such tests as his chief, if not his only function. When Alfred Binet was asked by the Paris Municipality about 1900 to sort children into those who could profit from the ordinary school curriculum and those who could not, he devised a series of short items which would be given orally and scaled them according to the age at which 50 per cent of the children could give the correct response. From this he calculated the mental age of each child, which taken as a percentage of his chronological age gave an intelligence quotient. When this quotient was found in a majority of cases to vary by only a few points over a period of years it was hailed as a powerful device for classifying children and predicting their future progress and the notion got about—not promulgated by psychologists—that the IQ was an inborn characteristic that could be displayed rather like fingerprints, and which would remain as constant, provided it were accurately measured. This remarkable idea, implying that mental growth should always proceed regularly at some multiple of the average rate, has since had to be drastically revised in the light of longitudinal research, and psychologists have become reluctant to quote exact IQs lest they be taken as eternal verities. Nevertheless, the intelligence test properly used and interpreted remains an invaluable asset, both as a measure (or set of measures) and as a setting for observation.

The intelligence quotient is sometimes regarded as an attempt to measure the g factor which Spearman identified as the general component of ability entering into all cognitive operations. Since no operation is determined solely by g, however, no test can be a pure measure of general ability: the best approximation was sought by adding up the scores on those items selected for their high correlations with the total pool. This criterion dictated the choice of items in several revisions of Binet's scale undertaken at Stanford University by Terman and Merrill in 1916, 1937 and 1960. The result is a miscellaneous assortment of items grouped by age level (six per level) with no attempt at consistency of content from one age to another. The level is found at which the child can pass all items and he is taken up until he fails all, adding credits between these extremes to establish his mental age.

Many of the items in the revised Stanford-Binet scales give revealing glimpses of the subject's thought processes and the scale has thus a clinical as well as a psychometric usefulness for which it is still sometimes employed. The succession of brief items suits young children and those with little staying power, but creates a fragmentary effect with older subjects and permits of no systematic analysis according to types of ability. The formula

$$\frac{MA}{CA} \times 100 = IQ$$

was found to require modification (included in the 1960 revision) to equalise the distribution of the IQ, and therefore its significance in terms of population percentiles, at different ages. A more serious criticism of the mental age concept is that it fosters the false impression that the thinking of a bright child of five, an average child of eight and a dull child of eleven, all with a mental age of eight, is equivalent, whereas qualitatively the three are poles apart. It may sometimes help to spell out *in what respects* a child resembles one older or younger than himself (e.g. in the complexity of ideas he can handle, speed of mental processes, etc.) and in what ways (e.g. ability to learn acceptable social behaviour and perhaps other skills) he should be treated at his own age level.

Some of the shortcomings of the Binet approach were eliminated in the series of intelligence scales by Wechsler. The first of these, the Wechsler Bellevue Scale, was designed to test adults, to whom the concept of mental age clearly does not apply. Wechsler therefore substituted a point scoring system which he converted to IQs (by then a part of everyone's thinking) by taking the average score at 100 and the standard deviation arbitrarily at 15 points. The same principle was applied in the later Wechsler Adult Intelligence Scale (WAIS), the Wechsler Intelligence Scale for Children (WISC) and the Wechsler Pre-school and Primary Scale of intelligence (WPPSI). The effect is that children's abilities are placed in relation to those of others of their own age rather than likened to those of a different age.

Wechsler's scales are made up of a number of subscales, each containing items graded in difficulty throughout the whole age range of the test. The raw score for each subtest is converted to a scaled score with a mean of 10 and a standard deviation of 3. The scaled scores are then added together and the totals converted to IQs with the aid of tables. Five subscales (in the WISC: Information, Comprehension, Arithmetic, Similarities and Vocabulary, with Digit Span as an optional extra) are combined to form a Verbal IQ, and five (Picture completion, Picture arrangement, Block design, Object assembly and Coding, with Mazes as an optional extra) to form a Performance IQ. The Full Scale IQ resulting from all ten (or twelve) subtests is separately standardised and not merely an average of these two. The verbal/performance dichotomy and the further breakdown by subscale scores permit of certain diagnostic inferences, although the differences between the subtest scores need to be rather large for reliability. Glasser and Zimmerman (1967) have written usefully on clinical interpretation of the WISC. The subscales do not correspond to specific abilities, however, and certain important functions such as verbal reasoning are under-represented. The scoring of certain items also raises problems which are not fully dealt with in the Manual.

However representative the sample may be on which a test is standardised in its own country and time, it cannot pretend to represent the population of a different country or a different decade. Limited surveys have indicated that the average IQ of British children in the 1950s and 1960s was probably between 106 and 113 on the Binet scale, depending on age (Sampson, 1959 and references cited therein; Pringle and Edwards, 1964; T. Moore, 1967; Phillips and Bannon, 1968) and between 103 and 107 on the WISC (S. Jones, 1962; Wright, 1972). See also p. 274. The relative difficulty of items will also probably vary from one culture to another. The New British Intelligence Scale due to be published soon (Warburton et al., 1970) has long been needed. This has been very thoroughly prepared by a team based on Manchester University with assistance from practising psychologists throughout Britain. Its rationale is much more sophisticated than that of the older scales and will, it is hoped, provide a sound theoretical foundation for diagnosis of a child's abilities. Its six main divisions— reasoning, verbal, spatial, numerical, memory and ideational fluency (or creativity)—are based on factorial analyses by many well-known investigators. These divisions are broken down into subscales measuring types of mental operation established through the work of Piaget and other students of developmental psychology. While a core of subscales will still provide a measure of g it is envisaged that this should be expanded into a profile of abilities, and that optional elaborations should provide for the more detailed investigation of individual strengths and weaknesses. If successful, this scheme should simultaneously improve psychometric validity, enrich and clarify test interpretation and foster a flexible research approach to the problems of individual children. How far these hopes will be realised can only be decided in the light of practice.

Some psychologists apply an individual intelligence test to nearly every child they see, because it has become for them a standard framework within which they can compare the child's responses with those of hundreds of others they have tested, and on this basis they formulate hypotheses for further investigation. Others prefer to start with a less formal approach, perhaps by observing the child in class and in free play or by talking to him and to his teachers, and then select the tests to be used in the light of these preliminary soundings. In cases of learning difficulty a thorough investigation of the subject's thinking is always desirable, and for this purpose the standard intelligence tests are still probably the best tools; but they should not be used without a clear purpose in mind. If one wishes to save time for other tests or less formal enquiries but nevertheless wants a measure of the subject's ability, one may choose between an abbreviated individual test and a paper and pencil test which the subject (if old enough) can do while the psychologist gets on with other work.

Abbreviated forms of the Binet and the WISC are offered in the manuals, with some indication of the additional margin of error they introduce. This should be allowed for in terms of the report, and the particular types of mental operation omitted from assessment should also be borne in mind. Glasser and Zimmerman (1967) survey the available evidence on the wide variety of 'brief WISCs'.

If more children have to be seen than can be adequately tested individually in the time available, it is better to take them in groups of up to four young or six older children and administer a group test of intelligence, followed by brief individual interviews with diagnostic, attainment or other tests as appropriate. Groups of this size permit of some individual observation and immediate detection of any failure to understand the test instructions, inhibiting anxiety or other condition which may stultify the child's performance unnoticed in a larger group. Group tests, of which there are many available, have been discussed in a previous chapter. Although they reveal less about the person's thinking than an individual test they are useful for screening purposes as described.

Again, with an adolescent seeking vocational guidance, when an extended programme of tests and interviews may be called for, the psychologist may decide to spend his time on personality tests, the discussion of interests, aspirations and life circumstances, and then to ask the subject to work his way through a written test of intelligence while he considers the rest of the evidence. In doing this he should ensure (a) that the test is of sufficient difficulty to challenge the subject's best efforts without unduly discouraging him, (b) that he has not taken the same test before, at least during the past year (this applies also to orally administered tests), (c) that he reads the instructions carefully at the outset and understands them, (d) that any time limit is strictly observed. If the subject remains in the psychologist's room note can be taken of his degree of concentration or distractability, self-sufficiency or tendency to draw the adult in, and other behaviours. If the psychologist leaves him alone, for example to talk to the parent or teacher, he should first see that the subject is equipped with a spare pen or pencil, is well embarked on the test and knows how long he has to complete it. It is best to return shortly before the time expires, to glance through the paper when it is done, checking on any illegible answers or omissions within the range of the subject's ability, allow him to express any worries about the test and make some suitably encouraging comment.

Group tests also designed for use with individual subjects include:

1. Progressive Matrices (Raven, 1960) Standard version for ages 6–14, coupled with the Mill Hill Vocabulary Scale; Advanced set, 1962, 11 and upwards; coloured version, 1963, for ages 5–11, coupled with the Crichton Vocabulary Scale.
2. The AH4 Test by Heim (1955), which includes verbal and performance scales for children aged 10 and upwards.
3. The Boehm Test of Basic Concepts (Boehm, 1967) for infant school children (supervision required) which reveals their grasp of classroom instructions.
4. Various other verbal and non-verbal tests published or distributed by the National Foundation for Educational Research and by Psychological Test Publications.

Tests of special functions

Intelligence can only manifest itself through action in response to stimuli.

This implies perception and movement. Any deficiency in either of these functions is liable to distort behaviour and to produce uneven performance on an intelligence scale. Where there is a wide scatter of successes and failures either between or within subtests, a reason should always be sought. In some cases it will be due to lack of experience of education in the culture for which the test was designed; in other cases, to anxiety or other emotional disturbance; but the possibility of distortion in the basic functions of perception or motor control, or in the links between them, should always be borne in mind. Such distortions may long go unrecognised and the resulting scholastic failures be attributed to laziness, perversity or stupidity. Tests of perceptual and motor skills enable the psychologist to correct these misunderstandings and to call attention to particular difficulties requiring remedial help.

Initial clues can be gained by watching a child's efforts on a performance test such as the WISC Block Design. These can be amplified if necessary by use of performance scales such as those of Alexander (1958) from age seven up, or Arthur (1955) from five to fifteen. For children up to six or seven the Seguin Formboard (Stutsman, 1931) is a useful brief adjunct to the Binet or WPPSI scale, revealing whether the child immediately discriminates shapes or has to proceed by trial and error, whether his movements in placing the pieces are deft or clumsy, his degree of preference for one hand over the other, and how much he can improve his performance on second and third trials. Being a quick and popular test with success almost guaranteed over the mental age of four, it is a useful one with which to begin the testing session.

Drawing is another skill which links perception and movement, although the representation of three-dimensional objects on a plane surface involves conventional transformations which depend to some extent on experience and cultural tradition. The drawing of a man (or a woman) has been used by Goodenough (1926, 1950) and D. B. Harris (1963) as a measure of maturity. Although not in itself a reliable measure of intelligence (Pringle and Pickup, 1963, Yule el al., 1967) it is a useful supplement giving insight into observation of the human figure, relative emphasis on its various parts, spatial organisation and the command of a pencil—all of which may be indicative of emotional as well as cognitive factors.

For some purposes it is useful to study drawing ability divorced from content. The Bender Gestalt Test consists of nine simple designs made up of lines and dots which the subject is asked to copy. The results when analysed according to the criteria set out by Koppitz (1964) can yield valuable insight into faults of spatial orientation and other forms of visuomotor disorganisation, some of them diagnostically significant for brain damage as well as for certain aspects of personality.

Difficulty in perceiving and copying designs can be distinguished from difficulty in reproducing them from memory after a few seconds exposure. The latter ability is explored by tests of Benton (1963) and Graham and Kendall (1960). Other aspects of visual perception and pencil control, which probably bear more closely on difficulties in writing than in reading, are covered by the Marianne Frostig Developmental Test of Visual Perception (Frostig, 1966).

The Embedded Figures Test (Witkin, 1969) measures an interesting dimension of cognitive style which, according to its author (Witkin et al., 1962), pervades both perception and behaviour as an ability to free oneself from hampering dependence on the environment (field independence).

Where general motor coordination is suspect, control of both large and small muscles can be assessed through the Test of Motor Impairment (Stott et al., 1966), derived from Oseretzky's earlier Test of Motor Ability. Imitation of gestures is used to assess spatial orientation, praxis and body schema by Bergès and Lézine (1963).

Superimposed on perception and movement, and making use of them, is language, another set of functions with its own development and pathology, some aspects of which can be independently measured. The verbal subtests of the WISC, with the exception of digit span, measure complex applications of language. An attempt to isolate its elementary component skills resulted in the Illinois Test of Psycholinguistic Abilities (Kirk et al., 1968, Kirk and Kirk, 1971). This scale yields a language age ranging from three to ten years, and more important, a profile based on three phases of the linguistic process—reception, organisation and expression; two levels—automatic (including closure and sequential memory) and representational; and two channels—auditory-vocal and visuomotor. There is controversy over the usefulness of this particular analysis (derived from Osgood) and over the validity of the subscales, for it cannot be assumed that separate measures of component skills which normally function in continuous interaction will necessarily have the practical significance in remediation that is claimed for them. The reliability and discriminating power of some subtests are questionable; nevertheless the scale does often suggest useful lines for further investigation of both linguistic and reading difficulties. A very useful technique for assessing the language of younger children (ages one to five) is that of Reynell (1969). By exploiting children's pleasure in play it seeks to elicit spontaneous conversation and comprehension of language in a naturalistic situation. A speech therapist (Renfrew, 1966) has developed a test of speech articulation which is simpler and better adapted to young children than the more exhaustive instrument of Templin and Darley (1960).

Comprehension, the receptive counterpart of spoken language, depends on auditory perception which, like visual perception, may be weak or distorted in various ways without the knowledge of the child or of the adults responsible for his training. At the level of sensory acuity, a degree of partial deafness, like astigmatism or other visual defect, may go unnoticed for years. Some psychologists learn to give simple audiometric and optometric tests as a screening for complete examination; others prefer to leave this to the appropriate expert while remaining alert to the possible need. Some individuals have difficulty in discriminating between similar speech sounds, owing to hearing loss over a limited range of frequencies. This may not noticeably affect their understanding of speech, in which contextual clues are probably much more important than precise hearing, but it is an obvious handicap in learning to read and spell. The Wepman Test of Auditory Discrimination (Wepman, 1958) systematically investigates ability to differentiate commonly confused phonemes. Comprehension of the meanings of single words (vocabulary of recognition) is measured by the English Picture Vocabulary Tests A (ages 5 to 8+) and B (7 to 11+) (Brimer and Dunn, 1962). Understanding of connected speech is tested by the Reynell Test and by the Boehm Test of Basic Concepts (Boehm, 1967) up to the age of school entry; beyond that level there seems to be no systematic measure of this important skill of aural (as distinct from reading) comprehension in isolation from other functions, so that it is often difficult to tell whether a test failure is due to poor grasp of the instructions or to some other cognitive difficulty (see below, p. 142).

Tests of scholastic attainments

Tests of scholastic attainments used with individuals (as distinct from the group tests discussed in chapter 5) include oral reading tests, some designed mainly for the assessment of the standard reached, usually in terms of reading age, others for diagnostic investigation of the types of error made, and tests of comprehension of the material read. Most of the tests in common use are seriously out of date and in need of revised norms.

Standard of reading is traditionally measured by the graded word lists of Schonell and Schonell (1956) or Burt (rearranged by Vernon, 1969); the Holborn Scale Sentences (Watts, 1948); or by the Neale Analysis of Reading Ability (Neale, 1958). Reading ages below seven can be misleading, since different methods of teaching produce very variable results in the early years, and there may be up to one year's difference in the scores of the same child on tests based on different teaching approaches (Bookbinder, 1970; Young and Stirton, 1971). The same probably applies to tests of spelling (Schonell and Schonell, 1956; Daniels and Diack, 1958).

Reading disabilities are among the commonest problems with which an educational psychologist has to deal. Their causation is various and usually complex, involving both cognitive and motivational factors: it will be discussed in chapter 9. Useful contributions on many aspects of this problem have been assembled by Reid (1972). No single test will enable a psychologist to diagnose the *cause* of a reading difficulty, but diagnostic batteries exist to help break the problem down. Various reading readiness tests are designed to discover whether a child has reached the requisite maturity in various functions to profit from formal instruction in reading. For those who are failing at elementary levels Daniels and Diack (1958) offer an analysis based on learning stages rather than ages, which may help to locate the particular processes in which an individual is finding difficulty. Alternative analyses are proposed by Moseley (1972b), Stott (1971) and others: see Reid (1972). Assuming the child is ready and willing to learn, these can be useful guides to the remedial teacher.

Reading comprehension is tested with young children by asking them standard questions about the passage they have just read: such questions are incorporated in the Neale Analysis quoted above. With older children written tests such as those of Schonell and Schonell (1956) and the Manchester Reading Comprehension Test (Wiseman and Wrigley, 1959) are generally employed.

Attainment and diagnostic tests also exist for the discovery of particular difficulties in conventional arithmetic (P. E. Vernon, 1949; Schonell and Schonell, 1957; Hebron, 1958); but scarcely as yet for the basic operations taught in the newer mathematical curricula, though the numerical tests in the British Intelligence Scale may provide a beginning. P. Williams (1970, pp. 489–92) discusses the position in a useful chapter covering the assessment of learning difficulties in general.

Tests of specific aptitudes for certain types of work are sometimes used in vocational guidance; they are classified in Buros's *Mental Measurements Year Books*. It has been found, however, that given adequate intelligence and freedom from specific deficits of a verbal, spatial or numerical kind plus interest and personal qualities suited to the work chosen, aptitude can generally be acquired, and specific tests are less useful than might be supposed.

Testing the very young

The testing of children under school age raises problems of administration, interpretation and rationale which differ considerably from those encountered at older ages. In the first place the predictiveness of test scores is much lower, as has been repeatedly shown by longitudinal studies over the past four decades. A full discussion of this topic can be found in Bloom (1964). Thus correlations between IQs at preschool ages and the IQs of the same individuals at maturity fall around +0·5 from age four,

+0·4 from age two and zero from age one—though Bayley (1949, 1955) has shown that these values can be raised by averaging the scores from several testings at intervals of a few months. Whatever scale is used, the younger the child the greater the likelihood of subsequent change; and the greater the interval between tests the wider the probable discrepancy. The basic reasons appear to be (a) change in the relative salience of sensorimotor and intellective functions, especially between infancy and school age, and corresponding change in the content of test items; (b) fluctuations in the actual rate of development, varying with individuals; (c) the difficulty of ensuring that a child's abilities are demonstrated to the best advantage before he is conditioned by school to display them on request. These results show very clearly that prediction from preschool tests to later intelligence is extremely hazardous, and this should be made quite plain in any psychological report; children may swing widely within the normal range, often for no apparent reason (Bayley, 1955). Definite subnormality of genetic or organic origin, however, can often be detected early and here one is on firmer ground in predicting that the child will not catch up to the average (Illingworth, 1961). Development is far more variable at the upper end of the range.

With normal children Hindley (1965) and others have shown that prediction can be improved to some extent by taking account of environmental factors such as the parents' social class. But prediction is not the most profitable use to which preschool tests can be put. They are better regarded as assessments of the child's current developmental status, giving clues to lagging functions which may perhaps be strengthened by the provision of suitable experience, and helping decisions for example in the selection of play material or the choice between nursery school and more adult company and conversation. Retests at intervals can teach the psychologist much about the malleability of early development.

The testing of young children calls for a much more flexible approach than that employed with those of school age. The first essential is to gain the child's trust and cooperation, for once he has decided to withhold it his decision generally prevails. If the child is found at play in the waiting room it is a good plan to join in with him for two or three minutes before suggesting that you have other toys in your room which he might like to see. In case he has not settled down, it is a good plan to have a small toy in one's pocket—a car for a boy, a small doll for a girl—as a medium of introduction. Nearly all children of two and three and many of four want their parents to come with them to the testing room, and this should be allowed at least until the child is happily engrossed in activity. If the child clings to his mother in the room, it is best to leave a few attractive toys on a table a few feet from her chair, indicating quietly that the child may use these but not urging him to do so, while one talks to the mother for a few minutes, preferably about positive things such as the child's play and interests at home. When he has sized up the psychologist and his attention has turned to the play material one may initiate a little game; simply rolling a car or a ball to the child's feet sometimes breaks the ice. Once the child has accepted the invitation to play, this can be discreetly merged into the more attractive items of the test, even if he insists on returning to the original toy at intervals. The mother may then be asked quietly to withdraw; if a shy child can allow this he often opens out to better advantage in her absence. If he becomes too upset, however, either at once or after a time, she may have to be visited, or if necessary recalled and asked to sit in the background to give moral support but not to urge the child (which usually has an inhibiting effect) and not to repeat or reword questions.

The psychologist too should avoid much urging: if a question or request spoken clearly and slowly twice does not produce a response, further repetitions are unlikely to do so. It is better to wait for a favourable moment and then to reintroduce the item in a conversational voice as though it were a completely fresh idea. Much more will be gained if the psychologist is prepared to follow any promising lead given by the child, and to elicit his voluntary cooperation through give and take, rather than attempting to impose too standardised a test situation.

Wechsler's Preschool and Primary Scale of Intelligence (WPPSI) has an age range of 4 to $6\frac{1}{2}$, overlapping with the WISC which is unsatisfactory in its lowest reaches because of paucity of suitable items. Verbal and performance subscales are presented alternately (a practice which this writer adopts in the WISC too) but there are still more questions in succession than some young children can take without getting bored and relaxing effort. There is conflicting evidence about the accuracy of the norms for British children (Brittain, 1969; Yule et al., 1969).

The Revised Stanford-Binet (Terman and Merrill, 1961) extends down to the two-year level. Its mixture of brief items, while permitting of no systematic analysis, does sample both verbal and non-verbal skills in fair variety. Command of language may be judged at the first few levels, but connected speech (beyond two-word utterances) is not essential before the $4\frac{1}{2}$ year series. The brevity of items is a distinct advantage with young children because of their short attention span. The items need not be given consecutively; thus, a verbally inhibited child can be allowed to enjoy the attractive toy material through free play, then asked to perform actions with it which will reveal his comprehension of language, before being asked to name, first objects, next pictures (naming having an intrinsic appeal) and finally to answer questions. Two items involve toys glued to a cardboard base, which is so frustrating to many children that reputable psychologists have concluded that they can only be used effectively it detached. The Binet tends to overestimate intelligence relative to other tests, particularly with verbally gifted children.

The Merrill-Palmer Scale (Stutsman, 1931) is a predominantly non-verbal scale for children from $1\frac{1}{2}$ to 6 years. Many of its items are scored at several age levels, often depending on speed of performance; but since speed can be affected by distractions, poor coordination or temperamental qualities as well as intelligence, this can be misleading. Some items call for the best of three trials, which again can be difficult to secure from a volatile child. But the material is attractive, most of the tests are interesting, and the scoring allows for items refused or omitted. There are a few verbal items but not enough to sample language adequately. Scatter is often wide, partly no doubt because the norms are based on limited American samples a generation ago. For these reasons an IQ should not be calculated from the mental age given. The test is useful as a non-verbal supplement to the Binet, for observation of the child's behaviour when faced with a challenging task, and for a rough assessment of visuospatial reasoning and motor skill in children with delayed or defective speech, or those who will not cooperate in a verbal test.

The New British Intelligence Scale (Warburton *et al.*, 1970) which will extend down to the two-year level, besides offering attractive material and using a playlike approach, includes subscales to assess progress through the cognitive stages outlined by Piaget. Assessment in terms of these basic mental operations, rather than of age-based quotients, is proposed by W. M. Woodward (1970), who urges a more flexible approach than that of the standardised test, using any object in which the child shows interest and any situation that will reveal his stage of development.

While babies and toddlers under two do not (yet) fall within the official scope of the education service, an educational psychologist occasionally, and a clinical psychologist more often, may be asked for an opinion about the development of a child in this age range. The testing of babies is a skill in its own right requiring specialised training and experience. Since instructions have no effect, we have to rely on observation of spontaneous behaviour elicited by material that stimulates the infant's natural curiosity, exploratory urges, vocal and social responses. The art lies in producing conditions in which these will display themselves, in noting them as they occur, and in tactfully interrogating the mother about the baby's habitual behaviour.

The classical developmental schedules of Gesell and Amatruda (1949) have been largely superseded in Britain by the Griffiths Scales of Mental Development (Griffiths, 1954, 1970), the earlier scale providing for very detailed assessment in the first two years, the later one for only slightly less detailed examination up to year eight. Dr Griffiths will supply the test material only to those who take her course of training (now available by correspondence). Elsewhere, the Infant Intelligence Scale of Psyche Cattell (1960) is often used.

These scales really assess not intelligence as such but general development, including posture and locomotion, fine motor (eye–hand) co-ordination, vocalisation leading to speech, attention to sounds leading to comprehension of language, self-help and other aspects of personal-social development, as well as the manipulation of materials leading to the solution of visuospatial tasks like those of later performance tests. They thus yield profiles of development in which these aspects can be compared with one another as well as with population norms. This analytic or diagnostic function of the tests can sometimes lead to early detection of sensory or motor deficits, defective response to persons, and other valuable warning signs; it is generally of greater significance than the overall score (DQ = Developmental Quotient, GQ = General Quotient) which, as already shown, is not a safe guide to prediction despite the wishes of aspiring parents and adoption agencies.

The assessment of social competence

So far we have been concerned with measuring ability. But a person's effectiveness depends not only on ability but on the use he makes of it in everyday life. Such effectiveness cannot be tested, but it can be estimated from information given either by the subject himself if he is mature enough or by a parent, houseparent or other adult living with him. The Vineland Social Maturity Scale (Doll, 1953) designed originally for use with subnormal patients, whose placement depends more on such practical competence than on purely intellectual capacity, has been found useful also as a supplement to intelligence tests with normal persons. In the Manchester Scales of Social Adaptation, Lunzer (1966) has modified, extended and restandardised the scale for British schoolchildren. The term 'social maturity' suggests interpersonal behaviour, but the scales in fact cover mastery of personal routines as well. The Vineland Scale includes self-help in eating, dressing and general matters, self-direction, occupation, locomotion, socialisation and communication, though not all of these extend throughout the full age range from infancy to adult life. The total score yields a social age which may extend from 1 month to 25+ years, and can be taken as a percentage of the chronological age to give a social quotient (SQ). Five of Lunzer's subscales cover much the same ground, while five more explore the subject's cognitive social perspective. Scoring yields not a social age but a percentile profile.

To ask directly how much a child does for himself is of course to invite a distorted reply. The question should be phrased, not e.g. 'Do you bath yourself?' but 'Who usually baths you?', 'Does mother help you to get dry?', 'Who washes your hair?', etc. assuming rather less competence than the subject probably has. (Lunzer proposes specific wordings and tests of certain items.) Even so, many children will tend to overestimate their competence, and a valid self-assessment can scarcely be expected at a mental age of less than seven or eight. Many parents also overestimate what their children can do, though a few err in the opposite direction. A psychologist should therefore record his impression of the validity of the replies, and who gave them. The purpose of this scale is to assess, not what the subject *can* do but what he *habitually* does (although a compromise score is allowed for those abilities which he is just in process of acquiring). Doll also suggests making allowance for those skills which the subject would have acquired but for lack of opportunity; but since lack of opportunity itself reduces competence, this seems to confuse the issue. A comparison of the SQ with the IQ can reveal whether an individual is failing to make effective use of his intelligence, perhaps because of impoverished background or parental overprotection, or on occasion that he is being forced into independent action without the intelligence to grasp attendant hazards.

A social maturity scale can also be used to obtain a picture of a typical day in the subject's life. For this purpose the questions are expanded so as to elicit, not merely what he does for himself, but who does things for and with him; how many friends he has; his favourite occupations and how often he can pursue them, and similar useful information.

Gunzburg (1968) uses progress assessment charts for the comparison of retardates with others of their own stage of mental development rather than with normal individuals. These yield a qualitative rather than a quantitative assessment, but are particularly useful in recording the progress of subnormals in the skills of real practical value to them, identifying areas in which they are tending to stagnate, and thus giving indications for the rethinking of training programmes.

Personality tests

The assessment of non-intellectual aspects of personality presents many problems arising basically from the fluidity of concepts in this area, lack of knowledge concerning the permanence or changeability of personal characteristics and consequent disagreements about the terms in which they can most usefully be described. It is not surprising that no test or diagnostic technique has been found to have very high validity for the prediction of behaviour tendencies which cannot themselves be shown to have permanent existence; or for assigning subjects unequivocally to categories or personality types too unsubtle to encompass the variability of an individual. Vernon (1964) closes his comprehensive review with the conclusion that such aims are largely illusory; but that the many ingenious approaches to personality assessment are nonetheless useful as aids to informed clinical judgment, which should take into account all available evidence and employ techniques selected according to the specific purpose of the enquiry. In trying to understand a person's behaviour in his current life situation, insight into his motives, feelings, self-concepts, interpersonal perceptions and fantasies is certainly important, even though these may (and should) change with changing circumstances.

Three types of observation are useful in the study of personality: for convenience they may be termed objective, subjective and projective, although these terms are not used identically by all psychologists. *Objective* data are here defined as what can be observed about the subject; *subjective*, what he observes about himself; and *projective*, what can be inferred from his perceptions of the world expressed through words or other media.

Objective data

The observations that can be made about a subject's behaviour have already been discussed. The psychologist who bears in mind his experimental training will keep these objective observations clearly separate in his mind and in his report from interpretations of their possible diagnostic significance, which he will base on a subsequent review of all the available evidence.

Certain tests are designed to facilitate objective observations, especially of the motor characteristics of behaviour. The Bender Gestalt, the Marianne Frostig and some of the Harris Lateral Dominance tests are all useful for this purpose. The Porteus Mazes (Porteus, 1952), originally intended as a cognitive test, were found to be more useful as a measure of planning capacity, impulsiveness and similar traits of personality and a qualitative scoring system was devised to highlight these aspects of performance. More recently Gibson (1965) has designed a simple spiral maze presenting no cognitive problems but scored for speed and accuracy in avoiding obstacles when urged to hurry; the relationship between these two variables may be relevant in the study of children who tend to act out their problems in antisocial ways, but probably much depends on the forcefulness of the examiner's urging.

Several objective tests were found by Himmelweit and Petrie (1951) to discriminate significantly (though less so than certain projective techniques) between children psychiatrically diagnosed as neurotic and normal controls. These included tests modelled on Eysenck's experiments with adult patients, measuring persistence, suggestibility and static ataxia. The fact that this pilot work has not apparently been followed up nor resulted in a published battery, suggests that the approach was found to be of limited value, perhaps for the reasons advanced by Maddox (1952): there is a danger that traits experimentally isolated and quantified may give too static a picture of the complex of ongoing processes which constitute personality, many of which can be expected to vary with the interpersonal situation in which the behaviour is observed.

Subjective data

Subjective reports, or self-assessments, do not escape the influence of the examiner for whom they are done; some examiners probably inspire a greater desire to appear in a favourable light than others. The subject's tendency to err in the direction of social desirability may be roughly estimated, but not offset, by the 'lie scale' built into instruments such as the Anxiety Scales of Sarason et al. (1960). It may be argued that no one can know a person as he knows himself. But self-knowledge is least subject to distortion where social evaluation is minimal, as in the field of interests, likes and dislikes.

Interest tests such as those of Rothwell and Miller (1968) consisting of lists of occupations or activities to be ranked in order of preference, are of obvious use in vocational guidance, while those for younger children such as the Devon Interest Blank (Wiseman and Fitzpatrick, 1955) throw useful light on their predilections, incidentally affording a pleasant task which a literate child can be left to do on his own.

Likes and dislikes among pictures, colours, words, jokes and musical excerpts have all been used in the assessment of personality, but to no great extent with children, whose tastes are notoriously fluid. The same can be said of opinions and attitudes. There is room for more experimentation in the measurement of children's views, however.

When it comes to ticking statements about one's habitual behaviour, a good deal of honesty and trust in the user of the information is called for; and feelings, being elusive, are perhaps the hardest of all to report on objectively—especially fears and worries, which are strongly taboo among boys. Nevertheless, personality inventories such as those by S. Eysenck (1965), R. B. Cattell and M. D. Cattell (1968) and Porter and R. B. Cattell (1968) are widely used with older children, because they are easy to administer and yield quantitative scores with which many psychologists feel at home. The first of these assesses personality in terms of the two main dimensions (extroversion/introversion and neuroticism) thrown up by Eysenck's factorial studies, while Cattell's series, based on a multifactorial approach, yield profiles of up to sixteen factor scores. These methods can be used 'objectively'—i.e. with emphasis on scores—as group tests for screening out deviant individuals for further investigation, or for equalising groups for research purposes. But they can also be used 'subjectively' with single individuals as a time-saving preliminary to discussion, which may take the test responses as a starting point and proceed to explore the subject's perception of himself.

A perennial difficulty in the assessment of personality by verbal methods is the fluid, ill-defined meanings of most words used in qualitative description; one cannot be sure they will mean the same to any two people. Semantic elasticity, treacherous to those seeking to anchor their concepts, can however be turned to good account in the study of those very differences in concept structure and affective value which make for individuality of outlook. The Semantic Differential (Osgood *et al.*, 1957) attempts this by getting the subject to indicate just where, in his estimation, key concepts (self, mother, work, sex, any idea that seems crucial to this particular person) fall on continua such as good/bad, active/passive, strong/weak, etc., which have been found to typify key dimensions of meaning. The Repertory Grid Technique (Kelly, 1955) obliges the subject to produce his own dimensions, or personal constructs, and then to rate or rank important elements in his environment (especially people) on each construct in his repertory. The resulting grid, or matrix, of rankings can be treated statistically to reveal individual patterns of person perception and other mental schemata in great variety. It is often especially revealing to compare the subject's perception of his actual self with his ideal self; and where time permits, to study the discrepancies between these and the views of him held by parents, teachers or others (Hargreaves, 1972). These methods have not been formulated as standard tests, but many psychologists find them valuable for the exploratory study of individuals and groups (Bannister and Mair, 1968). Ravenette (1968) has worked out ways of exploring children's personal constructs, which may be employed with or without factorisation by one of the simplified methods he proposes.

Quantification is not always necessary in the study of personality. The sentence completion method depends essentially on a straightforward scrutiny of the content of the subject's endings to incomplete sentences, the scoring or classification offered by Rotter and Rafferty (1950), for example, being of subsidiary importance. The same can be said of the word association technique originally used by Jung, of which Sutherland and Gill (1970) have recently devised an extension requiring sentences rather than single word responses and providing a system of classification. In these methods some stimulus words or openings may elicit subjective, others projective responses, while reaction times, if taken, contribute objective data.

The Family Relations Test of Bené and Anthony (1957) being likewise partly subjective and partly projective affords a link between this section and the next. The child first chooses from a number of cardboard figures, those that he needs to represent his family. To each figure is attached a posting box. He then reads (or the psychologist reads to him) messages printed on cards, which he is asked to post to the person the message fits best. A figure called Mr Nobody is available for rejected messages. About half the messages concern the child's (subjective) feelings towards other members of the family; the other half, his (projective) ideas of their feelings toward him or toward each other. Both sets include positive and negative sentiments of varying strengths. Most children up to ten or eleven accept this invitation to display their conscious attitudes with surprising readiness and their distribution of messages among family members can be quite revealing and often corrective of parents' misperceptions.

Projective data

In the projective techniques proper, the subject is not asked about himself directly but required to make up stories or scenes, to draw, play or arrange material, or to say what he sees in vague stimuli. It is assumed that by directing his attention outward rather than inward, resistance to frank admission of his problems will be by-passed and the problems projected, as they commonly are in everyday life, on to the characters and objects he sees, creates or imagines. There is no doubt that this does happen, that projective methods can yield a rich harvest of useful observations and that it is well worth while for every psychologist to have several of them in his repertoire. That attempts to validate projective responses against overt behaviour have met with only limited success is not surprising, since behaviour is defended to a variable and fluctuating extent by the very resistances that make the projective approach necessary; it is surely important to know how these defences distort perception and determine mental organisation even though their effects on behaviour cannot as yet be fully understood or accurately predicted. This unknown term in the equation, and the fact that no two persons' projections are identical, create a need for clinical insight in the interpretation of projective responses. Such insight can only be based on experience. A psychologist needs to use a test a good many times with children of varying ages, thus becoming familiar with the range of expectable responses, before he can judge the significance of an unusual one. It is best therefore to master one or two techniques thoroughly before going on to others. But it is worth while to add to one's tool kit from time to time, since different techniques throw light on different segments of personality, and none illuminates the whole. Rabin and Haworth's (1960) book covers more of these tests than can be mentioned here.

Of all the projective techniques, the Rorschach ink blots are both the best known and the most difficult to administer and interpret. Since children generally see fewer objects in the blots than adults, often only one per card, the test is less time-consuming with them; but since they cannot usually analyse their perceptual processes, a really satisfactory enquiry into the determinants of their perception is frequently impossible and interpretation must rest on criteria rather different from those used with adults. The younger the child the more problematic the test becomes; yet norms have been produced right down to the age of two (Ames *et al.*, 1952, 1959). Halpern (1953), Klopfer *et al.* (1956, vol. 2), Ledwith (1960) and Francis-Williams (1968) have written usefully on the Rorschach with children. Despite the difficulties, many clinicians consider this test to be unsurpassed for indicating the degree of contact with reality and the nature of any distortion of normal perception in children from six or seven upwards, and thus to be of great value where a psychotic tendency or organic damage is suspected, as well as revealing often unexpected facets of more normal personalities. But it requires prolonged study under expert guidance.

The numerous tests depending on interpretation of ambiguous pictures are useful chiefly for studying the subject's perception of interpersonal relationships. Of these, the most widely used with adult and adolescent subjects is the Thematic Apperception Test (Henry, 1956). For pre-adolescent children Bellak (1950) has produced the Children's Apperception Test which capitalises on children's tendency to identify with animals. Since these tests have no numerical scoring system, there is no obligation to present all the cards if time is short; a selection can be made according to the subject's problems. Bellak offers an elaborate system of analysing the stories given according to Murray's theory of needs and presses, but many children's responses are too short and simple for such treatment. Even if they merely describe the pictures, the terms in which they do so and the themes they introduce can be very revealing. In the Make a Picture Story Test (Schneidman 1960), the subject creates his own scenes by peopling empty backgrounds with any of a large number of human figures before telling his stories about them, the choice and placement of the figures being significant in itself. For those who prefer a more direct approach to parent/child relations, Lydia Jackson's Test of Family Attitudes (Jackson, 1966) and the Family Relations Indicator of Howells and Lickorish (1967) both offer pictures centred on this theme; the former suits young children; the latter can, if desired, be used with whole families to discover discrepancies of interpersonal perception. The Blacky Test (Blum, 1949) portrays a dog family in a series of situations intended to reveal the child's stage of psychosexual development in Freudian terms. One of the most interesting tests for older subjects, the Object Relations Technique (Phillipson, 1955) uses diffuse shading, chiaroscuro and colour, responses to which have been found in Rorschach studies to be diagnostic-ally significant, and systematically varies them over cards depicting one, two, three person and group situations; the structure and content of the subject's stories are interpreted in the light of his perceived relationships to others, including the psychologist; and the test situation itself, with the circumstances that led up to it, is acknowledged to be an important part of current life experience which will help to determine the responses.

Two tests that seek to provide quantitative measures of certain behaviour tendencies are of interest for their rationales although their predictive validities are not well established. One is the Picture Frustration Study of Rosenzweig (1947, 1948). In the children's form of this test the subject is required to supply the verbal responses of children undergoing various forms of frustration or accusation by an adult or another child. The responses are classified (a) according to emphasis on the frustration itself, on the frustrating agent, or on a possible solution, and (b) according to whether aggression is expressed toward others, turned back on the self or denied. In the Hand Test (Wagner, 1969) which is quick and easily scored, the subject is shown pictures of ten hands and simply asked what each hand is doing, scoring being in terms of behaviour tendencies associated with the attributed action.

With most children over six or seven, the more obviously pictures touch on painful problems the more likely they are to mobilise defensive manoeuvres other than refusal. While this complicates the relationship of test responses to life behaviour, it enables the psychologist both to identify areas of conflict and to study the defence tactics themselves, as part of the individual's personal coping style. This is usually revealed not so much in the overall scores, and not only in responses to particular items, but in the sequences or trends of response, perseveration, temporary disorganisation, recovery from stress and similar qualitative characteristics of the total record.

Children who lack the ability to construct stories in words can often express their fantasies freely through play, to such good effect that play has become the recognised medium of communication between children and their psychotherapists. Psychologists can learn its language too. One may have to do no more than present a young child with a family of small dolls and some dolls' house furniture in order to see his crucial preoccupations vividly enacted before one's eyes. The drama will be in terms of his fantasies, not of what actually goes on at home: if he makes the father doll kill the mother and eat the baby there is no need to alert the police, but one may begin to understand why he suffers from night terrors and feels impelled to provoke his father in order to discover the real bounds of his anger (T. Moore, 1964). The London Doll Play Technique (Moore and Ucko, 1961; Ucko and Moore, 1963) consists of a series of simple family scenes presented by the examiner for the child to complete in any way he wishes. Most young children respond readily, developing those themes they are ready to explore, rejecting or giving banal responses to those they are not, and incidentally revealing something of their individual style of coping with conflict.

Projective play need not be confined to family dolls. A method favoured by M. Lowenfeld (1950) is to provide as great a variety of miniature toys as possible from which the child can make his own selection to construct his 'world' in a sand-tray. Buhler *et al.* (1951) provided a standard 'World Test' kit and recommended a tabletop for the construction. In either case the project must be diagrammed or photographed, for diagnostic interest resides not only in the choice of elements, but in their arrangement: spatial characteristics such as expansiveness/constriction, order/disarray, balance and unity are considered alongside the thematic content, the child's comments on it and his behaviour in the course of its construction. A child's 'worlds', like other artistic products, can convey much about his developing individuality: one way to appreciate this is to obtain a series of them from the same child during a period of treatment or a critical phase of development and to note the changes. Bowyer (1970) has written on this technique.

The use of space and colour in purer form, without reference to concrete representation unless the child chooses to introduce it, can be studied through free construction in two dimensions with mosaics (M. Lowenfeld, 1954) or in three dimensions with kaleidoblocs, also due to Lowenfeld (Ames and Learned, 1954 a, b). Both types of material are of interest to subjects of all ages, but so far very little has been offered in the way of interpretive guidance.

Drawing is perhaps the most commonly used projective medium, though here again interpretation is usually at the intuitive level. The child's drawing of a person, given perhaps as a cognitive test, may reveal through disproportion or omission a feeling of the exaggerated importance or the inadequacy of some part of his own body. The House-Tree-Person test (Hammer, 1960) further explores the symbolism found to characterise drawings of these objects. As comparatively few children are inhibited by lack of drawing skill, one may sample their imagery by asking them to draw their family (Hulse, 1952; Burns and Kaufman, 1971/2), their class at school, or themselves as they would like to be. Size, spacing, emphasised details, posture and expression in the figures may give clues which can be followed up in discussion arising from the drawings. The Symbol Elaboration Test (Krout, 1950) offers, for development as the child wishes, a series of very simple linear configurations thought to embody symbols basic to our mental construction of the world.

The foregoing discussion of a limited selection from the great number of techniques available for the study of personality may give some idea of the scope of the field. Different approaches will appeal to different psychologists; no one can master them all. Since some of them reveal more about the subject than he realises, his welfare should always be the paramount consideration in their use and data obtained from them must be regarded as strictly confidential. In pre-adolescent children personality tests seldom call up more anxiety than the child can cope with by the normal defences of 'don't know', non-committal or facetious responses or diversionary tactics: if the item is omitted or postponed (with due note of the reason) the next item may restore equilibrium, or a different test may prove more acceptable. Some children have difficulty in accepting that there can be questions to which the answers are neither right nor wrong—a sign of anxiety for approval—while others may betray excessive self-criticism or give muddled contradictory replies revealing unresolved conflict in a particular area. Adolescents sometimes baulk at projective techniques, sensing that they may reveal secret thoughts: where suspicion is evident, it is always best to discuss the whole purpose of the test as part of a programme to understand and help the subject, and if he still seems unconvinced to shift to a more direct technique even though deeper insight may thereby be delayed. Personality tests are a short cut, not the only possible route, to understanding, and valid assessment cannot be obtained in an atmosphere of distrust.

On the other hand, many subjects find projective techniques interesting and rewarding, and may experience relief in expressing their conflicts through the media offered. For young children, play is well known to be cathartic in itself. Older subjects may wish to discuss their productions, and such a request cannot in fairness be denied; with adolescents indeed some discussion should probably be offered even if not requested. How far this goes must depend on the psychologist's experience and training, and also on whether he is handling the case alone or whether a psychiatrist or therapist is involved. In the latter case the psychologist should eschew any detailed interpretation, for it will tend to build up a transference relationship which is not readily shifted to a colleague and the subject may fall between two stools: having given vent to his preoccupations with one person the subject is less likely to feel inclined to repeat them to another. Used with these cautions in mind, projective techniques can enable the psychologist to write a report that will be of great assistance to the psychiatrist in calling his attention directly to crucial areas of conflict that might be evaded in an interview, and by providing a view of personality distinct from and complementary to his own. Harrower's (1953) imaginary dialogues between a psychologist and a psychiatrist develop this theme in a very readable way.

Assessment of special categories of children

We conclude this chapter by considering the assessment of four special categories of children:

(a) the mentally retarded
(b) the physically handicapped
(c) those with communication difficulties
(d) those from whom it is difficult to elicit sustained concentration on the task.

The aetiology of these conditions, their implications for the child, and their treatment and educational provision will be discussed in later chapters; (case studies on pp. 314–333). Here we are concerned only with assessment.

The general principles are the same as with any other kind of child: obtain as much relevant information as possible, be clear about the purpose of the referral, select tests as suitable as possible for answering the crucial questions, manage the situation with full awareness of its meaning to the child, establish good rapport, note as much as you can about the child from incidental behaviour and quality of responses. Adhere to the test instructions as closely as possible without allowing them to become self-defeating; if you have to depart from normal procedure, say so; report only what can be legitimately inferred from your observations, even if this amounts to saying only that the child refused to display his abilities.

Mental retardation

Amentia, or general failure of mental development, presents no special problems of assessment in itself, provided one has recourse to tests of a suitable range. With severely retarded children this may involve going down to the infant development scales. It is unsatisfactory to attempt an assessment too near the 'floor' of a test (and equally so too near the 'ceiling'): not only may there be insufficient items for the subject to display his full range of abilities and disabilities, but the items themselves may have been too close to the limits of the standardisation sample to achieve full discriminative power. Thus, if one has to go down to the lowest group of Binet items, the basal age of which, like that of the Merrill Palmer Scale, is eighteen months, it is as well to supplement them with the speech, eye–hand and performance scales of the Griffiths, which together provide thirty-six items covering the same six month period, with the possibility of going still lower if necessary. Indeed, the newly extended scales (Griffiths, 1970) provide for similarly detailed assessment up to year eight if desired.

Assessment in terms of Piagetian stages, as recommended by W. M. Woodward (1970), can be useful in formulating educational programmes, especially for those with a mental age of eighteen months or less, since the substages of the sensorimotor period have been studied in greater detail than the subsequent 'preoperational' period. Suitable educational placement for mentally retarded children depends as least as much on their social competence, temperament and amenability as on their testable intelligence. The scales of social competence (Doll, 1953; Gunzburg, 1968) were indeed developed primarily for this purpose, and should always be used to round out the picture of the individual's practical effectiveness: the informant will usually be the parent or whoever has been caring for the child recently.

A wide scatter of successes and failures within the test, or a very irregular profile of subtest scores, suggests either that certain abilities have failed to develop, or else that they are not being displayed to best advantage. The latter may occur where a certain type of test item produces a 'blank wall' reaction—the total rejection of a situation associated with repeated failure. The retardate may be unable to restructure the situation in such a way as to pick up clues to the relevance of what he does know. One may then try to elicit this knowledge through informal conversation; its existence, even though not available in the test situation, should be noted. If, however, certain types of ability prove to be genuinely stunted far below other types, questions of differential diagnosis may arise. Are there undetected sensory deficits? Is there a possibility of brain damage, perhaps of a kind that may lead to functional deterioration? Or is the uneven development probably due to a faulty environment, and if so how far is it remediable? Are the expectations of parents and teachers properly attuned to what the child can do, or are their demands too lax in some directions, too stringent in others?

Physical handicaps

In this section we shall be considering the problems of assessing children with impairment of sensory functions (vision or hearing) or of motor effectiveness. In so far as such impairment affects communication there will be overlap with communication difficulties and perhaps it will be best to look first at the common elements.

In most test situations it is taken for granted that the subject is capable of receiving and communicating information normally: the instructions are designed (with varying degrees of success) to make clear what is expected, the material to be adequately perceived, and the required responses, verbal or motor, to be well within the subject's range of capability. Unless perception, movement or speech is itself being tested, interest is usually centred on the efficacy of processes that go on between input and output. Where either input or output is faulty, however, it becomes problematic how far the intervening processes can be validly assessed.

If responses fall short of the norm, is this due to a failure (to perceive the material, to comprehend instructions or to express a response) which would not arise in other circumstances—in other words, is the subject capable of solving the problem if the difficulties of getting and conveying information are removed? Or have his problem-solving and other central functions been impaired?

In some cases it is impossible to answer this question on the basis of a single assessment, since chronic failure in exchange of information has deprived the subject of essential data on which to exercise his thinking processes; if such exchange is now facilitated he will need time to develop these. Whether such belated development is possible will depend very largely on the degree and extent of the deprivation, and probably on whether it occurred during a critical phase of development. It is therefore essential for the psychologist to have as much information as possible both about the current degree of sensory or motor impairment and about its history. Access to medical records in these cases is essential to effective work.

If defective vision or hearing is known or suspected but has not recently been assessed, it is useful for the psychologist to be able to give a screening test. For this purpose the Stycar tests of vision and hearing (Sheridan, 1968) are very suitable for young children. For older ones eyesight may be tested with an ordinary optometric chart. Hearing for pure tones can be assessed with an audiometer after a short course of training and some practice, but it is advisable to supplement this with a test for discrimination of speech sounds such as the Wepman or the Reed hearing cards. It should be made quite plain to the parent or teacher that this screening examination is no substitute for a full investigation, if one seems necessary, but it gives the psychologist a basis for estimating the extent of any deficit of sensory input. It is not uncommon for this to be seriously underestimated by those responsible for the child, with consequent strain on adjustment.

The psychologist has next to decide whether the subject's perceptual and motor equipment is such that a valid estimate of intelligence can be obtained by using the ordinary testing procedures, whether any modifications of these procedures are necessary or whether a special test is required. Special tests have been devised for blind, partially sighted and deaf children, and certain standard modifications of procedure with the Binet and WISC have also gained professional recognition. These are fully discussed in a pamphlet drawn up by a working party of the British Psychological Society which also deals usefully with more general problems of assessment of children with sensory and motor handicaps (BPS, 1966a). Because of the variety of their disabilities, few special tests have been developed for children with deficient motor control such as those with cerebral palsy, muscular dystrophy, spina bifida or missing limbs. One exception, The Columbia Mental Maturity Scale (Burgermeister et al., 1959) uses picture material on large cards designed for eye pointing where neither speech nor gesture is under control. Faced with such a child, often at short notice, the psychologist must be able to adapt his approach so as to obtain the most meaningful assessment of what is possible for the child and what is not. A global assessment such as an IQ may have little significance since it assumes basic conditions that may not be met. A profile of social competence such as that outlined by Gunzburg will generally be useful, amplified to reveal as far as possible (a) the thought processes that are unaffected or minimally affected by the handicap, (b) the operations that it renders difficult or impossible, and (c) the compensatory strategies, effective and ineffective, that the subject has developed for himself. The diagnostic programme may involve selecting or adapting items from existing tests or devising completely new procedures, perhaps on the basis of preliminary observation of the subject in familiar surroundings. It may thus become a protracted experiment, limited only by the time the psychologist can give. Prior experience with subjects having the same kind of handicap will make the difference between a pilot experiment and an expert judgment.

In practice, assessment of individuals with major handicaps such as blindness or severe cerebral palsy is usually undertaken by specialist psychologists working in the relevant units. Those working in the general community have not the opportunity to learn all that should be known about the range of possible adjustment open to such people in order to appraise the achievements of one of them. Any educational psychologist may, however, be asked to examine a partially sighted child, one with an unknown degree of hearing loss, speech defect, muscular incoordination or indeed any handicap that does not incapacitate the sufferer from living in the community. To do so effectively his chief needs are ample time and flexibility of approach. The comprehensive text book edited by Mittler (1970b) will be found very helpful.

Communication failure

Difficulties of communication can be classified as executive, receptive, cultural and motivational. The first two refer only to verbal communication; they may or may not involve a physical handicap in the mechanism of speech and hearing respectively. Minor disabilities of these kinds, which the psychologist may be the first to detect, have been noticed in chapter 6, under language observations (p. 110): here we are concerned with frank handicaps, which may pose problems of assessment of the mental ability which they can obscure.

Executive function

Speech defects include difficulties of articulation (dyslalia, dysarthria), stammering and difficulty in calling to mind the required word or form of expression (executive aphasia). The first of these can make a person's speech totally unintelligible to anyone who has not learned his individual code. Usually, however, this is not difficult to crack, consisting in fairly regular consonant substitutions. The mother and siblings will generally have learned to translate automatically, and the psychologist, if he cannot himself do so, may have to employ one of them as an interpreter. Failing this he must resort to tests not requiring spoken answers: performance tests of spatial reasoning, plus assessment of verbal concepts through paper and pencil tests or those using pointing (some sections of the ITPA, the EPVT, the Columbia and Boehm scales, all previously mentioned) or the execution of simple commands, as in Reynell's verbal comprehension scales. But it is worth noting the extent of the subject's speech, his readiness to use it, reactions when not understood, and recourse to alternative modes of communication. Such recourse is most likely to occur where the act of speaking requires a definite effort, as in some kinds of cerebral palsy or in cases of stammering.

A severe stammer may embarrass the psychologist more than the stammerer, and will certainly increase the time required for testing. Again, performance and written tests are a help.

In aphasia, by contrast, it is desirable to get the subject to talk as much as he will in order to assess the nature and extent of the handicap. But many asphasics are reluctant to talk, though some are able to write, and most develop a rich language of gesture and facial expression which distinguishes them from autistic children. These alternative channels of communication should of course be used to full advantage wherever speech breaks down.

Receptive function

Where a child fails to understand test instructions while coping much better with self-evident tasks, it is worth checking his discriminative hearing for speech sounds. If this seems intact, and assuming he is familiar with the language and not emotionally withdrawn, there is the possibility of receptive aphasia. It is important, though not always easy, to separate failure of verbal comprehension from failure of other mental processes required for success in each test presented. Try first using the standard instructions broken up into short phrases, emphasising the key words and looking for signs of comprehension at each pause. In most tests the instructions may be repeated as often as necessary. If this does not work, one may select a test which is unlikely to be used again (e.g. for official ascertainment) and test the limits of the subject's comprehension, first by rewording the questions or instructions in progressively simpler ways, and finally if necessary by demonstrating what is required. The results can be reported in terms of the levels reached with varying degrees of verbal simplification: this should be of value to any teacher. The ITPA can throw light on relative abilities in the decoding and encoding of verbal material up to a language age of nine years. The Boehm Test of Basic Concepts is also useful in discovering weakness in ideas of space, time and quantity at the infant school level.

Cultural aspect

A valid test of any sort depends on the subject's having some degree of familiarity with the basic data employed, whether these be words, pictures, geometrical shapes or toys. A person who thinks in another language cannot be properly tested with questions that assume more knowledge of English than he possesses, even if they are translated, though this may have to be done for purposes of approximation. Children brought up in bilingual homes are often found to be at a disadvantage; if they are attending an English-speaking school it is important to know how far they can cope with English instructions, but the score may well underestimate their intelligence. Immigrants whose language is a variant of English based on a radically different culture pattern, such as that of the West Indies, are often assumed to be in better communication than they are, for their usage attaches quite different connotations to many words and employs a different idiom, speech rhythm and pronunciation, so that English speech may be almost as unintelligible to them as a foreign language. In addition, some of the concepts taken for granted in the tests may be completely unknown to them.

But language is not the only barrier. P. E. Vernon (1969a) found that children reared in different cultures produced typical test profiles which varied widely from one part of the world to another and could to some extent be related to mode of life. Performance subtests were as much affected by cultural background as were verbal. This is one example of the familiar problem of finding a truly 'culture-free' or even a 'culture-fair' test, when the objects and activities of everyday experience, the patterns of child rearing and education and the resulting mental structures are so variable.

The influence of cultural life style on thinking, and therefore on test results, is significant in relation not only to immigrants but to children from different sections of our own society, as the work of Bernstein (1971) and others has shown. Since an adequate test standardisation includes all sections of the national population, the usual descriptive categories such as 'average', 'superior' and 'retarded' may be quite misleading to parents and teachers who know only one end of the distribution; these terms must be qualified and interpreted in relation to the standards of the family, school and neighbourhood.

Motivational aspect

Children who are capable of communicating normally may nevertheless be unwilling or unable to do so in some circumstances. Information from home and school will establish whether such failure is chronic, sporadic or confined to certain situations, and whether it affects only verbal communication (speech, comprehension or both) or other forms of personal interaction as well. Differential diagnosis between aphasia, more general asymbolia, autism and elective mutism or other psychoneurotic inhibition may pose intriguing problems for the psychologist. The aim will be to discover by systematic experimentation, observation and enquiry how far the subject is able to communicate under various conditions, and in what manner he does so. If a child withdraws from a normal friendly verbal approach it is generally useless to press for a response. As suggested with shy young children, one may produce play material and watch from a distance to see what the child will do with it while one talks to the parent or makes notes without appearing too interested. A neurotically inhibited child may take a long time to leave its mother's side or even to use toys put within reach, but will generally explore the room with its eyes and scrutinise the examiner so long as it is not scrutinised in return. Autistic children are more likely to wander round the room ignoring people or treating them as objects and betraying their preoccupation with particular things such as light switches or water pipes. They may ignore the play material or show exaggerated interest in one particular kind such as jigsaw puzzles, with which they sometimes exhibit exceptional skill; one should guard against estimating their general intellectual level from these islets of special ability. Other types of psychotic children often communicate in a limited and bizarre fashion revealing their distorted thinking; reversal of personal pronouns is one such symptom. Aphasia and asymbolia are not motivational problems; the sufferers may have become discouraged by the difficulty of conversing in words, but they are usually only too ready to do so in terms of play, and show interest in the material. Asymbolics have difficulty in recognising pictures and may use toys inappropriately through failure to understand what they represent.

Elective mutism is sometimes confined to the school, to the home or to the presence of the mother or some other individual; in other cases it is virtually complete. Like other neurotic defences it can become fixed outside the range of volition. The psychologist's task is to create a situation in which the profound suspicion and rejection of human contact dramatised in the symptom can be at least partially abandoned. Some children are known to talk to a sibling or a friend but not to adults; in that case it may be possible to arrange a joint play session, perhaps in a play room with screened observation and recording facilities, gradually entering into the situation as a third party before attempting to isolate the subject. Once cooperation is gained some children will produce speech, while others will respond in writing, drawing or gesture to test questions.

This glimpse into the complexities of communication failure is intended to do no more than stimulate the reader to inform himself adequately with the help of writers such as Mittler (1970a) and the authors he quotes.

Attentional difficulties

There are some children whose chief problem seems to be an inability to focus attention long enough to follow through any train of thought. This is not a diagnostic category but a recognisable source of difficulty for the psychologist in his examination, as it is for the parents, teachers and the child himself. Brain damage may or may not be detectable in such children.

'Inability to concentrate' is a frequent complaint from schools where the work is not geared to the abilities or interests of the child concerned. It is therefore important to distinguish between boredom with the situation and chronic distractibility. Enquiries may establish whether the child is capable of concentrating on tasks of his own choosing commensurate with his age and level of intelligence. To test this it is necessary to find a task that appeals to the child while presenting a challenge to his staying power. Sometimes a relatively difficult performance test will meet the need. If not, the World Test material may be presented and the subject asked to occupy himself with it alone while the psychologist busies himself but keeps an eye open for evidence of distraction by outward stimuli or inward daydreams.

Moment-to-moment fluctuations of attention can sometimes be noticed in the face-to-face situation. Where a child tends momentarily to lose track of what is going on, though otherwise normally in touch, the possibility of petit mal and the advisability of recommending an electroencephalogram should be considered.

Extreme physical restlessness can also be due to disorders of the central nervous system. The organically hyperkinetic child literally *cannot* sit still. If the test is done at all it will be done 'at the double' with frequent excursions, mental and physical, between items. With some young children any attempt at restraint of movement causes a tantrum; the psychologist can only go along with the child, watching his chance to present fresh items whenever its flitting attention seems ready for a new object. A combination of Binet and Merrill Palmer items usually suits such children better than a Wechsler test. While it is often difficult to be sure whether a child is incapable of passing an item when he cannot stop long enough to try properly, the net outcome, non-achievement, unfortunately mirrors the situation in his everyday life. Necessary medication for hyperkinesis or for epilepsy sometimes makes children drowsy and slows their mental reactions so that the test result is still of doubtful validity. Once again a detailed description of what was achieved and what was definitely failed, supplemented by a score for social competence on information from the parents, will be more meaningful than any tenuously estimated IQ.

Some children, instead of rushing from one thing to another, fix on one object or activity and resist all offers of alternatives. This behaviour is normal in very early childhood when the whole attention is apt to be engaged by some novel discovery, but not so normal at later ages when it may point to retarded development, obsessional preoccupation or, if the activity is stereotyped and meaningless, psychosis. One may try distracting the child and substituting other material; if the favoured object is demanded it is a good test of personality integration to see whether the child can wait for it while he does one or two other things at the psychologist's request, and then after another turn to try increasing the number of intervening items. One may also try suggesting variations on his play with the object to see how flexible or how rigid the obsession is.

The forms of behaviour described in this sub-section can all be produced or simulated as a result of personality disturbance without organic damage. Thus, impaired concentration frequently follows a bereavement or other emotional trauma; restless overactivity may be the result of frustration in a 'double bind' family conflict; limitation of interest to obsessional or compulsive actions may be a form of defence against unconscious anxieties. These and other abnormal forms of behaviour call for thorough investigation which may engage all the psychologist's ingenuity and extend far beyond the initial examination.

If he is to fulfil his function adequately and do justice to the scope of professional knowledge at his command, in order to bring it to bear most helpfully on the problems of children, the educational psychologist must insist on adequate time to investigate each case. This requirement very often competes with the pressure of a lengthening waiting list. In most areas where his services are appreciated the psychologist has to consider how best to keep up with the demands on his time. To try to do so by seeing four referrals a day, four days a week, will very soon lead him into a stultifying routine in which he has no energy for original thinking and no child receives the individual study its difficulties may merit. S. W. Gray (1963) has thoughtfully discussed this problem as it affects school psychologists in the United States, suggesting possible solutions equally applicable in Britain. The long-term solution undoubtedly lies in adapting the education system to the needs of individual children, a task to which psychologists should contribute, but only as one section of the whole educational profession. In the shorter run, some kind of screening procedure will have to be developed for the more efficient identification of pupils requiring psychological attention. Screening can be done in two stages. The first stage, using a survey, can best be carried out by head teachers or school counsellors following a programme suggested by, or agreed with, the psychologist. The second stage, involving a closer look at those who appear to be failing to profit from their schooling in some way, is best performed by assistant psychologists or specially trained teachers under careful supervision. Experienced educational psychologists can then look forward to a more specialised consultative role than they enjoyed in the past. This should enable them to follow up much more thoroughly, in selected cases, clues to the reasons for underfunctioning or maladaptive behaviour and to work out programmes for its remediation; tasks which may well lead them beyond the school setting, as discussed in the next chapter.

8

The educational psychologist and parents

An important aspect of the educational psychologist's work which is often understressed is his contact with parents. In child guidance clinics most of the ongoing work with parents is done by social workers, usually with a specialisation in psychiatric social work (until recently a separate profession) and the same is true in many school psychological services. But it can be argued that a psychologist should usually, perhaps always, meet the parents to explain to them the purpose and general results of his examination of their child. This may well lead to requests for advice about school placement or plans for the future, and often too about the methods and attitudes that should be adopted in dealing with difficulties of learning or behaviour. In some cases the psychologist may feel that the solution to the problem lies in helping the parents to view things differently and thus to modify their handling of the child: this may require a number of sessions and involve a counselling relationship, rather different from that of the social worker. In some cases the psychologist may be the first to meet the parents, perhaps at the school, and it may then fall to him to collect essential facts about the problem as they see it. Where a social worker is not available, he may have to take a complete history of the case and to see it through on his own. It is important, therefore, that he should understand something of the art of communicating with parents, the kinds of information he will need from them, the varieties of response he may encounter when he explains his findings and makes recommendations, and the ways in which he may be able to help. First, it may be as well to look a little at what is involved in being a parent, and especially in being the parent of a difficult or handicapped child.

Parents and children

It is fashionable, and all too easy, to write off children's problems as 'the parents' fault' and to stop thinking at that point. This attitude ignores a number of inconvenient truths. First, some children are born with temperaments which would be difficult for any parent to handle successfully; some with temperaments which, while they might suit other parents, grate on the susceptibilities of the individuals who happen to have parented this child (Thomas, Birch and Chess, 1963). Other children are born into circumstances beyond their parents' control which make their advent unwelcome, or destroy the harmony of family life in their early vulnerable years. Even if it is agreed that the parents' handling of the child is sufficient explanation of his difficulties, we are still left with the questions. Why do they treat him as they do? and (more important still), how can they be prevailed on to do otherwise?

To assume that parents are completely responsible for their children's behaviour is also to deny the significance for ill or for good of other influences, such as the school, the neighbourhood and the peer group. Moreover, parents could only be held so responsible if they were completely and constantly in command of their own actions. As we all know, being of adult years does not automatically confer infallible self-control. Many a parent is all to keenly aware that he or she fails to live up to his or her own ideal of parenthood. Some feel acutely guilty about their losses of temper or lapses into inconsistency. It means a good deal if they can admit this; those who cannot are liable to defend themselves against their guilt by rationalisation, denial or overcompensation of their errors, or by projecting the blame on to the child, the school, the doctor or the psychologist. It is in dealing with mechanisms of this kind that psychologists can often learn a great deal from the psychiatrist or psychiatrically trained social worker.

Even a writer as gifted as Winnicott (1964, 1965) cannot fully convey the subjective quality of a parental relationship. Those who have experienced it know that, to the normal mother and father, the firstborn child appears as a miracle of self-regeneration; especially, perhaps, many a father sees his eldest son as a fresh version of himself, offered a second chance of realising his dearest aspirations, and the same may often be true of the mother and her eldest daughter. Feelings for children of the opposite sex are different, but no less intense. The close identification or emotional participation in the child's life has obvious biological value in impelling the parents to defend their offspring with all their strength, to sacrifice much in freedom and convenience in order to rear them, and to treat the infant with that tender forbearance which enables him to love in his turn. A problem can arise however if this parental overinvolvement fails to wane at the normal time, sufficiently to allow the child to develop his legitimate individuality.

When the infant begins to assert himself and fails to respond exactly as

they wish, mature parents, without abrogating their educational responsibilities, will come to accept him as a separate person in his own right. This process may be aided by the arrival of further children, each of whom will behave
differently, gratifying some of the parents' wishes and frustrating others,
and thus dividing between them the burden of parental hopes and dis-
appointments. But where a parent, for reasons connected with his own
childhood experience, has unresolved conflicts, unrealisable ambitions
or rigid and inhibiting defences, he (or she) may well be unable to avoid
the attempt to mould the child in accordance with his own personal
needs, thus setting up tensions which will manifest themselves as behaviour difficulties or neurotic symptoms in the child or as problems of
relationships in the family. Tensions occur in all families, of course; those
parents who are adult enough to balance fairly their own claims and those
of the children will manage to resolve conflicts in ways which the children
will (later) come to see as helpful. Those who lack this gift will distort their
children's development to a greater or lesser extent, and will also distort
the information they give to any interviewer in accordance with their
misperceptions and the pressures of their personality structures.

Effective communication

Before we consider the specific purposes of the interview, there are a few
general principles governing communication in general and in the area of
interpersonal relationships especially, of which psychologists may usefully
remind themselves from time to time. First, let us always remember that
what we shall be discussing for the most part is the tissue of everyday life,
the moment-to-moment actions and reactions of people living together in
intimate relationship. Our purpose in enquiring about these details is to
find out not only the facts but how the people concerned see them and
feel about the situations that arise between them. We have somehow to
convey that our questions are asked not with the intention of criticising
or intruding unnecessarily but in an effort to understand the viewpoint
of everyone concerned. Indeed there is much to be said, once the topic of
concern has been opened, for keeping questions to a minimum and allowing
the parent to give his or her own view of the matter in his own way.
Where both parents can be met one may get two quite sharply contrasted
views and in some cases it is of great importance to hear both. An important part of the psychologist's work consists in interpreting to child,
parents and teachers, the discrepancies between their respective views of
the situation. This is a difficult task, in which he can hope for no more
than partial success and not always that; but the process can only begin
with any particular interviewee when that person is satisfied that his own
position has been sympathetically understood, even if not fully agreed with.

It is a good exercise of imagination to try to put oneself in the parents' place at the beginning of the interview when they have been obliged to consult the psychologist about their child's problems of learning or behaviour. To the extent that they see the child as a part of themselves his shortcomings will be felt as their own; while in so far as they feel responsible for moulding the child they may feel they have failed in the eyes of society. The parent who has been driven to punish a child impulsively, or has given him too little time and attention, or has exploited him in some way, is likely to feel guilty, perhaps disproportionately so; but guilt feelings are compatible with resentment if the child's demanding or naughty or sullen behaviour is seen as a form of punishment. By the time they reach the psychologist, many parents feel they have tried everything to solve the problem on their own without success and this is a last and often reluctant resort.

Psychologists share with psychiatrists (from whom they are seldom clearly distinguished) a vaguely sinister image in the eyes of many people. We are thought to have mysterious methods of 'reading minds', of analysing motives and of controlling or influencing others without their knowledge. It is disconcerting to find that someone who has encountered an educational psychologist in the past may have exchanged this picture for one of an individual who sees the child in unfavourable circumstances, administers irrelevant tests, assigns an IQ which is too low and decrees that he must attend a school which the parents consider quite unsuitable. We have to remember that anxiety and ego-involvement cause people to distort and misperceive what is said to them and one should be on one's guard against condemning colleagues (including those in other professions) for allegedly unkind behaviour which cannot be verified. Nevertheless, unwise and damaging things are too often said through carelessness and/or failure of empathy. Kindness, consideration and a careful choice of words will help not only our clients and their children but the reputation of our profession as a whole. With parents who readily complain about their treatment at the hands of doctors, teachers or others, extra caution is necessary in our own interest. Part 4 deals with communication in detail.

One must talk to people in their own vocabulary. Scientific jargon is a code for use with colleagues who are accustomed to thinking in terms of the concepts employed and understand their exact meanings. With anyone else such concepts have to be translated into ordinary English—a process which can be quite salutary for clear thinking. One's language should always be adapted in a natural way to the comprehension of one's listener. This is not 'talking down', it is talking as one human being to another, and it will serve, not hinder, the professional relationship. Of course, it helps if one is in a position to talk as one *parent* to another; a brief humorous reference to comparable experience with a child of one's own sometimes gives a useful fillip to the discussion. Failing that, one can generally find some other common ground on which to agree. It is important to establish points of agreement before one goes on to take up divergences of view. With any parent who is concerned for his child, one can emphasise that this in itself creates between you a joint aim for his welfare.

The setting

It is surprising what different people we are in different surroundings. Each of us builds up habitual patterns of behaviour which differ according to whether we are at home, at work, or in some other social group, and which must entail different concepts of ourselves in relation to the other people concerned. In an unfamiliar situation, the lack of any well-tried sequences of action leaves us uncertain how to behave, not knowing what to expect from others or how best to respond. This will make us guarded in our behaviour, unwilling to reveal much about ourselves until we can sense how such revelations will be received. This is especially true if the people we are meeting occupy positions of authority of which (despite ourselves, perhaps) we stand somewhat in awe.

To many parents their children's school is a domain ruled over by a head teacher who is just such a figure of authority, operating within the wider authoritative ambit of the educational system. Their attitudes will certainly bear traces of their childhood feelings about authority, overlaid to varying degrees by later experiences, including their relationship with the head teacher in question. It must be a great temptation to head teachers to foster any residual element of awe they may find among parents. However this may be, the parents' feelings about the school will tend to colour their initial attitudes to any official of the education service seen there, especially at the Head's instigation. If the psychologist meets them there he will see the front they habitually present in that setting, somewhat modified by their preconceptions about his own role and probable intentions regarding their child. It may be useful to see the head teacher with one or both parents in order to gain understanding about their relationships and the points at which communication fails. Whether the Head is present or not, the psychologist operating on his territory is likely to be seen as his ally and will be, to some extent, constrained by diplomatic considerations in conversing with the parents. If he can convey an attitude of unbiased sympathy and a desire to hear their views on the problem, something will have been achieved. He may then prefer to arrange the next meeting, usually after seeing the child, on his own ground, or possibly on theirs.

Home visits by psychologists can be useful in some cases, but one should always first obtain the agreement of any social worker concerned, and wherever possible, confirmation by the parents that it is acceptable at the time proposed. In writing to make appointments with parents, it is always advisable to enclose a stamped addressed reply card; even with this aid there will be some who will fail to reply, whether through forgetfulness, ambivalence or failure to appreciate the professional need to organise time. It is as well, therefore, to indicate whether, if no reply is received, you intend to make the call (being in the district) or not. To do so may be the only way of contacting a mother who may, nevertheless, prove perfectly cooperative. Even if one finds the house empty, it does not necessarily signify a refusal; the mother may not have mentioned that she goes out to work or visits a sick relative. A large section of the population is simply not in the habit of communicating in writing. In cases of real difficulty, the education welfare officer or the health visitor may have knowledge of the family situation.

Home visiting may be the only way of meeting parents who are either unable or unwilling to come to the psychologist's office. It may also be the only way of seeing a phobic child in a normal emotional state. Apart from these exceptional cases, it has advantages in other circumstances. Diffident, inarticulate or defensive parents generally feel more at their ease on their own ground; the role of hostess may give such a mother the confidence to speak more freely about her difficulties with the child. The child, too, will feel more at ease at home and one will get a truer picture of his personality and perhaps of his abilities than could be obtained in a school he dislikes or a strange clinic he fears. It may also be possible to see members of the family in interaction and although this will be affected by the presence of a visitor, it may yet be a more representative sample of their behaviour than would be obtained in unfamiliar surroundings. Finally, the opportunity of seeing for oneself the conditions in which a child and his parents live can be valuably revealing. The drawbacks to visiting are mainly practical: the exigencies of domestic routine, interruptions by callers or curious children and the inhibiting presence of others if a private room is not available. It is seldom possible to get really satisfactory conditions for testing a child in his own home, although sometimes one may have to do one's best if alternative arrangements would be less satisfactory still. Finally, there are paranoid parents who may resent and misconstrue the visit as an intrusion on their privacy or on their rights over the child, but such attitudes are comparatively rare and generally well-known to the head teacher and others concerned. In the great majority of cases, a psychologist prepared to adopt the role of a tactful, friendly guest can achieve cooperation and win a measure of trust from parents who might be unable to give it in an official setting.

From considerations of time and adequate testing conditions, however, the majority of clients will sooner or later be seen in the psychologist's office. The great advantage of this is that it is his own and can be arranged in whatever way he thinks best to dispel any false ideas of what a psychologist is and does. Its location—in an education office, a child guidance clinic or elsewhere—will colour anticipations, but these will quickly give way to impressions based on the atmosphere encountered on arrival. The reception should be welcoming; the waiting room inviting and supplied with play material beguiling to all ages served without being too difficult to leave: a rocking horse, slide, and large wheel toys are always popular with younger clients; comics and magazines suit older children and adults. But waiting should be kept to a minimum: reasonable punctuality in keeping appointments is one sign of that consideration for the individual which is fundamental to work in the area of human relationships.

The same principle of consideration for the person should govern the management of the situation throughout. Details such as ensuring that names are correctly spelt and pronounced, making drinks and toilet facilities readily available when needed, giving permission to smoke, seating the client comfortably where the light from sun or desk lamp does not shine directly in his eyes, and so forth—all these are important; much more so the interviewer's manner. Parents, no less than children, need to feel that they are accepted even if all their actions and opinions are not.

Recording and confidentiality

Rapport is best served by giving the impression of a free ranging conversation, even if one has unobtrusively to direct it from time to time. It is best to avoid constant writing while the parent talks, jotting down only essential data which must not be forgotten. The rest of the information can, with practice, be recalled and arranged after the interview in a logical order, together with comments on the parents' personalities and expressions of feeling on particular topics. But it is important not to leave the writing up, since memory for detail fades rapidly. To leave it overnight is generally too long. If it cannot be done at once, it is best to make rapid notes of the key points covered, for writing up at the next opportunity. Such notes should be made immediately after the interview and certainly before any other client is seen, or confusion can very easily result.

Tape recorders and oneway screens are not advisable in consultative work. If they have to be used for research, training or demonstration purposes, either with the parent or with the child, the parents must be asked for permission beforehand and given full opportunity to refuse.

It is extremely important to ensure the safeguarding of confidential records where they cannot be seen, e.g. by other patients or by cleaners or office keepers who might, by chance, be acquainted with the family. Even the names and addresses of clients should be locked away when the office is empty. Assurance can then be given, if required, that information will reach no one but the psychologist and his immediate colleagues, without express permission from the parents.

Resistance to the recording of personal information does not rest only on the fear that it may be divulged. Many parents who would welcome help with their children refuse referral for child guidance because they suspect interference with, or enquiry about, their own private lives, and this fear can easily be aggravated if they see extensive notes being written or a file being made about their case. It seems best always to keep visible records to a minimum and bulky files out of sight, having first extracted into a separate folder any notes, letters or reports to which one may need to refer. If one has to leave the parents in one's office for any reason, *all* records should be removed from sight, if only to avoid titillating natural curiosity.

Management of the first meeting

If a psychologist intends to see both the child and his parents, he has to consider how best to timetable the interviews. The easiest plan is to see the child first at school, if only briefly, to establish a friendly rapport and to get an impression of him; then to meet the parents by arrangement while the child is occupied in school, and arrange a further visit to his office or clinic to which both child and parents will come prepared. If the referral comes from the parents, either direct or through a doctor, they are likely to be anxious to present their problems before the child is seen. For this purpose a preliminary interview in the child's absence is useful. One may then suggest a form of words for the parents to use in explaining to the child the purpose of a visit to the clinic (the importance of an honest explanation was discussed in chapter 6) and may also obtain their permission to ask for a report from the school, or to visit it and see the child there.

If the parents bring the child to the psychologist without prior contact, it is highly desirable to have a colleague available to occupy him while one talks to the parents before and after the testing session. In a child guidance clinic, the social worker normally interviews the parents for the greater part of the time, but it is always appreciated if the psychologist sees them for long enough to convey the gist of his findings, either at the end of the interview (when the social worker may be interested to have a short session with the child) or on another not too distant day arranged at the time. If the psychologist is working without the benefit of a social worker or a receptionist trained to amuse children, the situation must be managed to minimise the time that the child spends alone, assuming he is old enough and independent enough to spend any. In such cases it is wise to obtain all the information possible by letter or telephone beforehand, and to ask whether both parents, or another member of the family, perhaps a sibling, can come to keep the child company. If he arrives alone with a single parent, the writer's practice is to see the child first and remain with him long enough to secure his trust, put him at his ease, and get him thoroughly absorbed in some task with which he can be left alone for a limited time, depending on his age and personality. This task should not be a test on which any important decision hangs, for he will certainly be wondering what is being said about him and therefore unable to give it his undivided attention. If the child seems too anxious or too suspicious to be left alone, one may have to abandon the idea of a private talk with the parent on that day, but may call her in at some point to say what can be said in the child's presence. In some cases, indeed, there is much to be said for including the child in the discussion, or at least allowing him to listen in while he draws, paints or constructs a mosaic or a 'world' in the corner of the room. But whether this situation proves helpful or embarrassing depends a good deal on the tact and the experience of the psychologist, as well as on the nature of the problem and the degree of mutual trust between parent and child.

Seeking information

The information that has to be elicited by the psychologist will depend on what is available or can be obtained by other workers. Most parents are very ready to talk about the problem as they see it, even if they have done so already to a number of people, but they may be less ready to fill in details of the child's history and family life, the relevance of which they do not fully appreciate, if they have recently done so for somebody else. If it appears that a social history has recently been taken it may save everyone's time to ask permission to obtain a copy of it (and likewise, if the child has been seen by another psychologist within the past year or so, one would always ask to be allowed to write for a psychological report, even if one decides to repeat certain tests). Equally, if it seems likely that the case must be referred for child guidance, it is wise to limit one's enquiries to points that are essential for one's own purposes in order to leave plenty of material fresh for discussion with the social worker.

What constitutes essential information will vary widely with the nature of the problem and how far the psychologist proposes to deal with it himself. It is impossible to lay down a protocol to fit all cases. It may however be of some help to give an outline of the kind of information that is often relevant, from which selection can be made to fit the occasion (see below). If desired, this outline may be mimeographed with a line or two for rough jottings under each appropriate item or heading (no more, since too much space will tempt to too much writing and disturb the flow of discussion). The psychologist can then, in the light of the information available at referral, mark in the margin those questions he thinks essential to ask; further essential points may emerge and be marked in the course of the interview. Where a point is discussed without note-taking he may convert the mark to a tick, and these ticks will serve to remind him of the points covered when writing up the interview.

This outline is not intended for administration as a questionnaire, but rather to serve as a list of headings for the psychologist's guidance. If the interview develops as a conversation, much of the information will transpire without specific questioning. On the other hand, where full detail is needed for the understanding of some crucial point, quite a number of supplementary questions may have to be asked. If this is done in the manner of a sympathetic friend and not of an inquisitor the questions will generally be welcomed rather than resented. Unnecessary questioning should be avoided, however, and some sections of the interview may be omitted altogether where they are plainly irrelevant or where it is felt better to postpone enquiries until a later date. In a brief initial contact there may be time only for the first section plus the child's date of birth and the family composition, further enquiries being reserved for a second meeting in the light of one's session with the child.

In a full diagnostic interview the psychologist may find it necessary to take a history in some detail. Since he will not be undertaking case work with the parents, however, he will enquire into their personal and family histories not routinely, as would a child guidance social worker, but only if some clue pointed to a possible connection with the child's problem which could be used to enhance understanding. Parents' own experiences are frequently very relevant to the current situation, but can only be usefully discussed when they are ready, and this stage is not always reached in the first interview. Most parents who consult a psychologist see the problem as residing in the child, and their confidence can best be gained by taking him as the main focus of discussion in the first instance; questions about the home and family should therefore be kept as brief as possible and it should be made clear that they are asked in order to view the child's behaviour in the context of his everyday life.

No two diagnostic interviews are alike, but they can generally be shaped approximately as follows. Having introduced himself, the psychologist invites the parents to tell him about the problem as they see it, keeping interruptions to a minimum. After a suitable time he explains that he now needs to fill in some details, and asks the necessary questions about the home, members of the family and the child's history, personality and general adjustment. This leads naturally back to the problem which can now be enquired about more systematically. Before closing it is important to check that one has the essential identification data and to ensure that it is clearly understood what steps are now to be taken and by whom. The outline given below is one possible way of expanding this framework. Valett (1963) offers an alternative form.

Outline of diagnostic interview

1. *The opening*
A. *Referral.* It is a good beginning to mention the referring agent, summarise in general terms the gist of any information received from him and ask if the parents would like to correct it in any way.

B. *Problem(s).* Ask them to tell you more in their own words about the problems, both those mentioned in the referral letter and any other worries they may have about the child. Listen without writing at this stage, and interrupt only if there is something you really cannot understand. In this initial presentation, manner, facial expression, behaviour and speech can give valuable clues concerning the parents' attitude to the child and his behaviour, their feelings about being referred and what they hope for in the outcome.

C. *Introducing structure.* After five or ten minutes, or at a suitable break, explain that you would like to ask some questions to give you a more complete picture of the child and his daily life.

2. *The collection of necessary facts*
(Select, expand, modify or omit items as required.)
A. *The Home.* What sort of accommodation—house, part of house, flat (what floor)? How many rooms for how many people? Child sleeps in own room/shares with whom? Shares bed?

Are domestic facilities adequate (own toilet, bath, heating etc.)? Is there a garden or play space? Busy/quiet street?

Does the home meet the family's needs and are they happy there? If not, any prospect of improvement?

B. *Family and others closely connected.* List (*a*) members of (nuclear) family, with ages, children's names, whether each member living at home or away, and whether at work, at school or neither; (*b*) others living with the family (relatives, au pairs etc.); (*c*) relatives living nearby and seen frequently. (i) *Father.* Age? Health? Occupation? (settled job? satisfied with it? Hours?) How much does he see of the children? How much does he do with them (especially this child)? Anything else volunteered, e.g. about his personality, background, history.

(ii) *Mother*. Age (estimated if necessary)? Health? Present and past occupations?

If at work now does she enjoy it? Hours? Arrangements for children when she is out (including school holidays)? How much does she do with the child?

If she worked when this child was under school age, what arrangements were made? How often did these arrangements change?

If not at work does she wish/plan to start? Feel frustrated?

Anything else volunteered about mother.

How often can parents go out together without the children?

(iii) *Siblings and others in household*. Any serious problems? Contact with child? Anything volunteered.

(iv) *Friends*. Have parents many/few/no friends within reach? Does the child mix freely in the neighbourhood/exchange visits with friends/have none?

(v) *Religion*. Any active religious affiliation of either parent; how does it affect the child?

C. *The child's history*

(i) Pregnancy and birth—any difficulties? Wanted child? Right sex?

(ii) Infancy—healthy baby? Contented or cried a lot? How well did he sleep? Any difficulty with feeding or weaning? Toilet training?

(iii) Any major illnesses? Operations? Accidents? Ever in hospital?—for what, how old, how long? Was he upset at the time or afterwards?

(iv) Any other separations (child away from home without parents, or either parent away for a week or more), how old, how long, with whom, how did he get on at the time, any difficulty afterwards?

(v) How has he taken to any changes in his life (e.g. a new baby, new home, death or departure of any family member, being looked after by someone different)?

(vi) How has he settled and how well has he learnt at each stage of school? (note names of schools, and dates or ages when attended; include nurseries and play groups).

D. *The child now*

(i) General health: good or poor? frequent colds, other ailments?

(ii) What is he like as a person? (cheerful, moody, irritable, nervous, lone wolf, etc.)

(iii) How does he get on with father? With mother? With siblings? With others in household? What happens when he is naughty? How often is punishment necessary? How and by whom punished? How does he take it?

(iv) How does he react if parents disagree about something?

(v) Is he happy at school now; any difficulties there? Are you satisfied with it?

(vi) What does he do in spare time? (interests, activities, pets, bicycle, etc.) Where and with whom does he play?

(In a full length interview it is often useful to administer the Vineland Scale of Social Maturity as a measure of independence training.)

Anything else volunteered.

E. *The problem*

Fill in gaps in the the parents' spontaneous account of the problem and any other difficulties by enquiring as necessary about the onset, course and frequency of the behaviour in question, methods tried in dealing with it, its effects on family life, the attitudes of family members, teachers and anyone else concerned, not least the child himself; and if not clear, just what precipitated the referral at this particular time.

What reason was the child given for coming to see the psychologist? (If it seems necessary to correct any false impression he has been given, discussion of the reasons for doing so may provide a useful starting point for an examination of the parents' attitudes to the child and his behaviour, which can be continued in later interviews.)

3. Rounding off

Shortly before the end of the interviewing time it is a good rule to shift the discussion on to a practical level in the following way.

A. *Check identification data*

(i) Child's date of birth.

(ii) Correct spelling of name, address and telephone number, if any.

(iii) Name and address of school, head teacher's name and permission to ask for a report on the child if contact has not already been made.

(iv) Name and address of general practitioner if parents are willing and if he may have to be asked either for medical information or for a referral, e.g. for neurological examination, or informed of referral to a psychiatrist.

(v) Name and address of any hospital or specialist from whom the child has had investigation or treatment relevant to the problem, and permission to contact for a report.

B. *Outline the procedure*

Outline the remaining steps in the investigation of the problem, explaining the purposes of psychological tests, psychiatric consultation or any other procedures envisaged. Try to allay anxiety about these procedures but do not be tempted to predict their outcome or to give advice before all facts are known.

C. *Agree on action*
Ensure that it is quite clear who is to take the next step and what it is to be. Give a written note of the date and time of any further consultation and of the name and address of any person the parents are to contact. If colleagues have to be consulted or report obtained before making the next move, allow enough time: without appearing callous to worried clients, it is kinder to avoid making promises of haste which may not be fulfilled.

Questionnaires
Where a psychologist is handling a case alone and the parent waits while he examines the child for perhaps an hour or more, a case can be made for employing the time by asking the parent to supply some of the information in writing. This is a matter that calls for considerable discretion, however. Those of us who take in our stride the completion of forms and the answering of written questionnaires may fail to appreciate the intense antipathy they can arouse in many people—those for whom writing and even reading may present real difficulty and may be still associated with the memory of failure at school; those who identify any printed form with soulless bureaucracy; and those who feel that to commit themselves in writing is to leave a permanent record which may misrepresent the case, may be seen by anyone and could damage them or their child in unknown ways. On the other hand there are some who welcome the opportunity to think out (and perhaps to edit) the information they supply. For them, sheets may be prepared giving space to answer a selection of the questions discussed below. The questions should be worded simply but explicitly, and the parent should be invited to leave blank, or mark with a query, any point she is uncertain about or would prefer to discuss orally. Enough time must be allowed both beforehand, to ensure that the forms are acceptable and clearly understood, and afterwards, for the taking up of points which have been queried, left blank, misunderstood, answered too vaguely or which raise matters of special interest.

Information that can reasonably be obtained in written form includes:

(a) *Factual data* unlikely to arouse strong feeling, i.e. points from the Outline Sections 3 A, 2 B and C, omitting the delicate questions about problems with members of the household and whether the child was wanted and the right sex. Written questions about living accommodation (2 A) can cause resentment, as the census enquiries showed. Open-ended questions will yield more useful replies if they are made as concrete as possible; thus for 2 C(v) one might ask: If any children have been born (or adopted or fostered) in your family since this child how old was he at the time that each newcomer arrived? Did he seem pleased, angry, jealous or what? Did his behaviour change about that time in any way? —and similarly for the other experiences listed.

(b) *Aspects of the child's personality.* There is a difficulty in that the qualitative data called for in Section 2 D, and still more in 2 E, can only be obtained as perceived and interpreted by the informant; these parental perceptions and interpretations reveal themselves in tone of voice and other incidental clues during conversation and may well be lost in the written replies. Nevertheless the more concrete aspects of a child's behaviour can be set out in the form of an inventory, as has been done for example by Stott (1963b) in his Bristol Social Adjustment Guide on 'The Child in the Family'. With a parent who really does not mind completing questionnaires, such an inventory can make a useful starting point for discussion as well as providing systematic scorable material for research purposes.

The Vineland Social Maturity Scale (Doll, 1953), already mentioned, is in fact an inventory of the child's everyday practical abilities (as distinct from the qualitative behaviour tendencies covered by Stott). While it might be thought time-saving to convert this scale to a questionnaire (for which purpose the items would have to be broken down and defined much more exactly than they are) the difficulty would be that most parents feel their child's competence to be a reflection of their own success in bringing him up, so that upward distortions of unknown extent would predominate, while a minority of infantilising parents would tend to distort downwards. Again, such tendencies can best be judged in oral discussion.

(c) *Parental attitudes and methods.* A similar danger of distortion would naturally apply to questions about the parents' methods of handling their child. Attitudes or opinions on child rearing policies in general, however, can be elicited with rather more objectivity. Various scales of this kind exist. The Parent Attitude Research Instrument of Schaefer and Bell (1958) yields scores for 20 variables of parental attitude and personality. Once again, instruments of this kind are best used, where parents are willing to complete them, as starting points for discussion rather than as ends in themselves. It has to be borne in mind that a parent's opinions about the best ways of bringing up children, what he actually does with his own family, and what he thinks he does are three very different things. Oppenheim in London has devised but not published a double scale calling on parents to distinguish the first (attitudes) from the third (professed practices). The second (actual practice) can be observed only in its public aspects; what goes on at home may be known only to parent and child, neither of whom is an unbiased witness.

While the invitation to express opinions on child rearing is generally acceptable to most parents, anything more directly in the nature of a test, either of personality or of ability, is not. However much a psychologist may want to assess parents in this way, he will be well advised to avoid jeopardising cooperation by treating them as subjects of investigation: he will need them as allies in his attack on the problem. There is of course nothing to stop him, if he is so minded, from devising a series of rating scales to assist him in recording his impressions of their personalities as an aid to research. Some workers however prefer to think less in terms of the ratable traits of individuals and more in terms of the mutual perceptions and interactions of people in a given situation, and of the changes that might be effected by altering that situation. This sort of analysis is more difficult to carry out but may lead to more effective diagnosis. A possible framework will be suggested below, in discussing the diagnostic summary.

Communication of test findings to parents

The reporting of psychological findings will be discussed in detail in chapter 12, but certain points must be made here, since the communication of these findings to parents raises special issues; it is an integral part of the continuous process which includes referral, examination, discussion and recommendations.

In the vast majority of cases parents' agreement to any special educational provision or to any therapeutic treatment of the child must be obtained, unless this is merely an extension of the ordinary process of education in the school he already attends. (Legal coercion in such matters is avoided by the authorities wherever any acceptable educational arrangement can be made.) To a large extent the effectiveness of such measures depends not merely on the parents' agreement but on their active cooperation. The way in which the psychologist presents his findings and recommendations may be crucial in eliciting this cooperation. His task is to present the child's abilities, behaviour and needs in a way that the parents can accept, even if it is at variance with their preconceptions, so that they will become receptive to whatever constructive suggestions can be made. This is not always possible in one interview; radical change of attitudes, modification of cherished aspirations, requires time.

The level of the child's general ability is best presented in terms relevant to possible educational provision. Parents usually want to know where the child stands, relative not to the whole population but to that section of it which embodies the goals they have been envisaging for him, explicitly or otherwise: the kinds of occupation they can 'see' him pursuing, and the kinds of education leading to such jobs. The term 'average', for example, will mean to any given parent the average of the children known to him or her, who are likely to move into the typical occupations for their social group. The standard category descriptions of test scores, based on norms for the total population, are therefore positively misleading both to professional class and to manual working class parents.

Sophisticated parents sometimes ask to be told their child's IQ. (Some independent schools ask them to ascertain it before admitting a child, but such schools will always accept a confidential report.) Policies vary, but the majority of psychologists would probably agree in withholding numerical assessments from parents—some also from doctors and even teachers—chiefly because the very general belief in their absolute validity and permanence can lead to false expectations. It is quite possible to explain that the profession is now regarding exact IQs with much less favour than formerly since they are known to vary from one test to another and to fluctuate over time. (Honzik, Macfarlane and Allen, 1948, found that the Binet IQs of 58 per cent of their normal longitudinal sample varied by 15 points or more between the ages of six and eighteen, and other studies have confirmed the variability: see Bloom, 1964.) The negative character of this reply should then be counteracted with appropriate positive information. One may be able to estimate the child's chances of getting into the school or passing the examinations envisaged; if these chances are low, it is best to say so and to suggest alternative goals. Undue pressure to succeed can be harmful, and every grammar school knows children who, having been forced through its entrance requirements, then wilt and fail at great cost in morale.

It is nearly always possible to find something favourable to say about a child, whether in terms of special abilities or of personal qualities. Where parents want to help, ways in which they can best do so should be discussed. If their efforts to teach the child are creating confusion, anxiety or resistance, some more useful shared activity can generally be suggested. Most parents can better accept professional help if they can feel they still have an essential part to play.

Extensions of diagnosis

Before he can make any recommendation the psychologist has to piece together information obtained from parents, from school and from the child, together with his understanding of all three as interacting elements in a complex situation. This understanding will not of course be complete after his first contact with each of the parties concerned. Investigation can seldom be as complete as one might wish because of pressure of work; it is therefore important to think clearly at each stage about what information is essential to an effective resolution of the problem. This may well involve seeing the second parent when only one was seen before;

further interviews with the parents or the child, alone or together, and follow-up visits to the school. In this process understanding will continually be enriched and any provisional diagnostic summary is likely to require modification and extension. Certain important questions can only be answered by observing the parents' reactions to interpretation and/or suggestion; the limits of what is acceptable will soon become apparent. Diagnosis thus merges into remedial action.

Experience will soon enable the perceptive psychologist, without the use of any tests, to gauge for practical purposes a parent's intelligence, his capacity for objectivity and for empathy in relation to his child, and many other aspects of his personality from the way he receives the psychologist's findings—always assuming that they are conveyed in a sympathetic and tactful manner. In so far as the assessment may frustrate parental hopes and aspirations, the rationale underlying Rosenzweig's categories of response to frustration can be useful (Rosenzweig, 1945):

'obstacle dominance'—is the parent overwhelmed and inhibited from effective action by disappointment? Does he strenuously deny this feeling? 'ego defense'—Does he openly or covertly refuse to accept the findings as valid? Does he react aggressively, seeking to blame the school, the other parent, the child; or intropunitively shouldering the blame himself; or is he concerned to exonerate everyone from blame? 'need persistence'—does he seek a solution from others; consider what he can do himself, or passively accept the situation as it is?

The type of recommendation most likely to prove effective will depend to a considerable extent on such attitudes as these in the mother or the father, whichever is the maker of decisions about the child; but the translation of attitudes into active cooperation will depend on a wider system of family and social dynamics.

There are of course straightforward cases in which the parents accept their child for what he is and cooperate gladly in whatever educational measures are suggested. But the comparative rarity of such an attitude among the parents of children with problems is not really surprising when one considers all that militates against it: natural parental aspiration aggravated in a competitive society by the knowledge that a child who falls behind in the race is at a permanent disadvantage; shame at having produced an imperfect child and fear of the opinions of neighbours; fear of 'tainted' heredity; guilt for real or imagined mishandling, sometimes projected onto a spouse or a grandparent; and the daily wear and tear of living with a child whose frustrations are almost bound to make him difficult in one way or another. Where any or all of these factors are operating to prevent the parents from looking at the problem calmly and openmindedly, they may reject the psychologist's findings out of hand and desperately resist any suggestion that the child should attend, for example, a special school or class. (For handling, see case studies, pp. 324, 325.)

Where the child is a slow learner without physical sign of subnormality, there may be a very strong desire to believe that he is just lazy, 'unwilling' to concentrate, temporarily retarded owing to early illness or bad teaching, or suffering from specific defect such as a speech handicap or dyslexia, and that the condition can be remedied by extra individual teaching while he remains at the ordinary school. Many parents will prefer a small private school, however ill-equipped, even if it is one in which their child may be allowed to sit and doodle or copy endless sheets of figures, to the most up-to-date school for educationally subnormal children. Nearly always the reason given is that if he mixes with children who are 'worse' (i.e. more handicapped) he will somehow be dragged down to their level either by imitation or by lowered expectations on the part of teachers. It is painfully difficult for these parents to accept that in any ordinary class their child would be far below the standard reached by all the others, and unable to understand much of what is going on, while in a slower learning group he could cope and blossom with confidence. The horror of subnormality is primitive and may not readily yield to reasonable arguments. The psychologist has to gauge its strength in each individual case and to be alert for signs of awareness that can be used to counteract it.

Where the problem is one of behaviour the primitive fear is that the child may turn out either mad or bad, and in either case beyond the parents' power to cope. Again, one frequently hears that he is 'easily led' by children of undesirable character (whose parents are usually held to blame); but where the problem has reached worrying proportions there may be readier agreement to attendance at a school or class for maladjusted children, together with discussions of the parents' own part in the treatment programme. Indeed they may come with the conscious desire, avowed or not, of having the child sent away to a boarding school, and it may fall to the psychologist to decide whether in the circumstances this course is to be recommended or not.

Beneath their feelings about the problem lie their feelings about the child: what he means to each of them in terms of their own needs and ambitions, ideals and antipathies; how they see his needs and their own ability to meet them; how he fits into the constellation of family relationships. This may lead to a consideration of the whole pattern of family life, with its internal and external stresses and its ways of dealing with them. In some cases a child can paradoxically hold a family together by acting as a kind of lightning conductor for the anger and hostility of other members. In other cases he may be a focus of common anxiety. On the other hand, a child whose behaviour is uncontrolled, or destructive, or threatening to cherished values, or one whose temperament clashes too sharply with that of a parent or sibling, can place a tremendous strain on the cohesion of his family. While to the outsider the problem may seem clearly one of mutual adaptation, to those personally involved it may equally clearly appear as one of right and wrong, requiring punishment or 'cure' of the offender.

Not very often will the educational psychologist singlehanded be obliged to investigate family dynamics in detail. His scientific training will keep him on his guard against making pronouncements more definite than the evidence will bear; but he can quite properly present the evidence, together with his own interpretative hypotheses, for consideration by a psychiatric or social work colleague. Unless appropriately trained or thoroughly experienced, he should not be tempted into explaining to parents, however sophisticated, the invisible forces he conceives to underlie their behaviour: the result may well be to alienate them from further professional help.

Diagnostic summary

Some kind of summary should be made of every case investigated, in a form helpful to the psychologist himself and to any colleague called in. There are many forms such a summary can take; that proposed below may be found useful in clarifying a complex problem but is by no means prescriptive. In simpler cases it may be much abbreviated.

The total situation can often be thought of as consisting of the interplay between the views of five main parties: the child, the mother, the father, the school, and the psychologist. Each of these parties has certain standards by which to judge scholastic attainment, personal competence, and the acceptability of behaviour. Each party also has his own perception of how the child is functioning in these areas. Where there is a discrepancy between standard and perceived functioning, the party concerned will have some attitude toward the possibility of reducing the discrepancy. He will also have his view of the causes of the problem. In summarising the case, the psychologist's task is to gauge as objectively as he can the standards, perceptions and attitudes of each of the parties concerned, to add his own assessment of the situation, and on this basis to offer an opinion concerning the causes of the problem, what changes he thinks desirable, how they may best be effected, and what difficulties stand in the way. The necessary information can be set out systematically in the form of comments under the following headings. (For a diagnostic *strategy*, see Wedell, 1972).

A form of diagnostic summary
1. *Identification data*
2. *Referral:* by whom and for what

3. *Psychological examination*

(a) Testing conditions satisfactory, or why doubtful? (child uncooperative, very anxious, unhappy, unwell, tired, sedated, etc. Language or cultural barrier, sensory/motor deficiency. External distractions, insufficient time).

(b) Abilities: tests used, results. Particular strengths, weaknesses, anomalies, wide scatter, etc.

(c) Attainments: tests used, results compared with general ability (over/adequate/underfunctioning in . . .). Any specific difficulties.

(d) Social competence, similarly.

(e) Personality structure, in terms of tests used or from observation.

(f) Quality of personal relationships, as shown in conversation, projective tests, observation, rapport with psychologist.

4. *Child's view* (elicited by psychologist/psychiatrist):

(a) How readily, freely, honestly does child discuss the problems? What forms of defence does he employ?

(b) In attainments, personal-social competence, behaviour and/or personal relationships, depending on the problem.

  (i) Are the standards he sets himself too high/appropriate/too low?

  (ii) Is his estimate of his own performance distorted favourably/realistic/distorted unfavourably?

  (iii) To what does he attribute the problem?

  (iv) Does he envisage a solution (what?)/want help/feel hopeless/not care/see no problem?

(c) What other factors influence his outlook?

5. *Parents' views* (elicited by psychologist/social worker/psychiatrist—from mother/father/both in joint/separate interviews). Record information for mother and father in parallel columns.

(a) How readily, freely, honestly does parent discuss the problems? What forms of defence does he/she employ?

(b) In the problem area(s):

  (i) Are the parent's standards for the child too high/appropriate/too low? If inappropriate, what is the probable reason?

  (ii) How seriously does the parent view the problem?

  (iii) To what does he attribute it?

  (iv) Does parent see himself as responsible for/aggravating/ameliorating the problem—in what way? How far is this realistic?

  (v) How does he see the other parent's part?

  (vi) Does he envisage a solution (what?)/want help/feel hopeless/not care/see no problem?

(c) What other factors in the family situation are relevant?

6. *The school's view* (elicited in conversation/in writing from head teacher/class teacher/both):

(a) What is the general attitude of the teacher(s) to the child?

(b) In the problem area(s):
   (i) are standards in the child's class too high for him/appropriate/too
     low? If inappropriate, would another class be more suitable?
   (ii) Is child's performance in school commensurate with his potential?
   (iii) To what do the teachers attribute the problem?
   (iv) Do they see the school as being able to help? how?
(c) In other respects is the school fulfilling the child's needs? Could it be
helped to do so better? Is a change of school indicated?

7. *Factors causing or perpetuating the problem* (inferred from the foregoing
analysis: several may apply):
(a) Inherent in child's personality (e.g. hyperkinesis)
(b) Self-dissatisfaction in child (admitted or denied, with or without compensatory misbehaviour)
(c) Discrepancies between views of child and parent(s)
(d) Discrepancies between views of mother and father
(e) Unwise handling by mother and/or father, due to:
   (i) misperceptions of causes of problem;
   (ii) misperceptions of effects of own methods;
   (iii) poor impulse control;
   (iv) rejection of child (not merely of his behaviour);
   (v) displacement of ill-feeling from other objects,
(f) Effect of wider family problems
(g) Discrepancies between views of child and school
(h) Discrepancies between views of parents and school
(i) Tensions within the school
(j) Inappropriate teaching or disciplinary methods
(k) Inappropriate school
(l) Social problems (e.g. poverty, delinquent community, racial tension)
(m) Other.

8. *Possibilities of management*
(a) List possible courses of action, with advantages and difficulties of each:
   (i) remedial teaching individually/in group, by a teacher in the school/
     by a specialist teacher elsewhere/by a psychologist
   (ii) therapy: individual/group, by psychologist/psychiatrist/therapist.
   (iii) speech therapy/physiotherapy in school/elsewhere
   (iv) referral for child guidance
   (v) referral to youth leader/probation officer/youth employment
     officer/social services department/other social agency
   (vi) work with parents by psychologist/social worker/psychiatrist
   (vii) support and advice to teachers/change of class/change of school/
     recommendation for special educational provision
   (viii) recommendation for holiday away/boarding school/hostel
   (ix) application for care by local authority.
     etc.

(*b*) Note what further information, or opinion, is needed to clarify the situation.

(*c*) Note what action required, and any contingencies, e.g. official approval, parental agreement, finding a vacancy, for each acceptable recommendation in order of preference.

Further work with parents

We will conclude this chapter by glancing at some of the ways in which a psychologist may, if he chooses, simultaneously deepen his diagnostic insight and help parents to find their own solutions to their child-rearing problems. Building on the rapport gained in his initial interview:

(*a*) He may encourage intelligent parents to make systematic observations of the interactions between their child and themselves, preferably with the aid of diary records.

(*b*) On this basis he can arrange regular discussions of events arising, of the feelings of the parties concerned, and of their methods of communication.

(*c*) From his knowledge of child development, he can explain children's mental processes and their implications for child rearing, including the expectations, training techniques, toys, etc. appropriate to each stage.

(*d*) As distinct from urging particular methods, he may point out the range of *possible* parental responses to given behaviour in a child, and may support the parents in any experimental modification they may decide for themselves to try, discussing difficulties as they arise.

(*e*) He may discuss the mutually complementary roles of mother, father, siblings, friends and teachers, and help them to coordinate the parts they play in relation to the child;

(*f*) He may discuss educational issues, explaining the ideas underlying methods used in the child's school which are obscure to the parents.

(*g*) He may mediate in disagreements between parents and teachers.

In addition to working with individual families some educational psychologists organise discussion groups where parents can meet and thrash out their problems together, often finding support in the realisation that others have difficulties similar to their own or even greater. Evening institute courses are one setting for such discussions; less formal groups can sometimes be organised at infant welfare centres, community play centres, parent–teacher associations, or with the staffs of children's homes. But this takes us beyond diagnosis and treatment into the realm of prevention.

Part Three

Children with special needs: educational and psychological approaches

The organisation of special education and the problems of the assessment of handicapped children have been discussed in previous chapters. In the following three chapters the difficulties of children who have learning problems or physical handicaps, or who are maladjusted or delinquent, will be outlined, and the educational and psychological treatment of these children will be considered. A comprehensive discussion of the psychology and education of handicapped children is not possible within the available space. There is now a vast literature on the subject, from which selected contributions are cited to illustrate trends in research and experiment in this field, with the emphasis on British rather than American research because of the differences in educational practice in the two countries.

It is important that the educational psychologist should be concerned to develop his diagnostic, counselling and therapeutic skills in the context of the growing body of knowledge relating to the developmental needs of both normal and handicapped children. How the assessment and education of handicapped children can be guided by an understanding of the principles of child development has been shown, for example, by M. Woodward (1962), who has applied Piaget's methods and theories to subnormal children (see also Stephen and Robertson, 1965). Although each child assessed will present unique problems, the psychologist, in making a diagnosis and appropriate recommendations for treatment, will be helped by a knowledge of the characteristic difficulties of the groups of children usually categorised as, for example, 'educationally sub-normal', 'cerebral palsied' or 'maladjusted'. However, he should avoid a rigid approach in using categories of this kind and be aware of changes in emphasis resulting from new knowledge. Although he will find it useful to classify the children whom he sees into widely accepted categories, these categories ought not to be regarded as clearcut and distinct. As already mentioned in chapter 2, the borderlines between one type of handicap and another are becoming increasingly blurred as the interrelationships between handicaps of different kinds are clarified by research and experience.

It is also essential for the educational psychologist, concerned as he is in the placement of children in special schools and classes of various kinds, to be familiar with research work on the progress of children in different establish-ments, and on the extent to which these establishments provide a satisfactory solution to the problems posed by children with special needs. Research on these topics has been very scanty, but sufficient has been carried out to question current practices and to encourage wide experimentation with new approaches.

9

Children with learning difficulties

Children who present learning difficulties of sufficient severity to warrant special attention constitute an extremely heterogeneous group; they not only range widely in intelligence but present a variety of associated problems, physical, social or emotional. As Cashdan (1969) points out, success and failure in learning are relative concepts, and terms such as 'dull', 'backward', 'subnormal', or 'retarded' do not have a precise scientific meaning; their connotations are affected by such factors as the population being studied and the skills under consideration.

The classification of children with learning difficulties, therefore, presents many difficulties. Here these children are, for the sake of convenience, discussed under the following headings (see also chapter 2):

1. *Educationally subnormal (severe) children*—ESN(s). Until the Education Act of 1970 these children were referred to in the literature as 'severely subnormal' (SSN), and the latter term will be retained in the ensuing discussion wherever it has been used in studies quoted.
2. *Educationally subnormal (moderate) children*—ESN(m). This term will be used to refer to pupils in special schools or special classes catering for a population with IQs mainly in the range of 50/55 and 70/75, though many of such schools or classes will also have some children with higher IQs (Chazan, 1964; P. Williams, 1966).
3. *Children 'below average' in ability.* Although most of the children in this group will not be brought forward for formal ascertainment, nor will they require special provision other than a suitable curriculum within the ordinary school, individuals within this category may present problems of learning or behaviour serious enough to warrant attention from the school psychological service.
4. *Educationally retarded children*, who do not show any marked deficiency in general intelligence but who are failing in a number of school subjects or in one specific area, for example reading or number.

It must be emphasised that, because of the overlap between the above groupings it will often be difficult, and indeed undesirable, for the psychologist to assign a child firmly to a particular category, and only the term 'educationally subnormal' has any legal significance. The concept of subnormality, as previously stated, has proved very difficult to define in precise terms. Neither the Education Act of 1944 and its subsequent Regulations nor the Mental Health Act of 1959 mentions intelligence quotients or specifies a range of ability in statistical terms within which individuals may be deemed subnormal. In view of research findings showing that IQs are subject to considerable changes over a period of time, this lack of reference to IQs is certainly justified, though it does draw attention to the difficulties in deciding on the criteria by which a judgement is to be reached that an individual is to be categorized as 'subnormal' in any degree. For some time past a single criterion of subnormality has been regarded as unsatisfactory (see Clarke and Clarke, 1966). Doll in 1941 suggested six criteria as essential to a definition of what was then termed 'mental deficiency' in the USA:

1. social incompetence (inability to manage one's affairs);
2. mental subnormality (low intelligence);
3. arrested development (i.e. not deterioration due, for example, to epilepsy);
4. deficiency at maturity (essentially permanent);
5. deficiency of constitutional origin (has roots in a hereditary lack of potential); and
6. essentially incurable defect.

Although psychologists still think in terms of several criteria rather than a single criterion of subnormality, they no longer find those suggested by Doll satisfactory. As the IQ as measured at a particular time is not necessarily an accurate predictor of future intellectual status, the psychologist usually confines himself to making statements about current intellectual functioning and hesitates to make other than tentative predictions about future development. Further, a variety of causes, both hereditary and environmental, of subnormal functioning are recognised, and few would venture to assert definitely whether any case of subnormality can be 'cured' or not.

Educationally subnormal (s) children

Now that the local education authority is responsible for providing education for all subnormal children of school age, there is no longer a need for the formal classification of children as 'severely' educationally subnormal. However, as the needs of 'severely' and 'moderately' ESN children are likely to differ considerably, it will be useful, in practice, to regard children as ESN(s) when they show, in daily life and (if testable) on the basis of tests, intellectual limitations of a severe kind as well as grossly inadequate social or adaptive behaviour; and when it is expected that they will be unable to achieve full independence and will need permanent support of some kind. It is essential that periodic reviews should be made of any child categorised in this way, as a change in educational or other placement may be advisable; and it is important that the predictions and expectations of the psychologist should not be allowed to exercise too rigid constraints on the education and treatment of the child. Although the IQ has increasingly come under attack, approximate IQ measures can still form part of an assessment and children in this category will usually have IQs below 50–55; but the psychologist must guard against fixing permanent labels on a child on the basis of a single test result, and should realise that test scores do not necessarily indicate how a child is eventually going to adapt to society. Test results need to be supplemented and confirmed, or challenged, by detailed reports on the child's reactions in a variety of situations, at home, in the neighbourhood, and, where appropriate, in school.

Aetiology

The causes of subnormality have in the past often been divided into *endogenous* (roughly equivalent to primary, inherited or familial) and *exogenous* (secondary, acquired or environmental). Sometimes exogenous causes are subdivided into *organic* causes (such as traumatic injury, disease, toxins or anoxia) and causes *relating to the environment* (severe restriction of cultural experiences). It is now well known that causation cannot be looked at only from the environmental angle or from the genetic point of view; the level of a child's intellectual functioning is always the result of the interaction between genetic and environmental factors. Even if some cases of subnormality are produced primarily by genetic causation, for example phenylpyruvic oligophrenia (caused by a single recessive gene) or mongolism (Down's syndrome, due to a chromosomal abnormality), some conditions can be produced by either exogenous or endogenous causes; for example, cretinism can be caused genetically or be due to a limited intake of iodine. Whether one emphasises physiological abnormalities, deficiencies in the environment or the complex interaction of cultural and familial causes, it can be said that in many instances the aetiology will not be definitely known. It seems the case, however, that factors such as genetic aberrations or prenatal, perinatal or postnatal disease or injury are more likely to be found in the histories of severely subnormal children than in those of ESN(m) children of limited ability. Marshall (1967), in a survey of 165 severely subnormal children (aged fourteen to sixteen) in nineteen training centres in three areas of England found the distribution of types of case to be as follows: Mongolism 45 per cent, familial defect 10 per cent, birth injury 10 per cent, mixed causes 10 per cent, cause unknown 25 per cent.

A knowledge of the causation of subnormality in any individual case will only rarely lead to action which is directly related to the ascertained causes. The treatment of phenylketonuria by a special diet, free of phenylalanine, has resulted in normal development; and milder cases of cretinism may respond to thyroid treatment. However, the progress of a proportion of ESN(s) children, whatever the specific aetiology, may be impaired by adverse home circumstances, and the educational psychologist, working in conjunction with the social services, should ensure that as much is done as is possible to improve the living conditions of these children.

Physical disabilities

Mental and physical defects tend to go together in ESN(s) children. In this group, physical development is often relatively slow, clumsiness and a lack of coordination is common, and physique is frequently ungainly (McDowall, 1964). Mongols and cretins have well-known physical stigmata. Some ESN(s) children will be suffering from cerebral palsy, perhaps in a mild form; and a number will have epileptic fits, often associated with some kind of brain damage. Marshall (1967) found that 48 per cent of SSN children in her survey had an additional physical disability, such as severely impaired eyesight, deformity of a limb, hip dislocation, or an abnormal heart condition, and 12 per cent of the sample had more than one such disability.

Although O. G. Johnson and Capobianco (1959), in an American study of the effect of physical condition upon learning in 'trainable mentally deficient' children, concluded that the general physical condition of the children studied did not affect the benefit they derived from their class training to any significant degree, it is important that ESN(s) children should have periodic thorough medical examinations. In this group it is easy to overlook such disabilities as partial hearing loss, and in individual cases even a slight physical defect may reduce the child's capacity to benefit from education.

Cognitive deficits

A great deal of research has been carried out in recent years to increase knowledge of the specific nature of the cognitive deficits which are characteristically found in severely subnormal children (A. D. B. Clarke, 1969). Cashdan (1968) draws attention to the 'behavioural rigidity' of subnormal children, who have a reduced ability to change activities for themselves and see little connection between similar activities (Kounin, 1943), and to the fact that subnormal children often spend much longer at a particular stage of development than normal children (Zazzo, 1960). O'Connor and Hermelin (1963) found that severely subnormal children can use concepts to a certain extent as a basis for classification, though they have great difficulty in verbalising such concepts. They emphasise that 'a verbal disinclination' as well as a verbal disability seems to be present in these children. In memorising, the severely subnormal tend to be inferior to normals in acquisition (e.g. of information, or learning new tasks) rather than in retaining what they have learned. Although SSN children are relatively poor at recalling sequences of words or pictures (Elliott, 1970), they are able to make use of clustering strategies in free recall tasks (J. M. Green and Herriott, 1971).

While SSN children tend to be highly distractable and to have a short attention span, with difficulties of comprehension, reasoning, judgement, insight and memory, possessing few interests, a lack of purposeful curiosity and little imagination (McDowall, 1964), the findings emerging from experimental work on the cognitive deficits of the SSN suggest that the learning efficiency of these children can be improved, at least to some extent, by appropriate educational procedures. A. D. B. Clarke (1969) summarises the implications of relevant research work in this field. Among the points which he emphasises are the following:

1. It is important to find ways of increasing the attention span of severely subnormal children. The attention value of relevant cues can be increased by such means as using three-dimensional objects in teaching shape discriminations, or introducing very brilliant colours (Zeaman and House, 1963).
2. Memory functions can be improved by, for example, making stimuli more intense or of longer duration and by simultaneous presentation of stimuli in multiple modalities (Baumeister, 1967).
3. A greater attention to verbal training might be worthwhile (Blount, 1968).
4. Distraction should be minimised in the early stages of learning a difficult task (Sen and Clarke, 1968).

O'Connor and Hermelin (1963) also underline the necessity of presenting material at relatively high intensity levels, stressing relevant aspects of stimuli, and presenting stimuli with sufficient frequency if SSN children are to begin to learn.

As yet there is little evidence of any wide application of experimental findings to the education of ESN(s) children (Marshall, 1967), and there is much scope for the educational psychologist in stimulating the introduction of experimental learning programmes into special schools for these children. The work being carried out at the Hester Adrian Centre (Mittler,

1970c), being based on psychological principles, is likely to offer guidelines to the educational psychologist in his endeavours in this field.

Language and speech

Mittler (1971) concludes that SSN children seem to show severe language delays in excess of what might be expected on the basis of their social or non-verbal development. Since the subnormal child is not as skilled as the normal child in communicating to others his failure to understand, it is difficult to tell whether he is failing on a learning task because this is too difficult for him or because he is unable to grasp the instructions. Further, SSN children are very deficient in using context in order to extract meaning.

Sampson (1968) also observes that a lack of age-appropriate, effective speech marks out the SSN more than any other single characteristic. The urge to talk seems lacking, and even when speech is achieved, it is often difficult to understand. Poor articulation may be aggravated by physical defects. The level of expression, too, of SSN children is crude and their vocabulary highly restricted.

In spite of the extreme difficulties which many ESN(s) children experience in the use of language, there is some evidence that their language and speech can often be improved, at least to some extent, both by direct training and by creating a stimulating child-centred environment (Lyle, 1960). The work of Jeffree (1971) has illustrated how the quantity and quality of a mongol child's language can be improved by the teacher systematically varying different aspects of the situation. She also emphasises that vague objectives such as helping a child to 'talk more' can be broken down into more specific aims, e.g. the use of longer sentences or an increase in the ratio of verbs to nouns. Jeffree and Cashdan (1971) have shown how the parents of severely subnormal children can be involved in a language facilitation programme, calling for a variety of approaches. Although the remediation of language deficiencies in ESN(s) children is still at the experimental stage, sufficient work has been carried out to date to provide guidance for the educational psychologist who wishes to encourage further experiments in special schools.

Behaviour problems

There is little systematic evidence available on the prevalence and nature of behaviour disturbance among ESN(s) children. However, most special schools for these children have to deal with some very difficult behaviour of a restless, aggressive, destructive and overactive kind associated with brain damage, although the most severe cases of hyperkinesis may need hospitalisation, being unmanageable at home and at school (McDowall, 1964). Mongol children are commonly thought to be placid and to present few behaviour problems, but Cantor (1958) does not support this stereotype. In general, ESN(s) children are prone to disinhibition, mood changes and antisocial behaviour caused by frustration or feelings of inadequacy. Behaviour problems may also be caused by the toxic effect of ailments such as infected tonsils, middle ear trouble or chronic catarrh.

Because of a difficulty in making interpersonal relationships, ESN(s) children may withdraw into themselves and refrain from participating in group activities. However, not all problem behaviour on the part of ESN(s) children should be regarded as indicating unsatisfactory development. McDowall makes the important point that compensatory behaviour responses which are a reaction to frustration, such as temper tantrums, may in some cases be a hopeful sign, indicating some degree of purposefulness and a striving towards 'identity formation' which is rarely well developed in the severely subnormal.

Mundy (1957) suggests that even severely subnormal children who are not psychotic or organically impaired can be helped by psychotherapy, but therapeutic help of this kind is unlikely to be available for most SSN children and the special school itself will have to bear the brunt of the behaviour problems presented by these children. Environmental structuring using, for example, operant conditioning methods, can, even in the case of some 'unmanageable' children, help to improve behaviour (Maier, 1971), and the psychologist trained in such methods should be able to assist school staffs in the management of behaviour problems.

Aims of education and training

The general aims of education and training for ESN(s) children with IQs roughly above 30 usually include enabling the children:

1. to acquire certain self-care skills (e.g. dressing, eating, toileting);
2. to protect themselves from common dangers in home and neighbourhood;
3. to communicate orally in a limited way;
4. to become socially adjusted at home and in the neighbourhood, learning to respect property and cooperate in the family unit; and
5. to become economically useful at home or in the community, in many cases in a sheltered environment under supervision (Kirk, 1957).

More specific curricular aims include the mastery of motor skills such as walking, running, climbing and dancing; developing visual and auditory discrimination; the learning of simple number concepts; learning to participate in group activity, for example of a musical kind; and the acquiring of certain occupational skills, such as running errands, using the telephone, setting the table, dusting and sweeping. Considerable stress is often placed on the achievement of a measure of social competence, and in this teachers have been greatly assisted by the work of Gunzburg (1960), who has clearly defined the important social skills which need to be mastered wherever possible.

It still remains, however, for special schools to work out precise objectives for individual children and for experimentation with various kinds of curricula (Mittler, 1971), with the particular aim of enabling ESN(s) children to make full use of whatever abilities they possess.

The effectiveness of education and training

The effectiveness of the education and training given to ESN(s) children may be assessed in two main ways, firstly by measuring the attainments of the children when due to leave school, and secondly by evaluating their postschool adjustment to life. Most of the research work in this country has been on subnormal children in the hospital setting rather than on children at junior training centres. However, Marshall (1967) provides information about the social competence of 165 ESN(s) children aged fourteen to sixteen (see above, p. 175), their language skills and general adjustment. The children had gained considerable progress in self-help tasks, but were poor in communication skills. Their vocabulary mean ages ranged, on different tests, from 5 years 6 months to 6 years, and little recognition of socially useful words was evident. Marshall concludes that the scope of the curriculum of the junior training centre could be considerably widened.

American studies of the effectiveness of programmes for trainable mentally retarded children in special classes have tended to conclude that the children fail to make substantial progress in socialization, intellectual development or self-care over and above the children who remained at home (Haring and Schiefelbusch, 1967). However, an enquiry in Minnesota (Reynolds et al., 1953) found that parents gained real relief from their children being in a special class and became more realistic in their expectations as the programme continued. An investigation in Illinois (Goldstein, 1956) confirmed the latter finding.

As far as the postschool adjustment of ESN(s) children is concerned, Saenger (1957) followed up 2,640 adults, formerly enrolled in special classes for trainable mentally retarded children in New York City during the period 1929–55. The main body of his report was based on interviews with over 500 parents. He found that two-thirds of the sample were living at home, one-twelfth were in institutions, and 2·5 per cent had died. One-quarter of the sample had worked or were working within the community (mainly those with IQs above 40); one in five assumed a major responsibility for household chores, and one-half looked after their own property and cleaned their rooms. Although the majority had made a reasonably good adjustment to their homes, a considerable proportion of the sample had physical disabilities and speech defects; few had any reading ability whatsoever. In this country, there has been little in the way of systematic follow-up of children in junior training centres, but Tizard and his colleagues have made a number of studies of subnormal adults, concluding that the great majority even of hospitalised patients were employable, and that their main need was for an effective rehabilitation and training programme (O'Connor and Tizard, 1956; Tizard and Grad, 1961).

The contribution of the educational psychologist to the education of ESN(s) children

Ways in which the educational psychologist can stimulate developments in the training and education of ESN(s) children have been mentioned above. As Mittler (1971) states, educational psychologists will be required to play a part in advising local education authorities and headteachers on the educational needs of the mentally handicapped in general, and of individual children in particular. In order to be in a position to give useful advice, educational psychologists will need to familiarise themselves with the research literature on the psychology, education and training of subnormal children and to reconsider the relevance of traditional assessment techniques and educational procedures to ESN(s) children. In recent decades, much progress has been made in the biochemistry and genetics of mental subnormality; it is to be hoped that in the next few decades there will be considerable developments in the education and training of the ESN(s), in which educational psychologists will play a part.

Educationally subnormal (moderate) children

The following discussion will relate mainly to children with 'pronounced educational backwardness' (Department of Education and Science, 1964a) and limited general ability, who usually require placement in special schools or their equivalent special classes.

Aetiology

'Subcultural' factors play a part in the case of a substantial proportion of ESN(m) children, that is their subnormality stems from a complex interaction of genetics and environment; they tend to have parents below average in intelligence as well as adverse environmental circumstances, both material and cultural (A. D. B. Clarke, 1969). At one time the genetic origin of subnormality at this level (IQ range approximately 50 to 75) was stressed, but now more emphasis is being placed on the effects of a poor environment, particularly on a lack of adequate stimulation in the early years. Stein and Susser (1960b) distinguish two types of ESN children:

1. a clinically heterogeneous group, drawn from 'high' and 'low' social classes, most of whom are 'brain-damaged', with detectable handicaps to learning;
2. a clinically homogeneous group, without brain damage or serious handicaps to learning, coming from the families of manual workers.

They suggest that the second group are likely to make better progress at school than the first group. The available evidence on the socio-economic background of ESN pupils suggests that the majority of those in special schools come from homes where the father is in an occupation in Social Class IV or V (semiskilled, unskilled or casual work) or unemployed (Stein and Susser, 1960a; Chazan, 1964; P. Williams, 1966). While, other things being equal, there seems to be a definite tendency for children in the lower social classes to be picked out for ascertainment to a greater extent than children of high social class, the relationship between a good home background and good school attainment is well documented in the literature, and there can be little doubt that many ESN(m) pupils are considerably disadvantaged by reason of a poor material and cultural background. The sources of disadvantage include membership of large families (Chazan, 1964), coming from broken homes (Stein and Susser, 1960a), and a frequent lack of stimulation and encouragement. The intellectual development and school progress of many ESN(m) pupils are, therefore, likely to be adversely affected not only by innate lack of potential but also by a combination of adverse environmental conditions.

However, Stott (1959, 1963c) has hypothesised that congenital impairment is often the main factor responsible for intellectual subnormality, accompanied by physical weakness and a proneness to temperamental instability. Tansley's work (1966) supports this view: in his study of 100 ESN children at a large residential school, 75 were considered likely to have been 'at risk' from an early age because of possible damage to the central nervous system after the occurrence of unusual prenatal, postnatal or perinatal conditions and physical trauma in infancy. It must, of course, be borne in mind that residential schools (at least outside rural areas) tend to accept pupils with the most severe problems, and further evidence is needed to support Stott's hypothesis.

Physical disabilities
Intelligence within the IQ range 50–75 is not necessarily accompanied by retarded physical growth. It is true that ESN(m) boys tend to be smaller, to deviate more from the usual growth patterns, and to have a greater tendency to fatigue, general muscular debility and postural defects than

their normal contemporaries, but a number are above average in height
(Oliver, 1956). Tansley and Gulliford (1960) distinguish between three
groups of ESN children, overlapping to some extent:

1. the allround slow developers, retarded both mentally and physically;
2. those who show uneven development, their physical development being
   in advance of their mental development; and
3. those whose capacity to learn is reduced by the effects of illness, minor
   ailments and defects, some of which result from poor home conditions,
   some from social and educational difficulties.

Chazan (1964) found that, compared with a control group, significantly
fewer out of 169 ESN boys and girls in special schools in South Wales
enjoyed good health and freedom from physical defect, as reported by
their teachers on the Bristol Social Adjustment Guide (Stott, 1966a).
The most commonly reported ailments among the ESN pupils were frequent colds, infected ears, skin troubles and headaches; the most frequently
recorded defects were poor vision, hearing and coordination. The junior
ESN boys (aged 9 to 10+) and senior ESN girls (13 to 14+) in the sample
were particularly prone to ailments of various kinds.

In making a recommendation about the educational placement of a
child considered to be ESN(m), the child's developmental age in the physiological sense (Tanner, 1961) will be of some relevance to the educational
psychologist. For example, where a child aged ten years is not only functioning intellectually at the six to seven-year level, but appears also
physiologically immature in relation to his age group, he is likely to need
the protective environment of a special school more than a child of the
same intellectual level but otherwise developmentally normal, who might
adjust satisfactorily in a special class in an ordinary school; but, of course,
other factors would need to be taken into account (see chapter 7).

Cognitive defects
ESN(m) children show a wide range of profiles on tests which offer more
than a global IQ, but typically the ESN(m) child performs at a low level
on both verbal and non-verbal intelligence tests. Those from culturally
deprived and linguistically poor backgrounds may do rather better on
performance than on verbal items.

Research has tended to emphasise the cognitive weaknesses rather than
the strengths of ESN(m) children. Retarded mental development at this
level usually means a general slowness in learning; a poor memory for
material whether presented mainly through auditory or through visual
channels; poor perceptual and conceptual abilities; very limited ability
to deal with abstractions; little imagination and creativity; and a relative
inability to transfer learning from one situation to another.

In Piagetian terms, many ESN(m) children remain at the stage of intuitive thought (approximately the four to seven year level in terms of chronological age in normal children) over a wide area of their experience during most of their school life, some just reaching the stage of concrete operational thought (normal CA range seven to eleven years) at thirteen to fifteen years of age (Lovell, 1966). According to Lovell, too, the thinking even of those who do reach this stage is rather rigid, the flexibility of the preoperational structures being far less than that of normal children of the same mental age. S. Jackson (1966b) confirms this view, finding that ESN children (with IQs ranging from 60 to 80) showed little increase in ability to perform Piaget-type experiments beyond the age of nine years and that they even tended to deteriorate slightly in performance between thirteen and fifteen years.

Much less experimental work has been carried out on the cognitive development of ESN(m) pupils than of ESN(s) children, and there is a need for much more knowledge about the specific cognitive defects of this group. A particularly important question for psychologists and teachers is whether the thinking skills of ESN(m) children, as measured by conventional intelligence tests or a Piagetian-type battery, can be greatly improved by appropriate stimulation and experience. Studies of changes in IQ among such pupils at special schools have not shown a consistent pattern and do not throw much light on this question. Rushton and Stockwin (1963) compared the Terman-Merrill IQs on entry to school of 111 ESN boys in a residential special school with the results obtained before leaving (at 14 to 16 years); they found a significant deterioration in mean IQ, from 71 at a mean age of 9 years 2 months to 66·0 at 15 years 6 months. The hypothesis which they put forward, to the effect that the deterioration was due to the increased verbal weighting on the test at higher age levels, was confirmed by an analysis of the proportion of verbal subtests passed in relation to the proportion of non-verbal tests on which success was recorded. Stein and Stores (1965) made a similar study of 75 boys and girls attending a day special school for ESN pupils in Lancashire. They found that 24 of the sample improved between 11 and 16 years to the extent of 4 to 22 IQ points, some children being lifted well into the range of intellectual normality; but 24 showed no substantial change, and 27 deteriorated by 4 to 18 points. These studies certainly confirm that the predictive value even of individual intelligence test scales is limited. Stott (1960c) suggests that a change in motivation over the years may be an important factor in causing fluctuations in measured ability, either up or down.

Language and speech
Tansley and Gulliford (1960) emphasise the importance of spoken language

to the ESN child. Yet an unstimulating linguistic background and limita
tions of ability often combine to cause severe language retardation in
ESN(m) pupils. Lovell and Bradbury (1967), on the basis of a study of the
morphology and syntax of 160 ESN special school pupils aged eight to
fifteen years, conclude that, whichever aspect of language is examined, the
same broad picture is seen—the slow growth of language and the poverty of
linguistic performance of ESN children when compared with that of normal
children considerably younger. Gulliford (1960, 1969) also draws attention
to the effect on language development of limited thinking skills. ESN
children show great weakness in the range of their vocabulary, particularly
in the acquisition of abstract words. Their expression is often lacking in
order and selectivity, the structure of language is less complex than in
normal children and less use is made of any except the simplest conjunc-
tions or of adjectives and adverbs. There is often confusion in the use of
prepositions and pronouns, and listening skills are usually poor.

The incidence of speech defects, particularly stuttering, immature
articulation and inaudible speech, in ESN(m) pupils is much higher than
in normal schoolchildren. Sheridan (1948) found that 41·8 per cent of the
boys and 24·5 per cent of the girls in a sample of 100 subnormal children
aged 11 to 13 had speech defects of some kind, and subsequent studies
have confirmed this picture. Tansley (1951) reported that of 155 boys and
92 girls (aged 7 to 16) in an ESN special school, 37·4 per cent of the boys,
20·7 per cent of the girls had defective speech. Similar figures were recorded
by Chazan (1964) and P. Williams (1966) in South Wales, and by Grady
and Daniels (1964) in Nottingham.

There is thus ample evidence to support an emphasis on language
development and speech therapy with ESN(m) pupils, who need to be
given a variety of stimulating language experiences both to widen their
vocabulary and to increase their understanding and usage of the basic
principles of grammar.

Emotional and social adjustment
The relationship between maladjustment and school failure has been
amply demonstrated (Duncan, 1947; Pringle and Bossio, 1958). The
cumulative effects of the lack of success which characterises the ESN(m)
child's efforts in his early years at school tend to produce unsatisfactory
attitudes towards the learning process and a low level of aspiration often
accompanied by symptoms of emotional disturbance at home or in school.
In many cases, primary disturbance, particularly in the early years, may
set up barriers to learning at school and lead to pronounced educational
failure. A high proportion of ESN(m) children are caught at some point in
a vicious circle of maladjustment leading to school failure, resulting in
increased disturbance and more pronounced failure.

Chazan (1964, 1965) carried out an investigation into the incidence, nature and aetiology of maladjustment among children in special schools for ESN children in South Wales. The ESN pupils were a complete sample of two age groups (9 to 10+ and 13 to 14+) in eight special schools. On the basis of the Bristol Social Adjustment Guide, over a third of the 169 ESN children were maladjusted, nearly three times as many as in a matched control group of pupils in ordinary schools. The ESN children showed considerably more symptoms of depression, hostility towards adults, inhibition and emotional tension than the controls. There was also a higher incidence of unsatisfactory attendance at school and delinquent behaviour in the ESN sample.

An intensive study of the thirty 'most maladjusted' ESN children in the sample, compared with a control group of the thirty 'best adjusted' ESN children, showed that significantly more of the maladjusted children showed some physical weakness or defect; were subjected to adverse psychological pressures and unsatisfactory discipline at home, related to parental instability; and had had interrupted or incomplete relationships with their parents. Significantly fewer of the maladjusted children had a positive relationship with their father; and maladjustment was, in many cases, associated with a lack of progress in the basic subjects at the special school. There was little difference between the two groups in respect of the incidence of adverse congenital factors, difficulties in early development and poor material conditions at home.

Maladjustment of the 'withdrawn' type tended to be associated with physical deficiency in the child and positive but weak parental discipline; aggressive behaviour was often linked with insecurity at home and hostile parental attitudes.

Robinson and Robinson (1965), in considering the causes of emotional disturbance in mentally retarded children, suggest that they are more dependent on their homes than normal children, yet their homes do not always provide the necessary support. Further, some are the unwanted offspring of parents themselves subnormal in intelligence. Feelings of failure resulting from experiences in school are often, too, exacerbated by discrepancies between the child's stage of psychological development, his physical size, and society's expectations of him.

Maladjustment among ESN(m) pupils may be caused also by their failure to find acceptance in the eyes of their more intelligent contemporaries. There is evidence to suggest that children of low intelligence are underchosen in mixed ability groups in the ordinary school (G. O. Johnson, 1950; G. O. Johnson and Kirk, 1950; R. V. Miller, 1956), and it is likely that this rejection is extended to out-of-school activities. Within the special school, ESN boys and girls are capable of forming coherent groups (Laing and Chazan, 1966), but Laing (1969) questions whether sufficient opportunities are given in special schools and classes for group relationships to develop.

In summary, it may be concluded that while intellectual handicap and emotional or behavioural disturbance are not related to each other in any simple way, and there is no evidence to show that subnormal children are characterised as a group by special personality patterns, the prevalence of some degree of disturbance is considerably higher in sub-normal children than in children of average intelligence or above (Garfield, 1963; Robinson and Robinson, 1965).

Aims of special education for ESN(m) pupils
The general aims of special education for ESN(m) pupils include the acquisition of basic skills and habits, the development of personal and social adequacy, the fostering of positive attitudes, the maintenance of sound physical and mental health, and the encouragement of vocational competence (Tansley and Gulliford, 1960). Important subgoals are the development of an adequate self-concept and self-confidence.

The range of subjects taught is perhaps somewhat narrower, but not vastly different from those offered in junior or secondary modern schools; it is the methods of approach and depth of study which differentiate special schools from ordinary schools (S. Jackson, 1966a). There is an emphasis on concrete materials, repetition, and ample illustrations, and on providing stimulating experiences; the approach is as practical as possible. It is, however, very difficult to generalise about methods used in special schools, as is demonstrated by the Association for Special Education's survey of methods of teaching reading in a sample of schools in Britain (Hibbert, 1969). Teachers varied greatly in the kinds of approach they adopted, and in the types of material they found valuable. It can be said, nevertheless, that the curriculum of special schools in Britain is based on a desire to give ESN(m) children a general education rather than vocational training (Taylor and Taylor, 1966).

The effectiveness of education for ESN(m) children

Attainments
The assessment of the attainments of ESN adolescents near to school leaving age has produced disappointing results which warn the educational psychologist against expecting too much from placing children in special schools. Moran (1960) studied the levels of attainment of 300 ESN adolescents, aged 14 to 16+ years (mean CA 15 years 2 months), comprising 12 per cent of senior ESN pupils in London special schools. The overall results showed a wide range of variation, but in general fell below those of junior school children of similar mental ages to the ESN sample in every

area tested except craft. Mean ages for different attainments were Reading 8:3 years. Mental arithmetic 7:6, Language 6:11, and Craft 11:2 (in some areas there were marked sex differences in achievement). A noteworthy observation made by Moran was that enthusiasm for a particular subject in a school tended to effect a relatively superior achievement in that subject, suggesting that an over-all rise in the general level of attainment of ESN(m) pupils could be realistically expected from better motivation, improved teaching techniques and sounder organisation. It is possible that in some cases teachers in special schools do not demand enough from their pupils.

Lovell, White and Whitely (1965) explored the reasons for reading failure among ESN pupils by comparing thirty pairs of children (mean CA approximately $14\frac{1}{2}$ years) from three mixed day special schools, one group being of good readers (RA 9+) and the other poor readers (RA less than 7 years). They found that the poor readers had more difficulties in visual perception and spatial orientation as well as in copying words, and hypothesised that these difficulties were possibly neurological in origin.

Studies comparing the achievements of ESN pupils in special schools and those remaining in the ordinary school have been made by L. F. Green (1966) and Ascher (1970). Green, taking a sample of thirty ESN boys and girls (mean CA $14\frac{1}{2}$ years, mean IQ 70) in ordinary schools and thirty ESN pupils in day all-age mixed special schools, found that the special school pupils were less maladjusted than those in the ordinary school, but there were no significant differences in social adaptation as measured by the Manchester Scale (Lunzer, 1967), nor in reading (attainments being at the 8 to $8\frac{1}{2}$ year level) or number. Ascher compared the progress of thirty-one children aged 11 to 13 years in remedial departments (with a mean IQ of over 70) with that made by a matched group of children in special schools for the ESN. He found that the children in the remedial departments were more advanced educationally and showed greater social maturity than their matched contemporaries in the 60+ IQ range in the special schools. In conservative terms, Ascher concludes that the special school children showed no particular advantage from their educational placement and also possibly suffered from being segregated from children in ordinary schools.

A. R. J. Lewis (1971), however, suggests that the social and emotional developmental aims of the day special schools for the ESN are being fulfilled. Comparing the self-concepts of the 100 ESN boys aged 12 to 15 years in special schools with a control group of academically average comprehensive school boys, he found that significantly higher mean self-concept scores were obtained by the ESN group, early admission to the day special schools being related to high self-concept.

Post-school adjustment

Most ESN(m) pupils can be expected to obtain a job and earn a living: a number of follow-up studies both in Britain and America show that about 60–70 per cent of ESN school leavers are reasonably successful in their work life. Matthew (1963), for example, found in a survey of sixty-two ESN boys, out of school for four years on average, that 60 per cent gave satisfaction in their jobs, 20 per cent had unsatisfactory employment records, and a further 20 per cent (compared with 3 per cent of a control group of ex-secondary modern pupils) had *very* unsatisfactory job histories, with more than half of their time being spent in unemployment. When employed, the boys could earn a standard wage, and the majority were reasonably content, not finding discipline at work oppressive. It is of particular interest to note Matthew's finding that neither measured intelligence within the limits of the IQ range of his sample nor the level of attainment in the basic subjects was significantly associated with success or failure in employment; but stability of character was significantly related to success. Matthew also found that many ESN ex-pupils were completely friendless, with no active leisure interests; and they were insufficiently competent in understanding the mechanics of everyday life. A quarter of the sample had appeared at least once before the juvenile court.

N. Jackson (1968), following up 188 pupils leaving five day special schools in Edinburgh, rated 32 per cent, on the basis of the number of jobs held and the number of months the school leavers were unemployed, as 'non-adjusted' vocationally, a further 12 per cent being 'borderline cases'. He concludes that, in view of technological progress, an increasing number of ESN pupils will be unable to compete on equal terms with their normal peers on leaving school, and that there is therefore a need for sheltered workshops designed specifically to cater for this group.

The contribution of the educational psychologist to the education of ESN(m) pupils

In recent years, psychologists have begun to use techniques which will give a profile of a child's strengths and weaknesses and which will give a better insight into the child's development (see chapter 7). There is a need for an extension of this approach, and also for relating findings to positive recommendations for action in the school situation. The educational psychologist can make a definite contribution to the reappraisal of the aims of special education for the ESN(m), of methods of teaching, and of the content of the curriculum. The high incidence of maladjustment amongst ESN(m) pupils suggest that special schools and classes need a great deal of support and help from the child guidance service, which should also be concerned with the establishment of an advisory and counselling service for parents. Robinson and Robinson (1965) comprehensively discuss the value and limitations of various forms of psychotherapy, individual and group, with subnormal children. They conclude that while there is still a pessimistic attitude towards psychotherapy with the retarded, and despite the shortcomings of research in this field, psychotherapeutic practices of several kinds have proved successful with some subnormal children. D. Evans (1956), for example, has shown that group therapy, adapted to suit children of limited intelligence, can be an appropriate form of treatment for maladjusted ESN children.

The ESN(m) school leaver also needs a great deal of guidance and support if he is to adjust successfully to the transition from school to work and lead a satisfying life in maturity. Psychologists have a role to play in the establishment of a comprehensive vocational guidance and after-care service, without which much of the value of special education will be lost.

Children 'below average' in ability

Children in this category, below average in general ability but not educationally subnormal in the sense in which the term has been used in the preceding discussion, require special consideration in terms of the organisation, curriculum and methods of their education (Gulliford, 1969). Where schools are staffed and equipped to give this special consideration, many of this group, comprising between 10 and 15 per cent of the school population, make adequate progress in school and do not require formal ascertainment or attention from an educational psychologist.

However, children from this group are not infrequently referred to the psychologist for learning difficulties or behaviour problems, or brought before the juvenile court on account of delinquent acts, though dullness, even when combined with deprivation and educational backwardness, does not necessarily lead to delinquency (McCord and McCord, 1959). Many of these children make a poor start to their school life from which they find it difficult to recover; often, for example, they are not ready to learn to read until they are due to enter the junior school, when they may fail to receive appropriate teaching. By the time these children reach the secondary school, they frequently have a hostile attitude towards school and form groups which are most difficult to teach and even to control. Some absent themselves frequently from school, and indeed controlled studies have found samples of truants to be, on average, inferior to regular attenders both in intellectual ability and in attainment in the basic subjects (Tyerman, 1958; Cooper, 1966). Many of the problems presented by children who are below average in ability are similar to those discussed in the next section, dealing with educationally retarded chldren.

When below average children require special educational treatment or therapy, their needs are usually difficult to meet. Remedial teachers, therapists and special schools for maladjusted pupils, faced with pressure from lengthy waiting lists, are willing to take on only children of at least average intelligence; some, indeed, feel that their methods are not suited to children below average in ability. This point of view is understandable, yet it is unreasonable to expect the ordinary school to bear the whole burden of problems which arise in the case of children in this category, and the educational psychologist must be prepared to offer support and help where this is seen to be necessary. There is also a role for the educational psychologist, yet to be worked out fully, in helping to shape school policy and to create a school climate in which below average children can flourish rather than deteriorate. It is clearly the responsibility of the head teacher and his staff to determine the policy of a school, but it would be valuable for the educational psychologist to be invited to engage in discussions with school staffs, and with parents too, in order to consider ways in which the school can contribute to the adjustment of its pupils, particularly of the not inconsiderable proportion of below average pupils for which most schools have to cater (Chazan, 1971). Many of the problems which arise in connection with these children can be prevented if education authorities and individual schools have a definite policy, supported by adequate resources, to meet their needs.

Educationally retarded children

'Underfunctioning' in school subjects will be found in children with a wide range of ability levels; here the discussion will mainly focus on children who need remedial education, being retarded in one or more scholastic areas but not as a result of limitations of general intelligence. The psychologist will see many cases of this kind, but will not find it easy to define the concepts of 'retardation' or 'underfunctioning'. Traditionally, the degree of a child's retardation has been assessed by comparing a child's attainment age or quotient with his mental age or intelligence quotient. In recent years, however, mainly on statistical grounds but also because intelligence and attainment tests overlap considerably in content, criticisms have been levelled against making direct comparisons between results obtained on attainment tests and those gained on intelligence tests (for a discussion of this question, see C. Graham, 1970). Various solutions have been proposed, such as standardising ability and attainment tests on the same population at the same time and including the results in the test manuals; making allowance for the regression to the mean phenomenon by calculating the level of achievement to be expected on any particular test at a specific intelligence level (Fransella and Gerver, 1965; Savage and

O'Connor, 1966; Yule, 1967); and using a coarse grading scale instead of numbers to avoid giving a false impression of statistical precision (Graham, 1970). Nevertheless, psychologists still find it useful to make a comparison of some kind between ability and attainment in assessing whether a child needs remedial education, taking into account that, for example, two years' retardation at the chronological age of eight is quite a different problem from two years' retardation at thirteen, and that a very bright child may be underfunctioning in relation to his 'mental age' but not require remedial education in any way. Retardation in reading has, mainly because of the serious implications in our society of failure in this area, received much more attention than retardation in other subjects. The present discussion will, therefore, focus on reading problems, after which difficulties with number will be briefly reviewed.

Reading

Size of problem

Although since the end of the Second World War standards of reading have risen considerably (Department of Education and Science, 1966), a substantial number of children have difficulties in learning to read adequately. Pringle et al. (1966) found that about 10 per cent of over 10,000 seven-year-olds in their final term of their infant schooling had still barely made a start with reading. This estimate would include children later to be categorised as educationally subnormal. M. Clark (1970), in a survey of 1,544 children aged 7+ in the County of Dunbartonshire, reports that 230 children (about 15 per cent of the sample) were without any independent reading skill after two years at school. Half of these children were still requiring assistance in the basic skill of reading even after three years at school, the majority of these children being of low average intelligence. When all the children who had been severely backward in reading at the age of seven and who were of average intelligence were retested at nine years of age, it was found that about 1 per cent of the total population (mainly boys) were two or more years backward in reading. In the Isle of Wight survey involving 2,299 ten- and eleven-year-old children, 86 children (nearly 4 per cent of the sample) were designated severely backward in reading, the criterion being a level of reading accuracy or comprehension (on the Neale test) at least twenty-eight months below that predicted on the basis of their WISC IQ (shortened form) and chronological age; the mean IQ of these 86 children was 93, that is within the average range (Rutter et al., 1970).

On the evidence of such surveys as these, it is clear that teachers in the ordinary school have to deal with many cases of reading difficulty who should not be transferred to special schools or classes for ESN or slow-learning children, but require the help of the school psychological and remedial services.

Causes of reading failure

Reading failure may have many causes, and in very few cases will a single causal factor be found to operate. Burt (1957) concludes that often four or five different factors may be active in a single case of educational backwardness, including retardation in reading. A useful framework for the investigation by the educational psychologist of the sources of reading retardation has been suggested by Applebee (1971), based on Eisenberg (1966):

A. *Extrinsic or social factors*
1. Quantitative and qualitative defects in teaching.
2. Deficiencies in cognitive stimulation.
3. Deficiencies in motivation associated with social pathology.
B. *Intrinsic or individual factors*
1. General debility.
2. Sensory defects.
3. Intellectual defects.
4. Brain injury.
5. Deficiencies in motivation associated with psychopathology.
6. Specific reading disability.

These headings can be subdivided further, and indeed the psychologist should attempt to make a diagnosis of the child's difficulties in as detailed and precise a way as possible; he should be careful, too, in searching for more esoteric causes of reading failure, not to overlook such causative factors as frequent absences during the infant school period (M. Clark, 1970); changes of school, teacher, or teaching method at a critical stage; child–teacher incompatibility; or severe illness or psychological trauma (especially bereavement), without suitable remedial action.

Rutter *et al.* (1970) found that the severely backward readers in the Isle of Wight sample, were, as compared with a control group, clumsier in their movements, had greater speech and language difficulties, and were more maladjusted, a particularly strong association existing between reading difficulties and antisocial behaviour problems. M. D. Vernon (1957, 1971) and M. Clark (1970) stress that defects and poor auditory discrimination are often associated with reading difficulty, but it is difficult to establish in most cases of reading failure whether any deficiency in auditory perception is not the result rather than the cause of the reading disability.

It is generally agreed that much reading backwardness in children of average intelligence or above is caused by such factors as already mentioned, especially inadequate or faulty teaching, absence from school, an adverse environment or emotional problems. However, a number of workers in this field have found the concept of 'specific dyslexia' a useful one to apply to children whose reading disability is associated with minor neurological dysfunctions or isolated maturational lags which are indicative of inherent developmental anomaly (Naidoo, 1971). Explanations for dyslexia put forward have included a genetic hypothesis (on the basis of the presence of reading disorders in other members of the family), the delayed or incomplete establishment of cerebral dominance, organic brain dysfunction, and unusual variations in the maturation of the brain.

Many psychologists have been reluctant to accept the concept of 'specific dyslexia' because of its vagueness and because they have preferred to look at each case of reading failure on an individual basis. Nevertheless, Lovell *et al.* (1964a, b) have concluded, on the basis of a controlled study of fifty backward readers with a RQ less than 80 but with a non-verbal IQ of 90 or more, in their third year of the junior school, that reading disability in many children of average non-verbal intelligence stems from some brain dysfunction, resulting in limited ability in the decoding and encoding processes involved in reading, and in some cases restriction or disturbance of visual input. Lovell and Gorton (1968) in a further study confirm this association between specific neurological impairment and reading skills. They stress the importance of looking at the clustering of test scores, not merely at the differences between means on single tests taken by backward readers and controls. Shearer (1968) also concluded that there is a group of retarded readers who show a complete inability to discriminate between right and left, a defective capacity for finger localisation, and mixed or weak hand preference. However, he emphasises that the nature of the relationship between this cluster of symptoms and reading disability is not clear—it may be the result rather than the cause of the reading failure.

M. D. Vernon (1971) considers that there is sufficient evidence to support the existence of a basic disability in the case of some backward readers. This disability, resulting from deficiencies in the capacity to associate visual and linguistic sequences, is characterised by excessive and persistent reversals, and by poor performance on tests of directionality, sequential ordering and the reconstruction of complex forms. The 'dyslexic' child finds it difficult to grasp the sequential spatial relationships of printed letters, and to perceive and analyse phonemes in words as well as temporal auditory patterns. Dyslexia may arise mainly in conjunction with poor linguistic ability or mainly in association with defective visual analysis of complex forms.

The concept of dyslexia has aroused a good deal of controversy which is not yet resolved, and, although there is already a wide-ranging literature on this topic, further experimental investigations of children showing all kinds and degrees of reading difficulties are needed. A comprehensive discussion of the concept of dyslexia is to be found in Bakker and Satz (1970) and in a symposium published in the *British Journal of Educational Psychology* (vol. 41, Part 1, 1971).

Remedial measures
Children selected for 'remedial education' are given help in a large variety of ways. Sampson's survey (1969a, b) of the methods used by a large sample of remedial teachers in Britain showed that four main approaches were emphasised, stressing

1. that the approach was entirely dependent on the *needs of the individual* and thus a variety of books, materials and methods should be used (15 per cent of sample); or
2. that the main aim should be to bring about a new *attitude* to learning on the part of the pupil (7 per cent); or
3. that the approach must have *pupil-appeal* (13 per cent); or
4. that specific *techniques* of teaching should be employed (65 per cent) with phonic methods predominating.

In a further study of remedial education practices in secondary schools (Sampson and Pumfrey, 1970) it was found that the methods used seemed to be geared to the particular context in which remedial work was done rather than to any commonly held principles. Of the sample of 280 remedial teachers from 270 secondary schools 38 per cent used 'straight-forward' methods, usually meaning fairly formal class teaching; 66 per cent stated that they used 'psychological approaches', but these seemed to mean 'child-centred' approaches, not therapy or casework, which were never in fact mentioned. Many teachers involved their pupils in centres of interest and projects (48 per cent); outside activities or visits (62 per cent); and programmed instruction (38 per cent). Teaching machines were used by only 7 per cent.

D. J. Williams (1969) discusses the function of the remedial teacher working in the context of a child guidance centre, being mainly concerned with cases requiring a primarily therapeutic approach. He emphasises that it is the quality of the relationship established by the remedial teacher with the pupil that is the most important factor in treatment. Play therapy is often valuable in bringing children to a point where they can accept the learning situation and associate this with a warm, accepting adult relationship. Pumfrey and Elliott (1970), in a review of the literature on the relationships between play therapy, social adjustment and reading attainment, conclude that there is no unequivocal proof of the positive or negative effects of non-directive psychotherapy on adjustment or reading attainment. This is, in their view, mainly because of the faulty design and poor execution of most studies in this field. Lawrence (1971), however, on the basis of a controlled study of the effects of counselling on retarded readers, concludes that in most cases of reading retardation it should be possible to increase the general level of motivation by planning a personal counselling programme. Methods of counselling used in the experiment included the establishment of an uncritical, friendly atmosphere; providing a sounding-board for the child's feelings, without any direct interpretation, in a child-centred interview situation; and the use of drawings and pictures to stimulate discussion. Many areas of the child's life at home, in school, and in relation to his peer group were explored during the period of counselling.

In addition to therapeutic approaches based on play or counselling, there have been limited experiments using behaviour therapy approaches (see chapter 11). Rachman (1962) considers that operant conditioning techniques are applicable to remedial reading cases. This approach is illustrated by McKerracher (1967), who reports on his attempt to treat a highly anxious, enuretic boy with several years retardation in reading by an operant conditioning technique involving both reward and avoidance conditioning and not requiring other than simple apparatus. Reward conditioning seemed more effective than supportive therapy or dual operant conditioning techniques.

Remedial teachers have a difficult problem when they try to combine the roles of teacher and therapist, since these roles tend to conflict with one another. However, they need to be skilled in a variety of experimental and therapeutic techniques, and those who have to deal with cases exacerbated by emotional disturbance or neurological dysfunction may need a great deal of support and advice from the educational psychologist.

Evaluation of remedial education services
Much has been written, from differing points of view, about the short-term and long-term effects of remedial teaching in reading (for reviews of the literature see Sampson, 1966; Chazan, 1967; and Carroll, 1971). The general conclusion from much of the research on the question of the effectiveness of remedial education has been that, while short term gains are often dramatic, there is a slowing down of progress on cessation of special remedial help. The long-term effects, therefore, when compared with the progress made by control groups not receiving remedial education, appear to be slight.

Several explanations have been put forward for these negligible long-term effects. These include the suggestions:

1. that the improvement of control groups is not so much spontaneous as

due to the extra help which is often given indirectly to children who are matched with remedial teaching cases in the same school (Cashdan and Pumfrey, 1969);

2. that inappropriate or inadequate methods are often used, for example, failing to deal with emotional blockages interfering with learning (Carroll, 1971); and

3. that remedial education ceases at too early a stage. As Cashdan and Pumfrey (1969) assert, many children in need of this kind of help require a continuous programme of remedial treatment as an integral part of their normal school activities if they are to achieve literacy by the time they leave the primary school.

Much work remains to be done in order to discover the personal, environmental and school characteristics of 'good' and 'poor' responders to remedial education (Cashdan *et al.*, 1971). However, both diagnostic techniques and remedial programmes have become increasingly refined, and the educational psychologist can help to make remedial education in reading more effective by more penetrating diagnosis and by relating diagnostic findings to specific remediation.

Difficulties with number

Aetiology

Considerable changes have taken place in methods of teaching number, especially in the primary school, since Schonell and Schonell wrote their book on *Diagnosis and Remedial Teaching in Arithmetic* in 1957. However, much of what was written then concerning the aetiology of backwardness in number still applies. Schonell and Schonell found both environmental factors and emotional causes to be of significance in addition to intellectual factors. The main environmental factors associated with number difficulties were listed as paucity of preschool experience, adverse home influences, absence from school, discontinuity of teaching and inappropriate teaching methods. Temperamental and emotional factors considered important included a lack of persistence, impulsivity, a low level of interest, the effects of censure or failure, disturbing thoughts due to anxiety, worry about work missed, and confusion arising from insecure knowledge.

Some children, especially those with some degree of brain damage, have difficulties with visual-spatial perception which prevent them from dealing adequately with concepts such as shape, size, and volume (Gulliford, 1969). Brenner (1967) found that nearly 7 per cent of a sample of 8-year-old children had significant visual-motor difficulties, which particularly affected progress in arithmetic in spite of good intelligence.

J. D. Williams (1970) points out that mathematics is particularly prone to promote attitudes and feelings of dislike and anxiety in those who find the subject difficult, and that these attitudes and feelings are likely to become self-perpetuating, since they make learning even more difficult than it originally was. Thus remedial measures must take account of motivational as well as cognitive problems.

Lund (1967) stresses that mathematics has a vocabulary of its own, and that this vocabulary may prove difficult to understand if insufficient attention is given to it.

Remedial measures in number
Sampson (1969b) found that, as compared with reading, little emphasis was given by remedial teachers to number work: only about 5 per cent of her sample considered it to be as important as reading. Most remedial teachers, however, do some work in number, emphasising the establishment of number concepts where these are lacking and the giving of practice in simple calculations. Special apparatus such as that devised by Cuisinaire, Stern and Dienes was found helpful.

J. D. Williams (1970) advocates programmed instruction as one means of helping children with difficulties in number, in that it enables pupils to work at their own rate and to suffer less from the effects of lapses of attention. Further, motivation is helped because failure rarely occurs and the task facing the learner at any stage will be a relatively easy one. The learner, too, is informed immediately of the accuracy of his response, and this helps him to judge his own behaviour realistically and confidently. Lund (1967) recommends that the mathematically retarded child should be taken back to a realistic starting point and given appropriate experiences, with the simultaneous introduction of the relevant language.

Evaluation
Little, if anything, has been written about the effectiveness of remedial teaching in number. Indeed, the lack of attention given to number retardation is surprising, particularly as a not insubstantial proportion of intelligent children seem to have specific difficulties in number which may cause them a good deal of worry and adversely affect their general school progress. This is a field in which a specialist contribution could be made by educational psychologists with an appropriate background.

The contribution of the educational psychologist to the treatment of educationally retarded children
The educational psychologist should regard it as an important part of his duties to carry out systematic surveys in order to ascertain, at the earliest appropriate stage, those children who are educationally retarded in the basic subjects; and in individual cases he will also make a consider-

able contribution to diagnosis, leading to recommendations for treatment (see chapter 7).

With the increase in the number of teachers specially qualified in remedial education, the psychologist is likely only in rare cases to carry out remedial work himself over an extended period, but there is still much scope for educational psychologists to contribute to the treatment as well as the diagnosis of educational retardation. As the Summerfield Report (Department of Education and Science, 1968b) suggests, the educational psychologist may himself find it helpful to experiment with remedial methods to establish their effectiveness; or he may need to explore and remove blockages to learning before educational difficulties can be treated by direct approaches. The major role of the psychologist in this field, however, will tend to be that of a consultant to remedial teachers, particularly where remedial education is closely associated with clinical treatment. The Summerfield Report recommended that remedial education involving treatment which is primarily by psychological methods should come under the supervision of educational psychologists, while in relation to other special classes it would be appropriate for them to act as advisers. The administrative arrangements for remedial education vary from authority to authority, and in some cases the educational psychologist will have the responsibility for supervising the whole remedial education service.

Whatever the administrative arrangements may be, the educational psychologist should play a vigorous and active part in encouraging the development of varied facilities for remedial education. In spite of the rather negative results reported by research investigations into the effectiveness of remedial education, both parents and children, as well as most teachers, are very appreciative of opportunities given to educationally retarded pupils to make good their deficiencies.

10

Physically handicapped children

The educational psychologist is increasingly being called on, in collaboration with medical and other colleagues, to advise on the education and treatment of physically handicapped children. He should therefore have a knowledge of the particular characteristics and needs of children with different kinds and degrees of physical handicap. It is not possible here to consider every type of physical handicap, and in this chapter consideration will be given to studies relating to the psychology and education of children with visual handicaps (both the blind and the partially sighted), auditory defects (the deaf and the partially hearing), cerebral palsy and epilepsy. To keep in touch with medical opinion on these and other physical handicaps, the educational psychologist will find it helpful to consult the official reports on the *Health of the School Child* issued by the Department of Education and Science at intervals. Although, as mentioned in chapter 2, blind and partially sighted children are sometimes educated together, their needs are sufficiently different for the two groups to be considered separately.

Blind children

As compared with other handicaps the blind have tended to arouse much pity and sympathy. Money has been given generously to promote their education and welfare, and for this relatively small group, social and educational services are more readily available than for most children with other forms of handicap. However, research studies relating to the education and psychology of blind children have been extremely scanty.

Physical difficulties
No differentiation is possible between blind children and others in terms of general physique, height or weight, except in cases where blindness is

related to such causes as prematurity, Rhesus incompatibility or maternal rubella (Telford and Sawrey, 1967). It is hardly surprising that blind children are restricted in mobility and do less well than normal children in tests of gross motor performance (Buell, 1950), but in many cases over-protection on the part of parents may exacerbate handicaps of these kinds. Many blind children show a heightened sensitivity to auditory cues which sighted children normally disregard, but there is little evidence of a special 'obstacle sense'.

Speech and language

Blind children do not show any language deficits or proficiencies specific to them as a group, but the lack of visual stimulation may cause greater attention to be given to the spoken word, especially in the case of the more intelligent among them. On the other hand, the language development of less intelligent blind children may be adversely affected by the absence of visual support which the sighted of all ranges of intelligence find so helpful. Research studies on the incidence and nature of speech defects in blind children have produced no clear picture, estimates of speech defects in the blind ranging from 7 to 50 per cent. Brieland (1951), survey-ing the literature, suggested that blind children tended to show less vocal variety than normal, to talk at a slower rate and with less modulation, and to make less effective use of gesture and bodily action. However, there is no general agreement that these characteristics apply to the major-ity of blind children.

Cognitive difficulties

Blindness itself has no direct effect on cognitive development, but in some cases the visual handicap may be associated with subnormality, for ex-ample when the cause is brain damage. Further, even in children of normal intellectual potential, their cognitive development is bound to be affected at least to some extent by the necessary restriction of their experience, their lack of mobility and their limited awareness of the self in relation to the environment. However, the intelligence test performance of blind children is not markedly different from that of sighted children. Hayes (1941) tested 2,372 blind children in residential schools in the USA, using a specially revised form of the Stanford-Binet Scale. He found the mean IQ of this sample to be 98·8, with a slightly higher percentage of blind children than of sighted children scoring above 120 and below 70. A similar distribution of intelligence was found (test used not stated) in a sample of 315 children tested as part of a Department of Education and Science survey of 817 pupils in twenty special schools for the blind in England and Wales (Department of Education and Science, 1968a). It is worthy of note that those children whose visual handicap was caused by tumours of the eye, diseases of the retina and choroid, cataract and some other conditions tended to have IQs higher than average, while those with optic atrophy and retrolental fibroplasia tended to have quotients below average.

Little work has been done on concept formation in the blind. Clearly cognitive functioning is restricted by the lack of visual perception and imagery. However, blind children are able to develop spatial concepts through the other senses, especially touch and kinaesthesis, and the available evidence does not indicate that the intellectual development of the blind is severely restricted by their visual handicap (Axelrod, 1959).

Social and emotional problems

Blind children obviously have special difficulties to face in making an adequate social and emotional adjustment. Kershaw (1961) points out that the blind are subject to overprotection and overpity, people being too ready to anticipate their needs. They are liable to develop habit movements such as head-scratching, nose-picking, eye-rubbing and masturbation, and are apt to become physically apathetic and emotionally 'shut-in' (Department of Education and Science, 1968a found 45 per cent of 817 blind children to have at least one such mannerism). Emotional development is affected by the inability to see facial expressions which often convey feelings more subtly than words, and the blind child who is frustrated in his social life may seek to gain satisfaction from himself, his own bodily sensations and his own imaginings. Adolescence may bring with it resentment, bitterness and depression.

The literature on the emotional and social adjustment of blind children between 1928 and 1962 has been reviewed by Pringle (1964), who emphasises the diversity of viewpoints and findings presented in studies undertaken during this period, few of which relate to blind children in Britain. Pringle also points to the need for a more adequate theoretical framework for experimental investigations, and for following up such studies as that by Sommers (1944) who, on the basis of personality tests, concluded that the frustrations and disturbed feelings of the blind arise from the attitudes and conditions surrounding the blind rather than from the visual handicap itself.

Since Pringle's review, a systematic and controlled investigation has been carried out by Zahran (1965), who examined the personality differences between blind and sighted children. Examining the existing literature, he differentiated between two main points of view about these differences. One view is that blindness leads to compensatory behaviour, often accompanied by maladjustment or excessive introversion; the other rests on the hypothesis that the process of adjustment in the blind is not significantly different from that of the sighted. In his own study, Zahran compared fifty blind children, aged 9 years to 13 years 11 months, with a matched control group of fifty sighted children, on a number of personality variables. Using the Junior Maudsley Personality Inventory (Furneaux and Gibson, 1966) he found that the blind children tended to be more introverted than the sighted and to have higher neuroticism scores. On the basis of a sentence completion test, the blind subjects were shown to be less well adjusted than the sighted; and a semantic differential test showed poorer self-evaluation and less confidence in the future in the blind children. Almost all the test results agreed with each other in showing a more favourable adjustment picture in the sighted group; but the differences between the groups were not statistically significant. The main conclusion of the study was, therefore, that there are no distinct personality problems produced by blindness (supporting the second view mentioned above), although problems frequently arise from the reactions of the blind to their social environment. The latter point is amply confirmed by D. R. Gray (1963) and Department of Education and Science (1968a). Gray studied the incidence and nature of maladjustment in a sample of fifty boys and fifty girls attending a school for both blind and partially sighted children in Wales. On the basis of the Bristol Social Adjustment Guide, he found 26 per cent to be maladjusted, and a further 31 per cent to be unsettled. There was a higher overall incidence of maladjustment and unsettledness in the older children, over 10 years of age, but more maladjustment was found among the younger children (32 per cent) than the older children (24 per cent). As many as 42 per cent of the totally blind children were maladjusted, with a further 21 per cent unsettled, these figures being higher than for the children with some vision, of whom 21 per cent were maladjusted and 33 per cent were unsettled. The maladjustment in the sample was mainly of an inhibited rather than an outgoing nature, particularly in the case of the blind children. In the survey undertaken by the Department of Education and Science (1968a), 36 per cent of the blind children studied were considered by their teachers to be emotionally disturbed.

Educational methods
The aims and content of special education for the blind are not essentially different from those of normal education (Telford and Sawrey, 1967). However, as visual media form the basis for the education of the sighted, and blind children are deprived of this kind of experience, the emphasis in schools and classes for the blind is on maximising the use of the other senses. Braille is used for reading and writing, and models and audio aids of all kinds (e.g. tape recorders, record players and talking books) are extensively employed. Further, intensive training is given in orientation and in gaining increased control of the environment. Special apparatus

has been constructed for number work, and embossed maps and relief globes are found useful in teaching geography as well as space perception (for a discussion of current issues relating to the education of the visually handicapped, see the Vernon Report: Department of Education and Science, 1972b).

Effectiveness of education for the blind

Direct comparisons of the educational attainments of blind children with those of sighted children are difficult to make, because blind children take attainment tests in Braille and need a good deal of time to complete them. A number of blind pupils do very well scholastically, and some achieve entry to higher education; but, in general, American studies comparing attainments by either chronological or mental age show educational retardation of about two years or more, especially in arithmetic (Hayes, 1941; B. Lowenfeld, 1945, 1963; Nolan, 1959; Ashcroft, 1963). The retardation is mainly related to frequent absences from school for medical treatment, lack of appropriate special educational treatment, and the difficulties inherent in learning Braille. The gap in attainment between the sighted and the blind appears to widen with age (Scottish Education Department, 1950).

Barnett (1955) estimated that many blind school leavers are unable to find work at a level appropriate to their capacities. However, greater opportunities are now available for employment of the blind than in the past, and new Vocational Guidance Centres for Young Blind Persons have been established in recent years (Richards, 1971).

Partially sighted children

Children with partial vision have considerable advantages over the blind child in learning, inasmuch as they can move with greater confidence, learn manipulative skills more easily and become independent earlier. However, their visual experience may be confusing and often disturbing; they are likely to become frustrated through making errors in judgment; and, seeing children without visual handicaps in action, they will want to do exactly what others do. The partially sighted are not always successful in either work or play in competition with sighted children, but it is generally agreed that they should be encouraged to mix freely with their sighted contemporaries in all possible activities in which they can participate without risk of further damage to vision (Scottish Education Department, 1950).

Intelligence

There is little difference in intelligence between sighted and partially sighted children. Pintner (1942) found the mean IQ of 602 partially sighted children to be 95 on the Stanford-Binet Scale, and Livingston (1958), giving the same scale to sixty children, aged 8 and 9, in classes for the partially sighted, found their average IQ to be 98·6. In this country, The Department of Education and Science Survey (1968a) found, in a sample of 567 partially sighted children, a greater proportion of dull children (22 per cent with IQs 84 or below) and a lower proportion of children above average in intelligence (11 per cent with IQs of 115+) than is the case in the normal population.

Social and emotional adjustment

The Department of Education and Science Survey (1968a) reports that 32 per cent of 1,374 children in schools and classes for the partially sighted in England and Wales were considered to be emotionally disturbed by their teachers. Mannerisms were found to be less prevalent in the partially sighted than the blind: in this survey 9·6 per cent of the partially sighted, compared with 45 per cent of blind children, showed mannerisms of some kind—rocking, head-nodding, hand-flapping and eye-poking being most common. Ashcroft (1963), in pointing out that the emotional and social characteristics of partially sighted children have not been clearly described and need to be studied more precisely, hypothesizes that (a) maladjustment is not a necessary consequence of limitations in vision; (b) maladjustment, when it does occur, is not directly proportional in severity to, nor necessarily directly related to, visual limitation; and (c) negative attitudes towards, and on the part of, the partially sighted are frequently found and may result in a disproportionate amount of maladjustment in these children.

Educational methods

In making special provision for partially sighted children, special attention is paid to good lighting and freedom from glare; the adjustment and positioning of desks; and the colouring of walls, ceilings and boards. Typewriters with specially large type, dictaphones and record players, books and other reading material with special print, and enlarged maps and graphs are all found of value. However, Kell (1967) describes how, in Britain, a rather negative approach to the education of the partially sighted, with an emphasis on sight saving, has gradually given way to more positive curriculum development. She comments on the importance of the recent improvement in variety and design of telescopic magnifying aids, and on the usefulness of projectors, illuminated miscroscopes, television and other audio-visual aids. It is also the case that many children, particularly as they become fluent in reading, can manage with ordinary text books.

Effectiveness of education for the partially sighted
Increasingly in recent years, facilities have been provided for the wide range of abilities shown by partially sighted children, and a growing number have successfully taken courses at CSE, GCE 'O' Level, or beyond (Kell, 1967). There is, however, little up-to-date information available on the attainments of the partially sighted. British reports which were made before the recent developments in the education of the partially sighted suggested that there was little difference between the partially sighted children and children with normal vision in arithmetical ability, but about three years retardation has been noted in English at the age of thirteen (Scottish Education Department, 1950). In the USA, Bateman (1963) found only slight reading retardation in partially sighted children studied at the ages of nine and ten years; the types of reading errors made by these children were not very different from those made by sighted children of similar reading ability.

Kershaw (1961) considers that the prognosis for many partially sighted children is quite good: by the late teens their condition has stabilised and they can succeed in many types of employment. Kettle (1966) carried out a survey of 623 partially sighted adolescents who had left special schools between 1962 and 1965. He found that these school leavers were engaged in a large variety of occupations, and that only 5 per cent were unemployed. Nicholas (1968) compared a group of twenty-two partially sighted ex-pupils of a residential special school in Wales with a matched control group of sighted adolescents, at the age of nearly nineteen years. Only two of the partially sighted group had been unemployed since leaving school, but most of this group took longer to find employment and had longer periods of unemployment than the sighted youth. In addition to visual handicap and lack of opportunity, the lack of academic qualifications was a major reason for the partially sighted failing to secure the employment of their choice. Richards (1971), making a similar follow-up study of twenty partially sighted school leavers from a special school for the visually handicapped, found that, up to about two-and-a-half years after leaving school, six of the partially sighted were unemployed, as compared with three of a control group of sighted adolescents. The partially sighted group were very poor attenders at youth clubs, found difficulty in making friends, and had only fleeting interest in any activity or interest.

Children with hearing difficulties

Children with hearing difficulties do not form a homogeneous group and present a wide range of associated problems—cognitive, emotional and social—the severity of which may be related not only to the nature and degree of hearing loss but to many other variables such as institutionalisation, other physical defects, or mental subnormality. From the educational point of view, a broad differentiation is usually made between *deaf* children, who require education by methods suitable for pupils with little or no naturally acquired speech or language, and *partially-hearing* children, whose development of speech and language, even if retarded, follows a relatively normal pattern (Handicapped Pupils Regulations, 1962). This distinction will be followed in the ensuing discussion, while recognising that there is no fine border-line between these groups and that the educational and psychological needs of each child with a hearing loss must be assessed on an individual basis. As Telford and Sawrey (1967) observe, the range of individual differences among the aurally impaired is as significant as the mean differences between the normal and the aurally impaired. Yet it is useful for the educational psychologist to be aware of the typical achievements and difficulties of children with hearing impairment, even if different samples in research studies may show conflicting results. Useful discussions of the problems of children with hearing defects will be found in Fiedler (1952), I. R. Ewing and A. W. G. Ewing (1958), Levine (1960), A. W. G. Ewing (1957, 1960) and Frisina (1967).

Deaf children

Cognitive difficulties
Children who have been born deaf or who have become deaf before the establishment of language and speech suffer from a severe degree of sensory deprivation, affecting perceptual organisation, cognition and language. Although there can be some development of thinking skills without language, and although deaf children without language can acquire concepts, compare sizes, remember sequences and solve problems involving forms and colours (Templin, 1950; J. B. Carroll, 1964; Furth, 1966), the cognitive ability of children who have not acquired language because of deafness is bound to be significantly impaired, however well endowed they are with intelligence and however advantaged in their background. Many concepts which seem to depend entirely on visually received information in fact depend upon the relationship between experience and an auditory factor (Reed, 1970). Furth (1966) emphasises that deaf children with little or no use of language may do as well as hearing children in a wide range of cognitive tasks, but M. M. Lewis (1968), while agreeing with this view, points out that deaf children are grossly retarded in the development of many specific cognitive abilities because of the inadequacy of their language. Even in the execution of certain motor tasks speech acts as a regulator and verbal control helps (Luria, 1961).

The cognitive development of deaf children has been assessed in a number of studies, mainly through individual intelligence tests of a performance type, though more recently through Piagetian-type tasks. The results of these studies are not always easy to interpret, because of the heterogeneous nature of the samples of children used, and indeed the value of a knowledge of the mean IQ of such samples may be questioned, unless variables such as the degree of auditory impairment, extent of distortion, age of onset, language ability, and socio-economic background are clearly specified (Telford and Sawrey, 1967). Most of the investigations to date suggest that when the need for verbalisation is minimised, deaf children do as well as hearing subjects (for reviews of the literature on the intelligence test performance of deaf children see Meyerson, 1963 and Ives, 1967). In the USA for example, Myklebust (1960) found the average Wechsler Bellevue (Performance Scale) IQ of eighty-five deaf subjects, aged twelve to seventeen years, to be 101·8, whereas their mean Verbal Scale IQ was 66·5. In this country, Kendall (1957) tested 392 'hearing-impaired' children, mostly severely or profoundly deaf, between the ages of eighteen and sixty-five months, and a matched control group of 328 children with normal hearing, on the non-verbal items of the Merrill-Palmer Scale. He found no significant difference in intelligence at any age level between the hearing and the deaf children, though more of the total sample of deaf children were seriously retarded. This finding was confirmed with older children by Gaskill (1957), who tested 465 pupils in schools for the deaf in Britain, obtaining a mean Wechsler Performance Scale IQ of 97 for this sample. The standardisation data for tests specially devised for children with hearing difficulties, for example the Snijders-Oomen Non-Verbal Scale (1959) and the Hiskey-Nebraska Test of Learning Aptitude (1966), have indicated that the overall mean IQ for deaf children does not significantly differ from hearing subjects on such tests.

Experimental investigation of the cognitive abilities and deficiencies of deaf children using Piaget's methods with normal children have shown the effects of a lack of a rich 'inner language' and limited educational experience on intellectual development (Ives, 1967), though Furth (1966) points out that deaf children can improve their performance on Piagetian tasks if care is taken to communicate the nature of the problem to them, and if they are adequately prepared beforehand for doing the tests.

Emotional and social problems

Little precise evidence is available about the emotional and social adjustment of deaf children, but it is suggested in the literature (reviewed by M. M. Lewis, 1968) that they are less well adjusted and more immature than hearing children. The characteristics of deaf children are said to include introversion and egocentricity, a lack of self-confidence and drive, and rigidity rather than flexibility. There is no doubt that language and personality are intimately connected, and that hearing and speech contribute to social acceptance as well as to one's feeling of personal security (Telford and Sawrey, 1957). Deaf children are deprived of what may be called the 'social sense' of hearing and are particularly handicapped in that they are cut off from the enjoyment of communicating with others in the fullest sense. The child who is born deaf has a very limited appreciation of the world of people and has to face dangers that do not threaten the hearing. For example, when left alone as a young child he does not hear any familiar and comforting sounds from afar. He is apt to misinterpret behaviour and to be misunderstood, since, instead of the more acceptable verbal protestations, he may seek an outlet for frustration through such means as temper tantrums, even as an older child or adolescent. Life may be so difficult that refuge is sought in isolation, with a progressive withdrawal from the world.

Kendall (1957) has shown that, from the early years of life, deaf children present more than the usual amount of problem behaviour. Investigating the incidence of behaviour problems in 180 deaf children aged $1\frac{1}{2}$ to $5\frac{1}{2}$ years, though interviews with the parents, direct observation and development ratings, he found that this sample had more difficulties than a control group over toilet-training, bed-wetting, sleeping, temper tantrums, over-dependence and social withdrawal. Murphy (1957) used a variety of methods to assess the adjustment of 300 pupils aged six to ten years in a number of day and residential schools for the deaf. He estimated that 22 per cent showed poor adjustment, needing remedial help of some kind, with an additional 4 per cent showing signs of serious instability. His conclusion that teachers of the deaf need to be given skilled guidance in dealing with the emotional problems of deaf children is of considerable relevance to educational psychologists. Bowyer et al. (1963) compared the personality adjustment of severely deaf and partially hearing children. In a pilot enquiry, three groups were studied, each of ten children, respectively severely deaf, with partial hearing and of normal hearing. Adjustment was assessed mainly by Lowenfeld techniques. It is of interest that the severely deaf were found to be above average in adjustment, while the partially hearing were below average, though not to a statistically significant degree. Lewis (1968), in a study of a sample of children with hearing impairment, highlighted the fact that the deficiencies in deaf children's vocabularies relating to personal traits (e.g. sad, depressed, glad, cheerful) may retard the process of the development of these traits in the children themselves.

Educational aims and methods
It is generally agreed that the aim of educating deaf children should be to enable them to become literate adults, well-adjusted in personality and

able to express themselves through generally understood media of communication (Department of Education and Science, 1968c). However, there has for some time been considerable argument over the disadvantages and advantages of using oral methods of teaching and communication with deaf children as compared with manual methods. The manual method involves the use of the hands for finger-spelling or signing; in the oral method, pupils are taught both to lip-read and to speak themselves (Department of Education and Science, 1967). Since the Second World War the oral view has been much in favour in this country, but recently it has been increasingly asserted that a more flexible approach is desirable and that individual children may not respond to oral teaching (Darbyshire, 1970; see also T. J. Watson, 1967, and Dale, 1967, for discussions of educational methods used with the deaf). For example, Montgomery (1968), making a factorial study of communication and ability in seventy prelingually and profoundly deaf school-leavers, concluded that oral and manual methods were not necessarily incompatible. He suggests that the present methods used for the development of speech in deaf children are notably unsuccessful with the majority of those without usable residual hearing, and that there is a need for alternative educational techniques to gear the intelligence of deaf children more effectively to academic achievement. The Lewis Committee, appointed in 1964 to consider the place, if any, of finger spelling and signing in the education of deaf children, while recommending that conditions should be made as favourable as possible to the oral education of these pupils, cautiously supported further experimentation with manual methods (Department of Education and Science, 1968c). Two members of the Committee, however, disagreed with this point of view, considering that pending controlled research studies, experimentation with manual media should be altogether discouraged (see also I. G. Taylor, 1971).

Effectiveness of the education of deaf children

Both in the attainment of speech and lip-reading skills and in scholastic achievement, results have proved disappointing (Department of Education and Science, 1968c).

A survey (Department of Education and Science, 1964b) of 276 children (aged 15 to 16 years) with marked hearing loss (over 70 decibels over the speech frequencies) showed that only 11·6 per cent had clear intelligible speech and good lip-reading ability. Further, a variety of studies of the educational attainments of deaf children have all testified to a considerable degree of allround retardation. As Burt (1957) observed, defects of hearing impose a particularly serious obstacle to educational progress, more so than defects of vision. Surveys in the United States have shown a retardation of three to five years in older schoolchildren, the gap between the deaf and the hearing increasing with age and being more marked in comprehension than in mechanical skills, such as number computation (Meyerson, 1963). In this country, Gaskill (1952) found a sample of 156 deaf children, average age 12 years 11 months, to be over four years behind the norms for hearing children on the Gates Test of Silent Reading, and over three years retarded in mechanical arithmetic (Schonell Essential Mechanical Arithmetic Test A). In a further study, out of eighty-six pupils aged 5 to 15 years, with a hearing loss of over 40 decibels, thirty-two were non-readers and thirty-six were retarded by at least one year (Gaskill, 1957). Wollman (1964) studied a representative sample of 14 to 16-year old pupils at thirteen schools for the deaf and/or partially hearing. He found that in both English (specially designed tests) and number (Manchester Mechanical Arithmetic Test) the pupils with impaired hearing were retarded when compared with hearing pupils in secondary modern schools. The mean scores in the English tests were significantly lower than those of the secondary modern pupils; in the arithmetic test, the hearing-impaired boys had a standardised score of 85, the girls 87 (norm 100, SD 15).

Although the degree of hearing impairment did not seem to affect performance in arithmetic, it did affect the results in English. Hearing-impaired pupils had particular difficulty with expression and with the comprehension of passages involving complex language structure. In English the severely deaf girls were significantly better than the severely deaf boys. It was further noted that there was no evidence of improved educational performance at fifteen as compared with fourteen years of age. The standards of achievement varied from school to school, and Wollman suggests both that the educational environment was an important factor in the standard of achievement reached and that this could be improved in a number of cases.

Partially hearing children

Many partially hearing children are able to attend ordinary schools with considerable success, especially when there are no problems additional to the hearing defect and when the degree of loss is fairly slight; others need special educational treatment in special units or day or residential schools (see chapter 2). Because of the wide range of hearing loss subsumed in the category 'partially hearing', and the variety of educational provision available for these children, it is even more difficult to generalise about this group than about the severely or profoundly deaf.

Cognitive difficulties
Studies of groups of partially hearing children have tended to show a

fairly normal distribution on non-verbal tests of intelligence, but consider-able retardation in verbal ability. J. C. Johnson (1962) found an almost normal distribution on Raven's Progressive Matrices in a sample of sixty-eight children, aged 5 to 16 years, with an average hearing impairment of over 30 decibels, but suitable for ordinary schools. Fisher (1965) supported this finding, with a sample of 83 children in ordinary primary and second-ary schools, with hearing losses between 20 and 64 decibels, while showing that these children had much poorer ability on the Crichton/Mill Hill Vocabulary Scales. Hine (1970) found the mean WISC Performance Scale Quotient of 100 children, aged 8 to 16 years, at a school for partially hearing children, to be 98·1 (SD 12·77), whereas their Verbal Scale Quotient was only 82 (SD 12·52), with the children with greater hearing losses doing less well on the verbal scale than the others. Thus while there is no reason why partially-hearing children with a slight degree of auditory impairment should have any specific cognitive difficulties, those with greater degrees of hearing loss are likely to have difficulties over verbal tasks of the kind discussed in the case of severely deaf children, though not necessarily to the same extent.

Social and emotional problems
There have been few studies in depth of the social and emotional adjust-ment of partially hearing children, but, in general, the evidence suggests a higher incidence of maladjusted and unsettled behaviour in this group than in hearing children. J. C. Johnson (1962), on the basis of interviews and home visits, estimated 9 per cent of his sample to be maladjusted, and 38 per cent to be unsettled; this estimate of maladjustment is not unduly high, but hearing children do not usually show unsettledness to such an extent (see Stott, 1966a). Fisher (1965), using the Bristol Social Adjust-ment Guide, found 20 per cent of his sample to be maladjusted and 27 per cent to be unsettled, significantly more than in a control group of hearing children (13 per cent maladjusted, 15 per cent unsettled). Hine (1970), on the same criterion, reports an estimate of 19 per cent maladjusted, and 37 per cent unsettled. Although Johnson found few cases of stealing or aggressive behaviour in the children studied, both Fisher and Hine challenge the stereotype of withdrawal being the main defence mechanism of partially hearing children, asserting that these children tend to adopt a demonstrative mode of expression when maladjusted. Fisher noted that children with lesser degrees of hearing loss were just as maladjusted as those with higher degrees of impairment, suggesting that a low degree of hearing loss can have disproportionate effects on emotional development.

Educational methods
In the main, educational methods appropriate for partially hearing are

similar to those used with normal children, except that partially hearing pupils need to be taught in small groups and to have sound amplified as much as is possible without causing discomfort. This is done through individual hearing aids, loop systems in acoustically treated classrooms and speech training units. Although most of the available special facilities for the partially hearing have been provided in recent years, educational technology is not yet being fully used to the benefit of these pupils. According to the Department of Education and Science report on *Units for Partially Hearing Children* (1967), there have been few serious developments in the use of programmed learning, film loops or film cassettes with or without synchronised sound tracks. One of the criticisms made by this report was, in fact, that clear aims in the education of partially hearing children seemed lacking, many teachers seeming 'unsure of the ultimate goal for their pupils and how best to help them to reach it'.

Effectiveness of the education of partially hearing pupils
Studies of the attainments of partially hearing have, as with the deaf, shown a considerable degree of retardation in this group. Johnson (1962) found 40 per cent of his sample to be 'seriously retarded' in reading (by two or more years) and a further 26 per cent to be 'markedly retarded' (by one to two years); in mechanical arithmetic, 25·5 per cent were 'seriously retarded' and, additionally, 31 per cent 'markedly' retarded. In Fisher's (1965) sample, the mean Reading Quotient on the Schonell Word Recognition Test was 85, with 30 per cent of the children having a RQ below 70 and a further 20 per cent a RQ below 85; in mechanical arithmetic, the mean Quotient was 81, with 26 per cent below 70, and a further 16 per cent below 85. Hine (1970) found the educational quotients of his sample of 100 children to be: Schonell Silent Reading 78·8; Schonell Mechanical Arithmetic 80·1; Schonell Problem Arithmetic 79·4. He concluded that not only are partially hearing children retarded relative to the normally hearing, but they also fall proportionately further behind as they grow older. However, M. D. Vernon (1971), quoting studies by Henry (1947) and Hamilton and Owrid (1970) which showed that partially hearing children can read up to the standard suggested by their non-verbal IQs, and in some cases above normal standards, suggests that impaired hearing may affect reading to a lesser extent than has been supposed. However, if children with auditory defects are to reach an adequate educational level, early detection of their hearing loss and the immediate institution of appropriate educational measures are essential.

Cerebral palsied children

'Cerebral palsy' refers to a group of conditions in which there are varying degrees of paralysis, weakness or incoordination as a result of injury or defect in the motor areas of the brain (Gulliford, 1971). The majority of cases of cerebral palsy suffer from *spasticity*, characterised by involuntary muscle contraction resulting in stiffness and rigidity. Most of the other cases are affected by *athetosis*, where the main features are involuntary or uncontrollable movements, or by *ataxia*, where there is incoordination of muscles and impaired balance. Although the degree of motor handicap varies from very severe to very mild, children suffering from cerebral palsy are often grossly handicapped in a number of ways. Unless the cerebral palsy is of a minor kind, there are likely to be serious cognitive, social and emotional difficulties additional to the characteristic motor disabilities. The majority of CP children also have associated handicaps of vision, hearing and speech which exacerbate the learning problems that result from their motor dysfunction, and, in spite of the progress that has been made in catering for their needs, the education of these children presents a formidable challenge.

Physical difficulties

The nature and extent of the physical disability of CP children will vary according to the type and degree of the palsy, but most of these children, whether spastic, athetoid, ataxic or otherwise classified, will be hampered in, or prevented from, making even simple movements necessary in school, for example picking up a pencil, opening books, or keeping the head still (Department of Education and Science, 1970a). In addition, a substantial number have visual defects which distort perception and may hinder reading. Although Cockburn (1961) found that only 4 out of 223 cases of cerebral palsy (aged 14 months to 21 years) surveyed in Scotland needed to be tested as blind, there is general agreement in the literature that a high proportion of CP children have oculomotor defects, affecting the movements of the eye muscles and the ability to keep to a line of print, and that a quarter or more have subnormal vision (Dunsdon, 1952; Hopkins *et al.*, 1954). The Department of Education and Science (1970a), in a survey of 343 CP children in special schools and units in England and Wales, did not find serious eye disorders to be common in this sample, but 70 of the children had a squint, and 58 wore glasses.

Hearing defects are somewhat less common than visual anomalies in CP children, and Cockburn (1961) found only 3 children in her sample of 223 needing to be tested as deaf. Even so, in the USA Hopkins *et al.* (1954) reported 13·3 per cent of 1,127 cases of CP to have hearing defects, and in this country Fisch (1960) found 20 per cent of 600 CP pupils to have hearing losses serious enough to constitute an additional handicap to the child. In the Department of Education and Science (1970a) Survey, 30 children (about 9 per cent of the sample), mainly the athetoids, had defective hearing to the extent that individual aids were required. High-tone deafness was the most frequent type of auditory defect met among the athetoids; Fisch also found this type of hearing loss most typical in CP children. A history of one or more epileptic seizures is found in about 20 to 30 per cent of CP children. Woods (1957) reports that 30 per cent of 301 cases had had such fits, and the Department of Education and Science (1970a) survey found an incidence of 21 per cent with fits in her sample.

Speech defects
Speech defects are very common in CP children. Floyer (1955) estimated that 46 per cent of CP children in Liverpool had speech defects, and both Cockburn (1961) and the Department of Education and Science (1970a) Survey found about one-half of their samples to have defective speech; 42 out of the 223 children in the former survey had no speech at all.

Cognitive and educational problems
There is general agreement among different investigators that, while a small percentage of cerebral palsied children achieve quotients above the average on intelligence tests, the distribution is heavily skewed, with approximately 50 per cent scoring IQs below 70 (Dunsdon, 1952; Hopkins et al., 1954; Schonell, 1956; Cockburn, 1961). Cockburn, for example, found 10 per cent to have IQs above 110, 16 per cent IQs between 90 and 109, 25 per cent between 70 and 89, and 49 per cent below 70 or not assessable. No significant differences have been reported between the mean IQs of athetoids and spastics, but Cockburn showed that the greater the extent of the child's physical handicap, the more he is likely to be mentally retarded.

The educational problems of cerebral palsied children are intensified by their impaired perception. They have particular difficulty in synthesising elements into wholes and in discriminating between background and pattern. Many cerebral-palsied children are prone to reversal of numbers and letters, have difficulty in spacing words, and have a confused sense of direction (Department of Education and Science, 1970a). They have a short span of attention, are easily tired and very distractible. Their lack of control over their movements produces much frustration and irritation.

Social and emotional problems
Behavioural problems frequently arise in the cerebral-palsied, either as a direct result of brain dysfunction or as a result of general developmental immaturity, often relating to overprotective handling at home. Floyer (1955) in a survey of CP children in Liverpool, found a good deal of tension, lack of drive, disinhibition or unnatural lack of reserve, and perseveration (a tendency to unusual repetition and a difficulty in changing from one

operation to another); other writers (Dunsdon, 1952; Woods, 1957) have also commented on the lack of emotional control found among cerebral palsied children. Ainley (1969), using the Bristol Social Adjustment Guide, found 40 per cent of 52 CP children in a special school for PH children to be maladjusted. Oswin (1967) illustrates with various case histories the types of behaviour problem commonly met amongst children with CP.

Educational methods

Kershaw (1961) points out that there are CP children with only minor degrees of handicap who can cope with ordinary schooling. However, most CP children need intensive individual teaching as well as physiotherapy, speech therapy and possibly other physical aids or treatment without which learning may be extremely difficult. Within the special school or unit a large variety of methods and apparatus are used. Hickey (1962) advocates constant stimulation, finely graded material, and short exercises: the child with little control over material should be given only a small amount of apparatus at a time. Pettican (1966) describes specially-constructed apparatus for remedial work in number, and R. I. Brown and Bookbinder (1966) describe programmed reading techniques suitable for spastics. Cotton and Parnwell (1967) give an account of 'conductive education', a method employed by Professor Peto in Hungary and aimed at enabling CP children to achieve total independence through the establishment of normal active motor patterns necessary for life at school and at home. Methods of educating CP children are comprehensively reviewed by Dunsdon (1952) and Schonell (1956), and the work of Strauss and Lehtinen (1947) and Strauss and Kephart (1955) on brain-injured children is also of great relevance.

Educational progress

Dunsdon (1952) estimated that only 40 per cent of cerebral palsied children are educable in the usual sense of the word. Schonell (1956) found two-thirds of 354 CP children in the Midlands to be non-readers (of these, one-third had IQs below 70 and over half were below age 7), only 23 per cent of those with IQs over 90 working 'to capacity'. Schonell considered that the more intelligent CP child was not always stimulated to the full. Cockburn (1961), testing 153 CP children over seven on the Burt-Vernon Word Reading Test and Schonell's Reading Comprehension Test A, estimated that only 15 per cent of the children could be considered 'not backward': 30 per cent of the sample failed to score on the Word Reading Test, and 52 per cent on the Reading Comprehension Test. On simple oral and written tests of arithmetic, only 6·5 per cent showed no degree of backwardness. Cockburn concluded that there was a tendency for poor attainment to be increasingly associated both with poor intelligence and a severe degree of cerebral palsy. Hickey (1962) suggests that many CP children are late readers, and considers that final decisions about the educable capacity of these children should not be made too early. Crabb (1965), comparing a sample of forty-two CP children with physically normal children matched for age and intelligence found, on the basis of Piagetian-type tests, that the number concepts of the CP pupils were significantly less mature, and that several were approaching school-leaving age without having achieved any understanding of number.

Post-school adjustment
The Department of Education and Science (1970a) Survey reports that of 156 CP school-leavers in 1965 and 1966 only 20 per cent went into open employment. Although some went on to higher education, the majority needed a sheltered vocational environment or remained at home unemployed. Cockburn (1961) found that of forty-five cases over school age, twenty one were considered unemployable, mainly because of subnormality. Of the twenty-four capable of working, only fifteen were actually in employment, mainly in work requiring little skill; no provision at all had been made for the majority of the unemployable who remained at home. Hellings (1964), studying fifty-four ex-pupils from a number of schools, mostly day schools for the physically handicapped, found that about 50 per cent obtained employment. However, a Spastic Society survey of 108 leavers from four residential schools for CP children, including a high percentage of severely handicapped pupils, over a period of six years, showed that only 15 per cent had obtained employment two to three years after leaving school, either in open or sheltered conditions (Gardner, 1969). Gardner suggests that educationists must face the fact that many CP school leavers will not obtain employment and should prepare them realistically for the life they will lead after school.

Epileptic children

The problems of epileptic children, most of whom attend ordinary schools, are often poorly understood in school and society. The effects of this lack of understanding on the adjustment of these children are highlighted by Bagley (1971), in a comprehensive review of the literature.

Cognitive difficulties
Because of the many variables involved, the relationship between epilepsy and intellectual development is not clearly known. While there is a relatively high incidence of epilepsy among the subnormal and of subnormality among epileptics, surveys of epileptic children have not shown their intelligence, on average, to be markedly below normal

(Telford and Sawrey, 1967). Halstead (1957) found the Terman-Merrill scores of fifty-six epileptics to be only slightly below those of a control group, and Nuffield (1961), surveying the intelligence of 288 epileptics referred to the Maudsley Hospital, found their mean IQ of 89 not to differ significantly from that of 100 non-epileptic children referred to the child psychiatric department. The Report of the Chief Medical Officer of the Department of Education and Science for 1960–1 (Department of Education and Science, 1962) pointed out that the risk of mental deterioration in epileptic children had been exaggerated: deterioration is sometimes seen in the rare cases of repeated major convulsions that have failed to respond to drugs, but generalised minor seizures of petit mal form, even if frequent, do not cause such deterioration, nor do anti-convulsant drugs prescribed in non-toxic doses. Bagley (1971), studying 118 cases of epilepsy, uncomplicated by other handicaps, referred to the neurological department of a London hospital, found a mean WISC IQ of 99·2 (SD 21·8). The distribution, however was significantly skewed, with a larger number of children than normal being of low intelligence, and a smaller number having IQs above average.

There is some evidence to suggest that impaired cognitive functioning may be associated with temporal lobe epilepsy, visual learning and memory being particularly affected (Milner, 1954), and that intellectual deficits are more likely to be found in cases of symptomatic epilepsy (where the fits are caused by a definite pathological condition in the brain) than in idiopathic epilepsy, where the causes of the cerebral dysfunction are not clearly known (Telford and Sawrey, 1967).

Adjustment difficulties
The Report of the Chief Medical Officer for 1960–1 (Department of Education and Science, 1962) was at pains to challenge the stereotype of the 'typical epileptic personality', seen as egocentric, antisocial, quarrelsome and moody. The majority of epileptic children, according to this Report, are as psychologically normal as non-epileptic children. However, about a third of those children who suffer from epilepsy of the partial, temporal lobe type tend to show personality disorders, related to the severity and diffuseness of the injury in the region of the temporal lobe rather than to the frequency or severity of the fits. Tension, irritability, bad temper, aggressiveness and hyperkinesis may be found in such cases.

Bagley (1971) using the Rutter (1967) teachers' questionnaire estimated that 43 per cent of his sample had a serious psychiatric handicap, as compared with only 7 per cent in the general population. On the basis of ratings by two workers, only 30 per cent of this sample were categorised as 'normal' behaviourally; 24 per cent were rated as 'anxious', 25 per cent as 'aggressive' and 21 per cent as presenting 'mixed problems'.

Bagley observes that some teachers react in a hostile or over anxious way to children with epilepsy. This attitude is likely to exacerbate any disturbance which epileptic children may have; it is not uncommon for such children to be in fear of having a convulsion, particularly in school in front of the class, and they need a considerable amount of sympathy and understanding from both teachers and schoolmates.

School progress

Epilepsy is usually controllable by sedative and anti-convulsant drugs, and only in rare cases is special educational treatment or placement necessary for the condition as such, though remedial help may be required for educational retardation and psychotherapy may help to reduce anxiety and conflict in the epileptic child. Hutt (1967) suggests that programmed learning devices may be useful for children who suffer from impairment in attention, learning and memory because of paroxysmal discharges, since the child is able to work at his own pace and any serious interruption will be quickly picked up by the programme. Rutter, Yule *et al.* (1967), in the Isle of Wight survey, found that 24·5 per cent of 61 children (aged 10 and 11 years) with epilepsy or neurological disorders were retarded in reading by at least 28 months, as compared with only 5·4 per cent of a random control group of 147 children. Bagley (1971) compared the attainments of his epileptic sample with a matched group of non-epileptic children attending a child guidance clinic. He found that retardation in reading in the sample was associated with psychiatric disorder rather than epilepsy as such, while the very high level of retardation in arithmetic in the epileptic children was associated with epilepsy rather than with psychiatric disorder.

Contribution of educational psychologist

The role of the educational psychologist in the assessment of the educational, emotional and social needs of the physically handicapped has been discussed earlier (see chapter 7, pp. 139–141). Although the value of an early and comprehensive psychological and educational assessment of physically handicapped children must not be minimised, it is important that the contribution of the psychologist to the education and welfare of these children should not be confined to assessment. It is true that specialised training and experience is a prerequisite for a full understanding of educational methods appropriate for children with visual or auditory defects, or with cerebral palsy, and that unless the educational psychologist has such training and experience, he is unlikely to be in a position to contribute to the development of the curriculum or to advise on specific teaching methods for children in these groups. However, those psychologists who have had a specialist knowledge of children with particular physical handicaps have already made a substantial contribution to special educational treatment, and it is desirable that some educational psychologists should seek to specialise in the education and psychology of specific handicaps. A number of in-service courses are arranged to help educational psychologists to specialise in this way, and it would be beneficial for these courses to be extended both in depth and duration.

Additionally, the educational psychologist can play a significant part in at least four other areas: counselling parents, advising teachers, helping to develop a vocational guidance and after-care service for physically handicapped school leavers, and evaluating the efficacy of special educational treatment.

Counselling parents

Parents of physically handicapped children almost inevitably find it difficult to accept the handicap and to understand all its implications for them and the child. They need support and guidance if they are to gain an insight into their own feelings about the child—feelings which are often suppressed—and they will also benefit through knowing how they should handle the child and what experiences they should provide for him. They will want to know what realistic educational and vocational aspirations they can hold for the child, and what his difficulties will be at home and in school. It is entirely appropriate that the educational psychologist should be directly involved in counselling of this kind.

Advising teachers

Neither the educational strengths and weaknesses nor the emotional and social needs of physically handicapped children are always fully understood by their teachers, especially those in ordinary schools who may have little contact with serious cases of physical handicap. Partially sighted, partially hearing and epileptic children, in particular, often fail to obtain the treatment they need. The educational psychologist, in close touch with ordinary and special schools, can do valuable work in spreading a wider knowledge of the psychological and educational needs of physically handicapped children among teachers. He will also, in the course of his normal work, be called upon to advise about individual problems of adjustment among physically handicapped children. As previously shown, teachers in special schools and classes for the physically handicapped face a high incidence of behaviour problems arising from a variety of sources. Teachers will welcome guidance and support from the psychologist and his colleagues in the Child Guidance Service in dealing with these problems.

Vocational guidance and after-care

During the past two decades the failure to meet the vocational and leisure needs of physically handicapped school leavers has been repeatedly highlighted (see Carnegie UK Trust, Report, 1964). Much of the work done on behalf of physically handicapped children and adolescents is vitiated by society's inability to find suitable employment for them, and by the lack of an advisory 'after-care' service which can help the physically handicapped to lead as satisfactory a life as possible. There is ample scope for the educational psychologist to be involved in the development of a comprehensive vocational guidance and after-care service for physically handicapped school-leavers.

Evaluation of special educational treatment
As the preceding review has indicated, there is a paucity of knowledge about the educational progress and emotional and social development of physically handicapped children. All school psychological services should consider it one of their functions to add to knowledge about the educational and psychological development of handicapped children, and to assess the efficacy of special educational treatment in their area. Even if numbers of physically handicapped children in a particular locality are limited, a combination of enquiries in different areas will increase knowledge considerably. In carrying out such enquiries, considerable sophistication in research technique is required, as many of the studies made in the past have given too little information about, for example, the precise nature and extent of the handicap, for the findings to be of much value.

11

Maladjusted and delinquent children

A high proportion of the children referred to a school psychological service or child guidance clinic will present symptoms of maladjustment—behaviour problems or emotional disturbance—or delinquency. In this chapter, the classification, aetiology and treatment of both maladjustment and delinquency will be considered, with particular reference to the part which can be played by the educational psychologist in dealing with these problems; the specific role of the educational psychologist in the areas covered will not, therefore, be dealt with in separate sections.

Maladjustment

Classification

The difficulty of defining maladjustment in precise terms and the problems of assessing it are discussed by Chazan (1970). It is particularly important for the educational psychologist to understand that the term 'maladjustment' has little psychological significance. The labelling of a child as 'maladjusted' does not give much information about the child: it merely indicates that the child is in need of help of some kind because he is emotionally disturbed or presenting a behaviour problem. A statement that a child is 'maladjusted' should, therefore, be amplified by precise details of the nature and extent of the maladjustment. It is helpful for the psychologist and his colleagues in the Child Guidance Service to identify and characterise the problem in such a way that those expected to help in treatment know exactly what feelings or behaviour they are aiming to modify. As yet, there is no valid and widely accepted system of classification of the symptoms of maladjustment in childhood and adolescence, but a number of schemes have been suggested. Hewitt and Jenkins (1946) and Jenkins and Glickman (1946) distinguished five main clusters of symptoms characterising 'over-inhibited', 'unsocialised aggressive', 'socialised delinquent', 'brain-injured' or 'schizoid' children. Himmelweit (in Eysenck, 1960a) categorised disturbed children in terms of 'conduct' (or more extroverted) problems and 'personality' (or more introverted) problems, and this distinction between 'neurotic' or 'emotional' disorders, characterised by inhibition, introversion and unhappiness, and 'behaviour' disorders, characterised by antisocial or aggressive behaviour, has been maintained in most classificatory schemes.

An attempt to draw up a system of classification of mental disorders in childhood has been made by the World Health Organisation, and a report on the third WHO Seminar on Psychiatric Disorders, Classification and Statistics is given by Rutter, Lebovici et al. (1969), who present a triaxial classification of mental disorders found in children between three and twelve years. The first axis relates to the clinical syndrome presented; on the second axis intellectual level is coded in broad categories; and the third axis is of 'associated or aetiological factors'. The outline headings under which the disorders are classified are supported by a glossary explaining the significance of the terms used. The main categories used for the classification of symptoms are: normal variation, adaptation reaction, specific developmental disorder, conduct disorder, neurotic disorder, psychosis, personality disorder, psychosomatic disorder, and other clinical syndromes. Some of these categories are further subdivided. The WHO scheme is clear and comprehensive, and, as the authors state, is worthy of being tried out and assessed on a wide scale. Further work is needed, in particular on the axis listing aetiological factors.

A revised scheme for classifying symptoms of behaviour disturbance in the school situation has recently been suggested by Stott (1971a), on the basis of results obtained in Canada with a new version of the Bristol Social Adjustment Guides. Behaviour manifestations are divided under the headings of 'underreaction' or 'overreaction'. The core syndromes of 'underreaction' are unforthcomingness, withdrawal and depression, while 'overreaction' includes the syndromes of inconsequence and hostility. Although a good deal of work has been carried out in this country with the old form of the Bristol Social Adjustment Guides (Stott, 1966a), the revised form has yet to be tried out on a large scale in Britain. The format of the Bristol Social Adjustment Guides has proved a useful one for obtaining information on children from teachers.

It is useful for a consistent scheme of classification to be used by a child guidance service, as this will help the service to assess the response to treatment made by children showing different kinds of behaviour disturbance. However, research has shown that many children show heterogeneous symptoms and do not fit neatly into definite categories (see Bagley, 1971, chapter 16), and much further work is needed on the problems of classification of symptoms of maladjustment in childhood and adolescence.

Causative factors

As Woody (1969) states, the theoretical orientation of the diagnostician will influence the way in which causative factors related to maladjustment are determined: the deeper the explanatory level used, the greater will be the influence of a particular theoretical inclination. A variety of theoretical positions are held by psychologists and psychiatrists working with malad-justed children. These positions may be divided, in the main, into 'psycho-analytically oriented' and 'learning-theory oriented', but within each of these two schools of thought there are many different orientations. For example, psychoanalytically-minded clinicians may be guided predomin-antly by the views of Freud, Jung, Adler, Erikson or some other psycho-analyst; learning theorists may follow Skinner, Eysenck, Mowrer or Dollard and Miller. Some workers in the field of maladjustment are greatly influenced by Carl Rogers's self theory, George Kelly's psychology of personal constructs or the 'competence motivation' emphasis of Robert White. Many clinicians seem to hold a somewhat vague eclectic position, choosing those insights from a variety of schools of thought which appear to be valid and useful. For a discussion of the various theoretical positions see Hall and Lindzey (1957), J. A. C. Brown (1961), Wepman and Heine (1963) and Mischel (1971). Most would agree that the causes of maladjust-ment are manifold, and that clinical practice shows that very rarely is there a single factor operative in any case of maladjustment, which tends rather to be the result of a combination of several factors. The most obvious causal factor may be a precipitating factor rather than the most important one: for example, a child may refuse to go to school allegedly because his teacher has shouted at him, but there is usually much more behind such a case of 'school refusal' which needs to be unravelled, and the main source of the difficulty may well be in the nature of the parent–child relationships.

The factors conducive to maladjustment can be classified in several different ways, but will be considered here under the following headings:

Temperamental and congenital factors
Early developmental difficulties
Physical factors
Intellectual and scholastic factors
Material and psychological factors in the home
Interrupted or incomplete relationships with parents.

Temperamental and congenital factors

In considering the relative contribution of heredity and environment to the causation of maladjustment, there has been a tendency to emphasise those factors which act upon the individual *from birth*, but clearly different children react differently to the same stresses. Not every child brought up in an adverse situation becomes maladjusted, and there are a number of children who show symptoms of emotional disturbance in spite of a favourable environment. As previously stated (p. 182), Stott (1962, 1966b) has placed much emphasis on *congenital factors*. He suggests that in many cases of maladjustment there are symptoms indicating neural damage, for the most part of congenital origin, and a susceptibility to stress often related to a disturbed pregnancy. He hypothesises that some children are, through congenital impairment, particularly prone to emotional disturbance of the 'unforthcoming' and 'inconsequential' types, showing a marked defect of motivation. Stott does not, however, underestimate the effects of an adverse upbringing and an unsatisfactory contemporary family situation, nor does he consider that congenital and family factors are independent of each other. In his view, the possibility must not be ruled out that the same general types of stressful family situations, with the physical strain and deprivation which accompany them, may also have been responsible for the neural damage to the children before or at birth.

Although a controlled investigation by Pasamanick and Knobloch (1960), has supported the idea that brain injury is an important factor in the aetiology of psychopathology in children, Werry (1972), in a comprehensive review of the literature on organic factors in childhood psychopathology, concludes that there is little evidence to suggest that brain damage or dysfunction is necessarily accompanied by psychopathology. He also finds no support for the hypothesis that all psychopathological conditions are organically determined, though there is some evidence that certain behavioural symptoms such as hyperactivity and distractibility, and certain patterns of behaviour such as the hyperkinetic syndrome, childhood psychosis or conduct disorders, tend to be associated more frequently with slight neurological and other indices of brain damage than in normal children. The validity of these indices is, however, not well established. On the basis of present evidence, Werry considers that brain damage or dysfunction is simply one of several variables, including temperamental proclivity as well as familial, social and educational experiences, that interact in a complex multivariate fashion in determining personality and behaviour.

Eysenck and his colleagues (Eysenck and Rachmann, 1965; Eysenck, 1967) stress the importance of knowing the individual's place on the introversion–extroversion continuum, considered largely a matter of inborn *temperament*. Eysenck postulates two major dimensions of personality—introversion extroversion and neuroticism–stability—which are powerfully determined by heredity and are likely to have some form of physiological, neurological or biochemical basis in the nervous system of the individual. His hypothesis is that most neurotic disorders (particularly anxieties, fears, phobias and obsessions) are *acquired* or *conditioned* emotional reactions. Since introverts are more easily conditioned than extroverts, introversion, anxiety, fears and obsessional behaviour tend to go together. This theory has implications for the treatment of maladjustment by means of behaviour therapy (see later, pp. 233–235).

Early developmental difficulties

A number of writers, particularly those with a psychoanalytical orientation, have stressed the adverse effects of some disruption of essential and basic personal relationships in the early years. Bowlby (1952) drew attention to the possible long-term effects of separation from the mother in infancy, suggesting that such separation could lead to lack of feeling, delinquent behaviour, and poor school work in adolescence. Later studies, including those by Bowlby himself (Bowlby *et al.*, 1956; Ainsworth *et al.*, 1962), have shown that separation from the mother is not inevitably followed by adverse effects either of a short-term or long-term nature, and that important factors are the care of the child *during* separation, the nature of the maternal care of which the child is deprived, and the experiences he has during the period of separation (e.g. whether painful or not). Age is also an important variable, separation before two years being likely to be more damaging than that experienced in later years. However, prolonged and traumatic separation can impair development, and Bowlby made a valuable contribution to the promotion of mental health in childhood in drawing attention to the dangers of maternal deprivation, to the need for frequent contact between hospitalised children and their parents, and to the necessity for individualising the care of deprived children in institutions. Rutter (1972) provides a comprehensive and critical review of the literature concerned with maternal deprivation.

Disturbances during the early years of life may also be related to weaning, toilet training and the child's urge to independence, which is not always understood by the parents. Also important is the way in which the parents handle such problems as early sleep disturbances, sibling rivalry and other psychological traumata which may occur in infancy (Sears *et al.*, 1957; Newson and Newson, 1968).

Physical factors

Poor physical condition tends to reduce a child's resistance to stress which might otherwise not result in emotional upset. It is not, however, easy to distinguish, in cases of maladjustment accompanied by physical ailments, between symptoms with an organic cause and those which are directly related to emotional disturbance. Maladjusted children easily take refuge in minor ailments such as stomach pains, headaches and feelings of sickness, and there seems to be a strong association between emotional disturbance and such complaints as catarrh or asthma (Nichols, 1959; Carré, 1961). Where the mother is overprotective or overindulgent, physical ailments may result in a child's frequent absence from school, which can cause difficulties with his school work and in his relationships with his classmates.

As shown in chapter 10, children with a marked physical defect are not always disturbed as a direct result of this, but the physically handicapped child is usually very susceptible to emotional disturbance because of his feeling that he is different from others and because of the attitudes of peers and adults to him. Parental attitudes to the physically handicapped child may be negative or even rejecting.

Intellectual and scholastic factors
Most work on maladjustment in childhood and adolescence has stressed the part played by the home background in the causation of maladjustment, and has tended to pay little attention to factors relating to the school situation. Even the Underwood Report (Ministry of Education, 1955), a report specifically on maladjustment within the educational system, concluded that, while the school might quite often be a precipitating or contributory factor in maladjustment, it was seldom the direct or chief cause. It is agreed that only rarely are adverse factors relating to home circumstances not to be found in cases of maladjustment, but, even so, there are many factors connected with the child's school life which may directly cause emotional or behavioural disturbance. Burt and Howard (1952) stated that in many cases the main, if not the sole, cause of maladjustment arose out of conditions at the child's school. They pointed out that, with younger children maladjustment not infrequently followed transfer from the infant school to the junior school, when the methods of teaching might be abruptly changed. Indeed, school seems to be a stressful experience for a considerable proportion of children. T. Moore (1966), for example, studying a sample of 85 boys and 79 girls, aged 6 to 11 years and in 115 different schools, over the primary school period, showed that about 80 per cent of the children experienced difficulties in the infant school of sufficient severity to warrant noting and that 18 per cent of the sample never became thoroughly reconciled to school throughout the primary school years. Not all of these children were overdependent, and some of the difficulties were clearly related to an unhelpful school atmosphere.

Difficulties which arise at school and cause disturbed feelings or behaviour may (a) be related to school work; (b) arise from the nature of the child–teacher relationship; or (c) be connected with the child's relationships with his schoolmates.

Difficulties relating to school work. The connection between educational failure and maladjustment has already been noted in chapter 10. A higher proportion of maladjusted pupils is to be found in special schools and classes for slow learners and in the lower streams of ordinary schools than in other classes (Chazan, 1963, 1964). In some cases, the educational failure is due to dislike of school, missed schooling, or frequent changes of school (Burt and Howard, 1952); in others, by emotional blockage caused by anxiety; in many cases, educational failure and feelings of inferiority and frustration may lead to maladjusted behaviour. Parental pressures and anxieties often add to the child's learning and emotional difficulties.

Difficulties over school work are most frequently found in dull and slow-learning children, but are not confined to these groups. Intelligent children faced with overpressure in school, sometimes exacerbated by undue parental aspirations, can react with symptoms of disturbance. There is little evidence that children who are highly gifted intellectually are more prone to maladjustment than others (Gallagher and Crowder, 1957), but the very intelligent child who is given too little or too easy work to do may become bored and troublesome in class.

There are some children, too, who have a stable home with sensible parents but who set themselves problems because of excessively high standards and aspirations. If they fail to reach the standards which they have set for themselves, they suffer much tension and anxiety, which may block intellectual functioning even in cases of high intelligence and cause a low output which is disappointing to the teachers as well as to the children themselves. Cases of this kind need very sympathetic and sensitive handling.

Difficulties in the child–teacher relationships. Difficulties in the relationships between the child and the teacher may stem from the personality and attitude of the teacher, or from the incapacity of the child to make satisfactory relationships. Teachers, in general, receive some training in understanding children as individuals and are usually sympathetic towards the children in their charge. But there are some teachers who are unable to make satisfactory relationships with their pupils in general, or with particular individuals, because of personality defects or insecurity in the classroom. Children referred to child guidance clinics occasionally complain about being smacked or caned at school, or about unfairness and sarcastic remarks. Often these complaints are exaggerated, but a sensitive child will react badly to an ill-tempered teacher, even if the teacher is not directing his bad temper at him personally. Such a reaction against a teacher of this kind can sometimes be generalised into hostility towards attendance at school, and when a maladjusted or otherwise handicapped child is picked out by a teacher for unkind attention in class, much damage can be done.

A small number of children are so deeply disturbed that they cannot make relationships with adults. Autistic or psychotic children fall into this category, but these children will rarely take their places in the ordinary school. Teachers in the secondary school may infrequently have to deal with psychopathic adolescents who have a cold hostility towards them, giving them little respect, being unconcerned about approval or disapproval, and therefore not caring how often they get into trouble.

Difficulties in the pupil–teacher relationship will also be caused by the boredom and apathy of whole classes in school, particularly of those with pupils nearing school-leaving age and with a high proportion of adolescents coming from disadvantaged backgrounds. So far, the educational system has failed to meet the needs of the adolescent pupil who does not have academic goals, and many adolescents who settle down later at work are troublesome in the school situation.

Difficulties with other pupils. As the child gets older, his relationships with his contemporaries at school become increasingly important to him. At about eight or nine, there is a sex cleavage and boys tend to become members of little gangs, which dominate their lives (Blyth, 1960). At this period, and for the subsequent school years, the child who fails to find acceptance in the eyes of the class group—the 'isolate', 'neglectee', or 'rejectee'—will almost certainly be disturbed about this (K. M. Evans, 1962). The most popular children tend to be the physically fit, well-adjusted children who are good at games and work (Belfield, 1963), and both the junior and secondary school periods can be difficult ones for those pupils who are educationally backward and physically handicapped. During adolescence, there may be over-close attachments between individuals which may cause some upset. These attachments are normally temporary and harmless but, if not wisely handled, may result in emotional disturbance.

A particular difficulty in establishing relationships with contemporaries is found in homes in 'delinquent neighbourhoods' where the parents have high standards and try to prevent the child from associating with other children in the neighbourhood because they belong to a delinquent subculture. These parents may need considerable help in providing their children with adequate social and recreational outlets.

Material and psychological factors in the home
In general, psychological factors in the home have been shown to play a much more important role in the causation of maladjustment than adverse material conditions. It is true that poverty or financial strain, overcrowding and dismal living quarters can damage family life and result in disharmony, and that there is a higher incidence of problem behaviour,

even in young children, in 'deprived' neighbourhoods than in 'residential' areas (Chazan and Jackson, 1971). But it is the quality of the relationships within the home that seems a particularly crucial factor in the emotional development of children, and where there is emotional warmth and security emanating from parental affection, many children grow up reasonably happy and well adjusted in spite of poor material conditions. In many studies, the most powerful factor to emerge in the causation of maladjustment in children is *faulty parental attitudes*, often related to parental instability and unreliability, but occasionally due to ignorance of the needs of children. Lack of affection, overstrict discipline, rejection and inconsistency are particularly damaging.

Hewitt and Jenkins (1946), analysing the behaviour traits of 500 problem children (average age eleven to twelve years; mean IQ 94) found the following patterns of cause and effect:

1. *Parental rejection* (unaffectionate or hostile parents, parents dead or separated, lack of contact with parents) was significantly related to *unsocialised aggression in the child* (violence, cruelty, defiance and malicious mischief).

2. *Neglect and bad company* (dirty ill-kept home, lax supervision, faulty discipline, parental incapacity) had often preceded *socialised delinquency* (truancy, stealing, staying out late).

3. *Constraint of a repressive regimen* (rigid or excessive discipline, hypercritical parents, lack of warmth within the family group) had been imposed on the majority of neurotic children (showing seclusiveness, shyness, worrying, sensitivity, inhibition).

They also found that illegitimacy and the mother being neurotic or psychopathic were factors significantly associated with disturbed behaviour in children; and there was also some association between a 'physical deficiency' cluster (CNS disorder, abnormal growth pattern, convulsions, auditory or speech defect, diseased tonsils and adenoids, chronic physical complaints) and over-inhibited behaviour. This study is a most valuable one, although it does not show to what extent these relationships are the result of environment or inheritance, and they did not apply in every case.

Burt and Howard (1952) mention, as the most important conditions in the home: lack of affection; overstrict discipline; presence of step-mother or foster-mother; death of child's own mother; drunken parents; illegitimacy; lack of adequate facilities for recreation.

Brandon (1960), in his survey of maladjustment in Newcastle upon Tyne, comments on the immaturity and young age of the parents of maladjusted children. These parents frequently lived with relatives and were unduly reliant on the grandparents, and in these circumstances it is not surprising that many of them had a disturbed marital relationship. A high proportion of the mothers of the maladjusted children had had an unhappy childhood themselves and had suffered from psychological stress during pregnancy. In the majority of the cases of maladjustment, defective parent–child relationships were found.

Interrupted or incomplete relationships with parents
Interrupted relationships with the mother have already been mentioned in the discussion above on *early developmental difficulties*. Clearly, the child who is deprived of a normal home life is 'at risk' with regard to maladjustment. Although the state looks after the physical needs of deprived children very well, and attempts to cater for their psychological needs, placement in a children's home (cottage home or family group) or in a foster-home has its difficulties. On the whole, the foster-parent is less tolerant of problem behaviour than actual parents are, and children must be less secure in a 'Home' than in the care of their own parents. Thus children in care, although they should never be treated as 'different', need tactful help and support in school, especially as they are often more backward educationally than they need be.

Treatment
Since the beginning of the twentieth century in the USA and the 1920s in Great Britain, the Child Guidance Service has developed a wide range of approaches to the treatment of maladjusted children. Although some clinics still emphasise the need for a psychoanalytic approach, the trend in child guidance, particularly as practised in local education authority clinics in this country, has been away from the stress on the individual treatment of the child as a 'patient' and towards the readjustment of the child through a modification of the home and school environment. The approaches currently adopted by child guidance clinics may be conveniently discussed under the following headings, though there is some overlap between the divisions listed:

Work with parents: counselling, guidance, and casework.
Psychotherapy with children: play or interview; individual or group.
Behaviour therapy with children, sometimes involving the parents.
Remedial education.
Changing the home environment.
Changing the school environment.
Medication.
Hospitalisation.

Work with parents
Treatment at a child guidance clinic, however limited this may be,

usually includes work with the parents of any child referred on account of behaviour or emotional problems. The clinic has, from its inception, always recognised that the child is a member of a family unit and that treatment must involve the parents and perhaps other members of the family if it is to be effective. Work with parents includes the giving of advice on methods of handling the child, reassurance, supportive therapy, or even prolonged and intensive treatment. The role of the educational psychologist in this aspect of treatment, and the ways in which he can cooperate with other professional workers in helping parents, have already been discussed in chapters 2 and 8. An examination of the dynamics of family interaction and casework will be found in *Relationships in Casework* (Association of Psychiatric Social Workers, 1963), Timms (1964), I. M. Cohen (1966) and Turner (1970); Ackerman (1958) gives an account of family group therapy, a procedure whereby all the members of the family are treated together.

Psychotherapy

Most child guidance clinics have continued to use individual psychotherapy as their main direct approach to the treatment of emotional disturbance. The term 'psychotherapy' covers a wide variety of techniques and may include persuasion, suggestion, counselling, listening and interpretation (Brammer and Shostrom, 1960; Clyne, 1966). Psychotherapy may be carried out in the play or interview situation, individually or in small groups. Play therapy is perhaps particularly appropriate for younger children, while approaches involving a great deal of verbalising of problems and conflicts are more suitable for older children and adolescents. In this country, group methods have not been much in vogue, though they offer a number of advantages over individual treatment. For example, a group context is a more natural one than the individual child–therapist relationship, and relates to the actual life of the child outside. Moreover, there is less emphasis on the child being a patient and having serious problems and more on the concrete formation of relationships with others; and group play or discussion is enjoyed by most children, providing an outlet for mildly aggressive behaviour or feelings. Slavson (1947) developed a variety of group techniques suitable for disturbed children, in particular activity group therapy and interview group therapy. Activity groups are considered appropriate for younger children, consisting of eight boys or girls carefully selected because of the therapeutic effect they may have upon one another. Age, personality-type and the nature of the presenting problem are all taken into consideration in the composition of a group. Groups are provided with a variety of materials, which they can use freely in a permissive environment. The group therapist assumes a neutral role, though he is not always passive. Slavson describes the aim of activity group therapy as the provision of spontaneous discharge of drives, lessening of tension and reduction of anxiety through physical and emotional activity in an atmosphere which encourages free interaction with other children. Interview group therapy is considered appropriate for adolescents. In interview groups, the presence of others with similar problems is supportive and encourages the member to speak freely. Adolescents, in Slavson's experience, make ready contact with one another in this situation, and once their defences are broken down, they easily talk about personal problems.

These techniques and others are discussed by Foulkes and Anthony (1965), who emphasise the importance of the verbal expression of feelings but recommend the use of play and activity to encourage verbalisation in younger children, and by Mhas (1970). It is not suggested here that group therapy is ever a complete substitute for individual treatment and it must be recognised that there are certain types of disturbed children who cannot fit into any group, and who would not benefit from group therapy. The educational psychologist does not normally undertake intensive individual psychotherapy with children, but much of his work with children and parents has therapeutic aims and involves a knowledge of therapeutic skills. With appropriate training, the educational psychologist can make a contribution to the development of group techniques of treatment.

Behaviour therapy

Although what are known as 'behaviour therapy' techniques are not yet widely practised in this country, they seem to a growing number of psychologists to offer scientifically valid ways of treating behaviour problems, being based on a sounder foundation of psychological theory than 'psychotherapeutic' techniques. Behaviour therapy covers a large variety of techniques designed to modify maladjusted behaviour; for a comprehensive review of these approaches and the principles underlying them, see Eysenck and Rachman (1965), Meyer and Chesser (1970), Bandura (1969) or Woody (1969).

Essentially, behaviour therapy relates to approaches based on experimental psychology and especially learning theory since Pavlov. The most frequently used approaches include positive reinforcement, negative reinforcement and social modelling.

In emphasising positive reinforcement techniques, which seem to be more effective in modifying behaviour than negative reinforcement approaches as well as more pleasant to use (Woody, 1969), unacceptable or undesirable behaviour is ignored, while desirable or approved responses are reinforced in a positive way. Positive reinforcement may take the form of concrete rewards, appropriate mainly for younger children, or social approval, based mainly on verbal conditioning. Attention needs to be given in using reinforcement to the timing and consistency of rewards or punishment.

On the basis of the work of Wolpe (1958), positive approaches have been developed to the reduction of anxiety in children using the principle of reciprocal inhibition: the aim is to encourage anxious children to behave in ways that are not compatible with anxiety. In particular, assertive responses may be encouraged in an inhibited child through direct training or simulation exercises, or relaxed responses may be evoked through systematic desensitisation. In the latter approach, the child is exposed, in as relaxed conditions as possible, to the anxiety-provoking situation to only a small degree. As the child learns to cope with the situation without undue anxiety, he is gradually exposed to stimuli originally arousing greater anxiety. For example, a child with school phobia will show extreme anxiety at the thought of going to school. He may, however, be willing to participate in a school-like situation at a child guidance clinic, remedial education centre, or tutorial unit. Later, he may be able to go to school for a short time after normal school hours; still later, he may attend school on a part-time basis; and eventually he may be able to attend school on a normal full-time basis. Clearly these graded steps will need to be planned very carefully, and the psychologist will have to undertake much liaison work with the child, his parents and the school in making the necessary arrangements.

Negative reinforcement involves the administration of an unpleasant stimulus when unacceptable or undesirable behaviour occurs, with the aim of forcing the individual to avoid the pain or discomfort by giving up this kind of behaviour. There has been little use in child guidance of such aversive stimuli as emetic drugs or electric shock, though the former method may be employed in serious cases of drug addiction in adolescents. In so far as aversive control is used at all in behaviour modification programmes for children, the techniques consist mainly of the withdrawal of rewards and privileges, or temporary removal from pleasurable situations.

Social modelling techniques have been developed by Bandura and his colleagues (Bandura and Walters, 1963; Bandura, 1969). The principle underlying these techniques is that behaviour can be changed and shaped by exposure to the behaviour of a social model. The techniques used to provide behaviour patterns for modelling include films and video-tapes, live demonstrations, or reading about the specific behaviour of others. Usually the modelled experiences are given in a hierarchical progression, ranging from behaviour which is only slightly different from the individual's usual behaviour to that which is very different.

Another technique of behaviour therapy which is sometimes used is negative practice or behavioural satiation. The principle underlying this method is that a response will be extinguished if repeated often enough, deliberately and under the control of the therapist. Negative practice has been found useful by some therapists in treating undesirable habits such as stammering or tics (Dunlap, 1932; Lehner, 1960) and obsessive-compulsive disorders (Eysenck and Rachman, 1965), However, according to Woody (1969) the technique has not yet been sufficiently widely used to assess its value.

Behaviour therapy, or to use the wider term, behaviour modification, techniques may be used both in the clinical setting and in the school situation. Behaviour therapy approaches in the clinical situation have been reported, for example, by Wahler et al. (1965), Patterson et al. (1967), Engeln et al. (1968), and Fischer (1968). These approaches have involved the precise identification of the variables functioning to maintain deviant behaviour and the systematic elimination of these variables in order to modify the deviant behaviour. In some cases, the parents as well as other members of the family have been involved in the treatment programme in addition to the child initially referred. Behaviour modification techniques have also been developed, mainly in the USA, in the school situation. The main aim of these techniques is to bring the overt behaviour of the child in line with standards required for learning in the classroom (Hewett, 1967). These standards may include the development of an adequate attention span; orderly response in the classroom; the ability to follow directions; tolerance for limits of time, space and activity; and appreciation of social approval and avoidance of disapproval. Hewett describes the kind of physical environment which is needed for this approach, and also the hierarchy of educational tasks which need to be mastered and the planning of interventions required to achieve the aims of the programme. Other American writers who have made a contribution to the development of behaviour modification techniques relevant to the school situation include Ullman and Krasner (1965); Whelan (1966); Dupont (1969), and Meacham and Wiesen (1969). In this country, Ward (1971) has reported pilot experiments based on the work of Becker et al. (1967); he discusses the benefits to be derived from using behavioural modification techniques in the classroom as well as highlighting some of the difficulties of using these techniques with teachers. As Ward states, the procedure typically employed involves the precise identification of the behaviour to be brought under control; a sequence of direct observations and the recording of baseline frequencies for the behaviour and associated reinforcement contingencies; practical advice to the teacher on extinction and shaping methods of behaviour modification; and periodic follow-up using further periods of direct observation. On the basis of the experiments reported, Ward stresses that the communicating of advice is a particularly demanding part of the programme, and that much time may be required to support a teacher over extinction and shaping programmes: unless the teacher is able to follow advice consistently, an attempt to introduce a systematic behaviour modification programme may result in considerable confusion for both teacher and children. In school psychological service work, therefore, it is important to proceed with care in the use of behaviour modification techniques, though, with adequate organisation, preparation and motivation, they can be effective.

Remedial education
Remedial measures for educationally retarded children, and the often-found association between retardation and maladjustment, have been discussed in chapters 2 and 9. Research on the link between reading difficulties and maladjustment is reviewed by Chazan (1969) and Yule (1969), and as previously mentioned, the specific problems involved in the treatment of maladjusted children with reading difficulties are considered by D. J. Williams (1969). Although in the treatment of some maladjusted children, it is advisable not to put any emphasis on scholastic learning, there is no doubt that in many cases of maladjustment a general improvement in emotional state is effected by a feeling of achievement in the basic school subjects, especially in reading. Wherever possible, therefore, attention to educational deficits serious enough to cause difficulties should be included in the treatment programme.

Changing the home environment
In cases where the home environment is contributing to maladjustment in the child, an attempt should be made, whenever possible, to modify this environment without taking the radical step of removing the child from it. Removal of a child from his natural environment should always be regarded as a last resort. Even when the home appears to be a very unsatisfactory one, it often proves that any alternative placement available for the child is even more unsatisfactory from the child's point of view. The importance of intensive work with the parents, mentioned above, is thus underlined here. In some instances, where the family are living in gross conditions of overcrowding or in accommodation unsatisfactory in other ways, rehousing of the family may be necessary before results can be expected from psychological treatment. (See p. 65)

There are cases, however, where it seems essential to remove a maladjusted child, temporarily or permanently, from his normal home background. This may be done through the placement of the child in the care of the local authority, or through arranging for the child to spend a period in a residential school or hostel. It should not be assumed that changing the home environment necessarily removes the child's maladjustment, and the change has to be made very carefully and with consideration of the child's feelings. Unless the child is too young, he should be fully informed of what is taking place and, in simple terms, the reasons for the move. Unless this is done, additional insecurity and disturbance may be caused. It is also important for the child guidance service to maintain contact with the child, at least until he is well settled in his new environment and possibly for a period thereafter.

Changing the school environment
In some cases, a maladjusted child can be helped by a modification of the school environment. As with an unsatisfactory home background, it is desirable to attempt, without removing the child, to modify a school environment which is not meeting the child's needs. It must be recognised that most maladjusted children will remain in their usual school, and that placement in a special school, class or unit will be possible, and indeed desirable, in only a very small proportion of cases. The educational psychologist will, therefore, have to devote a considerable amount of time to liaison with schools and to building up the kind of relationship with schools which will make any attempt at modifying the school environment a joint effort, shared by the school and the psychological service, rather than something which the psychologist seeks to impose on the school.

Where it is considered that the child needs to be moved from his normal school, a variety of possibilities exist, though special educational facilities for maladjusted pupils are still not well developed in some authorities (see chapter 2). It may be that a change to another ordinary school may give the maladjusted child the chance to make a fresh start; or that a transfer to a less demanding school life, such as is found in schools for the ESN or delicate children, may be appropriate. Considerable flexibility of approach is needed in considering the best educational placement for maladjusted pupils, particularly in areas where there is limited specific provision for these children.

The more serious cases of maladjustment (who do not require hospitalisation) will need placement in a special class or school, day or residential. Establishments of this kind for maladjusted pupils have performed a valuable function in containing and treating children and adolescents presenting major problems in school, at home, or in the community. Not a great deal, however, has been published about the actual methods used in special schools and classes for maladjusted pupils. A number of reports have been written on independent schools catering for disturbed children (e.g. Lenhoff, 1960; O. L. Shaw, 1966; Wills, 1960). Weaver (1968) has surveyed the treatment facilities available for maladjusted children in England, and Bridgeland (1971) has comprehensively reviewed the work of the pioneers in special education for maladjusted pupils; but still relatively little is known about the actual philosophy, aims and methods of local authority schools, which constitute the majority of the special schools for maladjusted pupils and have been recently increasing in number in many parts of the country. The Child Psychiatry Section of the Royal Medico-Psychological Association (1966) tried to obtain a picture of the work of special schools for maladjusted children in this country. A questionnaire was sent to fifteen day and forty-seven residential schools in the official list (42), and obtained replies from two-thirds of the sample. It was found that few of the teachers had special training and that not many of the schools had regular psychological or psychiatric support. The average stay at special schools was four years in spite of the fact that most of the children showed a rapid improvement in behaviour once they were placed in the special school. After-care was often unsatisfactory, and parent–child contact frequently insufficient. The report concluded that therapy was not sufficiently emphasised, and that too often placement of children in a special school was seen negatively, as removing them from an adverse environment rather than as giving them appropriate treatment. Since the report was published, many new schools for maladjusted pupils have been established.

The work of special day units is discussed in Therapeutic Education (Association of Teachers of Maladjusted Children, 1967), and Bartlett (1970) has surveyed the work of eleven such units in England and Wales. She found that these units catered mainly for cases of school refusal, educational problems and withdrawn and anxious children rather than aggressive or hyperactive pupils. Although these units are usually quite small, and are limited in scope, they perform a very useful function in enabling children who cannot easily settle down in the ordinary school to remain at home while receiving specialised attention either on a part-time or full-time basis.

The kind of investigation which is needed in order that the dynamics of the therapeutic community should be better understood has been indicated by N. Williams (1961), Petrie (1962) and Roe (1965). Williams and Petrie examined the factors related to a successful outcome to placement in a residential school for maladjusted pupils, the former emphasising the importance of improved educational attainments and attitudes and the latter stressing that improvement in parental attitudes was particularly significant. Roe suggests that not enough work is done in depth in schools for maladjusted children, where an adequate understanding of the reactions and feelings of both children and parents is often lacking.

Medication
Medication is used relatively little in the treatment of maladjusted children; in general, the pharmacological advances made in adult psychiatry

have not proved transferable to work with children (Hays, 1964). Never-theless, symptoms suggestive of brain damage may be amenable to drug therapy when other measures have no effect (D. Maclay, 1969). Even behaviour disturbances which seem to be related to 'minimal brain damage' on the basis of evidence provided by EEGs which suggest minor cerebral dysrhythmia, or by symptoms such as impaired motor coordination, restlessness or inability to concentrate, may respond to appropriate drugs (Wolff, 1969). Hyperkinetic children, in particular, may improve with medication. Campbell *et al.* (1971), for example, report an improvement in attention, response organisation and impulse control after the admini-stration of the energising drug methylphenidate to a sample of nineteen children diagnosed as 'hyperactive'. Strict criteria were adopted for admissibility to this sample.

Thus, while few maladjusted children in general will benefit from medica-tion, the educational psychologist should ensure that the possibility of drug treatment being desirable is not overlooked; whenever even slight evidence suggests that this may be the case, the child should have a specialist medical examination.

Hospitalisation

Although, when residential treatment is thought necessary for a mal-adjusted pupil, a school or hostel will usually be recommended rather than admission to hospital, severely disturbed or psychotic children and adolescents, or those with some physical disability or disorder requiring intensive medical treatment may be best placed in a hospital in-patient unit. As Warren (1971) points out, accommodation of this kind is very limited and unevenly distributed over the country, and the units vary greatly in their functions. Few are purpose-built, and some cannot take disruptive children because of their location. Accommodation for adoles-cents is particularly scarce, and little thought has been given to the ways in which 'adolescent units' should function clinically. Warren stresses the need for imaginative experiments in the psychiatric care and treatment of disturbed adolescents in the hospital setting.

Efficacy of treatment

Overall results of clinical treatment. There have been few systematic follow-up studies of maladjusted children in Britain, and we know little about how far those who show symptoms of maladjustment during childhood and adolescence are able to make a satisfactory adjustment to work, family life and society when they reach maturity. Most studies of the efficacy of treatment show that improvement follows treatment in the case of about two-thirds to three-quarters of children seen at child guidance clinics, but about the same proportion of children not receiving treatment show a similar improvement (Levitt, 1957, 1963; Eysenck, 1960b; Shepherd *et al.*, 1966). This evidence is, of course, difficult to assess, since so many different methods of approach are subsumed under the terms 'psychotherapy' or 'treatment', and it is never easy to know, in evaluation studies, to what extent untreated control groups are matched on basic variables with treated groups. Indeed, in the study by Shepherd *et al.* (1966), the most seriously disturbed children referred to clinics were excluded from the sample as unmatchable. Furthermore, ratings of 'improvement' are highly subjective and judgments made by different people using different follow-up techniques may not be comparable. Heinicke and Goldman (1960), for example, concluded, on the basis of a review of the literature on child psychotherapy research, that when compared with control groups, children who received treatment showed a significantly higher percentage of successful adjustments as opposed to partial improvements, and noted that a significant increase in the percentage of successfully adjusted children occurred after the close of treatment. Rachman (1971), too, while stressing the high spontaneous recovery rate among maladjusted children and the repeated failures to demonstrate therapeutic effects convincingly, agrees that this does not mean that all therapeutic intervention is a waste of time: the natural process of recovery may be accelerated even by brief supportive psychotherapy or other measures such as parental guidance. Children, parents and teachers often feel relief from pressure when a case is seen at a child guidance clinic; and there is also the possibility to be considered that some maladjusted children would regress without some treatment or support.

As stated above, a number of clinical workers see behaviour modification techniques as both more efficacious and offering a more controlled situation for evaluation than other current therapeutic methods. Since these techniques are varied and have been little used with children to date, it is premature to judge their effectiveness; but there is sufficient evidence to encourage psychologists to become skilled in using behaviour modification approaches with children, and also to involve others (particularly teachers) in their application (Woody, 1969; Ward, 1971).

Type of disturbance in relation to outcome. The long-term studies in the USA by D. P. Morris *et al.* (1954), H. H. Morris, Escoll and Wexler (1956), Robins and O'Neal (1958) and Robins (1966) are worthy of note, although the findings are not necessarily applicable to this country. These investigations suggest that it is the antisocial child rather than the neurotic who is in most need of help, if breakdown in adulthood is to be avoided. The prognosis for aggressive girls seems to be much worse than for boys; a larger percentage of girls become psychotic. The adjustment achieved at eighteen 'in almost every case showed little further change'.

In Britain, Wolff (1961) followed up a sample of forty-three children (twenty-four boys, nineteen girls) aged 2 years 3 months to 4 years 11 months, referred to the Maudsley Hospital. Symptoms on referral were mainly phobias, habit disorders and aggressiveness. Three to six years later, the boys had done less well than the girls, and the outcome was worse for children coming from broken or disturbed homes. Warren (1965), following up 157 adolescent in-patients six or more years after they had been discharged from a London hospital adolescent unit, found less further disturbance among the conduct disorders than the mixed neurotic and conduct disorders; nearly all those with psychotic symptoms had further illness. I. Maclay (1967) carried out a questionnaire follow-up of children who had been treated at a London hospital child guidance clinic ten to fifteen years previously. It was found that a satisfactory relationship with peers at the time of treatment was a good prognostic feature; poor prognostic features were membership of a large family, discharge to a residential school or hospital and an estimate of 'no change' or 'worse' on discharge. Children with psychosomatic disorders did well and those with psychosis and/or organic conditions did badly.

Such investigations as these are a welcome attempt to relate outcome to specific types of disturbance at the time of referral, though the some-times conflicting findings suggest that the relationship between type of disorder, treatment and outcome is a very complex one, and that sex and age at referral are likely to be important factors apart from other variables. All the studies show that children and adolescents presenting psychotic disorders show a poor prognosis and that many are resistant to clinical treatment, whatever methods are tried (see also Eisenberg, 1957, and Rutter, 1965), though Sands (1956), following up discharged adolescent psychotic patients from a mental hospital, found that depressives did much better than psychotics whose illness was associated with epilepsy or other organic conditions. As Rachman (1971) stresses, the most helpful course to take with psychotic children at present is to provide them with suitable psychological, educational and social facilities, as exemplified by the recent development of special educational units for autistic and other severely disturbed children in a number of regions (Furneaux, 1969) in addition to in-patient units for those who need to be contained in hospital.

Role of educational psychologist in evaluation of treatment
It is desirable that school psychological services and child guidance clinics should attempt to evaluate their own diagnostic and treatment procedures by a systematic long-term follow-up of at least a sample of the cases seen. The educational psychologist, with his training in research methods, can contribute much to our knowledge about the response of particular types of disturbance to particular approaches to treatment. Even if practice

varies from place to place, reports on the short-term and long-term effects of treatment will help to add to the very scanty knowledge on this subject.

Juvenile delinquency

Much of what has been written above about maladjustment also applies to juvenile delinquency. However, a vast body of literature now exists specifically dealing with the problems of delinquency, and a brief summary of the main trends in research and treatment follows, highlighting references of particular interest to the educational psychologist, who will normally see a considerable number of children and adolescents referred by magistrates anxious for advice about the best methods of treating individual young offenders.

The size of the problem

As West (1967) points out, deductions from official statistics on delinquency and crime have to be made with great caution, since there are many difficulties in the way of compiling accurate records. However, some idea of the extent of the problem of juvenile delinquency may be gained from the annual figures provided by the Home Office. In the year 1970, for example, 1·5 per cent of males, 0·20 per cent of females under fourteen years of age were found guilty of offences, either 'indictable' (more serious) or 'non-indictable'. In the age group fourteen to sixteen years (inclusive), 8·66 per cent of males, 0·77 per cent of females committed an offence (Home Office, 1971). To these officially-recognised delinquents can be added those juveniles who were cautioned by the police but not prosecuted: in the under fourteen age-group, such cautions are almost as frequent for males as prosecutions, and more frequent for females.

Looking at this problem longitudinally, a national study of a representative sample of children born in one week in March 1946 found that 14·6 per cent of the boys and about 2 per cent of the girls committed an offence by the time they were seventeen (Mulligan et al., 1963; Douglas et al., 1968). Of these, 10·4 per cent of boys, 1 per cent of girls committed indictable offences; 4 per cent of boys, 0·03 per cent of girls committed two or more offences (this group constitutes the repeaters or recidivists who give much cause for concern, as these are the adolescents who tend to find their way to Borstal or prison, with little chance of settling down to a non-criminal life). It is not clear why the delinquency rate among males is so much higher than among females. Differences between the sexes in aggressiveness and in strength have been postulated as possible explanations, as have the differences in opportunity to commit offences and the greater tendency of males to belong to gangs; but no entirely convincing explanation has been forthcoming.

The delinquency rates quoted above must be looked at in the light of the fact that in many cases of delinquency the offender is not detected (West, 1967). Particularly in the case of the younger children, the victim is unwilling to prosecute, and, with the growth of the social and psychological services, informal action is often taken in preference to legal action.

The nature of juvenile delinquency

Most of the offences committed by boys under seventeen consist of stealing or breaking and entering. Theft is also the most common offence committed by girls, but in later adolescence a different pattern emerges (Walker, 1965): young males turn from stealing to casual violence, females tend to come to the notice of police or social workers through associations of a sexual kind and being in need of 'care, protection or control'.

The peak period for male juvenile delinquency has in the past tended to be in the last year of compulsory school. When the school leaving age was fourteen the peak age for delinquency was 13 to 14; with the raising of the school leaving age to fifteen, the peak period for delinquency (or at least for indictable offences) became 14 to 15. It is difficult to say whether this association between delinquency rate and school leaving age has any definite significance. Among female offenders, the peak age has fallen from 19 in 1938 to 14+years.

Explanations of delinquency

Since Burt's classic study, *The Young Delinquent*, published in 1925, many studies have been carried out in order to throw light on the causes of delinquency. Yet there is still no generally-accepted explanation of delinquency. Wootton (1959), reviewing the literature up to that date, concluded that even the best studies had produced 'only the most meagre and dubiously supported, generalisations'. Wilkins (1963), too, commented that 'almost all features of life itself' had been put forward as explanations for juvenile delinquency, and that for every theory concerning the causes of delinquency a contradictory theory had been offered with equal conviction.

Apart from the heterogeneous nature of the individuals labelled as delinquents, and the difficulties inherent in assessing such factors as 'parental attitudes' or 'discipline', there has been a marked tendency for investigators to overstress particular approaches. In particular, a widening gap has been created between 'psychological' approaches, stressing individual characteristics, and 'sociological' approaches, stressing the role of the subculture in creating delinquent patterns of behaviour.

Examples of psychological theories about delinquency are those put forward by Eysenck (1964) and Friedlander (1947), themselves widely differing. Eysenck hypothesises that criminality is closely associated with a combination of characteristics predominantly determined by heredity. In his view, offenders are extraverted and are not easily conditioned; they also tend to be emotionally unstable and of mesomorphic physique (not fat, heavily muscled, broad-shouldered, and relatively narrow-hipped). Friedlander, using a psychoanalytic approach, emphasised that antisocial character was formed by factors operating mainly in infancy, particularly in relation to mother–child interaction. Bowlby (1952) has also stressed the importance of the maternal relationship with the young child, high-lighting the damage that can be caused to character development by maternal deprivation (see p. 226). Andry (1960) has drawn attention to the role of the father in the causation of delinquency in boys. On the basis of a comparison between eighty working-class delinquent boys aged twelve to fifteen, and a matched control group of eighty non-delinquent boys from London 'delinquency areas', he found that it was the inadequacies in the fathers rather than in the mothers which served to differentiate delinquents from non-delinquents. The delinquents tended to experience less adequate training from their fathers and to identify less with them than did the non-delinquents. The fathers of the delinquents had less adequate communication with their sons, shared their leisure time less with them, and showed less leadership than the fathers of the non-delinquent controls.

Sociological theories view delinquency as mainly caused by an environment which encourages criminal behaviour, 'the environment' referring largely to the home background, immediate neighbourhood, or wider subculture. They have also tended to stress that delinquency is often a reaction against conventional middle-class standards by the under-privileged members of society. It will not be possible to discuss these theories adequately here, but the major contributions will be mentioned briefly, especially as it is essential for the educational psychologist to understand the social context in which the children referred to him are functioning.

According to Durkheim (1939), crime itself should be viewed as a normal social phenomenon, though it flourishes in an atmosphere of anomie—a state of society in which age-old traditions and restraints have largely broken down. E. H. Sutherland (1960), too, considered that crime is inevitable in modern society. He developed the theory of 'differential association', hypothesising that the greater the opportunity an individual had for contact with criminal behaviour, the more likely he was to become delinquent himself. Merton (1957), developing Durkheim's concept of anomie and writing in an American context, viewed delinquency as predominantly the response of the lower classes to frustration. The under-privileged, seeing achievement and affluence denied to them, react by delinquent behaviour. A. Cohen (1955), too, hypothesises that lower-class boys seek compensation for their feelings of inadequacy and inferiority through membership of anti-social gangs, which gain satisfaction not so much through material gain as through causing 'society' a good deal of trouble by their negative and hostile reactions. W. B. Miller (1958), however, puts more emphasis on delinquent behaviour being more or less a natural part of life in lower-class areas than on frustration relating to status, a view similar to that of Mays (1954), who sees delinquency in the British context not so much as a symptom of maladjustment as of adjustment to a subculture very different from the dominant culture: for those who grow up in a delinquent subculture, it is very difficult not to commit an offence at some time or other.

The study of delinquent subcultures has been developed further by Cloward and Ohlin (1961) and Yablonsky (1962). Cloward and Ohlin suggest that the type and success of protests against middle-class values depend upon the opportunities offered for deviant behaviour by each subculture. Some localities encourage 'criminal' behaviour, some give opportunities rather for violence—the 'conflict' subcultures—and other localities, providing a 'retreatist' subculture, become the focal points for the gathering of failures and dropouts. Yablonsky, on the basis of a survey of aggressive gangs in New York, views the modern gang as a collection of inadequate, aimless failures rather than as cohesive groups of social protesters. Matza (1964), too, considers that the view of delinquents as opponents of society is a somewhat exaggerated one: they lapse from rather than oppose the accepted norms of morality. Making a study of delinquency in the east end of London, Downes (1966) concludes that there is little evidence to suggest that the theories of Cohen or Cloward and Ohlin provide valid explanations of delinquency in Britain. Juvenile gangs here lack coherent formal structure, and little opportunity exists for such gangs to become organised and well-established. Nevertheless, as Mays (1970) points out, social changes take place rapidly, and there are signs that organised adult criminal gangs are on the increase in Britain, though the relationship between adult gangs and gangs of young offenders is still not precisely known.

There is clearly a need, in the study of delinquency and its practical applications, for a synthesis between psychological and sociological approaches. Stott (1960a) points out that the disciplines of sociology and psychology tend to offer self-contained explanations of delinquency which are often considered to conflict with one another, but only by psychological investigation can variations of behaviour within culturally homogeneous groups be explained, and only through sociological approaches can the interaction between the individual and his cultural setting be fully understood.

Trasler (1962, 1970) suggests a possibly fruitful synthesis of various approaches. He sees delinquency as a partial failure of socialisation, dependent first, on the quality of the relationship between the child and his parents, and secondly, on the consistency of parental sanctions. Differences in delinquency rates between children from 'middle-class' homes and those from 'working-class' families relate to the differences between the classes in methods of socialisation. In the middle-class home, there is a long dependence on the parents, with 'love-oriented' discipline, while in the working-class home children rely from an early age on peers for social training, leading to great sensitivity to group pressures and group disapproval. The nature of the verbal interchange between parent and child when behaviour is corrected is particularly important, the use of a limited number of general concepts being more effective in socialisation than punishing offences with little or no explanation. Trasler also considers that further research into the relationship of individual personality variables (such as extroversion) and delinquency, already begun by Eysenck (1964), is desirable, and that this line of approach can be linked to ongoing work on social influences in the causation of delinquency.

Walker (1965) suggests that psychoanalytic theories more frequently seem to explain the more 'abnormal' or irrational type of offence, such as stealing objects of no value, sexual offences and sexual deviation, while the learning theory approach seems to explain delinquency of a more rational kind.

Intellectual level

Delinquents tend to come predominantly from the population with IQs below the general mean, but not excessively so, the average IQs of delinquent groups studies ranging from about 87–90 (Woodward, 1955; Eilenberg, 1961). This seems to be largely because they come from disadvantaged home and school backgrounds and larger families: below average intelligence as such does not seem to be an important factor in producing criminal behaviour or even, as popularly supposed, in the chances of getting caught. Nevertheless, ESN or severely subnormal children may get into trouble because they are easily led or do not foresee the consequences of their actions (T. Ferguson, 1952).

School attainment

Even though there is little difference in measured IQ between delinquents and matched groups of non-delinquents, delinquents show much more educational retardation (Wootton, 1959). Offenders tend to have poor school records and low basic attainments, to dislike school, and to be unpopular with their teachers. In some cases, the retardation is mainly due to dislike of school and missed schooling (truancy is often associated with delinquency); in others, educational failure and feelings of inferiority related to poor school progress may lead to delinquent behaviour, through which the backward pupil may feel some sense of achievement and win some approval from his contemporaries. In most cases, the retardation is remediable, if suitable help is available.

Emotional disturbance

As previously stated, delinquency is viewed by some as essentially 'normal' behaviour viewed in its social context. Several studies, however, have found a high degree of emotional disturbance among juvenile delinquents. Stott (1961) investigated the type and amount of general behaviour disturbance among first-time male probationers under fifteen in Glasgow during one year—415 in all, with a control group selected from the same schools as the delinquents. He found that the delinquents were much more prone to behaviour disturbance than the non-delinquent controls. Contrary to theories of cultural delinquency, the probationers in high delinquency areas were just as maladjusted as those in 'good areas', but the non-delinquents were considerably less well adjusted the greater the density of delinquency in their area. Stott suggests that certain neighbourhoods offer an unfavourable ecology to a proportion of their youthful inhabitants, which results in a higher incidence of physical, mental and emotional maldevelopment: the greater frequency of behaviour disturbance, including delinquency, is one aspect of this.

Ivy Bennett (1960), in a detailed comparative study of fifty delinquent children and fifty neurotic children (matched for age and intelligence) under treatment in a rural English child guidance service, found that certain kinds of behaviour commonly regarded as being typical of either neurotic or delinquent children were found equally in both groups. In particular, each group contained a considerable number of children who were unsociable, lacking relationships with others, retarded in attainment, and poorly adjusted to school life. Both groups had persistent nervous habits to roughly the same extent and the delinquent children showed as many disturbances of feeding, sleep, speech and bladder or bowel control as did the neurotic children. There were a number of differences in the backgrounds of the two groups. Delinquents, for example, tended to come from broken or unstable homes and to have parents with antisocial tendencies; neurotic children tended to come from homes with an unbroken family circle, but upset by psychological disturbances, with the parents showing neurotic tendencies. The delinquent children tended to belong to larger families. However, both groups showed character traits commonly associated with delinquent behaviour—irresponsibility, a lack of persistence, feelings of rejection, temper outbursts and precocious sexual behaviour.

This investigation was very thorough and combined both case study and statistical approaches, but the delinquents studied cannot be regarded as typical of delinquents in general, living as they did in an area containing little industrialisation. Furthermore, although an attempt was made to select delinquents without neurotic motivation, they had all been referred for investigation at a child guidance clinic.

Douglas *et al.* (1968) found the delinquent boys in their national sample to be badly behaved in school and to be prone to truancy. They tended to be seen by their teachers as aggressive or both nervous and aggressive, and by themselves as anxious. Both at ages thirteen and fifteen the delinquents were significantly less well adjusted than the non-delinquents in the sample. 'Repeaters' showed a higher incidence of maladjustment than those who had committed only one offence (Mulligan *et al.*, 1963).

The above studies indicate that, while a proportion of delinquents do not show any signs of emotional disturbance, no clear dividing-line can be drawn between delinquency and emotional maladjustment.

Physical health

Little evidence exists to show that delinquents are characterized by poor health. In a small number of cases, delinquency may be the result of illnesses such as encephalitis or meningitis, or a consequence of epilepsy. Gittins (1952) found that the stamina of his approved school boys was remarkable, and that gross physical defect was rare. However, he observed that minor infections, skin disease and running ears were quite common in new entrants and inevitably added to the irritating influences on the boys.

Home background

A vast number of studies have been made on the home background of delinquents, and the discussion above of explanations of delinquency has shown that many theorists consider the home environment to play a major part in the causation of delinquency.

It is well established that delinquency tends to be mainly concentrated in particular areas, chiefly in the slum areas of large cities, where low income groups predominate, but also more recently in some of the newer housing estates, which often lack adequate social amenities (Shaw and McKay, 1942; T. P. Morris, 1957; McDonald, 1969). There are streets in which practically every household has at least one child who is a recognized delinquent. However, even in the 'delinquency areas', juvenile delinquents tend to come most frequently from homes with squalid standards—'problem families' socially isolated and failing to teach the children how to control their impulses effectively enough to keep out of trouble (Sprott, 1954; Wilson, 1962).

Douglas *et al.* (1966) have found that there were considerable social class differences in the incidence of delinquency in the National Survey of Health and Development, especially in the case of 'repeaters'. The 'lower manual' working class stood out as having the highest incidence, about seven times that of the 'upper middle class'. However, other studies have suggested a more even distribution of delinquency over the social classes (Little and Ntsekhe, 1959; Palmai et al., 1967), and West (1967) considers that the class bias of young offenders has become less extreme in recent years.

Within the family, apart from poor material conditions, the most significant factors would seem to be (T. Ferguson, 1952; McCord and Mc-Cord, 1959; Glueck and Glueck, 1962):

neglect or cruelty on the part of the parents;
absence of a parent (e.g. through death, divorce or separation);
inconsistent or extreme discipline, especially on the part of the father;
the provision of a criminal model by the parents;
the failure of the parents to teach adequate standards of behaviour; and
size of family: delinquents tend to come from families of four to six children, as compared with three in control groups of non-delinquent children matched for social class.

School background
Phillipson (1971) asserts that the relationship between patterns of delinquency and structural differences within the educational system has been a neglected field of study: it has been too readily assumed in sociological studies that all schools mediate a common value system. That some schools may be successful in protecting children from delinquency, even though they live in delinquency areas, has been suggested by enquiries in the London borough of Tower Hamlets, which showed that delinquency rates varied widely, from 0·9 per cent to 19 per cent of boys between eleven and fourteen years of age, in different schools serving the same kind of social areas (Power et al., 1967). Why this should be the case remains to be investigated, but it is probable that the differential delinquency rate is related to the amenities of the school, the quality of teacher–pupil interaction, the tone of the school, and its success in adapting the curriculum and organisation to the needs of the socially disadvantaged pupils (Hargreaves, 1967; Phillipson, 1971). Further, Phillipson has found that the level of information about delinquency possessed by teachers tends to be low; they know little about the actual prevalence and character of delinquency within the community in which they teach, or even within their own school. As a result, they tend to accept that they are working in a 'normal' situation, about which little can be done; few teachers see the school as playing a part in reducing the patterns of delinquency in any way. There is, too, often too little liaison between the school and those agencies which have external responsibility for delinquency.

Treatment
Official reports and white papers over the past decade (Ingleby Report, 1960; Kilbrandon Report (applying to Scotland) 1964; *The Child, the Family and the Young Offender*, 1965; *Children in Trouble*, Home Office, 1968b), culminating in the Children and Young Persons Act 1969, have laid stress on preventing deprived and delinquent children and young people from becoming inadequate or criminal adults. More responsibility has been given to social agencies and less to the courts, in an attempt to provide parents with help and support and to make available a more varied, flexible and constructive range of facilities for young offenders. Court proceedings are seen only as a last resort, and regular consultation between magistrates, police, social workers and teachers is being encouraged. The age of criminal responsibility is gradually to be raised, but at present children of 10+ remain liable to criminal proceedings.

The procedures for treating young people are currently undergoing considerable change, but the following possibilities are either available or envisaged if a child is brought forward officially as a delinquent (of course, many delinquents are cautioned by the police, or receive help from social workers or the child guidance service, without being taken to court):

Care proceedings
1. parents bound over (help from social services being possible);
2. hospital or guardianship order (under the Mental Health Act);
3. placement of child in care of local authority (often leading to placement in a 'community home');
4. supervision order, with or without intermediate treatment (the child normally remaining at home).

Criminal proceedings
Possibilities as above, plus:
1. absolute or conditional discharge;
2. fine of up to £50;
3. payment of damages or compensation;
4. order to attend 'attendance centre' on Saturday afternoons;
5. placement in detention centre (for 3 to 6 months);
6. committal to Borstal (mainly for boys between 15 and 21, and only by higher courts).

Intermediate treatment (see Department of Health and Security, 1972b)
1. attendance (evenings, weekend afternoons, or weekends) at a place for training, treatment or recreation;
2. participation in a social service or adventure training project;

3. residence for no more than three months in a Home, hostel or with relatives.

Placement in a community home
A single system of 'community homes' to replace local authority homes, hostels, remand homes and approved schools is being planned by specially established regional planning committees.

Mays (1970) considers that the new emphasis on the guidance and discipline of children 'at risk' at the earliest possible stage is wise social policy, and he welcomes the growing awareness that this is mainly an educational problem. It is particularly important, in his view, that delinquents should not be stigmatised as criminals, that nothing should be done to encourage the growth of an antisocial self-image, and that peer group associations which promote delinquent activities should be broken down. The development of counselling in ordinary schools, linking youth work with the formal educational system, and improved vocational guidance services will all help to support the new trends in child care treatment. Institutional treament of any kind cannot expect to succeed unless there is an adequate after-care service.

West (1967) stresses that the situations leading to delinquency are so complex that approaches to delinquency control and prevention must be varied. No measures will result in the complete eradication of delinquent acts, but more positive social measures, improved educational methods and facilities (especially for disadvantaged children), and trying to reach the 'unclubbable' youth will all help to reduce the incidence of juvenile delinquency.

Although there have been a number of attempts to use psychotherapeutic methods with delinquents, and to make institutions for offenders more like therapeutic communities than penal establishments (Aichhorn, 1925; Polsky, 1962; D. Miller, 1964), these attempts have generally met with a good deal of resistance, both on the part of the delinquents themselves and often on the part of the staff of the institutions (Wills, 1971); and it is indeed much more difficult to use psychotherapeutic techniques in a penal context than in freer situations.

Eysenck (1964) advocates experiments using a combination of drug treatment and behaviour therapy techniques in the treatment of delinquents. He hypothesises that delinquents have inherited a central nervous system which conditions poorly, as well as an autonomic nervous system which tends to overreact, and suggests that the central nervous system can be directly influenced by the use of appropriate drugs. Since, in Eysenck's view, appropriate drugs can move a person's position in the introverted or extraverted direction, delinquents can be made more introverted than they usually are and thus more responsive to conditioning. As West (1967) points out, many people are hostile to such an approach because it may involve a manipulation of people against their will, but experiments with behaviour therapy seem, in our present state of ignorance about effective ways of dealing with delinquency, well justified.

Efficacy of treatment
It has been shown that considerable changes have been taking place in the treatment of delinquency, but it is doubtful whether these changes have occurred through the impact of scientific evidence on the efficacy of various methods of treatment (European Committee on Crime Problems, 1967). In general, the aims and strategies of research have been unsatisfactory, so the results obtained cannot be accepted with great confidence (Wootton 1959). Lodge (1967) points out that there is no indication that, for a particular offender, one means of disposal is likely to be more successful than another. It would seem that the characteristics of the offender, of his offence and personal background are better predictors of the likelihood of reconviction than anything to do with the treatment or disposal methods used. Although a high proportion of juvenile delinquents, found guilty once, do not commit further offences, this is hardly related to any specific measures of treatment; and the problem of recidivism has not yet been solved. As Lodge states, there is a need to define types of treatment as well as types of offender and to examine the interaction between offenders and treatments of the different types.

Prevention of maladjustment and delinquency

The importance of giving children a good start to life, the desirability of dealing with problems at as early a stage as possible, and the disappointing results obtained from the treatment of maladjusted or delinquent children all lend support to the view that increased resources should be devoted to the prevention of problem behaviour. There is growing evidence to suggest that children do not necessarily outgrow early behaviour problems (Macfarlane et al., 1954; Westman et al., 1967), and that both nursery and infant school teachers can help in the detection of emotional problems likely to be of long-term significance. That many children are 'at risk' because of the conditions in which they live, has been illustrated for example, by West (1969), who, in a longitudinal study of 411 boys from the ages of eight to nine years, found that poor social level (as indicated by the criteria of low income, poor housing, large families and dependence on support from welfare agencies) proved to be the most important single factor in discriminating the poorly behaved boys and the ineffectual parents from their peers and neighbours.

Prevention will be helped by the allocation of more resources of all kinds to areas containing a high proportion of disadvantaged families, including the wider provision of nursery schools and recreational facilities for young children. Measures to which the educational psychologist can make a major contribution include the screening of 'at risk' populations at the preschool and infant school stages, hopefully leading to early treatment where appropriate, the provision of guidance and support for parents and teachers and the initiation of other kinds of action which may seem necessary to meet ascertained needs (Chazan, 1971). The need for a comprehensive and imaginative approach to schemes of prevention is illustrated by the relative lack of success recorded in a number of programmes which have been put into operation to reduce delinquency. For example, in the well-known Cambridge-Somerville Youth Study (McCord and McCord, 1959) it was found that providing special help to 250 boys with high delinquency potential did not reduce the delinquency rate in that group as compared with a matched control group which received no extra help other than that routinely provided. The boys were eleven years old when the programme started, and it is possible that this is a rather late stage for effective measures to be put into operation for the first time. Similar results were reported by Hodges and Tait (1965) in Washington and Craig and Furst (1965) in New York City.

Prediction instruments to assist in the selection of children with high delinquency potential have been designed by Sheldon and Eleanor Glueck (1950, 1964) in America, and by Mannheim and Wilkins (1955) and Stott (1960b) in Britain. The validity of such instruments has yet to be established, and they tend to pick out a high proportion of children who will not become delinquent as well as those who will become offenders, but they merit use in longitudinal studies.

Part Four

Communication

In this part of the book, three chapters are devoted to questions of communication. It is easy for members of any profession to try to communicate with technical terms which have little meaning for persons with different backgrounds and different experiences. For any profession this is thoughtless: for psychologists, who recognize the importance of clear comprehension and who have studied the factors affecting it, it is unforgivable. So Chapter 12 discusses the principles of reporting findings intelligibly and sensibly.

Good reporting is an important condition for good communication. The existence of good relationships is another. Chapter 13 alerts the educational psychologist to some of the pitfalls which should be avoided and the positive steps to be taken in order to foster good relationships with colleagues in related fields.

In Chapter 14, the last of these three chapters, we present material which will illustrate and stimulate consideration of some of the points made in Chapters 12 and 13 and also earlier in the book. This is done largely through the use of case studies.

12

Reporting findings

This is an area of work in which the educational psychologist uses his psychological skill and knowledge to the full. It is also an area of work of considerable importance, to which psychologists give a large proportion of their time. The Summerfield report (Department of Education and Science, 1968b) contains an analysis of time spent by psychologists in different parts of their work. The time spent on reporting findings is given below (see also the summary in Table 1.1):

Table 12.1   Time spent on reporting findings

% of total no. of ed. psychologists	Activity	% of working time spent on activity
50	Report writing	6 to 10
33·3	Report writing	15+
50	Discussing individual children with teachers	6 to 10
33·3	Discussing findings with others	6 to 10
50	Discussing other questions with teachers	up to 5

All told, the majority seemed to spend at least a quarter of their working time in reporting findings to others, and some spent more. No matter how skilled a psychologist is in assessment and observation, or how learned he is in his knowledge of the reasons for children's behavioural problems, this is of no use unless he can communicate that knowledge to different people; it is, therefore, important at the outset to keep in mind the purpose of reporting.

Three kinds of reporting

1. Some reporting can be mainly concerned with passing on information

to other people so that they know what is happening, or what has been recommended. They may not need the full details immediately, but they require the basic facts so that, should a situation arise in which they are actively involved with a child, they know that he has been seen by the psychologist, and will seek further information if this is desirable. In some cases the information is necessary because administrative arrangements have to be made, e.g. information passed to the Education Office about the placement of a child in a special unit enables the Department's Officer to make the necessary arrangements for transport. This type of information is very basic; usually it consists of a short summary of what is intended, or what has been done, and is written in non-technical language.

2. Another area of reporting has a different purpose: that of keeping a complete record or store of information. This reporting may be in considerable detail. Usually it is not written for general circulation, but for staff closely concerned, or for the person who has responsibility for the child. This kind of information is mainly kept in files; frequently it is handwritten.

3. A third form of reporting is undertaken in order that someone else can more effectively treat or help the child. The aim here is to effect a change in handling the situation. Such reporting may be made to a parent, to a teacher, to other professional workers, or sometimes even to the pupil concerned. This presents problems of understanding the personality of the person with whom one is communicating, understanding the training and experience which that person has, and formulating the information in such a way that it can be understood and used effectively. It is in this area of reporting, above all others, that psychological skill and experience are most valuable, and one very important factor is the range of people to whom the psychologist may wish to communicate.

Some general considerations

Before we look at the range of recipients, two aspects of psychological science should be borne in mind.

Psychologists are used to thinking in terms of probability; they know, for example, that a test score has a degree of error, and what the probability is that a score is a reliable one. They appreciate that prediction is also to be expressed in these terms, so that a pupil with a quotient of 120 on a Moray House Verbal Test has a higher probability of achieving five good 'O' levels than one with a score of 100.

People not trained in this way tend to think in causal terms. Even those with some training in simple science may not be conversant with the concept of probability, and are inclined to think in the terms of nineteenth-century physics. They consider that there is a causal, and therefore certain, relationship between IQ and performance: some parents ask psychologists to assess a child's potentiality so that they can plan ahead. The psychologist needs to present findings stressing the probabilities of the situation. As many adults are used to life assurance which is based on probability thinking this is often a useful source for an analogy.

A further characteristic of psychological thinking is multiple causation rather than single causation. Parents are used to medical situations— tuberculosis is caused by a germ which can be destroyed, and hence a complete cure effected. Most psychological conditions are unlike this; they are the result of several influences. The retardation of a child in an ESN school is rarely caused by one simple factor such as dullness, but at least two or three major factors—adverse environmental circumstances, low ability, emotional difficulties may each play a part. It is frequently necessary to draw attention to this situation; even psychologists are not immune to the pitfalls of oversimplification, attaching all importance to emotional disturbance whilst neglecting the role that cognitive influences may play, and vice versa. In writing reports these two essential features of psychological science, probability thinking and multiple causation, need to be fully considered: to the man in the street and even to many professionals they are not yet understood; many still expect certain prediction and simple direct causation. The school pupil of today will have less difficulty when adult, for he meets these basic concepts in modern mathematics and in Nuffield-type science.

The most likely recipients

At the professional level psychologists send reports to psychiatrists, psychiatric social workers and social workers of the Social Services Department, head teachers, speech therapists, careers officers, school medical officers, general practitioners and consultants, education officers, educational welfare officers, probation officers and others.

Psychiatrists
Psychiatrists, especially those trained and working in child guidance, are likely to have a reasonable knowledge of most of the psychological terms which are frequently used. One of the advantages of working in a regular team is that the terms which are being used can be explained. If a psychologist is writing to a psychiatrist with whom he is not in a close working relationship then more attention may have to be given to the way in which the report is presented. It is very easy for psychologists to be so accustomed to using certain terms that they fail to appreciate that these cause difficulty for someone who is not in daily contact with them. It is as well

to remember, too, in this context that even communication amongst psychologists can be misunderstood because of slantings in terminology. For example, Kirk, in the Illinois Test, refers to certain mental processes as 'associative'; other psychologists explain these in terms of 'seeing and applying relationships': that is, as an eductive rather than as an associative process. Jensen uses the term 'association' more in the traditional sense, and talks of a process of thinking through *association* which does not involve *reasoning*. What, therefore, Kirk and Kirk (1971) call an 'associative' process Jensen (1972) would call a 'reasoning 'one. If this opportunity for confusion exists in the field of psychological terminology what can anyone who has only limited opportunity to study psychological terms make of some of these difficulties? The only safe approach is for the psychologist to explain his terms in ordinary language. Cattell (1950), explaining the dimensions of personality which stem from his factorial research, uses certain technical terms, but always includes a popular descriptive label. This can be a little misleading at times, perhaps, but it is less misleading than the confusion which can come from using a technical term which is not understood at all.

Psychiatric social workers and general social workers
Psychiatric social workers have usually had a training in basic psychology, as have the new generic social workers who have a certificate in social work. This basic psychology usually includes an outline of human development from early childhood to old age, together with some study of abnormal development. This involves some knowledge of terms used in child guidance and psychiatric departments. Most social worker training courses make use of psychoanalytic concepts such as defence mechanisms, projection, regression etc. Psychiatric social workers will have had a more detailed training.

Teachers
Teachers vary considerably in their knowledge of basic psychology. The British Psychological Society (1962a) made a survey of the teaching of psychology in Colleges of Education. It found that sometimes the students were provided with very little psychological teaching, often given by lecturers who had read psychology from a basic text book, but who were not themselves psychologists. It cannot, therefore, be assumed that teachers are necessarily knowledgeable about modern theories of intelligence, for example. Many of them still hold concepts which were made popular in the 1930s. There has, however, been a considerable improvement since 1962. Teachers who are likely to have the greatest knowledge are those who have been to one of the special courses run by universities and colleges of education, which provide a twelve-months study in child

development, or some aspect of special educational treatment or educational guidance. It is important to realise that certain teachers are very knowledgeable indeed in their specialist field. They expect from a psychologist much more expert investigation, and can appreciate psychological data in their field.

General practitioners
General practitioners on the whole know less psychology than the average teacher, although some of the younger doctors will now have had courses of basic psychology in their training. Recently medical training has been under review, and courses for medical officers will in future include more basic psychology.

School medical officers
School medical officers have a background of skills and knowledge similar to that of general practitioners. Some of them take a Diploma in Child Health, in which they will have some basic psychology; others have had a short course on the psychology of subnormality with some introduction to the use of the Terman-Merrill Test. If they have attended this course they will know something about the problems of measuring general and specific abilities, and a little about the use of personality tests, but the course was a short one, and their range of knowledge is therefore not likely to be very great. There are likely to be changes of training in the future. School medical officers may have special courses associated with paediatric developments. It is unlikely that they will have more training in psychological testing; the most likely development in the future is that this will become increasingly an area in which the psychologist carries out the investigations; the school doctor will attend courses to gain a background in child development, so that this and other material can be readily understood and the doctor can play his part in the general assessment teams which are evolving.

Education officers
Education officers, too, vary in the amount of psychology which they may have studied. Some will have had very little since their initial training, others may have attended an advanced course and could be very knowledgeable in a specialist area of educational psychology. There is little special training for administrative officers in education. They have usually been very able teachers, in the main with grammar school experience. Local authorities are developing good advisory services; those who advise in special education may have a very considerable knowledge of applied psychology in the field of handicap.

Speech therapists

Speech therapists have studied language development and the use of psychological testing in diagnosis, and are likely to be reasonably familiar with basic cognitive psychology. Some of them receive training in the use of certain psychological tests. The British Psychological Society has given some guidance about the use of tests by non-psychologists, and has classified those which may be used after a special training course has been undertaken. Thus, speech therapists may be trained in the use of the Reynell Scale (1969) for studying language development.

Careers officers

Careers officers, too, will have had some training in the use of psychological techniques for vocational guidance purposes, but they rarely have available the time to make any detailed study. They will, however, have had considerable experience in relating cognitive findings to personality development in formulating some kind of guidance for young people (Vaughan, 1970, Rodger, 1949).

Education welfare officers

As we have noted in Chapter 3 (pp. 57–8) education welfare officers are frequently untrained, although some have a certificate in education welfare taken through part-time study. Many, therefore, will not be familiar with psychological terms. Nevertheless their work is so important, and their contacts with parents so helpful, that psychologists should help them by writing non-technical reports, discussing cases regularly and running courses to give them an understanding of the terms commonly used.

Probation officers

Generic social workers of the social services are gradually taking over the case work for younger children, but probation officers may continue to have responsibilities for some of the older children (chapter 3, pp. 53–4). Like social workers, their training will have given them a background knowledge of psychological terms. They can be sent copies of most reports. Collaboration with probation officers is particularly helpful with some difficult adolescents.

This wide range of background means that psychologists should use discussion methods as much as possible to supplement written reports. There remains a formidable problem of finding time to write reports for different people. Ideally tailormade reports would be the most effective. In practice one has to rely on some kind of generic report, at least for certain circumstances, and this we must consider later. Professional workers in general have a problem of conveying their contribution to others who may know little of their work. One should, however, expect a higher standard of communication amongst psychologists, if only because communication depends so much on psychological understanding.

Parents

If the range of knowledge of professional workers is great, that of parents is much greater. We can assume that professional people have made some study of the subject, and that they are of above average or even well above average intelligence. Parents present the complete spectrum of personality and ability. They range from the mentally healthy to the mentally ill, some of them in psychiatric hospitals having children who need help, some not severe enough for this, but nevertheless showing signs of paranoia and depression. An example was that of a psychologist trying to communicate with two parents about their daughter, who was appropriately placed in a boarding school for educationally subnormal girls. Mother would go to the centre asking if her child could return home; a very careful explanation would be made showing her the value of her daughter's remaining at her boarding school; it was not unusual for the mother, after some twenty minutes of discussion, to turn to the psychologist and ask, as she had done at the beginning of the interview, 'Can Margaret come home?' (Mother was subnormal, and father was severely subnormal and attending the adult day training centre.)

It is extremely difficult, even for anyone skilled and experienced, to appreciate how some people, who are very different in their mental abilities, actually think. It can be equally difficult to communicate with the extremely gifted. Mildly paranoid parents can be particularly difficult, because they may see the intervention of the Education Department or of the psychologist as a threat, and may regard any findings about their child's abilities with suspicion. The psychologist may then find himself in considerable difficulties in trying to give the parents information which indeed would be helpful to them for the handling of their child. The need which emerges clearly from these observations is for the psychologist to have a wide knowledge of personality differences, including all forms of mental illness, not in order to assist the psychiatrist to treat the adults concerned, but sufficiently to enable him to understand them as parents, and therefore to be able to help them in their relationship with their children.

Although psychiatric social workers will have to do this much more than psychologists, and will undertake casework with difficult parents, the latter also like immediate contact; there are also situations in which the psychologist has to communicate to the parent, as social work may not be available or necessary. Chapter 8 treats this in detail. Parents with problems of mental ill-health, mental subnormality, etc., are likely to have a high proportion of children with problems of various types; the psychologist is likely to meet disturbed parents quite frequently in his career within the educational field, even though he may not be directly concerned with handling adult mental illness. The psychologist, too, has to meet the ordinary parent of average intelligence, with a very limited appreciation of psychological knowledge; in some cases these parents have pseudo-knowledge which is old fashioned or even erroneous. For example, some parents still regard test scores as something immutable and fixed, there-fore, if one gave such direct information to them they would be likely to misunderstand and misuse it.

The psychologist at times may not tell the parents some of his findings or may modify his presentation to reduce their impact. This will depend on his judgment about the use the parents may make of this information. The anxious parent may need reassuring, yet the reassurance should not be misleading. It does not help the parent of a severely subnormal child to be deluded for several years, hoping their child could become normal, and then having to accept for the child education in an ESN(s) school specialising in the severely mentally handicapped. Critical or rejecting parents may react to findings by becoming more aggressive to a dull child. Decisions in this type of situation can be difficult. Withholding of informa-tion can be justified if it will help the child's development.

Reporting to courts

Writing reports for courts constitutes a special problem; very often the reports are written by a psychiatrist as a member of the clinic team. He might well be the clinical director. In this case the psychiatric material will be integrated with psychological and social work information. Many courts like to have psychological reports and, for some children, feel that a psychiatric report is unnecessary. A growing body of psychologists consider that psychological information for a court should be presented by the person who has carried out the investigation; they see the real difficulties inherent in a report which is integrated by another professional worker. This point of view can be appreciated because of the difficulties we have already outlined in the background of other people who have not had a wide training in psychological work. On the other hand, child guidance clinic workers confer regularly in teams, and in most cases it is more essential for the director of the clinic, or the administrative director (in the latter case probably a psychologist) to write a general report, taking into account all aspects, and presenting a team point of view. It is probably fair to say that many children coming before the court and into care do not need the intense investigation of a psychiatric team. If the psychologist who gives a report on the child to the court or to the Social Services Department, thinks that psychiatric considerations should be taken into account, he will make this recommendation. Provided he is working regularly with a team which includes psychiatrists and psychiatric social workers he is unlikely to overlook such cases where intensive investigation may be necessary.

Magistrates in the court are well respected and intelligent lay people. One has to bear in mind that they have normally had very little preparation for their work, and may have no specialised knowledge of child development, child psychiatry or child psychology; they look for help and guidance from their special advisers. Basically they want some evidence to show whether a child can be helped by remaining in his own environment with, for example, support from a social services social worker or treatment by a child guidance clinic team, or whether some other supportive action should be considered. In addition they want to know whether there are grounds for removing the child from the family altogether, and placing him in the care of the local authority, and perhaps some suggestions as to the degree of care that the authority should consider. The Social Services Department itself may want some guidance on what to do when a child comes in care. Should the social workers, for example, seek placement in a community home which provides close control, or a community home which caters for mixed handicap, or in a school for maladjusted pupils, and so on? They may need to know a fair amount about the child and his educational development, and to have advice on the kind of education which would be appropriate should they move the child from his present school. They may wish to know whether they should try to maintain a child in his or her present school, even though the child may move to a local group home some distance from the present school. It is useful to appreciate, too, that there has been a change in procedure with the Children and Young Persons Act of 1969. Whereas in the past courts had to take a decision to send a child to an approved school they now have to take a decision whether or not the child should be placed in care. It is then up to the Social Services Department to decide what to do with the child. If, however, a child is placed in care, and has to be brought back to the court repeatedly, the court may ask the Social Services Department to take a different line of action. These are all matters about which the Social Services Department welcomes guidance and help; when writing a report these special needs should be kept in mind. There is likely to be extensive development of psychological support for Social Services Departments.

Methods of reporting

Discussion

Short discussion with the person who is going to use psychological material is an important ingredient of reporting back. It enables the psychologist to discover in the course of discussion the range of the other person's appreciation of psychology, and explanation of terms can be made.

Discussion with a teacher or social worker will often throw up a new angle on how material should be interpreted and used. Some educational psychologists work in schools with this very much in mind; that is, instead of asking a child to visit a well-furnished and well-planned consulting room they go into the schools and assess a child in whatever convenient room may be available, such as a staffroom, classroom or head teacher's study. There are disadvantages in using these in that there may be interruptions, and also the pupil may be a little apprehensive of a staffroom or head teacher's room. Modern schools tend to have a small room available for interview purposes, and these difficulties disappear. The great advantage is that the psychologist can have immediate discussion with the teacher and with the head teacher, always making sure that the head teacher's sanction has been obtained before holding any discussion with the class teacher. In this way schools get to know the psychologist. It may well be that a compromise can be made, if there are schools where facilities are not very good, by carrying out short initial investigations in the school. After discussion with the teachers the child can later be seen in one's own room. It is then essential to return to have a short discussion on findings, as well as sending a basic report on the child. Another great advantage of this situation is that information can be given which might well not be put in writing. This has to be weighed up very carefully, for valuable material which is passed on orally is often lost when a teacher changes; therefore, if no problem of great confidentiality is involved, it is better to write down the observation so that it can be made use of at some subsequent stage of the child's treatment. It is also well to bear in mind that, great though the advantages of discussion are, memory of what occurred is subject to all the usual distortions the psychological study of the memory process has made clear. These include summarising, weaving the material into a meaningful picture according to one's own schemata and so on. Valuable, therefore, though the discussion technique of reporting is, it must always be supplemented by some other means; written reports of the type we are to describe later, or even brief minutes of discussion, can be very helpful.

The case conference
The case conference is the traditional way of reporting information to members of a team. Usually the psychologist will present a written report; the conference provides an opportunity to elaborate on this, and to draw attention to any special terminology or any particular observations which might be useful to the team in formulating their approach to the problem before them. Case conferences are ongoing processes; and in addition to the report which outlines the basic findings the psychologist is able to make a

contribution through comment on observations by other members of the team and by giving a psychological appreciation on some of the points raised by discussion. The psychologist usually has a very good knowledge of the schools he visits, and can help the team by interpreting the information which will come from a school report. A conference is a situation in which the personalities of the various members play a considerable part. Some members may show dominant trends in a case conference situation, and wish to impose their points of view on other members of the team. Others show their insecurity about themselves by having to overjustify and elaborate any contribution they make. Most child guidance team members will have insight into the small group mechanisms that play a part in this and should be able, therefore, to resist some of these stresses that make discussion and conclusions difficult to reach. The members of the team who do best at case conferences are those who show the quality of leadership described by H. Harris (1949). This is leadership by contribution to help a team reach its goal. It was the kind of leadership looked for during the war when officers were being selected in the armed forces. The old concept of the dominant officer who gave commands was replaced by a notion of a leader who was sensitive to the needs of the group and the task in hand, and who played his part by making contributions which would enable a goal to be reached. It is not inappropriate to look at a member's role in a case conference in this way, regarding the latter as a team of people working together to solve a very difficult problem such as the treatment of a very maladjusted, disturbed child. In this case the psychologist adopting this role will avoid the pitfalls of trying to defend his profession or protect himself from losing prestige.

Courses

Courses may be a valuable way of reporting back case findings to teachers in general. This use of courses is a specialised one—that is, to help a professional keep up to date with ongoing research, new developments in the field etc. The psychologist is in the unique position of studying a large proportion of unusual children going through the educational network. If he restricts his findings to the teacher who is handling the case here and now this will be very good up to a point, but limited; it is extremely helpful if some of the findings, suitably prepared to keep confidentiality, can be given to other teachers who are interested, and who may prepare themselves for the possible occasion when they meet such problems for themselves.

Courses provide a way in which defence mechanism can be circumvented. If a teacher is handling a child in a particular situation, and it is fairly clear that a change of handling might achieve a better result, the whole procedure has to be presented with care and tact. This depends very much on the personality of the teacher involved. Some are extremely sensitive and would regard even the kindest comment as a critical attack. Others are able to discuss whether or not their particular approach is being useful to the child. In any case, however, discussion of approaches is useful; one Authority which used a series of discussions on activity approaches in Infant Schools with HMIs and teachers quite revolutionised the approaches being made in the local authority. Teachers identified with the newer approaches and, with some exceptions amongst the somewhat older group, tended to implement them. This provides a contrast with the strong defence put by the head teacher of a special school when the HMI suggested that the approach towards spelling was oldfashioned and slightly irrelevant. The head teacher in this case used to ask the children to learn lists of spellings whilst she was marking the register, a procedure which the inspectors regarded as neither interesting nor valuable to the children. The head teacher, however, at a meeting of the school governors to discuss these views, defended herself vigorously, saying that the men from London were not really in touch with the needs of the children as she was. The governors accepted the head teacher's view and no change was made. Direct comment, therefore, in this case failed.

A vigorous course on modern methods which this head teacher, who had a high regard for herself, might embrace, could have been more effective. These are examples from the field of curriculum development: psychologists can often be successful in obtaining an identification with psychological findings in a similar way. Courses, therefore, can be a very valuable part of reporting. It is also a way in which the psychologists become known to a larger group of teachers; if they present their material well, and it is interesting and useful, they can achieve very considerable prestige for the service, and hence a better use of it. It is important for the psychologist to bear in mind that there are some very good modern aids to lecturing, and these should be used fully. Also it is wise to adopt a team approach to general courses (as opposed to those reporting case experience), involving some of the more experienced teachers and advisers from other branches of the service in the lecturing. The image of the psychologist as being expert in all these matters is a false one. He has a very important contribution to make, but it should always be seen in a setting of other contributions, and just as a team works on the problem of a child it is advantageous for a psychologist to organise courses too on a team basis, and to work closely with teachers and others in the presentation of material.

Memoranda and letters
Memoranda are usually used for communication within a department; they are frequently short and meet the need of information for general action. With a team which meets frequently many decisions and informa-

tion are passed on orally, but it is important to realise that memoranda can also provide a reminder and a record. Even among colleagues working together it is not unusual for them to send memoranda to one another. These can be filed or kept for administrative purposes until action has been taken. This is one way of ensuring that ongoing information is kept in the file. Everything of importance in handling a child's problem should be recorded and dated. It helps subsequent discussion, making a summary of a file, and on handing a case over. Memoranda are useful too, for informing a colleague about a situation, even though the colleague will be seen in the near future. Busy educational psychologists often have a great number of things on their minds, and even though they intend to speak about some matter as soon as they see one of their colleagues, this can easily be forgotten. A short memorandum is one of the most convenient ways of communicating.

A letter tends to be used for communication outside departments. This is extremely flexible and can be comprehensive or just a short summary of information. Copies of letters sent can be used for the information of other people. The psychologist has to use his judgment and knowledge of the other people likely to receive the letter in considering whether it would be appropriate to do this. There is an advantage in sending a letter with a copy, in that the recipient who is not the person to whom the letter is written knows that this will have been slanted, say for the information of a medical officer or education officer, and will take this into account when interpreting the letter.

The psychological reports

The psychological reports summarise the main findings of psychological investigations for use of a clinic or other assessment team, for teachers, for courts, for boarding schools etc. Psychologists prefer to use the term 'psychological report' for a full report which covers aspects of the child's personality and indicates important features in the environment. They use a terminology like 'supplementary report' if they are only investigating one aspect, for example, the child's perception; or 'interim report' if they are presenting a few observations prior to making more detailed investigation. Psychological reports can be made generic, and therefore useful for a fairly wide professional consumer group, provided the terms used are all explained or the information given in non-technical form. Generic reports lose a lot in detail, and reports for other psychologists and for some colleagues with specialist knowledge should be much more specific and comprehensive. In practice, the generic report can be very useful if the psychologist is careful to remember that the aim of the report is to help the teacher or the general practitioner to do something about a child. The content of reports will be discussed later.

Team reports

Psychologists work in a variety of teams. They may work in a traditional child guidance team (v. p. 6), in a team with a school medical officer, teacher, and social worker for ascertainment of slow learners; they may work with a paediatrician in a child development type team, and so on. It is useful to be able to present the team's findings in all-embracing reports. So far as child guidance clinic teams are concerned it is usually the director of the treatment side of the work who will compile the report, taking into account findings of all members of the team. If it is a very important report he may well produce a draft form for discussion. On the whole, however, clinic teams are far too busy to tackle a problem this way.

The team has therefore to trust one of its members to produce the report. If it is a school psychological service type problem the psychologist may well write for the people who have contributed to the study and treatment, e.g. the social worker, the remedial teachers, class teachers etc. This may even include a reference to the work done by a child guidance clinic team, when, for example, applying for a child to be admitted to a boarding school.

At some stages, too, it is necessary to summarise a file in order to present an application for boarding school, or to give guidance to a careers officer, for example, when a child with a maladjustment problem is leaving school. This inevitably involves selection of material, the balancing of it, and presentation to give a reasonably coherent picture. This in itself demands considerable skill, and the way in which it is done will often influence very considerably, for example, the decision by a boarding school head teacher as to whether or not he will interview an applicant. It is important that the basic information should be there without omission of any fundamental feature. It would mislead a school not to reveal the nature of a child's aggression, and how extremely disruptive this can be in a classroom situation. On the other hand, to highlight too much the aggression which tends to stand out as the dominant feature may also mislead; the psychologist should always be very careful to point out all evidence of a positive type of behaviour, and any indications of growing adjustment, so that the chances of success in the handling of the youngster can be fairly accurately assessed.

Internal reports

Most school psychological services and child guidance clinics keep quite full internal reports. Sometimes these are not particularly well edited, simply because of pressure of demands on time available. It is not possible for carefully edited versions of internal reports to be made and also meet the demands of routine, everyday work.

It is important that the psychologist should not feel inhibited about writing down in some detail his findings and his views, making appropriate comment where these are rather speculative, or where the material gathered, or information given, is secondhand. The advantage of the internal report being fairly full is that one can outline hypotheses which can be checked up in some detail. It is rather less desirable to put these kinds of speculations in a report which is sent to other people, because speculation is so often taken for fact, and what is a hypothesis as far as the psychologist is concerned can be misinterpreted as a firm view, and the psychologist can then find it difficult to propose a somewhat different hypothesis later on, as a result of his observations or further information received.

General publication

Finally there is the question of communication by publication. The field psychologist carries out a considerable amount of research, but it is consumable and private research carried out on behalf of a particular person. On the whole psychologists have tended not to publish many of these findings; probably they are unable to devote much time to the preparation and editing which a published report would require. They may also well feel that, valuable though the material is for a particular child and its treatment, it may have less value for others. Nevertheless, publication of case material would be of great value. A useful example of this has been a publication by Pringle (1970) of *Able Misfits*. By publishing her material in this way she is able to attract the teacher's attention to this area of work, and by achieving a fairly wide readership communicate basic findings and attitudes to a large population.

It is very much to be hoped that, with the cooperation of teams of psychologists, more attention can be paid to the possibility of publishing case studies and details of methods employed in the treatment of children. Some journals, like that of the Association of Educational Psychologists or the Association for Special Education, cater particularly for this type of material.

Content of reports

Framework

It is useful, in writing a report, for the psychologist to have a broad framework. It is helpful to start off with a short paragraph explaining what the purpose of the report is. This can be followed by a number of paragraphs which will contain the basic observations made by the psychologist, a paragraph devoted to discussion and interpretation of findings, in which the psychologist may relate material to other workers' findings, and finally a paragraph of conclusions with suggestions for further approaches or even clearcut recommendations, such as recommendation for placement in special school or for full examination for this.

Purpose

This can usually be easily defined quite effectively by a short statement such as 'To investigate the causes of backwardness at school', 'to give teachers some help with a difficult problem'. Sometimes, however, the purpose for which a child is referred for investigation turns out to be minor compared with the real need. Indeed, sometimes the initial investigation reveals very rapidly that the problem is not one at all for the educational psychologist, but one which is really much more appropriately dealt with by another worker. Clinic teams in particular are sensitive to the fact that occasionally the real problem turns out to be different from that presented at the beginning of an investigation. A child may be referred because of backwardness, but the initial investigations may reveal considerable personality problems. The report may therefore shift in its purpose a little by not just exploring the backwardness of the child, but also the behaviour. It is possible for those studying the child to forget the original problem when they become involved with an allied issue. It is very important that the original reason for an investigation should be kept in mind, and an allied issue indicated as such. In noting the referral agency in a report the instigator should be included. A child referred by a parent after much careful discussion with the head teacher should be noted as referred by the parent through the head teacher. Head teachers are likely to be more cooperative if their contribution is appreciated.

Observations

Psychologists find it convenient to classify observations under two broad headings: personality and environment. They also subdivide under personality by looking first at the intellectual development of the child, secondly at the personality qualities in the orectic field, and thirdly at related physical factors.

On the intellectual side it is common for many British psychologists to use an hierarchical model in outlining their findings, that is, they will talk about general qualities such as general intelligence, influential factors such as verbal ability, and then draw attention to rather more specialised influences such as rote memory and perception (P. E. Vernon, 1960).

When considering emotional factors it is more difficult to present a convenient framework for marshalling ideas, although again a general quality of stability, broad influences like introversion and extroversion, and more specific attitudes and interests can be handled in turn. The importance of having a model in mind is not slavishly to report on every aspect, but to have a set of basic headings, which are very helpful in formulating the report in detail, and a reminder to include all relevant aspects.

Other conceptual frameworks can be just as appropriate, and might even be more effective than the one suggested here. Models based on communication theory such as that used by Kirk are frequently used.

On the physical side the psychologist will make use of findings from the School Health Service or general practitioner, paediatrician etc. Although he himself will be able to make some rough and ready observations on a child's hearing or vision, he will usually, with the cooperation of the school medical officer, see the medical notes and ask for further medical examination.

The environment of the child can be summarised under the two headings of past and present, each of these subdivided into home, neighbourhood and school. Very often it is a social worker who will make a detailed exploration of the contribution of environmental factors to the development of a child's personality, but he may not always be available and the psychologist may have to do this. It is essential that something is known of a child's environment; it is very difficult for a psychologist even to write a simple report on a child's intellectual ability without evaluating environmental circumstances. If anything has come out of modern research on the nature of intelligence it is that the child's environmental experiences play a part in the development of effective thinking; therefore, in reporting an intellectual level of functioning on a test like a Terman-Merrill, reference should be made to environmental circumstances, or else some false conclusions can be too easily drawn from the data.

Terminology

In writing the reports the psychologist will need to edit all his terms: even a term like 'intelligence' is frequently misunderstood. 'IQ' is now a well-known term, but should never be presented without the comment on the type of test, naming the test that was used and some interpretation of the finding. It is still inadvisable to quote figures without some explanation, and even when explanations are given the danger may remain that the figures will be interpreted without the knowledge of the probable error that most psychologists will have in mind. Some psychologists, therefore, prefer to talk in bands of general ability, rather than to give precise figures. Various bands of ability have been suggested, e.g. in the WISC and Terman-Merrill handbook. A common one accepted in this country is:

Severely subnormal below 55		Above average	115–130
Subnormal	55–70	Superior	130–145
Below average	70–85	Very superior	145+
Average	85–115		

Each threshold has a probable error of ±5 points. These figures are based on an average of 100 and standard deviation of 15. The WISC and Terman-Merrill have not been normed for a British population; a direct transfer of the data from these to the categories given will produce some misclassification. Phillips and Bannon (1968) and Wright (1972) have studied samples of children aged 11+, comparing scores on the Terman-Merrill with those obtained from Moray House. These agree in estimating the Terman-Merrill average for this country of 106, and the standard deviation 18. Comparison between the WISC and the Terman-Merrill (Wright, 1972) suggest a WISC average of 105: a study by Jones (1962) gave a similar result. Yule (1969) reported similar findings for the WPPSI. At the lower end of the ability range these test differences make only small variations, and taking into account the probable error of a test score they become unimportant. Thus the best estimate of a Terman-Merrill IQ score that is two standard deviations below the mean is 70; the WISC is only a point or two different.

Perhaps for this reason these tests have continued in use to help in making decisions about educationally subnormal pupils in spite of lack of British norms. At the higher ranges of ability the discrepancies are considerable. A Moray House score of 130 is equal to 142 on the Terman-Merrill. There is further complication in that rural children score some 5 points lower on average than urban children. It is not certain whether such differences are due to environmental differences.

Another way of dealing with the problem is to give some indication of how many children in a typical group of one hundred might make a higher score than the one the child has made; for example, instead of stating that the child has an IQ of 120, one can say that round about some 10 per cent of the population may score above this level and some 90 per cent below. This gives the teacher a better understanding than the vague comment that the child is 'above average'.

The mental age method of referring to intellectual status with respect to other children has been heavily criticised. The main criticism is that it can be overgeneralised by a reader, particularly an unsophisticated one, so that the interpretation made of a child who has a mental age of six is that he is like a six-year-old in many more respects than he really is. It is, however, untrue to say that he is only like a six-year-old in respect of the test given, as some critics seem to indicate. If a test correlates highly with attainments and performances in various intellectual tasks, a low mental age score has implications that are much wider than those referring to information about one test score. However, when mental age is used, and it is a very useful guide, especially in infant schools, one should point out in what way the child is of a certain age level. It may be helpful to say that, for example, 'he makes a mental age score which average children of six years make on this particular test, and in many respects his learning levels and achievements are those of an average six-year-old; he is much slower in general progress than they would be, and as far as emotional maturity is concerned he is very different'. It is better to use this kind of information which gives a teacher some help, rather than to give information that is too vague to be really of much use to him.

There are difficulties in the use of terms like 'weakness in visual perception' or 'weakness in auditory perception'. Sometimes when presented in reports these terms make it seem that this particular defect is of highly specific significance. This may well be true, but unless the general level of a child's development is known, it is difficult to come to any conclusion about this. Terms such as 'non-communicating children' also suffer from this difficulty. A non-communicating child may be a child who is severely subnormal and therefore does not communicate, or he may suffer from a rather more specific language handicap: for example, he understands perfectly well, but through some faulty mechanism fails to find the right words to express what he wishes to convey. Terms which are now fairly common in everyday speech, such as 'maladjustment', 'extroversion', 'introversion', must be used rather carefully; common usage, as all psychologists realise, does not imply understanding, and frequently its meaning in common usage will vary from that which the psychologist intends. This is particularly true of the term 'maladjustment', and a teacher may well say that he cannot see how Tommy is maladjusted (Tommy having stolen repeatedly, set fire to a school laboratory, and caused havoc in numerous classrooms), pointing out that he has such a hostile and difficult environment that it would be difficult for him to adjust otherwise.

Indirect information

Special care in report writing should be taken in treating information that comes from hearsay—for example, a mother says about a school that a teacher is particularly severe towards her child. She may be even more destructive in her criticism of the school. This sometimes can be a defence mechanism with just a grain of truth, if any, behind it. It is better, unless there is direct evidence to support hearsay statements like this, to record them with a careful note that they are the opinions of the mother, etc., in the general file, and not for communication outside.

An example of this was met a few years ago when a member of a clinic team wrote to the Chief Education Officer, stating that the teachers at a certain school were picking on a lad being treated at the clinic, and making things unnecessarily difficult for him. The officer who wrote asking that the Chief Education Officer take some steps about this matter was informed later that, as the boy had not attended school that term, it was difficult indeed to do much about it. It was not until this particular member of the child guidance team joined another service that confidence in the department was restored at headquarters.

There are sometimes difficulties in a particular school; teachers have a slightly below average distribution of mental illness and difficulties, but nevertheless teachers with personality difficulties, for example, paranoia, are found here and there. If one has to point out that there is a difficulty, however, this is best done in conversation with the head teacher. If anything has to be put on paper it has to be done with great tact.

Discussion and interpretation
In this section the psychologist can interpret the observations made so that the reader will be able to use them effectively. It also gives opportunity to suggest hypotheses on which to base future action. This part of a report provides the opportunity for the psychologist to stress the probabilistic nature of predictions and to emphasise the multidimensional nature of a problem if necessary.

Recommendations
Reports are usually completed with a short summary, followed by a number of recommendations or suggestions. Recommendations have to be carefully considered: teachers, for example, are professionals, and some may demand psychological information but not take kindly to further suggestions on classroom practice. This was the view adopted in the Summerfield Report. On the other hand there is not a clearcut difference between classroom practice and psychological approaches to learning. Sir Cyril Burt, in his address to the Association of Educational Psychologists on becoming their first Patron, remarked that the educational psychologist had contributed a great deal to diagnosis, but now was the time to turn attention to treatment, much of which would be teaching. A survey of the views of head teachers carried out in Hampshire and Portsmouth showed that a majority welcomed a contribution on actual classroom practice—they wanted the psychologist to relate his findings to the classroom situation and give advice on how to help pupils (Lowenstein, 1970). Some psychologists (e.g. Mittler, 1970b), see the educational psychologist as providing prescriptive-type reports based on profiles of ability and personality development, and on research into the most appropriate strategies for helping the children.

Recommendations can sometimes be misinterpreted as criticism; for example, it is sometimes difficult to make a recommendation that a child should change a school without inferring some criticism of the school concerned; this is best dealt with by discussing the advisability for having a change, so that when one writes a report one can say that this has been discussed with the head teacher, who is in agreement with such a recommendation. Many teachers are quite appreciative of the fact that if a child has been in some difficulties he may wish to preserve his self-respect by starting afresh with a different team of teachers. It is sometimes true, however, that the school may be uncongenial as far as the child is concerned.

In carrying out his researches on maladjustment Burt listed two main school factors: 'uncongenial teacher' and 'work too hard'. There are, for some children, uncongenial schools; the quiet, timid child may find it difficult to survive in a school where there is a lot of aggression freely expressed. Transfer can be treated quite sympathetically. Most teachers in discussion are quite willing to arrange for a child to have a transfer for his own good, and as it often happens that one will ask that same school to take in a child from another area, no criticism of the school is inferred by the teachers concerned.

So far as other recommendations go, much depends on the psychologist's own skills and knowledge and on the needs of the schools. Provided suggestions are made, and no implication that something 'ought to be done' is inferred, the psychologist should feel free to help the teacher with practical recommendations on classroom practice.

Confidentiality
Reports which contain confidential material should be so marked. However, it is not always clear how to interpret this term.

A doctor has an obligation to treat as confidential all material which his patient reveals. This is usually interpreted in the interests of the patient, the doctor making a judgment about what material should be passed on, and to whom. Some can be very conservative; one psychiatrist, director of a clinic, used to keep his data as secure as top secret government documents. Not even the other members of the team were allowed to see them. This very restricted view hindered the work of the psychologists and social worker, and many would consider that this was not in the best interest of the patient. Patients assume that doctors will keep confidential what they say, but are usually willing for the information to be shared by other professionals involved in the treatment situation.

Psychologists may be in similar circumstances, but they often have a dual role. They may be responsible to the local education authority, and hence to an education officer or head teacher to give help and advice in respect of a child's problem. On the other hand they may have a responsibility to the child they are helping. In the course of helping the latter they may have access to very confidential material. Should they include this in reports made to help the authority or the head teacher? Conflicts like this are rare; local education authorities exist to help the individual, so the ultimate goal is the same.

Decisions about very confidential material should be based primarily on how this affects the treatment of the pupil: if it helps to tell a head teacher of the promiscuous activities of a neglectful mother, then the head teacher can be regarded as a professional partner and given this information. Often, however, it will be sufficient to point out areas of neglect by the mother without comment on her promiscuous activities. Some of this may be given in discussion and not written into reports.

Most referrals to educational psychologists come from teachers anxious to have help and guidance on the treatment of a pupil. The psychologist has no conflict in this situation. If the teacher wants a general appraisal of abilities and attitudes for educational guidance purposes, this can be seen as an extension of normal school work, and the consent of parents need not be obtained, either for the child to be seen, or for the information obtained to be reported to the school. If further extensive investigations take place these are carried out with the consent of the parents; knowing that the school wants help, usually no difficulties arise.

There can be conflict when a parent seeks help for a child, but does not wish the school to know anything—or very little—about the problem. In this situation the child guidance clinic team will respect this, but do their best to achieve permission to cooperate with the school. If this is asked of a psychologist who has duties in respect of the school, he may decide not to accept responsibility for the case but refer it to the clinic which, having its main duties to help parents and children, need not be in conflict over this. Usually, when parents seek the advice of psychologists for their own guidance, they are quite agreeable for a report to be sent to the school.

Official documents for reporting

There are official forms for reporting on handicapped pupils (1 HP, 2 HP, 3 HP, etc.).

The 1 HP is a form certifying that a pupil has a handicap and describing its nature. This can only be completed by a medical officer who has attended an appropriate course. It is normally only used in cases of dispute with parents over special treatment (see chapter 13, p. 296).

The 2 HP is a form on which information can be summarised on a potential ESN child's development. Part I is a brief outline of social development and school history; Part II a section devoted to reports on intelligence tests, summarising those used previously, and those used at the time of examination, with opportunities for comments. This may be completed by a school medical officer or educational psychologist. Part III contains medical observations. The medical officer is required to state whether a child, in his opinion, is ESN or not, and to make suggestions for treatment. Form 3 HP is a school report form in respect of children who may be ESN Authorities need not use 2 HP and 3 HP forms: they may introduce their own. If there is a dispute the Department of Education and Science ask for information to be summarised on the official form. See also p. 296.

Shortcomings in the procedures and forms for discovering handicap and making recommendations for special education have been increasingly evident. A new circular on ascertainment is therefore being prepared, and new forms are being considered. Greater emphasis will be placed on the assessment of the needs of children. The new documents will not only aid diagnosis and placement, but will also help the teacher. The role of the doctor will be clarified; in the past he has been asked to record what are essentially educational decisions: these will now be left to educationalists, e.g. an educational psychologist. School medical officers and psychologists will both make essential contributions, and work closely with the teacher concerned.

The forms suggested are S.E.1 to 6. The 1 H.P. will be replaced by S.E 1: in this the doctor will certify the type and extent of a child's disability, but not the educational category. Form S.E.2 will be the medical form on which medical findings are summarised, and the implications of these for the teacher. The educational psychologist will give a full psychological report on Form S.E.3: in this he will relate emotional and intellectual aspects of personality to attainments and behaviour, and indicate the type of placement and teaching arrangements required. Form S.E.4 is to be used for a comprehensive school report. A new form, S.E.5, will summarise findings for case conferences or placement discussions. Form S.E.6 will replace 5 H.P. used for children whose parents are in the armed forces.

These forms are designed to outline the needs of all handicapped children, so that forms such as 4 H.P. for physical handicap or maladjustment will not be necessary.

13

Relationships with colleagues

We have already pointed out that the psychologist needs all his skills in some of the more general functions he performs, such as report writing. It is equally true that he needs to bring to bear psychological knowledge and skills in establishing the right kind of relationships with the colleagues with whom he works. Many of our field psychologists achieve their success in local authority work because they use their knowledge to help collaboration with colleagues in the pursuit of common goals. In this chapter we will make some general comments concerning relationships with other workers, and then look at the special contribution which psychologists make in the total field. In order fully to understand relationships with colleagues, it is important to set the scene in terms of the way in which the educational psychologist operates, and much of the chapter will be concerned with discussing the practical task of day to day operations of a school psychological service within which relationships with colleagues are so important.

We will be concerned with staff in the Education Department, in schools, in school health and health services, in social services, in allied professional organisations, and finally with other psychologists. The chapter will be concluded with some comments on the importance and use of team work in meeting the needs of young children and those who help them.

Relevant qualities of psychologists and their colleagues

Educational psychologists need some knowledge of a number of disciplines; for example, social psychology and occupational psychology are particularly important. The former helps the psychologist to a better understanding of personal relationships in the working situation, and the latter to appreciate the principles of management.

It is self-evident that the personalities of those who work with one another decide to a large extent whether cooperation can be achieved. Unstable personalities find it difficult to cooperate in any situation; highly neurotic individuals are so absorbed in their own problems that they fail to appreciate the needs of others, and those who feel insecure may be unduly critical of others. Psychologists with marked individual problems or difficulties are hardly likely to be effective with the children with whom they work, or the colleagues with whom they have to cooperate. Most units which select psychologists take these factors into account; there is no sound evidence to suggest that psychologists as a whole are less well adjusted than other members of the community.

A consideration of the importance of the personality of psychologists invites consideration of the personality characteristics that might be thought to be desirable in psychologists. Hardly any work has been done on this, although Cattell (1964) has attempted, using his Personality Questionnaires, to outline the characteristics of various professions, including clinical psychologists and professors. These tentative findings suggest that there may be different profiles for successful psychologists working in a therapy situation from those successful in diagnosis. The pattern for a successful research worker may well be different from that of either. No study seems to have yet been made of educational psychologists. There is room within the field for a variety of personalities: some will differ from psychologists who are highly successful in academic work. Indeed, the British Psychological Society recognises the difference in that it will award a Fellowship of the Society for outstanding practice in the field, as well as for academic contribution and distinction.

Similar comments are relevant to understanding colleagues with whom one works. They too have a wide range of personality differences; some are introverted, some more extroverted, and so on. They too have a wide range of mental health stability; the majority are stable and easy to get on with, others may go through periods of instability, and a small proportion may indeed develop acute mental illness. A good educational psychologist should show appreciation and understanding of the problem when a colleague becomes emotionally unsettled or indeed ill. Provided he is seen as an adviser and not as someone who has a duty to evaluate (see p. 290), the psychologist can often give support and help to a colleague, perhaps enabling him to seek the kind of psychiatric help that he may well require.

Psychologists too should be better able to appreciate wide variations of personality, and to be aware that others may be working towards the same goal, but have different methods of approach. It is reasonable to ask of any psychologist that the principles he uses in helping children should not be different from those he uses in approaching a colleague. It is inconsistent to help children, to be sympathetic to their special needs and difficulties, and yet be condemnatory or critical of a difficult teacher, for example. Even if one may not agree with a viewpoint or the way in which a teacher proceeds with his work, one may be in a position to understand why he may be motivated to do so, and to accept his point of view and outlook as one would accept the behaviour of the young people with whom one works.

Psychologists should also not forget the well-known principle, in giving advice to another person, to counsel rather than to direct, to give him an opportunity to reach his own conclusion rather than to force conclusions on him. In expressing these points of view one is not attempting to argue that the psychologist is in some way better off than his colleagues: indeed a particular psychologist, because of his personal difficulties, may be less well equipped.

One of the special factors involving personalities that psychologists will meet is that of ageing. They will meet this eventually in themselves as well as in their colleagues. Although the psychological studies of ageing are not numerous, there are some fairly well established findings. People, as they get older, whether they be psychologists, doctors or teachers, will become a little slower in assimilating new material. They may become, too, less able to adjust to those whose views they cannot share. However, old and new ideas may often cross-fertilise usefully when their exponents have finished debating.

It is reasonable to ask that anyone who has made a study of human behaviour should use his knowledge as much as he can in order to effect reasonable cooperation and working together for common goals.

The psychologist as educationalist

This leads us to the consideration of another basic principle in establishing effective cooperation, and that is identification with a common goal. Psychologists usually appreciate this particular aspect of cooperative work. Within the field in which the educational psychologist works he does share common goals with all those within the Education Department. All, including the educational psychologist, have a special aim, that of making an educational contribution to a child's development. Education has many goals, but above all it aims to help equip a young person to develop talents and abilities to the full, to satisfy his emotional needs and develop attitudes and interests, all in a manner which is reasonably compatible with the needs of other people. One way of looking at education is to regard it as an organised contribution made by professional and trained people to assist the family in the development of the individual child through the use of schools, youth organisations etc.

In this connection it is important to remember that when a psychologist joins an Education Department his first loyalty should be to education and its concern with the optimal development of each pupil. His special contribution is to bring psychological factors to bear on the problems with which he is presented. The priority for the local education authority psychologist therefore is to be an educationalist, as it is for any teacher. The latter may be an able biologist or an outstanding linguist, but when he is in a school he is first of all an educationalist, and those who are able to see that their language teaching or their specialist science is part of general education, are able to preserve a balance, to be sensitive to the needs of their colleagues and to avoid becoming extreme departmentalists. The end, therefore, as far as a psychologist in the Education Service is concerned, is to promote education. Education itself, however, is also a means to an end. It makes its contribution to the development of individuals together with the family and the other statutory departments, such as Health and Social Services. An educationalist who is sensitive to the ultimate aims of achieving mental health and physical health of the individual will see health and social services' workers as personal colleagues in a joint endeavour.

The basic issues are, then, 'How can I contribute?' and 'How can I help my colleagues in the contribution they are making?' Therefore, even though the special contribution of the educational psychologist is to apply his psychology to education, he can see this as being part of a total scheme to help towards individual mental health and individual development.

This awareness is particularly valuable in relating to other groups for, within the local authority services, there are a variety of professional groups which hold their own meetings from time to time. They may become conscious of themselves as a group, e.g. teachers, school medical officers, psychologists, social workers. The groups will exhibit some of the reactions typical of small groups. They may tend to perceive some other group as threatening to the area of work for which they have responsibility. They may tend to be critical of the contributions made by another group, sometimes to protect their own limitations. There will often be other reactions between colleagues due to defence mechanisms such as projection or rationalisation. The main need is to use group identification mechanisms to promote positive developments, but at the same time to reduce unnecessary irrational areas of conflict with others. A psychologist often has the opportunity to act as a catalyst in reducing group tensions. Greater cohesion and reduced internal conflicts can be achieved if there is identification with a common goal: this provides the opportunity to see oneself as contributing towards reaching this goal. Some educationalists feel that the early education of some of the professionals of today was imbued too much with competition, so that they aim too strongly for personal success.

This increases competitive elements within small groups. It seems likely that we have not yet paid sufficient attention in education to inculcating values of social cooperation. It is not so long since the Honours Board and the class lists in the primary school disappeared. People whose names featured on these boards are amongst the heads of our departments. One can understand some of the difficulties they may have in feeling positive about groups that they see as competitive. It is not only in local authorities' groups that one can find examples of failure in cooperation: it is not unknown at quite high levels in government departments for the opportunity for active and full cooperation to be missed.

The psychologist's particular contribution within education

We need now to consider the special role of the psychologist within the educational system. The British Psychological Society, in presenting evidence to the Summerfield Committee on the work of psychologists, considered that there was one main thread which distinguished the contribution of psychologists from that of others in the Education Service, and that was the specialised study of psychological science and its application to education and to other aspects of human development. The Association for Educational Psychologists outlined the contribution under three headings:

1. The assessment of psychological and educational development and needs of children.
2. Work as psychologist members of child guidance clinic teams.
3. Making contributions to those discussions of educational policy where specialist contribution from the academic and clinical psychological point of view could be useful.

These are useful guides and have not changed significantly since the Summerfield Report was published (1968), except for the development of other assessment teams in addition to the child guidance clinics, about which we will be making comments later in this chapter.

The day of the small authority employing one psychologist, and perhaps only one inspector, has come to an end with the new local government changes. There are now only about four authorities with total populations below 200,000 and about eleven with total populations below 250,000. This means that psychologists can attempt the kind of work described above with much more effect. In a small authority the psychologist has often been asked to undertake responsibilities which were clearly not his by virtue of being a psychologist, but given to him because he was the only member of the staff who might have sufficient knowledge to tackle this work. Some authorities have used psychologists as inspectors for special education. This, of course, they are perfectly entitled to do, but it should not be considered that, because the psychologist is trained as an educational psychologist, he is automatically suitable for this kind of work, but rather because he has had some relevant experience in addition to his normal training as an educational psychologist. On the whole an inspectorial role was not regarded by the Summerfield Committee as being an ideal role for the psychologist to play. It was felt that if he were regarded as an adviser he could be accepted more easily as a colleague, and confided in when there were difficulties of handling children, etc. To be considered as an inspector who might evaluate the school could inhibit some head teachers from referring problems, on the grounds that this might be considered an indication of lack of ability to handle the difficulties themselves.

Neither is pure administration a part of the psychologist's work. Some of the larger teams have an administrative officer who can look after day-to-day administration, such as seeing that arrangements are made for the transfer of children to special units, looking after orders for repairs or minor works to be executed. Effective help of this kind enables the more experienced psychologist, who is in charge of a service, to devote his energies to more appropriate work. There is, however, one aspect of administration which the psychologist may need to do: when he is promoting a new project it may expedite matters to help a busy office by working out some of the details. As an example, recently a chief educational psychologist was involved in looking at the regrading of psychologists, as their working responsibilities had changed. Details could have been left to an administrative officer to work out, but few had the available time to do this. The psychologist had also a distinct advantage in knowing the work and relativities, and could make appropriate suggestions about the salary levels, but not, however, until he himself was thoroughly aware of the various possibilities. This could be called temporary administration: it is a demand which occurs now and again, but is not a regular responsibility. If such administration is to be given priority the psychologist in charge has to do some of the work, even though it may not fall within the definition of what is a psychological contribution.

To sum up this section, the psychologist is one of a team of educationalists whose special contribution will be to apply psychological knowledge to the kinds of problems that emerge in an educational situation. These will mainly concern children with learning difficulties and other problems, but it is as well to point out that the specialised application of psychology is also of value to the average and above average, to the normal as well to the maladjusted. Psychologists should not be seen as part of special education only. They have important contributions to make to ordinary education, and may be involved, for example, in educational guidance generally, by making available the types of tests or assessment techniques which will help the teacher to assess and guide his pupils: they may also play a part, with other organisers and advisers, in applying psychological principles in the organisation of schools and curriculum development. They will contribute, too, by lecturing and running discussion groups for teachers, school welfare officers and others, including parents and staffs of children's homes, to help them to deal with the problems of children on their own.

It is important for the psychologist to consider the autonomy he should have. Within an Education Department the ultimate authority lies with the Education Committee. A great deal, however, is delegated to the Chief Education Officer and others, and within the educational system head teachers, for example, have considerable delegated powers. For job satisfaction a certain area of responsibility and autonomy is important; a psychologist who only advises and has to leave it entirely to others to implement his advice or ignore it, has a role that may not carry with it full job satisfaction. Most psychologists in the larger areas have scope for carrying out their own special educational treatment which they decide may be appropriate, and in some they may have responsibility for a small, specialised remedial service with a staff of teachers who work out specialised treatment in conjunction with the psychologist. All psychological services need to have available such a service, including having some units or classes for special difficulties, so that in the course of their work they themselves are able to meet the needs of some of the problems referred to them. This they would not be able to do if all the entries to special education were controlled by other officers. In a good authority there is considerable scope for initiative: few psychological jobs hold out greater opportunities for this.

Contributions of other colleagues

The education department

Education officers

We now look at the contribution of other colleagues, starting with the Education Department. The Chief Education Officer, and usually his deputy, are the two officers of the Department who have overall general functions, and who are likely therefore to be in continuous touch with all aspects of educational administration. They usually have working with them assistant education officers specialising in areas such as primary, secondary, further and special education. Educational psychologists are usually directly responsible to the Chief Education Officer or his deputy. because their functions are not restricted to one or other of the areas described. As has already been mentioned, they probably have their greatest area of contact with the officer in charge of special education, perhaps their smallest with further education, although there are likely to be developments in the latter, as indicated on p. 289.

The officer in charge of special education will be responsible for the staffing and general administration of special schools. He may, for example, act on the Chief Education Officer's behalf as Secretary for the Governors of Special Schools, and see that any resolutions they pass are implemented. He will make sure that estimates for special school purposes are given due weight by the committee. He may initiate projects for expansion of special education before an appropriate committee. The administrative officer in this section will, in a large authority, be assisted by an Adviser in Special Education, usually someone who has been a head teacher in one or more types of special school, and perhaps has one of the specialist qualifications in the education of handicapped children. As both primary and secondary schools refer children to the psychologist for study the latter will have an important contribution to make in the developmental organisation of special education as well as recruitment to it. He will also know a lot about slow learning and other handicapped children who are not receiving education in special schools.

In some areas it is the administrative officer in charge of one of the sections who may take a report on development to the committee. It is common practice, however, among authorities, for the adviser or the educational psychologist who is making the report to be present. The great advantages are, of course, that if the members ask detailed questions the professional adviser is most likely to be able to answer them satisfactorily, specially if in the case of the psychologist there are some technical-psychological issues involved. If it is the policy of the authority for one of the administrative officers to take the developmental reports to the committee, then the psychologist can effectively help by discussing the details and making fully available to that officer such information as may be required.

The relationship between the adviser for special education, or the psychologist, and the administrative officer can also overlap when deciding the admission of youngsters to special schools. According to the Education Act it is the duty of the education committee to decide what form of special education is appropriate, once doctors and others such as psychologists have made reports showing that a child has a special need. In practice this duty is delegated. It may be delegated to an administrative officer or to a special education adviser, or to a psychologist. In many cases the decision is made by a team which will involve these officers together with the head of the intaking school. Clearly the psychologist will have a major role to play in decisions which are taken about the desirability for the child to have special education. This essentially comes about because he will often be the person sent for by the head of the ordinary school to advise because the child is showing special difficulty. He will have made a close psychological study of the needs and personality of the pupil, and his evidence, together with that of the referring school, must play a major part in any of the decisions that have to be taken. The medical officer, who will also have seen the child and made a special study from a medical point of view, will have a great deal to contribute.

The administrator in charge of primary schools will have duties in respect of staffing, meetings of school managers etc. Some authorities intend to appoint advisers for primary education to work with these officers. Both of them again will be working closely with the psychologist, because a great deal of time is spent in primary schools, and a psychologist can become a very valuable colleague to those responsible for primary education. For example, the psychologist may have made a study of all the most difficult problems in the primary sector, and may have advised on the remedial procedures, and perhaps also run some special remedial classes. It is the primary schools' adviser who will encourage the schools to tackle reading and other problems in a manner that may be effective for the raising of standards generally, but his advice may be based on experience gained as a result of the psychologist's investigations, both of individual cases and of the needs of particular schools or districts. It must not be forgotten that the primary school area includes the provision to be made for nursery education.

A psychologist knowing a city and its needs may well be able to advise the primary officer on the priority that might be given to the setting up of nursery schools in particular areas according to their needs. The psychologist may be asked to undertake some kind of survey in order to make a better assessment of this.

The psychologist will find himself in contact also with the officer in charge of secondary education, and working with him in a number of areas. Until recently many psychologists were very actively involved in the 11+ selection machinery; where schools still operate this selective procedure they may turn to the psychologist either for help in general planning, in the choice of tests or in some of the administration and interpretation, or in the assessment of rather difficult cases; the psychologist may be asked to serve as a member of the selection team. The psychologist may find himself now much more involved in making suitable tests available for the secondary and primary schools. These will help in the internal educational guidance carried out by the schools. It will replace any 11+ selection and become increasingly important in the secondary school. The psychologist is also likely to be involved in policy making in respect of the development of school counsellors and their relationship with the school psychological and other services. Another field in which he may work with the assistant education officer and the adviser for secondary education is in advising on areas of development for slow learning children.

In its *Survey of Slow Learners in Secondary Schools* the Department of Education and Science (1971c), showed that there was a very wide range of provision in different parts of the country, and that by and large this was far from satisfactory. Psychologists in the schools, having studied slow learners, are well able to give information and help, so that the officer for secondary schools and his advisory colleague can take effective action based on information.

As yet psychologists have not had a great deal to do with further education. This may well be one of the growing points as psychologists become more numerous. It must be borne in mind that, under further education, education departments can provide for help for a wide range of people. Little so far has been done by psychological services to collaborate with those who help with the problems of young adults, either in advice on selecting an adequate further education programme or in help with personal problems. A student who is attending a university is not the responsibility of local authority services. But polytechnics, colleges of education and technical colleges are usually linked to local education departments. There could well be a development in the future with the local authority psychological staff providing some help and guidance. They have a potential role in colleges of education, both in helping to train teachers and in counselling those students who may need help in deciding whether teaching is their vocation, and deflecting them if it is not —a very important measure for preventing difficulties in the future. Some universities have begun the organising of courses for tertiary education counsellors: psychologists may be involved with these. Certainly if colleges themselves, as part of the local education authority, set up their own services, there should be very close cooperation with the Child Guidance Service and the local authority.

Administrative staff

Some comments are appropriate on the relationship between educational psychologists and other administrative officers. These will include the Chief Clerk and officers concerned with finance, including salaries and estimates. If a psychologist is concerned with developing a project which involves expenditure beyond that which is in the normal budget, then it has to be planned well in advance. Some idea of cost needs to be worked out. The architect's department may help by providing provisional estimates if buildings or adaptations are involved; usually this is arranged through the Chief Clerk or, with large projects, the administrative officer concerned with sites and buildings. Other budgeting, such as for new equipment, may have to be carefully prepared and submitted when estimates are made (usually in the autumn), together with the evidence for the value of the expenditure. Very large items need to go to a subcommittee for approval—the Chief Education Officer or one of his officers will usually advise on this. Invariably local education authority estimates have to be cut back and some items deleted or deferred. A psychologist may have evidence of the value for a special unit to be attached to a school: from the time the need is first established to the actual implementation a year or more may be needed. Sometimes developments can be planned to take several years. In all these activities it is always helpful to have informal discussion with the administrative officers concerned before embarking on details; they can save time by advising on the right approach.

Advisers and organisers

Most large local authorities have a range of inspectors, advisers and organisers, from those concerned with specialist subjects like physical education and music to advisers on educational technology. Advisers on educational technology are tending to replace the organisers of visual aids etc. This change places more emphasis on educational strategy in the use of apparatus and various aids, and on programmed learning contributions to education. There is an increasing tendency for these officers to be regarded as advisers rather than inspectors. One of these organisers is likely to be responsible for the activities of the teachers' centre which provides in-service training and which is likely to become of increasing importance with the future modification of teachers' training. The active participation of psychologists in the work of the teachers' centre is one of the ways already mentioned in which they can communicate findings and developments in the field.

There is bound to be overlap between the work of psychologists and some of the advisers, not so much in the specialist subjects but in the general field, such as special education and primary education, and perhaps curriculum development. All of these officers need to use a considerable amount of psychology. The psychologist will not find himself in great conflict if he bears in mind that his role is to bring to bear specialist psychological knowledge, a large amount of which will come from his own special study of young people in his area. For example, one of the great contributions that can be made to the field of special education, working with the adviser, is the knowledge that comes from studying a wide range of handicaps. Some advisers in special education will have come from the ranks of head teachers of special schools, and some will be knowledgeable in all areas of handicap. They will usually have had some years of teaching and organising experience with one or more of these groups. Few will be really knowledgeable in all areas. Psychologists may not have had the same degree of teaching experience—indeed are most unlikely to have had—but they will have studied a variety of children at different levels in all types of schools, ordinary and special. A special contribution, therefore, can derive from their knowledge of a wide range of psychological characteristics that the various handicaps carry with them, as discussed in Part Three.

Education welfare officers
Education welfare officers are an important source of referrals to the school psychological service, frequently making first contact with school refusers and the delinquent-prone and sometimes developing a sort of counselling role with a problem family, in which they may well need support from a colleague with psychological knowledge. They may know more about some families than anyone else, and their knowledge can be extremely valuable. In some areas, as we have already seen (chapter 3, pp. 46, 58), their work has been amalgamated with that of the social services but most areas are maintaining their own services. With increased training opportunities their work will become more skilled and more closely integrated with school psychological work.

Careers officers
Careers officers work with teachers in advising pupils on their future careers. They will have a good knowledge of local work opportunities as well as the qualities needed for a profession or skilled work. Their approach is very similar to that taken by an educational psychologist in studying children referred with problems—an allround assessment of personal and environmental factors—but, as they have to see large numbers of young people, it has to be abbreviated. They are limited, too, in the availability of confidential material about families. Psychologists can cooperate with them in providing information on the strengths and limitations of handicapped children in making special studies of referred cases, and in working with them to introduce more effective vocational guidance in schools. There is a natural link between their activities and the work of occupational psychologists. Large authorities might well use an occupational psychologist for specialist work with careers officers and educational psychologists.

Her Majesty's Inspectors
It is appropriate here to make reference to the work of Her Majesty's Inspectors. Although not part of the local Education Department, they are in close and regular contact. Their knowledge of a wide range of educational practice in different parts of the country is particularly valuable. If an educational psychologist wishes to have the help of an HMI from another area, e.g. to take part in a course for teachers, it is normal for this to be requested through the HMI for his own area. The inspectorate includes a wide range of educational experts, including educational psychologists.

With a change of emphasis formal inspection has almost disappeared, and HMIs are making valuable studies of special areas of work, drawing attention to useful developments or lack of provision, for example. Psychologists will always find them very helpful and approachable. It is advisable for HMIs to be consulted when any major development is envisaged. This is usually arranged by the Chief Education Officer, but the educational psychologist may initiate a discussion, always making sure that the Chief Education Officer supports this approach. Suppose, for example, an education committee is considering the building of centres for mixed special educational treatment. An allocation of central funds from the Department of Education and Science pool for special education may be involved. Prior discussion with HMIs in the area, who would involve the HMI for Special Education, would be essential on two counts. The plan may well need to be modified in the light of the HMI's knowledge of similar projects. Secondly, when the request is made to the Department of Education and Science for a grant, the administrators there will ask the local HMI what is known of the local situation. If the HMI is already aware of the suggestion this will save time: if it were not regarded favourably he would have said so earlier, some modifications have been made, and the plan postponed or pursued with all the positive evidence of its value clearly expressed.

School staffs and youth service

The head teacher
The statutory power to develop a school psychological service is derived from the Education Act 1944, and the duty it imposes on all local authorities to see that children are educated according to their ages, abilities and aptitudes. This concept may now be regarded as needing some modification; abilities and aptitudes are seen more as phenotypes and less as basically genotypes. It is also appreciated that children have special emotional needs that have to be taken into account in their education. This is seen explicitly in the provision made for maladjusted children, and it is implicit in much of the work carried out in schools today, even though it was not specifically stated in the Education Act of 1944. It is not always easy for teachers to carry out their obligations for some of these children. It is not unexpected, therefore, that by far the majority of requests for help in local authority services come from head teachers and teachers. Psychologists from the school psychological service, who give advice and help to the head and the class teacher on problems that arise, find themselves in a strong position if there is a child guidance case referred from other sources, but which require the help of the school. In this country the local education authority delegates considerable powers to

the head teacher of a school, and he has rather more autonomy than he has in other countries. If the head has invited the psychologist to give him some help, then the situation is clearcut. If, however, a child needs to be followed up because he is a handicapped child for whom the medical officer would like some advice, or he is a maladjusted child, and the psychiatrist who is organising his treatment wants some help, it is essential to approach the school, asking the head teacher if the child may be seen. Even though a child may be regarded as someone's patient, it does not give an automatic right to see the child at school. Most head teachers are extremely cooperative, and if asked to do so will be only too pleased to make the necessary arrangements. So far as primary schools are concerned, the psychologist usually makes direct contact with the head teacher and with the class teacher concerned. It is very important that the latter is brought into the picture, although not all heads see this as necessary. Some of them like to discuss the case thoroughly with the psychologist, and then themselves act as interpreters to the class teacher involved. Very few, however, refuse to let psychologists have direct contact with a class teacher if asked. There is always some practical difficulty in that the class teacher has a large class to look after, and it is not always convenient for someone else to look after the class whilst he has a discussion. Special arrangements frequently have to be made, but these are well worthwhile; a common criticism of some services is that the class teachers themselves rarely get to know the psychologist.

The teachers and their classes
Although all teachers are regarded as trained teachers, i.e. not as infant or junior teachers, there are differences in the approaches and the classroom environment, according to the stage of education the child is entering. Our infants' schools are small, junior or middle schools large, and secondary schools larger still. With the tendency for education authorities to develop comprehensive schools, some are very large indeed. There are differences, too, in approach. Nursery and infants' schools tend to be more orientated towards child development. Children work on independent assignments and activities for much of the day; a great deal of the learning is individual. Some schools group children in family-type groups: few tend to use the rigorous streaming that was popular in the fifties. The head will know all the children quite well, and can liaise directly with the psychologist when a child has a problem. Because of the smaller range of individual differences of ability and the flexible approaches of today, only a small proportion of infant school pupils need to have special help away from their own schools. A small proportion (about 4 in 1,000), may need the help of diagnositc remedial units, which can be invaluable. Even if the approach is flexible classes can be large, and the very difficult child may best be helped in a

special unit. The research at University College of Swansea (R. Evans, *et. al.*) on identifying disadvantaged children has produced useful material for earlier and better diagnosis of infant school children needing help.

With reorganisation, in many areas the infants' schools will cater for children up to eight years of age; junior schools will be replaced by middle schools taking pupils to twelve or thirteen years. The middle and junior schools have changed their approach considerably over the last decade; there is now much more emphasis on individual activity, on learning from experience, working in mixed groups. Many schools favour team teaching and non-streaming. It is in this progressive climate that the needs of the child who requires special educational treatment have to be appreciated. Individual differences become sufficiently wide in middle schools that not all needs are met without special help. The psychologist can help the teachers by working with them on special programmes within schools, by advising on groupings to meet special needs, or recommending for special treatment elsewhere if the school cannot fully meet the needs of the child, or if the child itself disrupts too severely the development of others. Some schools have special educational treatment classes, which the children who are very slow learning attend for part of the day, or even whole time. Others provide special learning bases within an open plan type of group provision. Others give specially trained teachers responsibility for seeing that needs are met within an unstreamed system.

Whatever techniques are used it is essential that those requiring special help should get it. The psychologist is particularly sensitive to the large number of children needing special attention because of the referrals made, both at school level and at Education Department level. Estimates indicate that approximately 20 to 25 per cent of primary school children need special help. Not all can be studied by a psychologist or school medical officer. There is a need for teachers to play their own part in identifying special cases. A well developed educational guidance test service, and some training for teachers in special diagnostic techniques that lie within their scope can be promoted by the school psychological service. It is in the junior and middle school stage that many of the intellectual difficulties become clearly identifiable.

The environment of the new comprehensive schools provides a very different background from the others. Teachers are more specialised, seeing many different groups of pupils. Head teachers cannot be expected to know every child. Other provision becomes necessary to meet some of the special needs of the children. Some schools have a tutorial system, in which a teacher has special responsibility to get to know a cross-section of the children and see that their needs are met. Others are using school counsellors (see chapter 3, p. 58), who may have three types of function:

one, to have responsibility for the general educational guidance procedures, another to help with personal problems, and the third to provide
vocational guidance in cooperation with careers officers. Smaller schools
may use teachers to fulfil these functions, large schools will appoint
specialists for each area. In such schools the psychologist will have specialist teachers with whom to liaise; indeed, the training course for counsellors,
especially those working with personal problems, stresses that they should
be sensitive to the contribution that can be made by the child guidance
clinic, the school psychological service and the school health service, and
call them in as appropriate. Psychologists will find these teachers particularly involved with school psychological service work. Their development is likely to increase the demand on special studies of secondary
school children.

Grammar and independent schools have some special problems in
dealing with the pressures that bear on pupils whose ability does not match
up to the school standards or to parental aspirations. Many of them are
too small to have their own counselling services, and seek help directly
from the school psychological service.

Youth Service officers (see also chapter 3, p. 58)
The Youth Service does not merely provide for the leisure of young people,
but also gives a very vital and important service which enables young
people to achieve need satisfaction which they otherwise could miss; it has,
in short, a significant bearing on the mental health of young people.
Psychologists can find themselves working with the youth officers in
courses in leadership training, and indeed for other in-service training
work. They may also be involved in working with certain clubs in the
rehabilitation of youngsters who are in difficulty. The great problem which
has not yet been solved by the Youth Service is how to get the delinquent-
prone, antisocial youth effectively involved in club life.

Health services
The general role of the Health Service, including the School Health Service,
has been described in chapter 3. Here we will look at relationships between
the educational psychologist and some of the different professional
colleagues who work in the service.

General practitioners and health visitors
Local authorities have a duty, under the Education Act 1944, to find out
children who are handicapped and to make special educational treatment
available for them as appropriate. This they can do for any child from the
age of two years on. In assessing the needs of these children the educational
psychologist has the important role of making psychological observations,

and relating them to special educational provision which may be needed. Until children have to go to school the education authority relies on the Health Service to help it perform its duties. General practitioners, maternity and welfare clinics and health visitors are the main source of referral. Some local education authorities make special arrangements for the assessment of preschool children: an example will be given later. Health visitors are key personnel in finding children with handicaps at an early age. Most have had some training in appreciating early signs of maladjustment, as well as other more evident handicaps. They have all been trained as nurses, and have had a further training in health visiting. Originally mainly concerned with physical health, they are increasingly concerned with mental health problems. Their contribution and that of general practitioners, together with improved early screening through nursery schools, will do much to ensure early ascertainment and enable preventive steps to be taken. They should be invited to take part in suitable local education authority conferences and courses.

School medical officers (see also chapter 3, p. 55)
Once statutory age has been reached the local education authority is in a good position to find all pupils needing help. They themselves can be a source of referral to the Health Service. School doctors are increasingly making use of selective medical examinations to supplement routine screening of all children, which does not then need to be so frequent. Teachers draw to their attention children who, in their opinion, need to be seen. The children who have learning disabilities are usually at risk medically; a greater proportion than average of educationally subnormal children have physical handicaps. The psychologist, therefore is in close liaison with his school medical colleagues (see also chapter 2, pp. 20 and 25). He usually sends the school medical officer a copy of any psychological report made; he may wish to defer making a final report until a medical officer has seen the child, and they have discussed needs. Some work with a basic team of school medical officer, educational psychologist and social worker, supported by teachers as appropriate.

The school medical officer has a special role to play if there is disagreement between the authority and a parent about the need for special educational treatment. The local education authority may initiate action under Section 34 of the 1944 Education Act, and request the parents to present the child for a medical examination. If, for example, there is a dispute about the need for a school for educationally subnormal pupils, the doctor and the psychologist examine the child, completing Form 2 HP, which has three parts; part I for a basic social work type report, part II for a psychological assessment, and part III for the medical report with recommendation about the child's condition (whether he is educationally subnormal or not). The doctor will then tell the parents his opinion about the child's handicap and its need for special education. If the parents challenge this, the doctor issues a form 1 HP, which states what handicap a child has, and what his educational needs are. The parents can then write to the Department of Education and Science contesting this; they have three weeks in which to do so. Only doctors with recognised training can sign the certificate. It is only needed when parents refuse the special education offered, and the local education authority officers feel it is essential, for the sake of the child or in the interest of others. Apart from the appeal situation 1 HP, 2 HP and 3 HP are not required. The local education authority can arrange its own documentation, but it will normally make sure that all the children requiring special help, either in their own schools or through transfer, are given adequate medical, social and psychological investigations. In the case of physical handicaps forms 1 HP and 4 HP are used. For maladjusted children there are no forms; a consultant child psychiatrist can sign form 1 HP, but in practice they rarely use this procedure, as treatment without the cooperation of the parents is not effective; only if a child really had to be placed elsewhere, in another school or in a boarding school, and the parents refused, would this be considered.

It is sometimes thought that the school medical officer alone is empowered to decide whether a child should go to a special school, but this is not the case. The Act (section 34) makes it clear that it is the duty of the Education Committee to decide this after they have had medical and any other relevant reports. Sometimes they delegate this to a school medical officer, an educational psychologist or an education officer, but it is a growing practice to use a team consisting of the first two of these officers and the head teacher of the appropriate special school. The medical, social and psychological contributions made when deciding a school transfer should not be regarded as geared to that only; they are even more important to the teacher and others responsible for day to-day handling of the child, whether he goes to a special school or remains in his own.

The special courses for school medical officers in mental subnormality, which have run for many years, mainly at the University of London with the aid of the National Association for Mental Health but also at other centres, are now to be discontinued. The old courses equipped school medical officers to test children, using the Terman-Merrill test of intelligence, and gave them a broad course on subnormality and its implications. As the number of psychologists has grown it is now a practical proposition to have the psychological assessment carried out by them. In addition to finding out what children have handicaps, there is the need for ongoing assessment: children and their environments change. The school medical officer and the educational psychologist should therefore be regularly supporting diagnostic and assessment units, special schools and units providing special education.

Hospital staff

Some hospitals have assessment teams particularly for multiply handicapped children. The Health Service memorandum on comprehensive assessment centres for handicapped children recommended two types—a general assessment unit in area hospitals, and a more specialised one for a region. These are not the same as assessment units described in Education Survey 9, mentioned in chapter 2, which dealt with assessment to evaluate educational needs; the hospital teams look at general development. Such teams will need the help of someone from the education authority who has firsthand knowledge of the educational provisions and of the needs of handicapped children; someone who has the resources to initiate action and to follow it through. The educational psychologist is the member of the education staff most qualified to do this; he is likely to be concerned with the children when they are in a school setting. He is likely to work with a local education authority team, such as a preschool study group, when carrying out this work. Important in this work will be his cooperation with hospital-based psychologists, to which reference will be made later.

The educational psychologist may therefore find himself working increasingly with a hospital team headed by a paediatrician, or other consultants concerned with children. In one large authority the consultant in physical medicine has a preschool assessment team for neurologically impaired children, for which the local education authority supplies the psychologist and the social worker. This team recommends the entry of children to the specialised unit provided by the local education authority, or forwards reports to the local education authority's preschool study group for appropriate action in other cases. There are considerable advantages in this type of arrangement, but until there are sufficient educational psychologists this is not likely to be a universal pattern, and the local educational psychologist may need to keep good contact with the hospital clinical psychologist. The educational psychologist may have a useful part to play in establishing special treatment units for preschool children, because psychological study has shown the importance of preschool learning situations; neglect of these can aggravate a handicap such as partial hearing or cultural deprivation.

Social services

Much has already been said about social services' departments. Social workers are key colleagues with educational psychologists, and all school psychological services should have very good social work support. If there is any main implication of the modern concept of intelligence and other psychological characteristics being phenotypes, it is that one needs to know the social history of the children with whom one works. Social information is essential in diagnosis. Social work support is needed to ensure the cooperation of parents for treatment measures, not to mention casework for those families where inadequate family relationships play a part in a child's maldevelopment. It would seem that these social workers should be part of social services, but if this is not possible the school psychological service needs to set up its own, perhaps in conjunction with school welfare officers, and to establish good working relationships with the social services' departments. The latter usually organise their casework services in areas, with teams of basic social workers headed by seniors. Psychologists meet both frequently; if the school psychological service has an independent social work service it is not difficult to discuss with social services who will work with a family when there is overlap. If a social services officer is actively involved with a family he usually carries on. Difficulties do arise when there are within a large city some seventy social workers to about five psychologists and two psychiatrists. The senior, or chief, educational psychologist can reduce the difficulties in getting to know the large group of people concerned by lining up his zoning with that of the social services. This facilitates joint conferences and maximises the chances of officers getting to know one another and their methods of approach. It would be extremely difficult for a psychiatrist to work with a large number of different social workers, hence the child guidance clinic or child psychiatric team will continue to need its social workers to be fully employed in the team, so that they can work effectively with the other members of it. If they are permanently based in the clinic, seconded by the social services' department, they can effectively liaise with team leaders in that department. A looser organisation, in which the social worker handling a family teams up with psychologist and psychiatrist, would only be used on special occasions; to make it the main model for working would mean that no consistent team existed.

Educational psychologists should be working to help the social services' department in various ways. It is preferable for the school psychological service to provide for their needs rather than to set up an independent service. One way of achieving good cooperation is to have a senior psychologist within the school psychological service responsible for seeing that the social services' needs are met. Not all of the work with individuals need be done by the senior; it may be appropriate for the psychologist who serves the school which the child attends to carry out the work. Educational psychologists can also have a major part to play in helping with in-service training of social workers, particularly in the field of child development.

Professional organisations

Educational psychologists will find many opportunities to get to know other field workers by joining some of the allied professional organisations. The Association for Special Education, now incorporating the Guild of Teachers of Backward Children, is a broadbased association which includes a wide range of professional people concerned with handicapped children of all sorts. The Association arranges for head teachers, teachers, social workers, psychologists, speech therapists, medical officers etc. to meet together to discuss common problems and to hear about recent developments in research and practice. Membership of such groups can make a considerable contribution to better working relationships. Another group fundamental to work with children is the National Children's Bureau, which now has a number of local groups. This brings together representatives of various disciplines working with children (paediatricians, psychiatrists, social workers, teachers, probation officers, etc.) with the intention of improving cooperation amongst them; it involves voluntary agencies as well as statutory. Some local authorities run a social workers' group, to which membership of psychologists, teachers etc. is welcome. This again provides an excellent opportunity to get to know others in the field, as well as keeping abreast of current developments.

The National Association for Mental Health has a large number of local associations. Like the headquarters body itself, these often pioneer projects which are then taken over by the statutory bodies. Psychologists can contribute much to the work of local associations; they may well also gain their support for mental health projects in education. It was a local association that financed the first purpose-built training unit for educationally subnormal school leavers (the Cliffdale Project). They are, too, a major group which brings together members of the public and professional workers. Other voluntary associations like that of the National Society for Mentally Handicapped Children and the Autistic Society have more specific aims. Voluntary bodies of various types, including parent–teacher associations, can have a considerable part to play in local affairs.

The Association of Child Psychology and Psychiatry is a national association which facilitates intercommunication and cooperation between members of these disciplines. It produces a highly valued journal and arranges meetings, mainly in London. Active participation in such associations does demand some sacrifice of time, but psychologists who take part in these make a substantial contribution to better cooperation and communication with other colleagues.

Other psychologists

With the increase of psychologists, and the development of different types of professional work within psychology, it is appropriate to make some comments on the relationships between psychologists. At local level the educational psychologist will come into contact with clinical psychologists employed by the Health Service, and less frequently with occupational psychologists and those working in polytechnics and universities. Clinical psychologists mainly work in psychiatric hospitals, or in general hospitals which have a psychiatric department. Usually they provide a specialist psychology department which serves the hospital, and it is likely that future developments will lead to departments in general hospitals. They have more work with adult patients than with children, but it is in the latter area that their work may overlap with educational psychologists. Although there is a temptation to guard one's role jealously (it has been known for a local education authority to refuse a clinical psychologist the opportunity to visit freely the schools of the children with whom he works), there is so much to be done that it is a loss to the total work done for children if such barriers are set up. It is better to give scope for initiative and effort, but to ensure through regular consultation a partnership in the fieldwork. The clinical psychologist going to a school will not be able to effect a change of school for a pupil or decide on special treatment: this must be done by the educational psychologist or other educationalist. The clinical psychologist will be able to give some useful information about the child, but he will not advise the school generally about educational psychological matters as the local authority psychologist does; he will, in any case, be unlikely to wish to do so. One can, of course, never cover all possibilities; difficulties can arise, not so much because a person is a clinical or educational psychologist, but because he is a difficult person anyway. These individual and personal problems should not be allowed to interfere with the establishment of a desirable policy.

Psychological help is needed to meet those requirements of the social services not supplied by educational psychologists, e.g. for adult handicaps and those of the elderly; such needs may be met by clinical psychologists who are trained to evaluate adult needs. Some social services are experimenting by appointing community psychologists, but there is as yet no official training for such posts. An educational psychologist is well equipped to help with children's problems, but not to meet the other demands of the social services.

The other major group is that of occupational psychologists. Although largely employed in industry, some may well work closely with local education authority psychologists and careers officers, and bring specialised knowledge to bear on vocational guidance problems. Some industrial rehabilitation units have psychologists who may liaise with the local authority service.

The British Psychological Society with its professional boards and divisions provides opportunities for psychologists of all types to meet. The Association of Educational Psychologists is a body which, in particular, is concerned with negotiations on salaries and conditions of service as well as professional matters. Again, membership brings not only personal benefits but also the opportunity to cooperate with other psychologists. As an affiliated body of the National Union of Teachers contact with professional teaching groups is facilitated.

Team work

We conclude this chapter by considering in more detail team work in a local authority, and the value for professional cooperation of setting up teams. Team work is essential for the adequate diagnosis, assessment and treatment of pupils with special needs. The early child guidance clinic teams were set up to deal effectively with severe behaviour problems (Healy's approach to delinquency). The extension of team work to all forms of handicap is steadily growing. The Department of Education and Science (1971a), in their pamphlet *Education Survey 9—Diagnostic and Assessment Units*, refers to the basic team of teacher, educational psychologist and doctor, supplemented where necessary by other specialists and consultants.

The clinic team

The basic child guidance or child psychiatric team deals essentially with children with behavioural or emotional problems. Since the publication of Circular 347 (Ministry of Education, 1959) authorities have been recommended to set up child guidance services which include child guidance clinics, a school psychological service and the contribution of the school health service as outlined in chapter 1. The clinics enable the authority to carry out its duty in respect of maladjusted children, but they do more than that. They provide a service for children and parents who have problems, even though these do not involve any school handicap. The approach in the clinics is team based; child psychiatrist, educational psychologist and psychiatric social worker work together. Treatment is directed by the psychiatrist. Communication is largely through conferences and discussions, and ideally a team decides its policy after each member has made his contribution. Close cooperation with colleagues in this area of work takes up a large part of the educational psychologist's time, up to about a half. His relationship to his colleagues is therefore vital. There was at one time some rivalry between educational psychologists and psychiatrists for leadership of the team, and at times this was interpreted to mean leadership of the whole child guidance service. Circular 347 did much to clarify the situation. The school psychological service was for the first time officially mentioned as an independent service of which the educational psychologist is the head. The clinic team was defined as one of the Principal School Medical Officer's clinics, and under the direction of the psychiatrist. The psychiatric social worker, although often having general administrative responsibilities, was never the head of the team.

With the introduction of social services' departments and the recognition of social work as a profession, and with the reorganisation of the health service, the background from which members work is changing. Social workers in the social services department carry responsibilities for the families they help, and may indeed have full responsibility for planning for children in their care. In areas where the social workers in a child guidance or child psychiatric team are seconded by the social services they carry with them some delegated powers of that service. The psychologists, who are education-based, carry similar responsibilities on behalf of education. The situation is therefore favourable for the emergence of new style teams, with each member bringing not only diagnostic skills, but also executive powers to deploy resources to contribute to treatment. Hospitals will need child psychiatric teams based in hospitals to deal with their problems, to maximise the use of other medical facilities and to provide training facilities for psychiatry. They will need the support of departments of social services and education to help with diagnosis and treatment. Similarly, education departments need a team approach to meet their obligations to ascertain and give special educational treatment for maladjusted children. Social services departments need this approach to assess the needs of children placed in their care.

One problem is to maximise cooperation and reduce overlap. If the psychiatrists are seconded from a hospital base this can lead to effective interrelationship of the psychiatric work. Similarly, if educational psychologists work in each department continuity of educational contribution can be achieved. Social workers in hospital clinics also may not be under social services; again, they need to work out their relationships. It does not appear to be an answer to have one general clinic serve all departments; each department has responsibilities that necessitate a team approach, and which cannot be delegated to other departments. Overlap can be reduced by having a common register of pupils seen, which is checked whenever a new one is presented. This can be extremely helpful, and save considerable time.

Although the child guidance clinic has been under attack—the Seebohm Report (Home Office, 1968a) was critical of its effectiveness, and a sociologist Rehin (1972) suggested the team approach was outdated—medical associations are quite clear about its value, stating: 'Child Psychiatry, almost more than any other speciality, involves multidisciplinary cooperation. The clinic, or department, team must include psychiatrist, psychiatric social worker and psychologist' (Report of the Tripartite Committee, 1972). The Summerfield Report (Department of Education and Science, 1968b) said that 'interdisciplinary collaboration with the psychiatrist and psychiatric social worker is a necessary background to the work which educational psychologists undertake in Child Guidance Clinics and School Psychological Services; it is highly desirable and should be fostered wherever possible'. A multidisciplinary working party of the Royal College of Psychiatrists, the British Psychological Society and the British Association of Social Workers and the Association of Child Psychotherapists endorsed this point of view (1972). Those experienced in working with children know they cannot work on their own and fully meet the child's needs—this is what determines the need for collaboration. The Secretary of State for Education and Science wrote to the Association of Educational Psychologists: 'As each of the professions making up the Child Guidance team is likely in future to be based separately a more varied pattern of organisation is to be expected; the important thing is to maintain the active cooperation between the different members of the team.' A child guidance team is essentially a working partnership, not only concerned with diagnosis and assessment, but with ongoing treatment over a period of time.

Other teams

Child psychiatrists are the specialists within the Health Service for the treatment of mental ill-health in children. The specialists for dealing with health problems of children in general are the paediatricians. School medical officers are increasingly being trained in developmental paediatrics, and undoubtedly a basic working team of the future will consist of paediatrician or school medical officer with special training, psychologist, social worker and teacher concerned with the handicap; it may also include other specialists (neurologist, for example) as appropriate. In the past such teams have not been as numerous as child guidance clinics. There are, however, examples such as the Wolfson Centre, of a specialist hospital team serving a region and examples of paediatricians taking part with school medical officers and educational psychologists in giving support and help to local authority assessment units.

Certain areas of work demand special assessment teams. In one city there is a preschool case conference—a team looks at the needs of all preschool children who are brought to its attention. Membership consists of a school medical officer, medical officer for maternity and child welfare, senior health visitor, audiologist, educational psychologist and speech therapist. Some of the children on the list will have been seen at a hospital assessment centre, and a comprehensive report will be available. The team can then suggest appropriate special educational treatment. If some aspect of investigation is missing further assessment can be arranged. With other children the panel arranges medical, psychological or social investigations and considers the report. There are preschool assessment and infant school diagnostic units available to assist in the work. Many children can be placed without needing to go either to a hospital assessment unit or to special local education authority units. The panel acts as a clearing house, making sure that all facilities are coordinated, including education.

Some units have their own admission panels because of their specialist nature; admission to educationally subnormal schools is on a team basis, with school medical officer, educational psychologist and head teacher of the intake school acting as a team; specialised units such as those for specific language handicap include on the panel a speech therapist and hearing specialist; the unit for neurologically impaired children has the help of a consultant neurologist. Admission panels for schools for maladjusted will include a child psychiatrist, and partially hearing units involve an audiologist.

We have stressed that assessment is an ongoing process, and towards the end of the handicapped child's school career assessment for vocational purposes becomes important. Two types of panel may be organised, one for the educationally subnormal school leavers, and one for children with other handicaps. These panels do not necessarily have to see all the children; they do, however, make sure that necessary information is available, and if relevant arrange specialist investigation. The panel of the former consists of the usual basic team plus head teachers, social services social workers and careers officers. For the other handicaps specialists such as audiologists and child psychiatrists may ask to be present, and the disablement officer from the Department of Productivity, who may be concerned with the specialist training of a handicapped young person, may also attend.

In addition to these specific teams there are coordination teams. They make sure that various departments concerned with a child work to a coordinated policy. An example is the clearing house run by the local education authority. This has fortnightly meetings chaired alternately by the senior school medical officer and the chief educational psychologist. The panel has, in addition to these officers, representatives from the Health Service (senior health visitor), from the Social Services (area team leaders), from the Child Guidance Service (head social worker), and a child psychiatrist when necessary. Head teachers and school welfare officers also attend, according to the agenda. This regular coordination of activities is invaluable. Cases on the agenda include, for example, those which concern more than one service, and need a planned total approach. The school psychological service and the school health service may be concerned with a child in the family, but need to discuss with the social services the needs of the family as a whole and to decide on policy. It may be that social services will be able to intervene and help the family as a whole. Often, however, there are no grounds for them to do so in face of parental resistance, and other place for action can be evolved. A school phobic child who remains at home having some psychiatric help may well be on the agenda, so that his social and educational needs are regularly appraised. These are the types of problems that can be overlooked when there are heavy caseloads. There can, too, be differences of professional viewpoints about the total approach to such children that are best resolved in team discussion, and an agreed policy determined. The psychiatrist will carry responsibility for medical treatment, but the local education authority still has its responsibility to see that every pupil receives adequate educational provision. Sometimes a child's needs are being discussed elsewhere—at the area Social Services conference, for example. In such a case 'clearing house' may simply keep the name on the agenda for review, or remove it altogether if it is satisfied that all effective help is well looked after. Head teachers or school welfare officers sometimes refer children as they feel more should be done for them; for example, a child may be irregular in attendance because the parents condone this. Without the planned support of the Education Department the Social Services Department may not be able to take action. Another very useful function is to help children for whom a long-term plan is necessary by keeping their names on the agenda, so that action at a future date is not overlooked. A child may need placement after a period of observation, or may be waiting for a boarding school place, and alternative plans need to be drawn up if it is not possible to find a suitable school.

Boarding school placement may present special issues, and for this some authorities use a Residential Treatment Panel (Education). The school health service, school psychological service and social services personnel combine to look at the needs of the children and decide whether residential provision should be made via the social services department or not. Not all children requiring boarding help will be discussed at the panel, only those with which social services personnel may be involved, or when this latter service feels educational boarding provision may be more appropriate for one of the children for whom they have responsibility.

Social services personnel themselves have their own case conferences to which school psychological service and school health service members are frequently invited. They also have assessment teams for children taken into care. In addition they may organise a policy coordination committee with representatives from health, education and voluntary services discussing broad issues in which cooperation can be made more effective.

Chairmanship of these teams may well vary according to the main purpose, a head teacher, educational psychologist, medical officer or social worker may each in turn be the official leader. Leadership qualities in the sense of helping the team reach a goal successfully are not the prerogative of the official leader; individual members showing these qualities will ensure effective cooperation.

It will be noticed that membership varies according to emphasis. This is an economical way of using specialist time. A general team involving all specialists could be wasteful of time, e.g. a child psychiatrist is not necessarily involved in a decision about a partially-hearing, backward child. If, however, members of one team are also members of another, then they are likely to become sensitive to specialist approaches and ensure that suitable cases are referred on. If a partially-hearing backward child does show emotional problems, then the educational psychologist and the social worker concerned who also works in a child guidance team are likely to pick this up.

A problem of a coordination type panel is how to review the cases without too cumbersome a committee. A handicapped school leavers' panel may find it difficult to involve all the personnel actively concerned: thirty headteachers, forty social workers may be involved. In this case senior and experienced representatives act on their behalf, referring back for more 'grass roots' discussion if this is necessary. These problems do not arise in working case conferences, although even in these, e.g. in child guidance clinics, problems can arise. Thus the educational psychologist, with his knowledge of the schools and close contact with head teachers and class teachers may have to act on their behalf in a case conference, especially if this is concerned with a number of cases.

There is an area in which the educational psychologist can be autonomous, or work with a class teacher or social worker. He will, however, find that in a large number of the cases he has to handle he will be involved with a range of other disciplines, each making its contribution to the common goal—that of helping a child towards effective allround development. He will, with reorganisation of the Health Service and the Social Services, find himself very much the representative of the Education Service in interdepartmental cooperation. His initiative and his leadership (in the contributive sense) can play a very considerable part in making interdepartmental cooperation really work.

14

Principles in practice

This chapter will be concerned with illustrations from practice of the principles which have been discussed in this work. It is not intended that any of the illustrations should be taken as models; much improvement can and should be made on the approaches described. Each, however, will provide opportunities to highlight certain aspects of the work carried out by educational psychologists. The first four illustrations are fairly detailed examples of very different kinds of problems. The rest of the chapter presents some shorter case studies.

Cooperation in planning a project

This first example is of cooperative work between a school psychological service and its Education Department, the Regional Hospital Board and the Department of Education and Science. It illustrates how the educational psychologist may initiate and then take part in the joint planning of a project, in this case the building of a school for a hospital department of child psychiatry. This department was planning a diagnostic and assessment unit with residential accommodation for twenty-five emotionally disturbed children, for whom education was to be provided. The psychiatric unit had close contact with the school psychological service; there were weekly conferences which the staffs of both units attended, and the Director of the Psychiatric Unit, and other psychiatrists on his staff, gave sessions to the local education authority child guidance service. The chief educational psychologist acted as honorary consultant for special educational treatment for the hospital unit. When, therefore, the initial plans for the new unit were being considered the psychologist was consulted about the educational provision.

At that time the Ministry of Education had published a circular pointing out that education authorities would make provision for hospital schools, namely, building, staff and equipment. The school psychological service had already pioneered the development of local authority classes for maladjusted pupils and a day school. This interest by the school psychological service was a natural outcome of the psychologist's work with the schools, which revealed the need for this kind of provision to help both the individual child and the schools, where it is extremely difficult to provide adequately for disturbed children in an ordinary classroom environment. The original plan for the hospital school envisaged a single teaching space (mainly for work in the basic subjects), and supplementary provision for activities to be undertaken by occupational therapists.

The educational psychologist pointed out the possibility of the local education authority making full provision for all the work of the school, and discussed this with the chief education officer on behalf of the unit director. Further discussion followed between members of the education department, the school psychological service and hospital representatives. School psychological service experience suggested that the numbers justified a small school: this, of course, needed discussion with the Inspector for Special Schools of the Department of Education and Science Medical Service. (In a larger authority the adviser on special education would be involved in this, working with the educational psychologist and others concerned.) It was finally agreed that a school with a head teacher and three teachers would be appropriate, and a further meeting was held at which the local authority and hospital representatives discussed plans for the building with the architect. The concept now was of a school which made an allround educational provision through satisfying a child's needs, developing abilities and interests, and especially establishing a positive relationship with a sympathetic teacher. This modified architectural planning considerably, and the notion of specialist rooms for art therapy and pottery was dropped in favour of multipurpose classrooms. Plans were submitted to the Department of Education and Science, and a further meeting took place with DES medical, inspectorial and architectural representatives. The latter brought their wide experience of school construction for handicapped pupils to bear on the problem. They wanted a more flexible open-plan type of design, with greater use of corridor and other space. They preferred non-specialisation of rooms, but recommended some special location of equipment such as a pottery wheel and furnace. The hospital board's architect and the DES architect had a final meeting to draw up plans for the school. The result was a building giving considerable scope for modern educational practice and a strong base for education and psychiatry to contribute jointly in helping disturbed children. The educational psychologist's role in this was partly catalytic in making sure that matters beyond his immediate action were referred on to appropriate officers, and partly contributory, since his experience of working in the special educational field in the local education authority enabled him to make direct suggestions.

A small epidemiological study

The second example shows how the educational psychologist can help in planning by undertaking a survey of special needs. The Department of Education and Science had published a circular which recommended that local authorities should review their provisions for educationally subnormal pupils and consider whether these were adequate. Circulars like these provide opportunities for work which has long-term effects. However busy with day-to-day cases a psychological service may be, it must be ready to take time from this work so that good planning can be achieved. Although some individual children had to be kept on a waiting list longer than usual, the long-term effect on many children was considerable.

The aims of the study were:

(a) to survey the distribution of educational handicap in the schools of the city;
(b) to attempt to break this down into types of special handicap such as specific reading disability, general allround slowness;
(c) to try out suitable tests which might help in diagnosis, and to obtain city norms for subsequent use;
(d) to derive from the data, and other sources, some suggestions from which a development plan for helping children with educational handicap could be drawn up.

An estimate of the amount of educational handicap amongst fourth year pupils in a city was made using the Moray House 11 + English Test scores, which were standardised using the raw scores of city children and compiling a conversion table direct from them. (This Moray House itself, the test producers did, as part of their service when supplying large numbers of tests.) Similar calculations were made for second and first year children, using the National Foundation for Educational Research sentence reading test, again standardised on city children. This test had NFER norms which would give a different mean from a city sample.[1] To achieve a local norm the cumulative frequency (c.f.) of each NFER standard score was calculated for city children: this enabled a correction table to be calculated. A sample of three selected points in the correction table is given below.

---

[1] It was assumed that this would be the main difference and that the age allowance of the NFER norms could be used without serious error.

Table 14.1   Example of correction table (expressed as a percentage)

c.f.	NFER	City score
75	115	110
50	104	100
15	77	75

The numbers involved (over 2,000) seemed large enough to justify direct use of c.f. scores corrected to the nearest whole number. The incidence of standard scores of 80 or below was calculated for each of three successive years to give an ESN incidence. As 9 per cent of the total population studied made such scores meaningful, comparisons could be made of different schools.

A selection of the findings is summarised in Table 14.2.

Table 14.2   Incidence of ESN children in eight schools

School	Percentage of ESNs		
	4th year pupils	2nd year pupils	1st year pupils
A	42	43	25·4
B	36	24	35·8
C	25	11	15·5
G	19	37·5	29·8
J	2	0	0
K	2	2	0
L	2	0	1
M	0	2·5	10·2

The four schools which had the highest proportion of scores below 80 are here contrasted with the four schools which had the lowest: the first and second year data on one year samples show the same cluster of schools with the problem. The degree of contrast shown between schools with backward children and those with virtually none is striking; few teachers had realised quite how marked it was. The administrators had appreciated the problem, but the actual figures enabled a much more realistic appreciation of the amount of extra help needed. This led to a differential and planned growth of special educational treatment according to the needs of the schools, so that, for example, school A was the first to receive this help and was given facilities to enable two special classes to be established.

A survey was also made of children with severe reading difficulties in their last year of primary school. They were given Schonell Reading Tests by members of the remedial teaching staff. There were 2,650 pupils in the age group; of these 25 had reading ages of 5+, and 46 of 6+. This total of 71 was regarded as showing the need for very special provision in secondary schools. This survey was repeated eight years later to see if the problem was more or less severe. There had been considerable publicity about the apparent decline in reading standards in some areas, and some teachers in secondary schools had expressed concern about lower standards. The results of the survey showed a significant reduction in the number of children with acute difficulties. Of a population of 2,621 there were 13 with reading ages of 5 + years, and 36 with reading ages below 6 years, a total of 49. It can be very helpful to keep careful records of surveys carried out and to repeat them to check on progress made.

A study was also made of retarded children, and the report summarised thus:

> Children are regarded as retarded who do not come up to the level of their general ability. There are difficulties in measuring this, but nevertheless some approximate estimate can be made, using group tests of general ability; thus, on the first year test, calculations were made of the number of children who differed significantly in their scores on the reading test and on the picture intelligence test when each had been restandardised into city norms. Of the children who were not educationally subnormal, 334 scored between 10 to 19 points below their Moray House Picture test score; 166 scored 20 to 29 points below, and 57 scored 30 to 39 points below. Some of these differences will be explicable in terms of the differences in special talents measured by the various tests. [There is now available a better test for juniors which measures the verbal factor. D. Young, 1964.] It would not be correct to assume that all children ought to make scores almost the same in both tests. However, quite a number of them, including those with the largest discrepancies, will probably be underfunctioning to a considerable degree. It is interesting to note that underfunctioning occurred in children of all levels of intelligence. The second year survey presented a similar picture: in this case a different test was used, namely the Cornwell instead of the Picture Intelligence Test. On these findings there were 72 children who were both ESN and retarded in the second year. There were 280 children who were retarded by 10 points or more, and 50 who were retarded by 20 or more, based on the Cornwell test. These figures were substantially lower than those of the first year, and may indicate that the amount of retardation was substantially reduced in the second year. The number of children scoring 75 or below on all tests was 33 in the second year survey. These are the children who do need to be looked at further and carefully considered for transfer to a special school.

There were obvious limitations in this tentative survey, e.g. a better measure of general ability could have been made using individual tests, but it was difficult to find time to do this. It was, however, sufficient to point out that there was a considerable number of children whose attainments were well below their general level of development, and that remedial and diagnostic services were needed to help with these.

The data obtained from these studies, together with evidence from research in other areas, enabled a programme to be suggested to the Education Committee. This included

(a) Encouraging regular surveys and use of the Educational Guidance Test service by teachers to pick out children for further study or special help.
(b) Giving priority attention to schools with special needs, including making a provision for twenty 'special educational treatment' teachers in the estimates.
(c) Establishing some special units in selected secondary schools.
(d) Reviewing remedial provision to include
  (i) Expansion of the service.
  (ii) Greater use of remedial teachers in advisory work in schools.
  (iii) Greater use of the permanent exhibition of books and remedial material.
(e) Giving priority to preschool provision in the areas with the highest proportion of educational handicap.

The evidence for priority for preschool provision did not come from the survey, but from research known to the educational psychologist. An appreciation of the significance of ongoing research and its relevance to local education authority work is of considerable value when preparing reports of this nature, but it is not always enough to generalise from this research without carrying out one's own investigations. For example, the mean performance of children in different authorities vary considerably.

It is essential that policy plans should be based on demonstrated needs of the children in the area concerned. In special cases long-term planning may need to depend on other sources, e.g. when the principal school medical officer and the chief education officer studied the increase of incidence of spina bifida it was useful to refer to national figures as a first approximation to need, but even with this condition there were inexplicable local differences, so that information from paediatricians and neurological surgeons in the area was needed.

The educational psychologist may well initiate this kind of survey. Clearly it affects his work, as well as that of inspectors and advisers, particularly those concerned with special education. In some areas the psychologist may find that the local adviser himself will initiate a survey, or be willing to take part in its organisation. See P. Williams (1970) for a discussion of survey methods for educational psychologists.

A case of multiple handicap

This third example will illustrate the contributions made by the educational psychologist to the development of a boy with multiple handicaps. It illustrates also the contributions made by other specialists.

Arthur was referred whilst he was at a special unit for cerebral palsied children, as his teacher found his behaviour extremely difficult and his general educational progress so limited that she thought he might not be suitable for education. He was, she felt, quite unsuited for the unit. He was troublesome to get round the room, threw toys and other material into the nearby street; he pushed some of the other chairbound children and heavily handicapped children over and was generally disruptive.

Medical records which were available showed that Arthur was a rhesus baby. He suffered from a moderate degree of athetosis; an athetoid tongue made speech difficult. An audiological report showed the following decibel losses for one ear (the losses for the other ear were similar).

Frequency	Decibel loss
128	20
256	30
512	40
1024	70

He could hear a conversational tone from five feet, and certain consonants from a few inches. There was a considerable amount of hearing present with a fairly good hearing for low frequencies.

The consultant in physical medicine reviewed his case and considered that the athetosis was minimal, and that his problem was more associated with hearing difficulties. This was supported by the audiologist. The speech therapist who had treated Arthur over a number of years said he had made little progress because his spasticity affected the muscles concerned with speech; his complete inability to make the necessary tongue movements was such that it was impossible, even for an experienced person who had worked with him for years, to understand what he was saying.

Arthur was eight years old when he was first seen by the psychologist. He would not respond to verbal questions and had no reading or writing skills. He did, however, respond to performance items in the WISC. He produced a nearly average score on block design, and showed evident delight in his success. It was clear that he had areas of average ability and that he was not severely subnormal.

The family background was good. Mother was positive and affectionate. Father had had a period of depression following long years of difficulty with Arthur, but had recovered from this.

The psychologist felt that the behaviour problems stemmed in the main from Arthur's frustration in not being able to communicate his needs effectively. The psychologist supported the audiologist's and consultant's view that emphasis in special education should be on Arthur's hearing, feeling that, given help in this field, he was clearly educable. Fortunately the LEA had set up a unit for partially hearing children in a local primary school, and Arthur attended this.

At 11+ his needs were again reviewed, as he could no longer remain in a junior school. At that time he scored above average on the Nebraska and Columbia tests which are designed to help assess the abilities of children with hearing difficulties. Areas of average ability were therefore confirmed. On the Coloured Progressive Matrices and the WISC performance scale he scored in the low average zone. His reading age was 7+ years on a sentence reading test (silent), and 7·1 years on a word recognition test. His mathematics performance was at the level of an average child of 7·4 years (P. E. Vernon, 1949). His behaviour was still causing some concern because he interfered so much with the work of others, but it was much improved. In his speech he had made only a little progress, and it was still very difficult to understand him. Unfortunately the authority did not have a full-time unit for older partially hearing children—only special sessions at one of the secondary schools. There was therefore the problem of choosing an appropriate secondary school. Boarding school was ruled out immediately because the parents would not consider this in any circumstances.

A decision was finally made after joint conferences with the audiologist, school medical officer, psychologists and teachers. Clearly his attainments were in line with those of ESN secondary pupils; his behaviour, it was thought, was reactive and different from that shown by maladjusted children of the local special school. It seemed, therefore, that Arthur would best be helped in an ESN school. The psychologist was not completely in accord with this, as the problem of language was different in Arthur's case, but agreed that a compromise could be made if as much supplementary help as possible were given by one of the teachers for partially hearing children.

The placement was a success. Arthur became a pleasant and enthusiastic member of the school. He learned to type, and showed his practical superiority by his achievements in woodwork and metalwork. By the end of his secondary career he had a reading level of 10+ years, but still had difficulty in communicating through speech. He had been seen several times by the psychologist, who had discussed his progress with his teachers.

Arthur's progress was again reviewed towards school leaving age by a panel which included a careers officer as well as a medical officer, educational psychologist and teachers. It was felt that his communication problem was such that he would need some special help to adjust to work—just to find a job would be insufficient. The school ran an end-on course to prepare immature ESN school leavers for work, and it was felt that Arthur should be helped in this setting until suitable work could be found.

The psychologist again became involved, this time when Arthur reached an age at which it was no longer practicable to keep him on at school as a pupil. Contact with the local branch of the National Association for Mental Health obtained a grant so that he could be employed as an assistant. The psychologist's knowledge of the young man's needs was instrumental in obtaining this. Arthur was suitably placed in a job after some four months as an assistant manager in the unit.

This case illustrates the long-term contribution made by the psychologist in a series of assessment procedures. Assessment is an ongoing procedure, for children with special needs require frequent reassessment and evaluation of a suitable programme.

A hyperkinetic boy

This study will show the help given to a boy showing hyperkinetic behaviour problems. He was first referred to the educational psychologist shortly after he entered school, and was helped up to and including further education. The salient features of the case are:

(a) In the initial stages the full clinic team was involved—How valuable was this?

(b) The psychologist had different roles at different times.

(c) A crucial decision was to seek boarding school placement.

An alternative could have been to plan a behaviour modification approach, although this procedure was not prevalent at that time. It is doubtful however, with the continuous instability of the family relationships, whether this could have been effective.

Bill was first referred in June 1961, when he was five years of age. An unusually tall boy, he was restless, physically uncontrolled, and failing to make the usual positive learning starts the other children were showing. The headmistress of his infant school had made some pertinent observations:

'Mother said on entering him, in his hearing, that he was a very naughty boy. I took this with a grain of salt, but she proves to be absolutely right. He is always in trouble for something, making loud and peculiar noises (copied from another boy), being in the wrong place, writing on the classroom wall, interfering with other children, but not in an aggressive way; the main impression he gives is lack of physical control, although the writing I have just seen seems to be normal for his age.' 'Fell over step from grass, upsetting his milk. Fell off his chair three times, sat on a stool, returned to chair and fell off backwards' (6 June). 'Chased children on grass with his shoe' (8 June). 'Took handful of pegs from number apparatus and deliberately scattered them over the floor' (15 June). 'Fell off his chair four times. Mother said yesterday she was at her wits' end, and would welcome help' (26 June).

The head teacher then referred to the school psychological service. The psychologist who saw Bill eliminated the possibility of low ability—indeed he was above average ability with a good vocabulary: early failures on the Terman-Merrill test were of a practical type, such as folding paper to a pattern. It was judged that it would be helpful to have him referred immediately for full child guidance clinic observation. His restlessness suggested a possible medical condition, and the school notes pointed to some degree of maladjustment.

The social history revealed some inadequacy in parent–child relationships. There were early environmental stresses when the family occupied a small top flat, where they felt no noise or commotion would be permitted. As an infant Bill was active and restless, and the kind of restriction deemed necessary provoked resistance. Mother had always felt inadequate and had relied on Father' s help in the early months. Always an anxious, worrying woman, her relationship with her stepmother had never been really satisfying, and they frequently quarrelled. The maternal grandmother had died after a long illness which had restricted the mother's development. Father was away for long periods in the Air Force; an anxious man, described as moody and impatient, he was discharged from the service with a duodenal ulcer. Mother said she was worried to death, and felt so hopeless that she was in a continuous state of tension and anxiety.

Bill was born full term, a much wanted baby after four years of marriage. Mother was unable to breast-feed, and bottle feeding was difficult. He had gastro-enteritis at six months and was hospitalised for three weeks. He was circumcised at ten months, and at eighteen months had an operation for hernia. Developmental progress seemed average in all areas, and there was no apparent change in primary behaviour pattern after the birth of his sister when he was three years old. She was an active, self-willed, outgoing child, but never aggressive; Bill was said to be affectionate towards her.

The psychiatrist felt that the behaviour problems were mainly reactive to handling. The team accepted this, and it was arranged for Bill to attend a play group under a therapist, and for mother to have the continuous support of a social worker.

Follow-up at Bill's school six months later by the psychologist showed continuing difficulties. He had started to read and was making a little progress academically, but he was always restless and wanting to be the centre of attraction. He showed uncoordinated movements in Music and Movement lessons, and his drawings were disjointed. Further psychological testing using the WISC gave a verbal quotient of 113 and performance quotient of 83, with a full scale quotient of 99. He showed clear and significant difficulties with practical material, the difference between his practical and verbal abilities being significant. Mother had become disturbed and depressed, so that the psychiatrist arranged for Bill's admission to a psychiatric hospital unit. It was considered that observation in a residential setting might help to decide whether he was a hyperkinetic boy, or just reacting to the handling situation. It would also provide a short period of relief for mother. He was admitted in May 1962, and discharged three months later, being described as 'Happy, rather active and fidgety, but not presenting any major disciplinary problems.' He returned to his infants' school in September 1962. The psychiatrist felt that the home tensions had improved only slightly, and enlisted the aid of the GP to give Largactil treatment to help mother. The clinic team continued to support the family.

The psychologist carried out a review in February 1963, as the head teacher again referred Bill because of a deterioration in his behaviour, which was giving cause for grave concern. 'Cannot keep still. Upsetting work and possessions of others. Constantly hitting people. Always falling off his chair.' The psychologist followed up the observations, in previous studies, of marked practical difficulties. On a test of perceptual[1] performace Bill showed gross perceptual immaturity, drawing every figure with widely separated parts. On another diagnostic figure drawing test[2] he performed at a subnormal level, with an exceptionally high error score of 27. A hypothesis of possible organic condition such as brain damage was postulated, and the views of the psychiatrist sought. He, however, did not feel that there was enough evidence to support a hypothesis of brain damage. He thought the boy had well above average energy, and was overactive.

The syndrome of brain damage has been put forward to explain certain characteristic patterns of disability in learning and behaviour (Strauss and Lehtinen, 1947). Birch (1964) has shown that this concept has limited application when there is no neurological evidence: there is no clearcut syndrome. Nevertheless the possibility that there was an organic factor playing a part was important. An alternative hypothesis to brain damage is that of constitutional differences (Bax and Mackeith, 1963). It could be that Bill was at the end of the curve of distribution for practical ability, which neurologically seems to be located in a different hemisphere from verbal ability (McFie, 1972). In this case his poor ability in space perception and spatial relationships and his clumsiness would be as natural

[1] The Bender-Gestalt test.   [2] The Benton test.

to him as being short is to another child. It would also indicate that he himself could not control his clumsiness, nor were the parents or the school to blame for not remedying it. The behaviour problem would then be seen to result from parental handling, not from the clumsiness. The earlier observations made when he was in the residential setting supported this. It was agreed that Bill should be readmitted to the residential unit in March 1963 if his behaviour deteriorated, and that meanwhile consideration should be given to special class placement. Shortly after this the school reported that he had tried to strangle a child and that he was unmanageable. He was readmitted in March 1963.

After a further period of observation and treatment a conference with psychologist and hospital staff recommended that he should be admitted to the day school for maladjusted pupils in February 1964. By March 1965 the home situation was breaking down completely (father had had an operation and was away convalescing) and urgent admission was sought at the hostel for maladjusted pupils, which worked closely with the school. The hostel arrangements enabled contact with home to be maintained.

Bill stayed in the hostel for two years, and at the day special school for a total of four years. Improvement was slow but positive. The head teacher, however, asked if more could be done for the boy, and at a panel meeting at the school he was referred for a review. The psychologist saw him, and found that he had a reasonable grasp of basic subjects, although he remained slightly retarded (CA 12 years, reading level 10 years, arithmetic level 9+ years). On the WISC the same marked contrast between verbal and performance levels was again evident, although his general verbal level seemed to have dropped slightly, but not significantly (Verbal quotient 100, Performance quotient 83). Bill had considerable difficulty with block design, and undoubtedly his ability to deal with spatial material was very poor. This and his clumsiness were still characteristic features of his skills. Emotionally still distractable, with poor attention span, he was making positive relationships with other people. At interview he was very friendly and relaxed. The psychiatrist reported him much improved, but suggested that boarding school provision be sought.

After team discussion it was decided to proceed with this, mainly on the grounds that, although the situation was much improved, the parental relationships were still unstable, and the pressures of adolescence might prove too much for them. As Bill himself had a positive attitude to boarding school, having enjoyed his stay in the hostel, a placement was arranged at a school for maladjusted children by the school psychological service. Regular follow-ups were organised, so that Bill came for an interview during each holiday with his parents, who saw a social worker during term-time. Some very valuable discussions took place between the social worker and the parents, particularly his mother, who eventually confided at length about her feelings of inadequacy and her anxiety about her son. Bill was usually given an opportunity to talk about the school, and from time to time his development was reassessed. His attainments showed a steady improvement. On the HSPQ personality test (Cattell and Cattell, 1969), given when he was fourteen years old, his traits were mainly in the average zone, except for factor D, on which he scored 9 stens (excitable, impatient, demanding, overactive). The normality of most of the scores was reassuring. The Maudsley Personality Inventory given on another occasion indicated slight extraversion and normal neuroticism. A sentence completion test gave some interesting replies, such as

'When I was a little child . . . I used to be bad.'

'Other people . . . are nice to me.'

'The future . . . is good for me.'

'I need . . . lots of help.'

'My greatest worry . . . is Dad.'

(His father had just been in hospital for an operation.)

In his report the school emphasised his clumsiness, and when the psychologist visited he was told that Bill was the clumsiest boy in the school, forever knocking things over or breaking them. He was friendly and fitted in well with the school. At his interviews in the clinic he always spoke well of the school and was clearly identified with it.

When he was approaching fifteen years of age his needs were discussed at the School Leavers' Panel for Handicapped Pupils. The psychologist gave a review report. The proposal that Bill should remain longer at school had already been discussed with him and his parents, all of whom were positive to this, and the panel recommended continued attendance. During that year there were two incidents, the school became worried about his sexual precocity and arrangements were made for the psychiatrist to see him. No further problems of this nature were reported. During a holiday he stayed overnight with some friends (young men with whom he worked on a holiday job), without the permission of his parents, who became very anxious. The police, who were informed, made enquiries through the social services (Form P 15 (b)). The opinion of the psychologist was asked for, and he wrote a detailed letter to the police, who were satisfied that the boy was receiving adequate treatment. It would have been most unfortunate had Bill been taken to court; certainly the new procedures for seeking special help and treatment worked effectively in this case. The incident itself, and the parents' anxiety, made it clear that a return home at sixteen years could be premature.

During the holidays in his last year at school the possibility of going on a training course was discussed with Bill and his parents. School reports had indicated a positive interest in cookery. His clumsiness would handicap him a little in this field, but by now it was not severe enough to prove a real drawback unless manual dexterity as such was called for. Bill wanted to join the Army, but it was felt desirable to keep options open; his scholastic levels might not have been sufficient, and his manual performance would not endear him to any drill sergeant. Bill was told about a possible unit which provided training of about eighteen months duration in a number of jobs, including simple cookery. It also specialised in helping the somewhat immature, and had the services of a consultant psychiatrist. The Handicapped School Leavers Panel discussed this and agreed that the authority should be recommended to seek placement there for Bill. An interview was arranged, at which he was offered a place, but told that he would have to ask for it; this he promptly did. Progress at the unit has been good. Bill has discussed problems with the psychiatrist there, including his feelings about homosexuality. Clearly he now regards the adults with whom he comes in contact as sources of help and guidance. During his time at the unit he will have detailed vocational guidance and relevant training. There is a good chance that he will then find employment, perhaps away from home, maintaining regular contact with his family.

On reviewing this case and its treatment several points of significance stand out. Firstly, the decision to call in the full child guidance team was well justified. It would have been impossible for a psychologist to relate the psychopathology of the family to possible organic factors solely on the strength of his own skills. This was a problem that demanded a team approach. The contrast between verbal and practical skills was well established, and continued through to school leaving age. This was not tackled by any special drills to reduce his clumsiness, but by accepting that there were natural deviations. There were indications that this was successful in his positive attitude to adults. New advances in treatment techniques may enable these problems to be alleviated through direct treatment, but there is no convincing evidence of this as yet. Whatever remedial techniques are undertaken it is important that attitude development is continuously watched, and positive attitudes fostered. The boarding school placement proved to be a success, the important factors in this being the boy's own identification with the placement and his positive progress there. Failure is more likely if a pupil is feeling rejected and does not identify with the placement. In this authority the school psychological service had been given delegated powers to find boarding schools for maladjusted and slow learning pupils (not physically handicapped), and the responsibility to keep in touch with the school and pupil. Opportunities were taken to improve the relationship between Bill and his parents during his periods of absence from home. This was successful to a point, but it became clear that the parents' deficiencies would make it difficult for them ever to become completely adequate, as indicated in their handling of Bill's night out. There was also evidence from school that the boy himself still needed help, hence the decision to seek further education for him.

Residential placement involves consideration of the role of the social services in making this kind of provision available. They have to provide this if a family is without support, or if children are placed in care by the court. They can also take children into care if the parents ask. If, however, the home is intact, but it is desirable to provide a different environment, as in Bill's case, then there are difficulties in evoking social services' help. Had Bill's parents requested that he be taken into care, boarding placement could have been effected by the social services. However, in this case the parents would not have wished to do this, and it was beneficial to their own feelings about themselves that provision could be made without the inference that they were incapable of providing a suitable home.

This then illustrates a situation in which the education authority was justified in making boarding school provision.

Some short case studies

In this section some case studies are described with less detail than those previously reported. They have been selected to illustrate various aspects of field work.

A slow learner needing special school help

Christine was noticed as a slow learner in her infant school. She was not, however, a difficult child to manage, and in the flexible organisation of the infant school she presented no undue difficulties. Nevertheless, as the time approached for transfer to the junior school the head teacher doubted that Christine would adjust, and thought her needs might be met more adequately at a special school. The educational psychologist found that Christine had very little reading knowledge—just two or three words—and could only manage number work using concrete aids, such as counting and adding with bricks, but was not able to perform simple addition on paper. On the Terman-Merrill test she scored an IQ of 75. She came from a poor family living near the town railway station, and was the oldest of four children. Her father and illiterate mother were themselves very limited; father worked in the local fruit market. Medical records showed only minor defects, such as a slight occasional hearing loss due to a catarrhal condition. Although Christine clearly needed special educational treatment, she belonged to a fairly large group of children, some of whom could manage in an ordinary primary school, especially if there were special provision for them. Christine's junior school had two special units, staffed by teachers with an interest in slow learners and it was decided that she could go to the junior school. It has been found, in any case, that girls have a better prognosis than boys in terms of overcoming early reading handicap. At this stage no further investigation was made, for it is not practicable to make an intensive investigation of all children showing slowness in learning. At Christine's new school the teacher in charge of the unit observed her carefully, but in spite of special help she was still showing such marked lack of progress towards the end of the year that, in the teacher's opinion, it did not seem that her needs were being met there. Follow-up testing, using the WISC, gave a verbal quotient of 72, performance quotient of 63. This provided confirmation of slow allround development. It is interesting to note that the performance quotient was below the verbal quotient, although statistically this was not significant. This, however, reinforced the hypothesis that Christine's slowness was not simply a by-product of her environment. Slow learning pupils were usually discussed by all the educational psychologists to ensure that the places at the ESN school were not filled by any single enthusiastic psychologist, but were made available to those children with the greatest difficulties. Christine presented no problem in this respect, for her needs, although not as great as many, were sufficiently strong for her to be considered for transfer. Notification was therefore sent to the Chief Education Officer recommending consideration for placement, with a copy for the principal school medical officer, who then arranged a medical review. Both doctor and psychologist then reviewed the child's needs, and after discussion agreed to recommend that Christine should have special school help. Christine's parents had been seen by a social worker who had explained the possibilities without promising anything. The parents had expressed some concern, but had not refused to cooperate. Discussion with the head teacher of the special school about Christine and other children brought agreement to admit Christine, and an invitation to the parents to visit the school. This they did, and after seeing the provision (the school was purpose built, and had attractive facilities) they readily agreed. Christine settled well at the school, and by the time she reached the end of her junior school period she had made considerable progress, so much so that the head teacher asked the psychologist to assess whether she could now transfer to a secondary modern school. Some four pupils a year were successful in this. Home circumstances, however, were not favourable; two more children had been born, and Christine's two immediately younger siblings had both been admitted to special school. It was felt, therefore, that Christine would not have the resources to cope with a normal secondary school's demands. Follow-up testing had confirmed a good level of effective ability for special school work, but even had she scored higher it would have been a little risky to transfer her.

A comment on the repeat of intelligence tests is appropriate here.

Bloom (1964) has shown how the repeat of tests can improve prediction. This particular local authority liked to have both Terman-Merrill and WISC scores for pupils. These were placed with the educational history, and the record of medical and social conditions to provide the data for discussion. Although the intelligence scores alone are far from decisive it is helpful to have a reasonably reliable estimate of effective intelligence and of special abilities, such as practical or verbal skills. A great deal of misplacement of children has occurred in the past because of reliance on one measure of intellectual ability.

An appeal case

Freda was a girl who had been admitted to special school when she was eight years old. When she was thirteen her mother started to keep her at home, and demanded that Freda should attend an ordinary school. The neighbours, mother insisted, expressed great surprise that Freda, who was always neatly dressed and was a very good-looking girl, should be at a special school. The head teacher advised strongly against any change, for he maintained that Freda was not even an average performer in her class; she fitted in well in her special school, but he was sure that she would flounder in a secondary modern school However, mother persisted, so the advice of the educational psychologist was sought: he confirmed the headmaster's findings. Freda's looks were deceptive. Her reading level was that of a seven-year-old, and her arithmetic level lower still.

Although the psychologist explained Freda's needs very carefully, mother refused to accept this, saying she was sure that the local secondary school would admit Freda. Mother said that she knew some of the girls who attended the school, and she maintained that Freda was quite their equal, if not better. In a case like this there is an outside possibility that a secondary school could accommodate a pupil, so the head teacher was approached. Meanwhile mother was asked to ensure that Freda attended the special school regularly while further possibilities were explored, and this she did.

When the head teacher of the secondary school was acquainted with Freda's work she said that she had no group that could possibly meet Freda's needs, and this she told the mother at a joint interview arranged by the psychologist. Again mother demurred, and said that she intended to write to her Member of Parliament. It was quite clear that Freda's needs were best met in the special school, and it was put to mother that the teachers and the psychologist had to say what they thought would help Freda most, just as mother felt impelled to insist on a different viewpoint. She was told that she could appeal to the Department of Education and Science. She decided to do this and as she could not write very well she was given help to write the letter.

The Department asked for full information on the problem, and after considering this they wrote to mother, saying that they thought the authority's viewpoint was quite reasonable. Mother accepted this, and Freda attended school regularly from then on, eventually reaching the heights of miming the Madonna in the school's nativity play. It is rare for parents to appeal once they have accepted special education, although there used to be the temptation to do so when special school pupils left school later than pupils in ordinary schools. Most authorities are flexible in their procedures: if a child would be helped best in a special school, but the parent objects, or a secondary school can fit her in, they are prepared to advise the parents and let them make the final choice. Where, however, it is markedly to a child's disadvantage, or a secondary school cannot cope, they act in the child's interests by using their powers. This was Freda's situation. It may be that mother's possible feelings of guilt about her daughter going to a special school had been dealt with by helping her to exercise her right to appeal.

A borderline ESN(s) boy

A rather unusual case was that of Tom, the son of a schoolmistress. He was noticeably backward at the start of his infant school, and a psychological investigation revealed an IQ of 50 to 55 on the Terman-Merrill test (he was then $5\frac{1}{2}$). When the parents were seen to discuss this and the possibility mooted that Tom would need special help, mother refused to accept it. Tom, she insisted, just needed proper teaching and all would be well. She was convinced that no one could believe that children could be slow by nature, and Tom was destined for university. In spite of explanations about the nature of the special help, and that chances of improvement would be increased by this, mother remained adamant. She thanked the head teacher and the psychologist for their interest and withdrew the boy from the LEA, placing him in a local private school. Four years later a harassed head teacher of a small boys' preparatory school phoned the psychologist (who had seen some of his pupils on other occasions) to say that he had admitted a boy who just could not cope at all, and was a soiler and bed-wetter. Apparently the mother had persuaded the head to admit the boy, not telling him of any difficulties. Tom was smart, well dressed and had a good middle-class accent; mother was a teacher and father a business man, and they had apparently dominated the interview. The head teacher had never met anyone as backward as Tom. Most of his pupils were fast learners, and a slow boy, to him, was one with just above average ability. The head was advised to ask mother to seek the help of the school psychological service. She, however, negotiated a place for Tom in a boarding school that took slower pupils. On intake the head reported that Tom seemed quite intelligent, and he felt he could help him. Mother wrote to the authority asking for his fees to be paid, as they were more than she could really afford. The school medical officer and the educational psychologist were asked to advise the authority about this request, and this gave the opportunity for a full medical and psychological investigation. On the WISC, Tom scored only an IQ of 45 on performance, and 55 on the verbal scale. He had not made a start with learning to read. He appeared to converse well, and gave a superficial impression of verbal fluency, until one realised that he was just repeating phrases, evidently culled from home. The medical officer was concerned at his small stature, and initiated investigations into this. The social worker was able to make positive contact with the family. The psychologist visited the school to see if it could meet Tom's needs. It was run on public school lines, and took pupils who had failed the common entrance examination. There was some attempt to help slow learners through practical activities in the spacious grounds. No member of staff had had any special training for teaching slow learners. The head teacher said he felt that Tom could fit in. The psychologist felt that, whereas the school was not ideal, it was not totally inappropriate, although he would never have chosen it himself. He therefore recommended that the views of the Department of Education and Science be sought as to its suitability for special educational treatment.

Before investigations were completed Tom was discharged from his boarding school as 'mentally defective'. His headmaster lacked any real knowledge of very slow learners, as his use of outmoded terminology suggested. The initial superficial impression gained from Tom's verbal fluency and smart appearance had misled him. The parents were therefore obliged to seek the help of the authority at this stage. Because of the possibility of an organic factor, or even some psychotic condition, arrangements were made for Tom to be admitted to a hospital school atttached to a psychiatric unit. There a diagnosis of subnormality was confirmed, and no organic defect was discovered; nor was he thought to be psychotic. A recommendation was made that Tom should go to the local day school for ESN(m) pupils, and this he did, at first on trial. The parents had by this time, with social work help, accepted Tom's low level of ability. They found the amenities at the special school far better than they had expected, and much superior to those for which they had paid expensive fees. Tom was allowed to remain. At first the school felt they could get more out of Tom than test scores suggested, but they proved unable to do so.

At times it was suggested that Tom would fare better at the special school for SSNs (then called a day training centre). This the parents could not accept, and as the school grew fond of Tom with his bizarre, meaningless chatter they kept him on. Finally at school leaving age he scored, on tests, in the severely subnormal zone. The local authority ran a special end-on course to help immature leavers from the special school to adjust to a working situation. This seemed an admirable chance to provide Tom with opportunities to try out some working situations. He arrived daily, neatly dressed and carrying a little attaché case, an apparently promising pupil. He could carry out extremely simple operations, e.g. stamping a code number on boxes, but he never showed any initiative or consistency, giving up after short periods to chatter aimlessly to the supervisor. In spite of a careful operant conditioning approach Tom made little progress. The manager felt sure that he would not be able to cope in ordinary work, and asked for psychological evaluation. This confirmed the low level of ability previously seen, although now Tom's scores were below 50, and he seemed to be a severely subnormal young adult. Social and Health Services were sent copies of the reports and recommendation, and the parents accepted the offer of social services' guidance.

This was a case of borderzone severe educational subnormality where the psychologist found his advice ignored at one stage, but gratefully acted on later. It was a case, too, in which medical opinions played a vital part. Difficult though the parents were, the authorities' officers continued to advise and help, although one does wonder if the boy would have been helped more if the authority had used its powers in the early days to insist on special education. On the other hand, the psychologist and the other advisers to the LEA may well consider that they have done their job effectively if they have taken every reasonable step to make their opinions and knowledge known. Parents do have a part to play in decisions, and frequently a compromise has to be achieved.

A case for educational guidance

Philip, the son of a consultant in the hospital service, was not making progress in his grammar school. He seemed to lack identification with his work, and was in the lowest set of his age group. The parents expressed concern that he would fail to achieve any O levels, yet they felt that the boy had ability, and therefore sought help from the educational psychologist.

At home Philip was a cheerful, outgoing boy who presented no problems to his parents. The family relationships had been stable. Both mother and father appeared to have reasonable attitudes to their son.

When Philip took the 11 + tests his quotients were as follows: verbal reasoning 110, English 113, and arithmetic 120. The mean scores for the LEA compared with other areas taking these tests were 102 for arithmetic and ability tests, and just above 100 for English; it was, therefore, an average type of borough. The threshold for admission to the school was an aggregate of approximately 330. A few boys with scores lower than this were also admitted. Nearly 30 per cent of the intake had lower aggregates than Philip. His birthday, too, was in October, which meant that he was older than most of his age group—a factor which favours educational adjustment in the early years at a grammar school. This, together with his home background, would lead one to expect a better academic performance. His school, however, although having no complaints about his behaviour, rated him as one of their least able pupils. He seemed, they felt, to have little interest in most subjects. He scored well in engineering drawing, and not too badly in metalwork and sciences, but he was very weak in foreign languages and in English. When tested on the WISC his quotient of 115 was very near his 11+ average. It was, however, the pattern of his subtest scores rather than the average that merited attention. His verbal quotient was only 108, but in performance material he showed his strength with a block design scaled score of 14 and object assembly of 17, indicating a very high level of success. This indication of high potential in the practical field was confirmed by his score of well over the 95th percentile point, on a 'matrices' test. On an arithmetic attainment test he showed a good grasp of mathematical concepts, and at fourteen years of age had a score of 17 years on Vernon's A-M Test. He had a good but not outstanding vocabulary.

Observations already made pointed to a marked practical bias in the boy. He commented that his major interests in school were metalwork and science subjects. At home, his parents said, he spent hours making models and enjoyed working on his bicycle. An attitude test (the Devon Interest) gave an attitude score of 122 for practical and 90 for academic interests. All the evidence collected up to this stage suggested that the lad was biased in the 'km' or practical factor. It is possible that the relatively poor development of the 'v ed' group of abilities, may be linked to poverty of experience, or some personality difficulties. Certainly the home environment was favourable to academic development, as both parents were graduates. Poverty of experience was therefore an unlikely explanation. Interview with the parents did not reveal any evidence of circumstances that could lead to personality difficulties. To check on this Philip was given the HSPQ; his score for extroversion was 8 stens, and for anxiety $3\frac{1}{2}$, and on this evidence he seemed a stable extrovert. Subtest scores were mainly in the average band, but he was venturesome (socially bold), with a sten score in this dimension of 9 (Cattell's P factor). On the guilt proneness dimension he scored at a 3 sten level, i.e. he was self-assured and secure, rather than guilt prone. Outgoing and warm-hearted, his sten score was 8 on cyclothymia. It was his scores in these dimensions that showed him to be extroverted.

It seemed on this evidence that Philip was a stable extrovert, with marked interest and ability in practical subjects. The local authority had a technical high school which approached secondary education from a practical workshop base. The possibility of a transfer was discussed with the head teachers of the schools, the parents and the boy. The grammar school head was quite positive about it: had his school been comprehensive no doubt he would have had some very suitable course options, but he agreed that the technical school would be likely to have a wider range. The head of the technical school invited the lad and his parents to see what his school could offer: Philip agreed at once, and the parents agreed to a transfer. The change suited Philip admirably. He liked studying in a workshop setting, and from this developing his academic skills. He was relieved that he did not have to tackle so many literary type subjects, although his school did not neglect these. He succeeded well with his O levels, subsequently proceeding to A levels in Science and Engineering subjects.

A case for individual remedial treatment
Reg was ten years old and a non-reader. He came from a good middle-class home, and had one sister a little younger. His ability was above average—on the WISC his verbal quotient was 108, and his performance quotient 106; he showed no visual perceptual or auditory weaknesses, and his motor control was good average. The only test findings that seemed significant were in the memory field. He was poor at remembering digits both forward and backward, and when given sentences from the Terman test again he performed badly. Both visual memory and auditory memory (Sibwell 3-letter word test) scores were at least three years behind his chronological age. His teacher said of Reg, 'I take ages to teach him some-thing—he's got it, and then to my dismay within a few days he has for-gotten it all.' He could not remember either the year or the month in which he was born, and he could name only five of the days of the week—nor did he know the months of the year. Christmas Day, he informed his examiner, was some time ago, but when exactly he could not remember. When first observed he failed to tell left from right in a number of short tests, and a year later was still unable to do so. Exploration of emotional difficulties did not reveal anything of significance. At school he enjoyed model-making sessions; he caused his teacher no disciplinary problems. It seemed therefore that Reg had a severe memory difficulty, and con-sequently could not assimilate enough basic knowledge on which to build further skills.

Reading is a complex process, one component being the formation of arbitrary associations of sounds with written symbols. To many children, provided they can discriminate the sounds and note the details of a visual pattern, the association causes no problem; a few repetitions and the material is learned. If, therefore, the hypothesis about Reg was a correct one, he would need considerable repetition of basic material. At the same time emotional factors had to be borne in mind. Sheer drill can be tedious and may not succeed. The psychologist discussed the possibilities with an experienced remedial teacher, and Reg was enrolled in a small group which attended four days a week for an hour each day. The following (quite well known) approach was used: firstly, an exploration was made to find a suitable rhyme or jingle that Reg knew well (in his case it was the kerb drill rhyme). The material was carefully printed; Reg, of course, could 'read' it immediately because he knew the rhyme by heart; this was reassuring. He could also pick out individual words (usually he would pause and then after a while point to the word). Clearly he worked through his rhyme each time. The next stage involved printing each word on card, and getting Reg to match the words with his copy. Then the words were mixed up and Reg picked them out and made the rhyme without a copy. Games were then played with the words, e.g. if Reg read the word he was the winner and got the card. In a short time he was regularly the winner. Individual words were then consolidated using the Fernald training method. This work produced a small stock-pile of words that Reg knew— look, left, right, cross, before. These were used to teach the sounds of letters and digraphs, and to derive new words. Eventually Reg was introduced to the words of a basic reader. All this took a considerable time, and short lessons were interspersed with other enjoyable activities. At the end of about two years Reg had still only consolidated a few words, reading at the 5 to 6 year level. Suddenly his reading leapt to the 7 year level, and three months later to 9 +, and by the end of that year he was an average reader. It seemed as if at last Reg had secured enough data from which to make quite rapid strides. Psychologists usually work with remedial teachers by helping with the diagnosis and planning approaches, ex- perienced remedial teachers are generally left to work out a programme themselves.

Johnson and Mycklebust (1967) describe a range of approaches suited to different types of difficulty. Reid (1972) has edited a very useful selection of articles on reading failure, diagnosis and treatment. Some educational psychologists become interested in experimenting with different types of reading approaches and undertake some of the remedial work themselves. Burt, in the 1920s, used to teach groups of children using different approa- ches in order to test their efficiency. An inventive teacher may ask for help in evaluating a new approach, or a psychologist may formulate a technique for a particular difficulty and evaluate it.

A highly intelligent boy with emotionally determined learning difficulties
This study illustrates the importance of emotional factors in learning; the treatment has involved a multiple approach, using both LEA and Regional Hospital Board facilities. The hospital psychiatric department

was the one referred to at the beginning of the chapter, where the co-operation of departments in setting up the school facilities was described; in this section continued cooperation in using the facilities is shown.

Donald, aged $7\frac{1}{2}$ years, was referred by a school medical officer, who had given the boy a medical examination at the school, and was concerned about the boy's asthma, which was accompanied by nervousness and failure to learn. He sought the opinion of the psychologist, having pres-cribed medication for the asthma, feeling that further investigation would be helpful.

Before seeing Donald the psychologist asked for a report from the head teacher, who described his behaviour as excellent, but timid and with few friends. He was attentive and yet had great difficulty with reading and spelling, although his mechanical arithmetic was nearly average. His teachers thought him to be of low average ability.

Mother proved to be a tense, anxious woman who cried copiously during the early interviews. She found Donald difficult to manage—he was often awkward and rude, he was timid about going to school, and once he was there was conforming and quiet. Mother had high expectations of Donald. Father was not a positive figure; he had left home when Donald was a year old, and returned a year later. Relationships between the parents had been tense.

When the psychologist saw Donald he was surprised at the ready re-sponse to his individual test of ability (the Terman-Merrill). Indeed, the boy achieved an IQ of 145, with correct responses to the reasoning item and reconciliation of opposites in year 14. No difficulties were found in memory, or in visual or auditory perception. The Raven's Projection test was used to probe attitudes. This provided suggestions of strong feelings of inade-quacy, and a wish to compensate for these. Donald was small: the boy he described wanted to be big and acclaimed for physical prowess, and had dreams of becoming a king. The psychologist felt that Donald's problems were mainly emotional, and sufficiently complex to justify using the full resources of the clinic; the school medical officer was agreeable to this and the boy was referred to the clinic.

Further observation confirmed the mother's inadequacy in handling Donald, which the psychiatrist felt had left the boy with considerable insecurity about himself and his mother's feelings about him. After team discussion it was agreed that Donald would be admitted to the hospital school, where the psychotherapeutic approach would be beneficial, and his mother would have intensive help from the psychiatric social worker. The psychologist would keep in touch by attending the monthly case conferences on day pupils, which were attended also by the psychiatrist who saw Donald and his mother from time to time. A great deal more was learned about the mother's demands on Donald, and his defensive reactions.

At school he enjoyed the relaxed atmosphere; he could play games such as draughts, and soon became interested in other games which involved the recognition of words, such as Monopoly, although initially he needed help with this kind of activity. His main progress, however, was social and emotional. He was at ease in school and liked his teachers; their approval of him gave him confidence. After a year it was felt that Donald could return to a normal school for part of the week, and arrangements for this were made by the psychologist. Donald's reading progress was still very limited, but a psychological review, carried out this time by a clinical psychologist at the hospital, confirmed the previous finding of high ability and no noticeable defects in intellectual functioning. A later conference at the hospital unit reported a good adjustment at the junior school, but still little reading progress (RA 6·6 years, CA 10 years.) It was felt, however, that he could now be given specialised direct remedial help, and the educational psychologist took over responsibility for following him up at his school. During the next year he started to make noticeable gains in reading. His remedial teacher commented on his friendly and positive attitude towards her. A Bristol Adjustment Guide gave a few pointers towards unsettledness, and none towards maladjustment. On the Cattell test he appeared slightly introverted (3 stens) and a little anxious (7 stens). Outstanding in the individual factors was low schizothymia (tendency to be very reserved), high ergic tension (tendency to become tense), rather high excitability and guilt proneness. He was, in this test, obedient and somewhat shy. These observations fitted well with what had been learned about Donald. They showed his areas of strength and weakness, and guided teachers and psychologists in planning a school approach. The school further cooperated in helping the boy by keeping him on for an extra year in an ordinary, not a remove, class. At the end of this period he was reading up to his chronological age level and the remedial teacher discharged him as an adequate reader who should do well. Under the remedial teacher he had progressed from reading levels of 6+ years to levels of between 9 and 11 years, depending on the skill assessed.

The psychologist alerted the boy's secondary school to Donald's previous problems, and he was reviewed at the end of his first term there. Mother said he was rather anxious about his French (he could still not spell very well in English), but his teacher reported satisfaction at his progress. He was given an A grade for history, his oral work in religious education was regarded as quite exceptional, and in science he was commended for enterprise and initiative. Follow-up after a further term showed still more adjustment.

The psychologist's role in this case was at times crucial (in the initial assessment), then similar to that of a touchline observer when the psychiatrist was in charge and the therapeutic school and social worker provided treatment. Finally the psychologist was very much a guide and counsellor on return to normal schooling.

When a child is referred to an educational psychologist continued guidance is expected. Although the clinic treatment of a case may be in the hand of a psychiatrist, this does not mean that the educational psychologist relinquishes responsibility. He maintains contact and continues to liaise with the school. The same psychologist first interviewed the boy and followed him up to secondary school. He visits the school regularly, and a watching brief can now be kept on Donald. This boy appeared to have temperamental traits that made him vulnerable in making personal relationships, and endeavours to improve these were highly successful. It is characteristic of Donald (as of Bill, p. 316) that he now perceives adults as friendly people ready to support him. The success in achieving this is undoubtedly due to combined operations.

Part Five

Future developments

This final part of the book consists of a single chapter. It looks at some of the ways in which practice is changing under the twin influences of the demands of the consumers and the pressures of research findings.

15

Future developments

As Seth (1972) has pointed out, educational psychology seems to go through a ritual decennial examination. In 1952, 1962 and 1972, symposia on the role of educational psychologists and on the training of educational psychologists have been published by different journals. This concern is not confined to this country. In Australia the *Australian Psychologist* has recently discussed current issues in the training of psychologists (e.g. A. M. Clarke, 1972; Lovibond, 1972) and American journals often contain papers discussing the role of the school psychologist and ways in which training requirements need to alter (e.g. V. D. C. Bennett, 1970; Barclay, 1971; Hartlage, 1971). We cannot tell exactly how the practice of educational psychology, as outlined in this volume, will develop. This is as much an exercise in clairvoyance as a study in prediction. But we can attempt to define trends and consider their implication, in particular for training. In this final chapter we examine some of the influences which are likely to affect the development of the profession and we end with a brief look at the implications of these trends for training.

It can be argued that developments are influenced from two major sources. On the one hand lie the demands of society, that is the demands consumers make on the profession for the kinds of services society requires. On the other hand there are the new skills and new knowledge which have arisen within the discipline of educational psychology itself. These frame the approach and determine to some extent the problems which the educational psychologist feels that he can help to solve. The achievement of a fair balance between these sometimes competing influences so that the scope of the work of educational psychologists can develop on a reasonably sound basis, is not always easy. We discuss them in turn.

Society's demands

Changes in the demands of society have already had marked impact on the educational psychologist's work. The social and educational pressures which have led to the virtual abolition of the 11+ examination have removed what was at one time an important part of the educational psychologist's skills. Few educational psychologists today play much part in selection procedures at eleven. But it is not only diminishing demands that lead to disappearance of skills; so too, paradoxically, can increasing demands. Thus the great demand for remedial teaching services in the 1940s and 1950s was such that educational psychologists themselves could not fulfil it. So a body of remedial teachers was established, and most remedial teaching is now carried out by skilled remedial teachers working with special classes or with withdrawal groups in the ordinary school. The work the educational psychologist does in relation to children with reading and learning disabilities has changed. The educational psychologist is now more particularly involved (Department of Education and Science, 1968b) with the special problems of the educationally retarded child whose learning difficulties require a carefully planned psychological programme of training and therapy.

While the need for some skills has been removed or modified by virtue of changes in society, at the same time new skills are required. One of the emphases in recent educational thinking has been the concern for the deprived and disadvantaged section of the community. This has shown itself in the demand for 'positive discrimination', so that a higher proportion of resources are diverted towards these sections of the community. One result of this is the demand for educational psychologists to design programmes which help the development of 'at risk' children. These programmes can then be used in educational priority areas, with educational priority children. The need to possess this kind of skill has implications for training. One inference is that the training process should take some account of sociological studies.

This concern with deprivation is one example of the current emphasis on the idea of schools as instruments for social change. Another example is the extension of the concept of education to include a wider age-span. There is now not only a great concern for the education of the very young but an equal concern for the re-education of the young adult and the middle-aged person. Education is no longer something which happens to most people between the ages of five and sixteen. This change affects all professions concerned with education, including educational psychology. The educational psychologist is starting to be heavily involved in the educational procedures which are now beginning to be established for the young child. But what about the older adolescent and the adult learner? The provision of short courses for teachers and other interested colleagues has always been an activity in which educational psychologists have been involved. But will the idea of *éducation permanente* mean that in the retraining and extended education that will take place there will be an extra role for the school psychological service? These are questions which have yet to be resolved, but it may be that other types of psychologists, with different skills and experiences from those of the psychologists in school psychological services, will work with the older age groups. These may be vocational and counselling psychologists for example.

The kind of work required by the so-called 'preschool child' is much more in tune with the skills that educational psychologists already possess. Most psychologists are indeed working with young children in this age group already. But a large extension of work with children in the 0–5 years age group will demand a reappraisal of the training curriculum. Thus the very young child is firmly attached to his family, and in particular to his mother. The diagnostic procedures and treatment methods needed in this situation are different from those appropriate to older children and should involve parents far more.

So far, two examples of changes in the demands of society have been considered. The third example is not so much the development of a new demand as a marked increase in an existing one. The number of children for whom a school psychological service opinion is required grows continuously. This demand seems insatiable. Waiting lists for school psychological services today seem quite as long as they did twenty years ago. Yet the number of educational psychologists in post is very much greater (Department of Education and Science, 1968b).

One way of meeting this need is to continue to increase the number of educational psychologists until the demand is satisfied. Another way is to seek methods of diminishing the demand, and of educating the referring agencies so that their own skills in dealing with children with problems increases. This latter development is attractive and is consonant with the ideas of Himmelweit (1963) on the need for the profession to develop its preventive skills. There are signs that the profession is beginning to extend its skills in this direction, as in the school-based therapy advocated by E. M. Moore (1971), Acklaw and Labon (1971).

Let us now turn to the second influence on the development of the profession, changes in the knowledge which the profession has available.

New knowledge

Dubin (1972) has recently analysed the rate of increase psychological information and knowledge are showing. He did this on the basis of the number of abstracts published in *Psychological Abstracts* each year from 1967 to 1971 inclusive. Of the eleven specific areas of *Psychological Abstracts*, educational psychology showed a greater increase than any other. There was a 100 per cent increase over the five-year period. Not all these abstracts will be of relevance to the field of work of educational psychologists. But it is interesting that developmental psychology, which is perhaps the nearest branch of psychology in relevance, showed the second highest increase in numbers of abstracts, increasing by 90 per cent over the five-year period. In other words it is not unlikely that educational psychologists, more so than clinical psychologists or social psychologists, for example, will have difficulty in keeping up with the flood of new knowledge. Using the idea of half-life, that is the time after completion of professional training when practising professionals have become half as competent to meet their work demands as they were upon graduation, Dubin estimates that the half-life of the psychologist is approximately ten to twelve years. Since the rate of new material produced in educational and developmental psychology is much greater than that for any other branch of psychology, then it seems not unreasonable to infer that the half-life for educational psychologists is appreciably less than this.

This large increase in new knowlege, containing within it new skills, new applications, new insights resulting from the accumulating experience and research of a large body of skilled individuals working in different contexts have various implications for the future development of educational psychology and the school psychological service. One is the need to establish different kinds of educational psychologists. Burt (1969) has already argued for the development of three kinds of educational psychologists which have been referred to in chapter 1. But Burt's analysis is not the only one possible. Manning and Cates (1972) have recently factor-analysed the competencies reported by a large number of members of the American Psychological Association. By this method, thirty-one factors, or groupings of competencies, were isolated. An examination of these thirty-one factors suggests that nine of them can be found to a greater or less degree among the tasks carried out by educational psychologists. These nine factors and the specialities which each one includes are given in Table 15.1 below.

Table 15.1   Factorial breakdown of educational psychologists' competencies

Factor	Specialties and loading
8. Personality development	Personality development (0·68), socialisation (0·37), individual assessment (0·36), childhood and adolescence (0·33), personality and learning (0·28)
9. Early childhood	Nursery and preschool (0·66), infancy (0·60), cognitive development (0·47)
10. Cognition	Cognitive functioning (0·71), visual processes (0·71), language theory (0·63), cognitive development (0·45)
11. Special education	Special education (0·58), mental deficiency (0·54), speech pathology (0·40), exceptional children (0·39)

Table 15.1—*contd.*

12. School—clinical	Behaviour problems (0·72), pupil assessment (0·69), exceptional children (0·63), therapeutic processes (0·56), reading problems (0·36)
13. School adjustment	School learning (0·63), school adjustment (0·60), reading problems (0·34), childhood and adolescence (0·33)
14. Educational administration	Teacher personnel (0·68), curriculum development (0·56), student personnel (0·37)
15. General counselling	Vocational problems (0·67), assessment (0·59), educational problems (0·56), personal adjustment (0·50), student personnel (0·45), counselling theory (0·42), therapy (0·29), rehabilitation (0·28)
16. Educational measurement	Test construction, validation (0·66), educational measurement (0·63)

It is not difficult to find ways of relating this breakdown of the educational psychologists' activities to that suggested by Burt. Thus the first three of Manning and Cates's set of factors could well be described as a further breakdown of the skills required by Burt's child psychologists. The second three could be regarded as a further breakdown of the skills required by Burt's remedial psychologists. The last three could be considered as the set of skills required by Burt's organisational psychologists. In short, as we look ahead, three kinds of educational psychologists may be insufficient: in the more distant future these three specialist kinds of educational psychologists may themselves give rise to subspecialisms.

New knowledge may require specialisation. But knowledge itself may appear in different guises. There is little point in discussing in this chapter the likely emergence of new kinds of individual test procedures; there will undoubtedly be new opportunities for educational psychologists to assess different kinds of abilities as new measures appear. More important are the newer approaches which the educational psychologist is likely to have to adopt as different ideas permeate the field in which he works. For example it can be argued that the measurement of cognitive skills of individual children is receiving less emphasis whereas the assessment of other personality qualities is growing. This may follow from the establishment in recent years of acceptable measures of personality qualities, qualities that have eluded satisfactory measurement hitherto, enabling the links between the cognitive, affective and motivational aspects of personality to be better appreciated.

It is likely, too, that educational psychologists may turn their attention from the measurement of the child, whether cognitive or personality factors are involved, to a much more careful assessment of his environment.

The importance of assessing the child in his environment has already been mentioned in earlier chapters of this text. But the techniques available so far for accurate assessment of important environmental variables are limited. Some exceptions to this criticism occur in work with the disadvantaged child, which has led to the development of new techniques for assessing the background in which children grow (R. Evans, unpublished) and also the school environment in which their skills are fostered (Laing, 1971). These new developments have been mentioned in Chapter 5.

Treatment, too, is likely to change in the wake of new developments. Child guidance clinics are under attack, and there are indeed suggestions for abolishing the concept of the child guidance team (Rehin, 1972). It will be clear that this is not a suggestion that this book supports, and in chapter 11 we discussed the ways in which the range of approaches to treatment offered by child guidance clinics has extended. Alongside this lies an emphasis in treatment literature, certainly in the educational psychology field, on the development of behaviour modification techniques such as those described in chapter 11. All these points are examples of new knowledge which has implications for the training of educational psychologists.

Training in educational psychology

Educational psychology, like psychology itself, carries a double meaning. It is in one sense a body of knowledge, taught to a wide variety of different professions, for example teachers, counsellors, social workers, etc. It is also the name given to the practice of a set of definable professional skills, employed by people called educational psychologists who work in school psychological services. This ambiguity and the problems that it poses are mentioned by T. Moore (1973). It is more with the set of professional skills and not so much the body of academic knowledge that most of this book has been concerned, although even this narrowing of range has not permitted more than a brief reference to the practical techniques of behaviour modification, counselling, psychotherapy, remedial teaching, etc. Readers interested in these approaches must consult the specialist texts. In talking of training in educational psychology we refer to the training of workers for the practice of educational psychology, people called educational psychologists in this country and school psychologists in United States. What is said does not apply to educational psychologists with 'academic' qualifications in educational psychology, e.g. persons who may be highly competent and skilled lecturers in the subject in universities and colleges of education. Nevertheless it would be a pity to draw attention to this division solely for the sake of clarity. There is much to be said for this division to disappear. The 'academic' lecturer gains from a background of practical experience, as do his students. The practitioner, too, has a real contribution to make to the teaching of his skills.

In chapter 1 the educational psychologist was described as an honours graduate in psychology, usually with a postgraduate qualification in education, some years of teaching experience and a postgraduate qualification in educational psychology. This defines the structure of the present training programmes. This required pattern of qualification and experience was discussed at some length in the Summerfield Report (Department of Education and Science, 1968b), which suggested that a variety of training routes should be available to enable educational psychologists to qualify. In particular, the Summerfield Committee advocated the abolition or shortening of the required two-year period of teaching experience for some educational psychologists. One of the main reasons for this recommendation and indeed for the existence of the Summerfield working party was the major difficulty in recruiting suitable students into the training centres for preparing educational psychologists. This difficulty has now been very much reduced. In the last few years there has been an expansion both in the number of well qualified applicants and in the number of training places available for people wishing to take the professional qualification in educational psychology. Figure 15.1 gives the number of such training centres existing over the last fifteen years. But more important than the number of establishments is the number of places they made available. The number of these places is indicated in Fig. 15.2 below. The figures are taken from the British Psychological Society's current pamphlet on postgraduate training for educational psychologists and from the Summerfield Report.

It is clear that the Summerfield recommendation of minimum expansion of training places from 36 to 108 between 1968 and 1975 is likely to be met. But how can the structure of training accommodate the new developments which new knowledge requires and changes in society's needs impose? There is no doubt that each part of the four-stage package—that is (1) degree, (2) education qualification, (3) teaching experience, and (4) educational psychology qualification—can be modified. Few psychologists would want to query the necessity of acquiring a degree in psychology as an essential part of training. But many would wish to ask whether the content of the psychology degree could be sharpened to allow for some specialisation even at this early stage (Murrell, 1969). While few departments of psychology run strong courses in educational psychology for their undergraduates, there is an increasing move towards the establishment of education as an undergraduate discipline in many British universities. A study of education usually includes a strong component of educational psychology and it might be advantageous for intending education psychologists to pursue a pattern of courses that allows them to choose

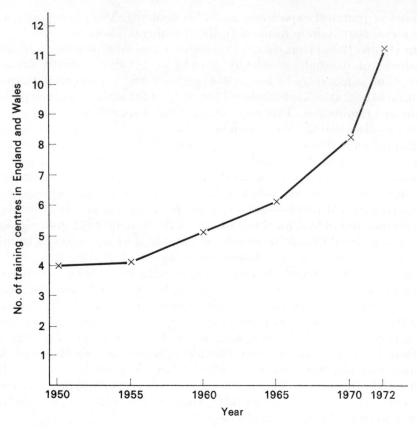

Fig. 15.1   Number of educational psychology training centres, 1950-72

some components from educational departments and others from psychology departments. A joint honours course is one obvious solution, but
there are others.

The importance of what has been the education year, that is the year
of training for teaching, has again been fairly well agreed (e.g. Seth, 1972).
But there is no doubt that for intending educational psychologists, and
perhaps for psychology graduates generally, the normal content of the
education year offers opportunities for making more relevant experiences
available to intending educational psychologists, opportunities that have
not always been grasped. The period of teaching experience has been most
severely criticised. There are those who would wish to abolish the teaching
experience requirement entirely, and there are those who would wish to
modify the teaching component so that the intending educational psychologist becomes sufficiently aware of the process of education to be able to
work satisfactorily as a psychologist in it, without having to qualify and

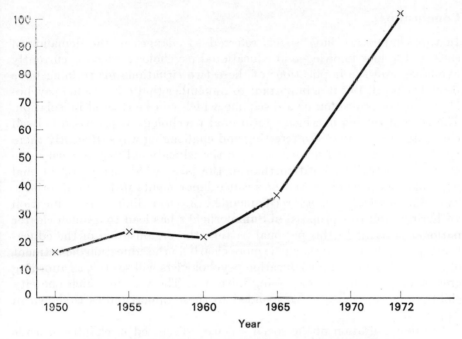

Fig. 15.2   Number of places available for training educational psychologists in England and Wales, 1950-72

gain experience as a teacher. There is of course a danger in this, exemplified by American school psychologists, for whom the teaching requirement is no longer obligatory. Thus V. D. C. Bennett (1970) describes the school psychologist as 'a guest in the house of education'. The views of teachers on this point are of some relevance but seem to have been relatively neglected. And there is a body of opinion which feels that a wide range of experience with children, of which teaching experience is only a part, is the most essential prerequisite.

It is probably the fourth rung of the ladder that has been more changed than any other. In recent years we have seen the gradual extension of this fourth step from a six-months period of training, through a time when all postgraduate courses in educational psychology were an academic year in length, to a time when nearly all postgraduate training required a full calendar year, until more recently we have seen the appearance of the first two-year courses of postgraduate training in educational psychology. Parallel to this development there has been an increase in the academic standard required of students, so that the introduction of diplomas in educational psychology has been followed by the appearance of courses leading to Master's degrees in educational psychology, child psychology and education.

Conclusions

In this chapter we have so far referred to changes in the demands of society, the new knowledge in educational psychology which is currently available, and the implications of these two situations for training have been discussed. But it is important to remember that educational psychology is not a profession or a discipline which can be treated in isolation. The current setting in which educational psychology is practised is itself changing in a number of interesting and challenging ways. Recently there has been an increased tendency to see the educational psychologist more closely linked with education than in the past, when many educational psychologists were employed by health departments in local authorities. The Summerfield Report recommended a clear link with education authorities and this proposal of Summerfield's has lead to a much clearer national pattern. In this national pattern the organisation of the educational psychologist's work will lie more clearly in the education department of local authorities. Many education psychologists will see this as affording greater opportunity for exercising initiative. The way in which one city child guidance service has responded to these opportunities is shown in Appendix I.

The reorganisation of the social services, discussed in chapter 3, leads to social workers having much more support from their social service departments. Similarly the tendency for psychiatrists to be based in hospitals makes available to them a whole range of hospital resources which previously were not so readily at hand. This situation means that in collaborative teams, members have much more to offer to the cooperative process than has been the case hitherto. It also makes the psychologist increasingly shoulder the responsibilities of an educational specialist in the teams of workers from different disciplines collaborating in trying to tackle the problems of individual children. At the same time as the changes in the health service there have been major reorganisations in local government. This has led to a much smaller number of local education authorities and the disappearance of the small boroughs who might have employed no more than a single educational psychologist. This leads to a situation in which groups of educational psychologists will be the norm in all local education authorities. The pressure to employ specialist educational psychologists will grow, and the implications for advanced training are clear. At the same time as the groups of educational psychologists grow, so will the groups of educational advisers and organisers enlarge. These too are partners in the task which the educational psychologist is tackling.

A White Paper on education (Department of Education and Science, 1972c) has once again emphasised the importance of the preschool years.

Much more effort will be put into the education of young children and the demand for the skills of the educational psychologist in working with them will increase. This too has implications for training. It also has implications for work with other psychologists. The boundary between child psychology and education psychology is a narrow one. It begins to disappear in the early years of childhood. With increased specialisation, the advent in the near future of significant numbers of research psychologists, and of specialist child psychologists working alongside educational psychologists, there is a real prospect of a greatly improved professional structure for all psychologists in education services.

Another significant development, which will have considerable impact on the practice of educational psychology, was the publication in March 1974 of Circular 3/74, on Child Guidance.

This circular, which is issued jointly by the Department of Education and Science, the Department of Health and Social Security and the Welsh Office, appears as Appendix 3. It replaces circular 347, (see p. 7) and advocates a network of services:– child psychiatric services, school psychological services, health and social services working together in a variety of settings. Arrangements will be flexible, with permanent and regular teams, as well as temporary and occasional ones, functioning to meet needs as they arise. Each service will have its own specialised resources, which will be shared in the interests of children whose problems demand an interdisciplinary approach.

The service described in Appendix 1, although based on Circular 347, provides examples of development which illustrate the beginnings of this kind of organization. To some extent the new 1974 circular reflects changes that are already under way. It will, however, be influential in spreading these changes more widely, and in clearing the way for the next stage of professional growth.

Appendix I

Notes on a city child guidance service and its relation to other services

These notes describe a child guidance service based on a total population of just over 200,000 people, residents of a city in the south of England. It has developed a wide range of services. These illustrate many of the points made in the text about the school psychological service. Apart from small modifications, such as place names, the material is published in booklet form as another activity of the school psychological service.

The child guidance service described here is organised as recommended in Circular 347 of the Ministry of Education (1959) and illustrated diagrammatically in chapter 1. It comprises:

    A. The school psychological service
    B. The child guidance clinic
    C. The school health service.

The school psychological service

Advisory service to the local education authority
The service makes a major contribution to the work of the Education Department by advising on policy when relevant problems are under discussion. The Chief Educational Psychologist attends meetings of the Schools' Sub-committee as required; is an adviser on aspects of special educational treatment; attends meetings of Special Schools' Governors and Managers of the Hospital School, and represents the Service at staff meetings of education officers and advisers.

Policy developments in which the Service has played an active part with other officers over the last ten years include:

(*a*) Expansion of special schooling for educationally subnormal pupils, including an end-on industrial training unit.

(b) Development plan for the child guidance service, culminating in the provision of purpose-built headquarters.
(c) Development plan for maladjusted children, including the setting up of tutorial classes, a day school and hostels.
(d) Development plan for dealing with educational handicap (slow learners in primary schools).
(e) Plan for the development of a hospital school in which the Regional Hospital Board, the Department of Education and Science, the local education authority and the department of Child Psychiatry cooperated.
(f) Policy in respect of children with severe reading and behaviour difficulties.
(g) Development of preschool special educational treatment.

Contributions have also been made from time to time on the problems of adolescence, sex education and training for personal relationships. There has been participation with the careers advisory officer in evaluating vocational and educational guidance, and with the youth service in examining special needs of the unattached youth who does not attend any club. Recently the Service played a part in discussing developments arising from the proposed reorganisation and special developments in middle and comprehensive schools. There are therefore opportunities for the Service to play a part in general matters and to cooperate with organisers, advisers and education officers. Although the major demand is for advice and help over children showing difficulties an appreciable contribution to educational developments for normal children is also made.

Schools' advisory service
This is the basic work of the school psychological service. Head teachers and class teachers can ask for the help of psychologists either to discuss problems and advise them, or to make a special study of children who are presenting problems. The psychologists usually visit the school for their initial work. The pupils' personalities are studied, including both intellectual and emotional aspects. Where necessary the background environment is considered, the head teacher having first asked the parents for their cooperation. Social workers and psychiatric social workers play a valuable part in this. The psychologist uses a wide range of diagnostic tools to help him in his study, such as tests of intellectual development, social abilities, attainments, emotional stability, interests and attitudes.

As a result of the study action is discussed with the teachers; a full psychological report is then sent to the school with recommendations. Sometimes the Service refers on for further specialist help to the school medical officer, the audiologist or the child guidance clinic, or refers the child for special educational treatment.

General advisory service

Over recent years there has been an increasing demand for help from professional workers other than teachers, and from parents. The former includes school medical officers, paediatricians, education officers and officers from other departments, especially Social Services.

They require from the psychologist information about a child's development, usually with respect to educational adjustment as well as that in the home, or they want some further help, either by referral or for appropriate special education, or clinic treatment, or they ask for advice or direct help for the child from the psychologist.

A senior educational psychologist is responsible for organising the work for the Social Services' Department.

Social work department

This service, headed by a principal social worker who is a psychiatric social worker, provides the case work and diagnostic facilities for the child guidance clinic. For the school psychological service it provides help for the parents to understand and cooperate with special educational treatment, and also provides the service with valuable information concerning the environment and development of a child. These social workers cooperate with those from the social services; if a member of the latter is involved, responsibility for continued support is decided after discussion.

Service for handicapped pupils

Ascertainment of ESN children is a joint decision of the school medical officer and the educational psychologist, in consultation with head teachers.

Boarding school provision for maladjusted and ESN children is arranged by the school psychological service after consultation with the school medical officers, psychiatrist and teachers.

Admissions to the school for physically handicapped and to partially hearing units are made on medical grounds, but psychologists often help with studies of cognitive skills and personality.

Admission to other units is made by appropriate panels on which the educational psychologist serves.

For those already ascertained as handicapped and in special schools or units, the service provides weekly visits. A special diagnostic unit for the preschool cerebral palsied children has been set up and psychological contributions are made by the school psychological service.

One of the senior psychologists specialises in working with children who have specific language difficulties or neurological impairment.

Special educational treatment provided by the school psychological service

This service provides special educational treatment for children who are backward in their school subjects, but for whom there is evidence that this is not due to lack of general ability. The children are referred to the service after the psychologists have studied their needs. Some of the children have special intellectual disabilities, some have faulty attitudes or some degree of emotional maladjustment, some have missed earlier learning opportunities through absence or home circumstances which do not provide sufficient stimulation. Usually the children range from low average to above average ability. The units like to have the children as young as possible, but many cannot be ascertained until the end of the first year in the primary school.

The treatment given ranges from individual sessions several times a week to daily group sessions. There is growing evidence that a few need more full-time approaches than those given at present, and arrangements for these are under review. This particularly applies to the older junior and young secondary modern pupil.

The specialist teachers have all had special training for this work, and are available to help schools in their area, they are able to call in to discuss teaching approaches with interested teachers. There are eight remedial centres, one of which houses a permanent exhibition of a wide range of books and apparatus available to help slow learning children.

Service for behaviour problems

Tutorial classes. Six tutorial classes have been set up to help with behaviour problems, and two further units for secondary school children are being considered.

Three of the units provide part-time preventive work for juniors, two provide a service for difficult adolescent girls and boys (with full-time provision if necessary) who for some reason cannot be placed in fulltime day or boarding schools but need special educational provision away from their own schools. The Headquarters Unit provides for emergencies, for diagnostic study and for phobic children: these children may later be placed at units nearer their homes. The units are all small and work through the teacher establishing a supportive relationship and a curriculum which provides for satisfaction of interests and needs, such as those for success, appreciation, etc. In this way the child is led to a better control of his actions. Whenever possible the children are reintegrated into normal schooling. With the younger children this can be achieved by part-time attendance, but with older pupils it has been found that full-time attendance is needed usually, at least in the initial stages of re-adjustment.

Every attempt is made, however, to ensure a minimal attendance at ordinary school.

A domiciliary service has been set up for those children for whom there is no other provision, for example extreme school phobics, children excluded from school but not suitable for tutorial units.

Special units within schools. Two experimental tutorial classes have been set up in secondary schools. These provide for the pupils who are slightly less maladjusted than those who go to a special school or external tutorial unit. They have close association with the School Psychological Service but remain essentially a part of the school. The Service provides special help with equipment, and general advice and support.

Hostels. A mid-week hostel takes up to ten maladjusted children: the aim is to help them to adjust to their environment by providing mid-week support in addition to any therapy or special schooling they may require. Usually the children go home at weekends, and close contact is maintained with the home; most of them attend ordinary schools. A further hostel has been established as part of the treatment provided by the day school for maladjusted children. The authority aims to make full use of this type of provision, and hostels for the two schools for ESN pupils are under consideration.

Department of English for immigrant children
This caters for approximately seventy pupils, most of whom attend a centre for daily sessions. In addition to teaching English to children from five to eighteen years who arrive without any knowledge of the language, further special educational treatment is provided for some who are of very low general ability. A diagnostic and advisory service is provided for schools. The school psychological service provides regular support and has opportunities to research into the learning difficulties experienced by immigrant pupils. Special liaison is made with the School Welfare Department.

Services for infant school pupils
Three remedial/diagnostic units have been set up for children from five to seven years. They are for children who do not fit into their infant schools because of immaturity, very low general ability, emotional instability, and very occasionally physical handicap. They attend for mornings only in some cases. The atmosphere is of a nursery type. The children are given opportunities for a wide preparatory experience and are carefully observed. Some make marked progress and can be resettled in ordinary schools, others need continued special treatment in schools for the educationally subnormal, maladjusted or physically handicapped.

Referrals are made to the school psychological service by the head teachers. Some go direct to the unit as they have been recommended by the principal school medical officer's preschool conference. Final recommendations for further treatment are made by a team, consisting of teacher, educational psychologist and school medical officer (and psychiatrist if the problem is one of maladjustment).

Special units for preschool pupils
A purpose-built unit provides special education for twenty-five preschool children who need this mainly because of emotional or intellectual deprivation. There are three classes, each with a teacher and ancillary helper. The unit is headed by a teacher in charge, and is directly administered by the school psychological service. In addition, a small unit for children suspected of having specific language difficulties is located at the centre.

Educational guidance service
Tests of attainment and ability are kept at one of the remedial centres. The advisory panel for this service meets annually and agrees tests for general use in primary schools. These are the tests which are in common use and which are recorded on school record cards. A wide range of tests is available for schools on demand.

Selected tests (reading, and a non-reader's intelligence test) have been agreed to help with the screening of ESN children at the end of the infant school and the first year of the junior school, so that a systematic check on the needs of the children can be made. The head of the Remedial Department administers the test service, and his staff help with the use of screening tests.

There has been growing demand in secondary schools recently, both for tests to help in general educational guidance and for vocational guidance tests.

The school psychological service sees children for individual study if they present any difficulties about placement, e.g. children from abroad.

Research activities
The Service undertakes research activities, and in recent years the following topics have been studied:
Distribution of educational handicap in the primary schools.
Value of tests for vocational guidance (with the careers advisory officer).
Contribution of i.t.a. to remedial work (with the Institute of Education, London University).
Comparison of WISC and Terman-Merrill Form L-M (with a working party of the British Psychological Society Division of Educational and Clinical Psychologists).

Study of the reading problems of school leavers.

Evaluation of the industrial training unit for immature school leavers.

Help with the evaluation of tests for the early identification of disadvantaged children (University College of Swansea Schools' Council Project in Compensatory Education).

A study of changes in reading levels of infant school leavers during the summer holiday.

There are therefore opportunities for developing research interests. A research officer is likely to be appointed to help to carry out a three-year evaluation of the service.

Programmed learning unit

This unit has been set up to provide knowledge about programmed learning books and teaching machines, so that schools can be informed and make full use of this new development in education. It stimulates research in schools and the writing of programmes by teachers. Courses and lectures are provided. An advisory committee has been set up with representatives from the college of education, the psychology department of the polytechnic, together with the adviser for educational technology, the curriculum developments officer and an educational psychologist with special interest in this field. It is chaired by the head of the unit.

Training contributions

A senior educational psychologist is responsible for helping with the field training of psychologists from various centres. He also works half time for a university course for the MSc in Educational Psychology, helping with fieldwork and seminars.

Courses for teachers are organised regularly, usually in cooperation with the college of education and at the teachers' centre. Subjects covered have been vocational and educational guidance, behaviour problems in the classroom, the slow learner in the ordinary school. Two full-term courses for teachers interested in work with maladjusted pupils have been organised, and one for work with slow learners. A combined course for teachers wishing to work with slow learners and/or maladjusted children is to be a regular feature of in-service training.

Lectures are given to social workers, education welfare officers, parent groups etc. Recently the Service has cooperated with the In-service training of staff of the Social Services Department. Field training work is also provided for the social work training course of the polytechnic.

The child guidance clinic

By advising and helping parents and by giving treatment to the children, the child guidance clinic helps children who are developing in ways that are unsatisfactory to themselves or others with whom they may come in contact. A wide range of problems is investigated by a full team consisting of psychiatrist, educational psychologist and psychiatric social worker.

Referrals are open and come through:

Teachers	Probation officers
School medical officers	Speech therapists
Education welfare officers	Social workers (Social Services)
Paediatricians	Magistrates
Parents or guardians	General practitioners

Treatment available consists of counselling, psychotherapy, family casework and various forms of special educational treatment including the use of the day school for maladjusted children and the hostels, the tutorial units and boarding schools. A psychotherapist is shared with the Regional Hospital Area's Unit for Children and Parents, and provides individual therapy.

There is thus a wide range of facilities for maladjusted children. The LEA Child Guidance Service works closely with the the regional unit, and joint conferences are held. The chief educational psychologist is honorary consultant educational psychologist to the unit. The clinical psychologists meet the educational psychologists frequently, and work with the schools over problems referred to the hospital unit. If these problems have special educational treatment implications, the unit uses the school psychological service facilities. Recently, with parental coopera-tion, arrangements were made for some treatment to be given at the nearest clinic, irrespective of sources of referral, i.e. children who live near the regional unit may be seen there rather than at the child guidance clinic, and vice versa.

The school health service

The school health service has links with the Department of Public Health which is involved in basic preventive work, both with mothers at child health clinics giving early advice on child development and behaviour problems, and at a much later stage when several schools have help with courses for older boys and girls on personal relationships, family life and child development.

The Service has links with the hospital consultants in paediatrics, in neurology etc. The Education Department relies heavily on the Health and School Health Departments for discovering, before they reach statu-tory school entry age, children who need special educational provision.

In addition it plays a considerable part in child guidance. The LEA clinic is one of the Principal School Medical Officer's clinics, and one school medical officer gives sessions to the clinic, working closely with the child guidance teams.

School medical officers carry out preventive work by advising parents and teachers about children seen at medical examinations. Through the activities of health visitors, the medical officers of the child health clinics, referrals by consultant paediatricians and general practitioners, the Medical Officer of Health and Principal School Medical Officer come to know about preschool children who may need special help. Such children are studied by a team consisting of medical audiologist, school medical officer, educational psychologist, medical officers in the Department of Public Health, speech therapist and health visitor. Specialist examinations are arranged as necessary, including psychiatric investigations.

The service has developed an audiology unit for ascertainment and treatment of partially hearing children, and has set up, with the Education Department, special classes for the partially hearing in a primary school and a secondary school. Units have also been set up for the observation and treatment of children with developmental difficulties of communication, one for infants and one for junior school children.

The school health service is closely concerned with advice and help to handicapped school leavers, including ESN and other forms of handicap, and has set up teams which include medical officers, psychologists, teachers, careers advisory officer, social workers (Social Services), representatives from the Department of Employment, to advise on the problems.

A regularly fortnightly joint conference of the school health and school psychological services is held, which the Social Services' representatives attend. Head teachers are invited to attend this when special cases are being discussed. Health visitors and speech therapists also attend.

School health and school psychological services work closely together in ascertaining the needs of ESN pupils, and with the child guidance clinic in determining the special treatment necessary for maladjusted children.

The school health service will shortly be administered through the National Health Service, but services for children are likely to continue, with some differences of emphasis, e.g. more emphasis on training in developmental paediatrics for medical officers working in this field.

Centres used by the Child Guidance Service

Headquarters
A purpose-built unit was completed in 1968, with the school health service in one wing and the school psychological service in another, thus providing for close cooperation between the two services and an excellent base for the full child guidance service.

Rooms include a child study centre, which gives opportunity for study of child development, including child psychology and special educational treatment.

There are consulting rooms for psychiatrist, psychotherapist and four rooms for educational psychologists, four social workers' rooms and one for students. There are two playrooms, one large for group treatment and one smaller, with a one-way screen for observation to supplement the treatment facilities. The remedial centre has rooms for individual and small group treatment, and the tutorial centre is a large multipurpose classroom.

Other centres
There are nine other centres in different parts of the city. Two of these are branch child guidance clinics situated in health centres. These provide contact with general practitioners. Parents bringing children have relatively short distances to go. Although the clinics are only in session for one or two days, the advantage to parents with young children is considerable. These centres also act as bases for the educational psychologist and social workers of the child guidance service in the area. The development of these, with records centred at headquarters, fosters some specialisation in the central clinic, and enables expansion of services without overcrowding the headquarters accommodation.

A principle in organising other centres which mainly provide special education is to form clusters of units. One cluster has units for remedial work, tutorial work and a department for teaching English to immigrants. Clustering offsets the isolation that could obtain in single units.

Other clusters include a unit for infant school pupils, remedial and tutorial. There is no overall head of these clusters as they serve rather different purposes. The teachers serve under the appropriate head of department.

One centre houses a permanent exhibition of materials for helping backward pupils. It is hoped to move this to the teachers' centre when there is suitable accommodation.

Another cluster includes the educational test service and is the headquarters for the training unit and the research unit.

Because of difficulties in obtaining sites in a built-up area these have not been planned ideally. Experience has, however, suggested that permanent clusters of educational services near to the schools they serve would be invaluable. *Ad hoc* accommodation useful to pioneer developments rarely provides the conditions for good remedial work of all types. Purpose built, attractive premises facilitate parental cooperation and encourage the pupils.

LEA provision for special educational treatment for which regular support is given

Type of school or unit	Number	Number of pupils	Psychologists' visits
Primary ESN	1	160	weekly
Secondary ESN	1	200	weekly
SSN	1	100	weekly
Physically handicapped	1	120	weekly
Maladjusted (day)	1	50	weekly
Hospital	1	25	when required
Cerebral palsy	1	50	weekly
Special classes (SET)	22	440	when required
Partially hearing	2	40	weekly
Developmental disorders of communication	3	20	when required
Hostel for maladjusted	2	22	when required
English for immigrants	4	70	when required
Diagnostic nursery	3	25	when required
Hostel for SSN	1	18	when required

The school for physically handicapped has special facilities for spina bifida children and a nursery unit.

In addition to the above units there is a peripatetic teaching service offering help to children with hearing loss who are placed in normal schools.

The LEA uses private and LEA boarding schools which cater for maladjustment, educational subnormality and/or other handicaps. The school psychological service arranges visits and regular follow-ups for ESN and maladjusted boarders. The school health service arranges follow-ups for other handicaps. Approximately 100 children are currently placed in boarding schools.

Speech Therapy Department

There are four speech therapists and one part-time under the direction of a senior. They provide speech therapy and work closely with the school health service and the child guidance service, referring cases and taking part in team work with the audiology service and the unit for developmental disorders of communication at the clearing house conferences, at conferences for handicapped school leavers and preschool case conferences. The part-time therapist works in nurseries taking handicapped children.

Contribution of allied services

Hospital unit for children and parents
This caters for psychiatrically disturbed families and children of all ages in terms of diagnostic assessment, therapy and specialised education. It is officially recognised for the postgraduate training of child psychiatrists and clinical psychologists.

It includes out-patient clinics, a forty-bed complex consisting of three separate residential sections, a day centre, a therapeutic school and an experimental nursery. The unit is purpose-built: where appropriate parents and children can be admitted on a joint basis.

Social services department
This department is playing an increasingly important part in preventive work with children, providing substitute home care or taking action to prevent a home breaking up. A child guidance clinic psychiatrist gives regular help to the department and psychological work is given on request. A senior educational psychologist provides help for children taken into care and needing study to help with planning, placement and handling, and sees that the psychological needs of the Social Services Department are met.

Recently a joint committee with the child guidance, school health and social services has been set up to review the needs of children who require residential provision. This will enable full use to be made of social services' provision for child guidance cases as appropriate.

The social services department provides excellent facilities for SSN and SN adults, an adult centre with special educational and sheltered workshop provision, and a special hostel.

The school psychological service provides psychological assistance for the department and assists in follow-up work.

Probation department
The Probation Services give considerable supportive help to delinquent or delinquent prone children. Probation officers are frequent attenders at meetings of clearing house, child guidance clinic conferences etc., and joint case work on difficult problems is practised.

Health department
Educational psychologists work with preschool study groups on advising on very young children.

Reference has been made to other units with which the school psychological service is associated in order that the work of the service can be seen as part of a wide range of services designed to help children.

Factual details

Basic data

School population
30,000 approximately

Establishment
Psychologists
  1 chief educational psychologist responsible to the CEO for the direction
    of the Child Guidance Service, and to the PSMO for the administra-
    tion of the CGC
  1 senior educational psychologist (training)
  2 senior educational psychologists
  3 educational psychologists
  1 trainee educational psychologist
Social workers
  1 principal social worker
  4 social workers (PSWs if available)
Remedial teachers
  1 head of department
  6 full-time teachers
  3 part-time teachers
Tutorial teachers
  1 head of department
  5 full-time teachers
  1 ancillary helper
  1 part-time teacher (domiciliary)
Teachers of English to immigrants
  1 head of department
  3 teachers
Preschool unit for children with communication problems
  1 teacher (part-time)
  1 ancillary (part-time)
Remedial/diagnostic units for infant school children
  3 teachers
  3 ancillaries
Preschool unit diagnostic/remedial
  4 teachers
  3 ancillaries
Research unit
  1 research officer (3-year project)
Psychotherapists
  1 shared with hospital unit

Administrative and clerical staff
  1 administrative officer shared with School Health Service
  1 clerk—secretarial duties for chief educational psychologist
  1 shorthand typist
  2 audiotypists
  1 clerk (receptionist)

Consultant and medical staff
Consultant child psychiatrist 1 session
Child psychiatrist   8 sessions
School medical officer

Regular conferences
  1. *School psychological service staff*—alternating with separate psychologist and social worker staff meetings
  2. *Clearing house*—fortnightly
     Chairman: Senior school medical officer and chief educational psychologist alternate
  3. *Intake conference of the hospital unit for children and parents*—weekly
  4. *Psychologists, remedial and tutorial teachers*—twice a term.
     Chairman: Chief educational psychologist or department head

Special teams to which school psychological staff contribute
  1. *Ascertainment for ESN pupils and planning of special treatment*—school medical officer, educational psychologist and head teacher of special school
  2. *Preschool case conference*—monthly conference to review needs of preschool handicapped children
     Chairman: Senior School Medical Officer
     Members: School medical officer, medical officer for maternity and child welfare, senior health visitor, social worker (child guidance), social worker (play groups and day nurseries), audiologist, educational psychologist, speech therapist
  3. *School for maladjusted and hostels admission panel*
     Chairman: Chief educational psychologist
     Members: Head teacher, school medical officer, psychiatrist, psychiatric social worker, health visitor, warden of hostel, head of tutorial department
  4. *Handicapped school leavers* (other than ESN)
     Chairman: School medical officer
     Members: Educational psychologist, health visitor (welfare services), careers advisory officer, medical officer for audiology service, disablement resettlement officer, careers officer

   5. *Handicapped school leavers, ESN*
      Chairman: Head of special school
      Members: Careers officer, educational psychologist, school medical officer, medical officer, social worker (Social Services), class teacher
   6. *Admission panel for unit for developmental disorders of communication*
      Chairman: Deputy principal school medical officer
      Members: Audiologist, teacher in charge, education officer, senior speech therapist, educational psychologist, school medical officer, social worker (child guidance)
   7. *Committee for deaf and partially hearing*
      Chairman: Assistant education officer
      Members: Audiologist, school medical officer, educational psychologist, teachers of the deaf, health visitor
   8. *Cerebral palsy admission panel*
      Chairman: Consultant in physical medicine
      Members: School medical officer, teacher in charge, educational psychologist
   9. *Children's residential treatment panel*
      Convenor: Social worker of school psychological service
      Members: Senior medical officer in charge of school health service, chief educational psychologist, social worker (Social Services), psychiatrist, administrative officer
  10. *Area Social Services Department coordination meetings*
      Educational psychologists and social workers of child guidance service attend meetings for their area
  11. *Adult day training centre*
      Conference with consultant psychiatrist and staff

Committees attended by the chief educational psychologist
   1. Schools' subcommittee and education committee—as required
   2. Special schools' governors—once a term.
   3. Hospital school managers—once a term
   4. City coordinating committee (policy on problem families)—once a term.
   5. Council of Social Service research group—once a term

Training activities (of psychologists)
   1. Area school psychological service meetings—once a term
   2. Area inter-clinic conference—once a term
   3. Attendance at courses such as Division of Educational and Clinical Psychologists refresher course, British Psychological Society Annual Conference, child guidance inter-clinic conferences
   4. Senior educational psychologist (Training) organises in-service training activities for the educational psychologists (visiting lecturers, special visits)

Voluntary associations to which staff of child guidance contribute
1. *Social and Welfare Workers' Group*—monthly
   This provides excellent opportunities to meet social workers over a wide field and discuss common problems.
2. *Association for Special Education*
   This provides meetings and visits to discuss special education; teachers, doctors, psychologists, speech therapists and social workers participate.
3. *Association for Mental Health*
   This involves all aspects of mental health, and especially preventive measures which particularly concern Child Guidance and Education. Lay and professional members work together and support LEA endeavours.
4. *National Children's Bureau*
   This group promotes cooperation in the field of child care. Representatives of every discipline playing a part in children's work are members. Open meetings as well as closed group discussions are arranged.

Appendix II

The interpretation of score differences

The interpretation of score differences is an essential part of the educational psychologist's diagnostic skill. His clinical knowledge, experience and imaginative thinking are vital to his understanding of the situation that the score difference reveals. Nevertheless, in interpreting a score difference he must also be aware of the limitations imposed by the psychological tests themselves.

The principles which apply to the interpretation of single test scores apply with equal force to the interpretation of score differences. Just as a score obtained on a single test has meaning in the light of the test's mean and standard deviation, so must we know the mean and standard deviation of the difference scores obtained through the use of two tests in order to interpret one difference score. In this way we can estimate how often any difference score is likely to occur. Clearly the intercorrelation of the two tests helps to determine the standard deviation of the difference scores. The less well two tests correlate, the more likely are we to find some large difference scores, whereas the more closely they correlate the smaller will be the difference scores obtained when we test our population on the two tests.

The formula which tells us σd, the standard deviation of the difference scores, is $\sigma d = \sqrt{\sigma A^2 + \sigma B^2 - 2 r_{AB} \ \sigma A \ \sigma B}$ where σA and σB are the standard deviations of the two tests A and B and r_{AB} represents their intercorrelation.

Consider two hypothetical tests A and B where $\sigma A = \sigma B = 15$ and $r_{AB} = 0 \cdot 778$. The test scores are normally distributed.

$$\sigma d = \sqrt{225 + 225 - 2 \times 0 \cdot 778 \times 15 \times 15}$$
$$= \sqrt{450 - 350}$$
$$= 10.$$

Now the mean of our difference scores will be 0. (Remember that we are calculating the value of $A - B$ for each child—there will be negative values as well as positive ones.) So two-thirds of our difference scores will lie between $\pm$ 10 points (i.e. $\pm 1\sigma$). A psychologically significant difference score (in the sense that it occurs less often than 1 in 20 times, i.e. the 0·05 level) would be a difference score of $\pm 19\cdot6$, or 20 to the nearest integer $(10 \times 1\cdot96)$.

As another example consider a child of $10\frac{1}{2}$ who on the Wechsler Intelligence Scale for Children (Wechsler, 1949) obtains a performance quotient 105 and a verbal quotient of 90. How might the educational psychologist interpret the difference?

The WISC manual shows that the standard deviations of both verbal and performance scales are 15 points and that their intercorrelation at age $10\frac{1}{2}$ is 0·68.

So
$$\sigma d = \sqrt{225 + 225 - 2 \times 0\cdot68 \times 15 \times 15}$$
$$= \sqrt{450 - 306}$$
$$= \sqrt{144}$$
$$= 12.$$

So two-thirds of the difference scores obtained when the WISC verbal and performance scales are administered to a population similar to that of the standardisation sample are 12 points or less. A difference score of 20 (i.e. $1\cdot645\ \sigma$) or more in either direction is obtained by 10 per cent of the population. So the difference score of 15 points is not very unusual.

Note that this approach represents a psychometric contribution to the evaluation of differences between test scores, a contribution which is complemented by the educational psychologist's clinical skills and insights. Note also that Table 4.2 will enable us to estimate probability of occurrence of any difference score, once we have calculated the standard deviation of the distribution of difference scores. As with the interpretation of a single score, there are some basic points to bear in mind in interpreting a difference score.

The administration
The administration of both tests must have been carried out in accordance with the instructions of the constructor.

The standardisation population
The distribution of difference scores is applicable to the population from which it was obtained. This renders accurate interpretation of difference scores a particularly hazardous operation; since sometimes standardisation data and intercorrelation data are available only for different populations.

The reliability of the difference score
Just as a single score represents a measurement taken from a band of

inaccuracy so does a difference score represent a measurement taken from a band of inaccuracy located in this case on the distribution of difference scores. The standard error of measurement of difference scores will depend on the standard error of measurement of both tests and the formula for calculating it is

$$\text{SEd} = \sqrt{\text{SEm}_A{}^2 + \text{SEm}_B{}^2}$$

where SEd represents the standard error of measurement of the difference score and SEm_A and SEm_B represent the standard error of measurement of the two tests A and B.

Consider again the two hypothetical tests A and B mentioned above. Let us assume that A has a reliability $r = +0\cdot90$. Let us assume that B has a reliability $r = +0\cdot80$.

Then $\text{SEm}_A = 15\sqrt{1-0\cdot90}$

And $\text{SEm}_B = 15\sqrt{1-0\cdot80}$

(Remember that the standard deviations of both tests are 15 points.)

So $\text{SEd} = \sqrt{225 \times 0\cdot10 + 225 \times 0\cdot20}$

$\qquad = 8\cdot2$

This figure of 8 points is our best estimate of the standard deviation of the distribution of difference scores which would be found if a child could be given both tests a large number of times. Pursuing the analogy with the discussion on p. 82, let us consider a child with a difference score of 5 points. We can estimate that on retest his difference scores will be normally distributed with a σ of 8 points about a mean of 5. Thus we can estimate that there is one chance in 20 that on a retest our child will obtain a difference score outside the range 21 to -11 ($5 \pm 1\cdot96 \times 8$, i.e. 5 ± 16, to the nearest integer). Again, confidence bands appropriate to other probabilities can be derived from Table 4.2 (see p. 82.). The width of the confidence bands appropriate to the three most common probability levels is given in Table 4.3 (see p. 84.).

Look again at the WISC example on p. 365. We have already established that the difference score of 15 points is not infrequent. Let us now consider, in the light of our discussion of reliability, whether we can attach any weight to the difference at all. How justified are we in concluding that the child is more able on the performance scale than the verbal scale?

The WISC manual gives reliabilities of 0·96 and 0·89 for the verbal and performance scales respectively at age $10\frac{1}{2}$. Entering Table 4.3 at $r_m = 0\cdot925$ we can estimate the 10 per cent confidence band as lying about $9\frac{1}{2}$ points on either side of the difference score of 15 points that we obtained. Thus even at its lowest value of $5\frac{1}{2}$ points ($15-9\frac{1}{2}$) the difference score is still greater than zero. So we can be reasonably certain that, allowing for test unreliability, the child is more able on the performance scale than on the verbal scale.

Effect of score value on interpretation[1]

So far we have considered the question of the difference score in relation to its error of measurement and its likelihood of occurrence. There is a third factor to consider, that is the effect that the *value* of the two scores has on interpreting the difference. To illustrate this from educational psychology we can consider two children, both of whom obtain identical difference scores when a test of ability (*I*) and a test of attainment (*A*) are given; possibly as part of a survey designed to initiate remedial teaching procedures, where we are interested in *I*–*A* scores only.

First child $I = 130, A = 105$
Second child $I = 100, A = 75$

Let us assume that both tests have a mean of 100, a standard deviation of 15 points and a reliability of 0·99. Further, let us assume that the tests correlate $AI = +0.68$.

Now the interpretation of these scores *as difference scores* is identical.

(*a*) We can show that the standard error of measurement of difference scores obtained from these two tests is

$$\text{SEd} = \sqrt{225 \times 0.01 + 225 \times 0.01}$$
$$= \sqrt{4.5}$$
$$= 2.12.$$

Thus our differences of 25 points are indeed stable ones.

(*b*) We can show that the standard deviation of the difference scores obtained (from the standardisation population) is

$$d = \sqrt{225 + 225 - 2 \times 0.68 \times 15 \times 15}$$
$$= 12.$$

Thus our differences of 25 points are both more than 1·96 times the standard deviation of the difference scores and are both unusually high.

(*c*) Here we begin to diverge. Let us deal with the first child. First let us predict the *A* score that we would expect a child with an *I* score of 130 to have. (This is the same as the mean *A* score of all children with *I* scores of 130.)

$$A_{\text{pred.}} = r_{AI} \frac{\sigma A}{\sigma I} (I - M_I) + M_A$$

Therefore $A_{\text{pred.}} = 0.68 \dfrac{15}{15} (130 - 100) + 100$

$$= 120.4$$

---

[1] When a difference score is considerably different from zero then a better estimate of the band within which retest difference scores are likely to fall can be obtained by following the procedure outlined on p. 84.

Now the $\sigma_{\text{pred.}}$ (the standard deviation of the distribution of predicted scores) is given by

$$\begin{aligned} \sigma_{\text{pred.}} &= \sigma_A \sqrt{1 - r_{AI}{}^2} \\ &= 15 \sqrt{0 \cdot 5376} \\ &= 11 \cdot 0. \end{aligned}$$

So our score of 105 on Test A, which is 15·4 points less than the mean of the distribution of predicted scores is between one and two standard scores below this mean (15·4/11·0, standard scores, to be precise).

We now have to multiply this standard deviation of 11 points by the appropriate figure for telling us the score which is exceeded once in 20 times in our distribution of predicted scores. Since we are concerned with a difference in *one direction only* we do not use 1·96 (critical ratio at 5 per cent level for two tails of the distribution) but 1·65 (critical ratio at 5 per cent level for one tail of the distribution).

So a score of $120 \cdot 4 - 1 \cdot 65 \times 11 \cdot 0$

$= 102 \cdot 25$ would be significant at the 5 per cent level.

Our score of 105 is one which we can predict would occur more frequently than one in 20 occasions, and is not therefore all that unusual *for children with I scores of 130.*

Now let us adopt the same procedure for the second child.

Here $A_{\text{pred.}} = 0 \cdot 68 \times \dfrac{15}{15} \times (100 - 100) + 100$

$= 100.$

σ_{pred} as before, $= 11 \cdot 0.$

A score of $100 - 1 \cdot 65 \times 11 \cdot 0 = 81 \cdot 85$ would be a significantly lower A score in this case.

Our obtained A score of 75 is clearly well below this, and in the case of the second child the difference is indeed unusual *for children with I scores of 100.*

Note again that the difference between statistical significance and psychological interest must be realised.

Exact probabilities can be discovered, if required, by making a conversion to standard scores and using the data of the normal distribution given in Table 4.2. (See p. 82.)

Note also that one of the main implications of this approach is for large scale surveys aimed at selecting children for remedial education. Consider surveys which took no notice of predicted scores but only of I–A scores to produce a group of children for remedial education. Would the group selected by this method be predominantly a group of children of above average intelligence or below average ability?

Table 4.4 gives score differences which would be significant at the 1 per cent and 5 per cent for tests with intercorrelations between $+0 \cdot 50$ and $+0 \cdot 75$. (See p. 85.)

Appendix III

Circular 3/74
(Department of Education and Science)

Circular HSC(IS)9
(Department of Health and Social Security)

Circular WHSC(IS)5
(Welsh Office)
14 March 1974

Joint Circular from the

DEPARTMENT OF EDUCATION AND SCIENCE, ELIZABETH HOUSE, YORK ROAD, LONDON SE1 7PH

DEPARTMENT OF HEALTH AND SOCIAL SECURITY, ALEXANDER FLEMING HOUSE, ELEPHANT AND CASTLE, LONDON SE1

WELSH OFFICE, PEARL ASSURANCE HOUSE, GREYFRIARS ROAD, CARDIFF CF1 3RT

Child Guidance

Introduction

1. This circular gives advice to local authorities and health authorities on the provision and organisation of child guidance. It replaces the advice which was issued in 1959 to local education authorities as Circular 347, and sent to hospital authorities under cover of HM(59)23.

2. As a consequence of the transfer of the medical inspection and treatment functions of the school health service from local education authorities to area health authorities on 1 April 1974, there is a need for specific

guidance on transfer of certain staff and premises, and on child guidance arrangements in the immediate post-transfer period.

3.   But apart from this, it is opportune to take a fresh look at arrangements for providing child guidance in the light of developments and to ensure that the best possible use is made of scarce resources, particularly of manpower. Part I of the circular suggests the future concept of child guidance towards which authorities should aim, and asks that the Joint Consultative Committees to be established under Section 10 of the National Health Service Reorganisation Act should review existing services and draw up plans. Part II sets out the arrangements for transfer of staff and premises arising from the NHS Reorganisation Act, and recommends that, until new plans are agreed, the present arrangements for existing child guidance services should be disturbed as little as possible.

Part I — Current Developments and The Pattern for The Future

4.   The following paragraphs set out the pattern of the services as they exist and as it is envisaged that they should develop, so that the interim arrangements in Part II can be seen in the context of longer-term aims. The full development of the future pattern will however be contingent on the availability of resources for the purpose; in the present climate of financial stringency it is not likely that resources for immediate development can easily be made available, so that the pace of change may be slower than we would otherwise have wished.

5.   Any pattern for the future needs to take account both of experience of existing child guidance services, and of developments in other services which have a bearing on the handling of behavioural, emotional or learning difficulties in children, and on the management of associated family problems.

Existing child guidance services

6.   Although there is no specific reference in the Education Acts to child guidance services, local education authorities have long considered it essential that they should be able to obtain help for and advice about pupils with such difficulties. They have regarded the duty of securing that child guidance services are available as being part of their general responsibilities for the education of pupils and of their specific duties, under Sections 34 and 48 of the Education Act 1944, to ascertain which children require special education and to secure the provision of medical treatment.

7.   The arrangements for child guidance recommended in Circular 347 envisaged that local education authorities should provide premises and

employ psychologists and psychiatric social workers, and that Regional Hospital Boards should provide the services of psychiatrists. It was also recommended that a child guidance clinic should form part of the general responsibility of the principal school medical officer and be under the medical direction of the psychiatrist. This has been the usual pattern. In some areas however other arrangements have been adopted: for example some clinics are in premises provided by Hospital Boards, while some psychiatrists have been employed by local education authorities, and some social workers by local health and social services authorities.

8.   The School Health Service Sub-Committee of the Working Party on Collaboration recognised that changes in organisation might be needed as a consequence of the transfer to the National Health Service of the responsibility for providing medical treatment services for school pupils; but the Sub-Committee made it clear that they did not want local education authorities' powers in relation to the provision of child guidance to be in any way limited as a result.

9.   Experience has shown that there are many more needs to be met than was at one time thought. For example, there are many more children with behavioural, emotional or learning difficulties than was previously assumed; a high proportion of these difficulties arise at pre-school age; and frequently there are related family problems which need to be tackled at the same time. Although expansion has taken place over the years in the number of child psychiatrists, educational and clinical psychologists and social workers, there are still serious shortages, especially in certain parts of the country; the number of child psychiatrists in particular is unlikely to match the demands made for their services.

10.   There have also been differences of approach. While some clinics give each child referred to them a detailed psychological, social and psychiatric investigation and provide prolonged and intensive treatment for selected cases, other clinics have tried to reach a larger number of children by concentrating more on assessment and consultation, both in relation to individual children and general problems.

Developments in related services

11.   School psychological services. During the last decade school psychological services, staffed by educational psychologists and remedial teachers, have been established as an integral part of local educational provision. It is now recognised how much success or failure at school and acceptance or rejection by his peers affect a child's development, and how close the interactions can be between home and school. The psychologist usually has many more calls for his services than he can respond to, but he seeks to spend part of his time on visits to schools to discuss general problems with staff, in addition to seeing individual children with difficulties of

personal adjustment or learning, and advising staff about handling them; he also sees some of the parents. Increasingly too, educational psychologists are extending their help to children below the age of 5 in nursery schools and classes, children's homes and elsewhere. Educational psychologists are also involved in the assessment of children with handicaps of all kinds and the organisation of remedial work, as well as in curriculum development, in-service teacher training and a variety of other activities. The growth in school psychological services has been made possible by an increase in the number of educational psychologists employed by local education authorities in England and Wales from (in whole time equivalents) 324 in 1965 to 638 in 1973.

12.   Child psychiatric services. A marked increase in child psychiatric services both in hospital and elsewhere in the community has taken place in the last decade as a result of growing recognition of the need for specialist psychiatric services for the diagnosis, assessment and treatment of mentally ill and emotionally disturbed children (some of whom may also be mentally handicapped) and help for their families. Interim advice on child psychiatric services was issued to hospital authorities in 1964 (in HM(64)4) with more recent reference in HM(71)22 issued in 1971. A discussion paper has been circulated recently by the Department of Health and Social Security which puts forward suggestions for the way in which child psychiatric services should be organised, and how they should relate to adult services and be extended into the community. The number of child psychiatric hospital units has increased from 18 in 1964 to 39 in 1973, and the number of in-patient places from 370 to 640. A further 41 units with some 800 places are planned. The number of consultant child psychiatrists (whole time equivalent) with contracts with hospital authorities in England and Wales has increased from 80·9 in 1963 to 162·7 in 1972. Day and out-patient services are also expanding, and there is increasing emphasis on developing links with services in the community, particularly with the education and social services.

13.   Child Health services. In recent years there has been a substantial increase in the provision of facilities for multi-disciplinary examination and assessment of handicapped children and a number of comprehensive assessment centres have been opened, usually in general hospitals but sometimes elsewhere. There has also been an increase in the number of clinics held jointly by consultant paediatricians and child psychiatrists. The medical and nursing staff of local authorities have participated and, with their special knowledge of local authority services (including educational provision), have provided an important link between hospitals and the local authority health services as well as between the local authority health and education services.

14.   Social work services. Psychiatric social workers have been an integral

part of child guidance services since their inception in 1926. They have contributed to the development of services for children and their families, and the experience and expertise gained in this work has made a considerable contribution to social work training. The Local Authority Social Services Act 1970 and the setting up of local authority social services departments have brought about fundamental changes in the provision, organisation and training needs of the social work services. The comprehensive nature of the services required for all clients has called for a widening of the scope of social work and of the skills involved. The social services departments have assumed new responsibilities for children and their families, among them those resulting from the Children and Young Persons Act 1969. Residential, day care and other social work services for children have expanded, and regional plans for community homes call for the extension of assessment facilities in those establishments. A recent further development is that as from April 1974, local authorities will be responsible for making social work staff available to the health services.

The pattern for the future
15.   Ways must be found to extend help to more children with behavioural, emotional or learning difficulties and their families. In a situation where resources of staff with specialist skills are very limited, more flexible arrangements for seeking and providing assistance are needed to ensure that the time of scarce staff is used to the best advantage. Further, services must be concerned not only with providing assessment, diagnosis, consultation, and treatment for children with difficulties but also with providing help and general guidance about problems of child development and behaviour to parents and to other people in regular contact with children, including health visitors, general practitioners, teachers, social workers, and residential child care staff. It is plainly desirable for difficulties that at present are not brought forward until they become aggravated to be dealt with at an earlier stage—and indeed if possible prevented from arising at all.
16.   Rather than a self-contained, highly specialised child guidance service which has operated in some areas, the concept of child guidance that now appears appropriate is of a network of services, each providing help for children with difficulties and their families, which collaborate in such different combinations as may be required to handle individual or general problems. Such arrangements will clearly need to be flexible; but this makes it the more important that they should also be well defined and understood.
17.   The school psychological services, the child psychiatric services, the social work services and the child health services, are seen as constituting a network of services each having its own independent organisation and

functions and its own premises in the community, but having joint working arrangements for dealing with those children and their families whose problems call for a combined approach by more than one service. This combined approach is most appropriately carried out by members of a recognised team and entails identifying individuals from each service who will work together for this purpose. In some cases this will be on a sessional or regular part-time basis, and in others on an occasional basis. A full-time commitment may be appropriate in the case of some social workers. In order to achieve cohesion as a team, to provide continuity of treatment and to afford opportunities for interdisciplinary training, the same individuals will need to work together regularly over a period. While doing so, they should develop common aims and approaches which will inform their other activities. The work that they do during their time as members of their own service will give them a firm professional base from which to operate and a larger pool of resources on which to draw. It is also envisaged that they will work more often than at present in schools, community homes and other places where there are groups of children.

18.   It is implicit in the independent operation of each service in the network that staff should be employed by the authority responsible for the service involved—medical and nursing staff and psychotherapists (non-medical) by the health authority, educational psychologists and social work staff by the local authority, in the education[1] and social services departments respectively.

19.   The premises in which the team would meet would also need to be identified. In principle it is not important whether these are educational, health or social services premises. The important factors are that children who need multi-disciplinary assessment, diagnosis or treatment should not have to go from one place to another for it; that premises should be readily accessible to children and their families; and that premises and supporting services should be easy to administer. The place or places selected might thus be in the headquarters of one of the participating staff or in some separate premises.

Planning

20.   Proposals for future arrangements for child guidance in each health and local authority area[2] should be drawn up as soon as is conveniently

[1] In Inner London, the Inner London Education Authority.

[2] Outside London the boundaries of the health authority areas and the local authority areas will normally be the same. The Report of the London Sub-Committee of the Working Party on Collaboration recommends that the particular situation of London, where in a number of instances the area served by an Area Health Authority comprises more than one London Borough, should be met by local agreement between the authorities concerned as to whether they would wish to participate in a single Joint Consultative Committee covering

possible after the reorganisations of the NHS and local government in April 1974. These proposals should give effect to the concept set out in paragraphs 16–19 above and take into account the points outlined in paragraphs 21 and 22 below. There may be cases where the existing arrangements for child guidance services already reflect this concept, and in such instances the authorities may wish to continue with them, perhaps with some modifications. The Joint Consultative Committees[1] which are to be set up in each area should be asked to draw up agreed proposals for the consideration of the two authorities. The local and shared responsibility for drawing up plans should be the best guarantee of co-operation between the different services involved in the network on which the effectiveness of the arrangements for child guidance depends. The Joint Consultative Committees should also be asked to keep the arrangements agreed between the authorities under regular review.

21.   Careful planning will be required to determine the pattern and arrangements appropriate for each health and local authority area. Some of the points to be borne in mind are:

   i. planning should take account of the prospective development in the area of each of the services referred to in paragraphs 11–14;
   ii. the proposals should be related to the needs and resources of the area as a whole, but different arrangements may be appropriate for for different parts of the area according to local circumstances;
   iii. responsibility for maintaining premises and providing administrative and supporting services is most suitably vested in the authority responsible for the building in which the premises are sited.

Detailed points of organisation
22.   It is suggested that all plans should cover the following detailed points of organisation:

   i. routes of referral of children and families;
   ii. determination of responsibility for cases at different stages;

all boroughs in the Area Health Authority area or whether instead they would prefer to have an individual Joint Consultative Committee for each borough or for particular groups of boroughs. The Report also recommends that the Inner London Education Authority should be represented on all Joint Consultative Committees which cover an Inner London Borough. (Acceptance of these recommendations by the Working Party is subject to consultation on them with interested parties).

[1] The Joint Consultative Committees which are to be set up will comprise members of the area health authority and the local authority (the latter in both its education and social services capacities). In broad terms the functions of the Joint Consultative Committees will be to act as a means whereby the health and local authority can jointly examine the needs of each area, co-ordinate the plans of the two authorities for meeting those needs and review progress in implementing them. Circular HRC(74)19 (Welsh Office Circular WHRC(74)14) describes these functions in more detail.

iii. arrangements for communicating with, and reporting back to, referring agencies and others concerned;

iv. arrangements for keeping case records, and for access to them.

Notification of arrangements in each area

23. The Secretaries of State will wish to be informed of the arrangements for each area as soon as they have been agreed but in any event not later than the end of 1976.

Part II — Interim Arrangements

Future employment of staff

24. The NHS Reorganisation Act, although it repeals the relevant provisions of Section 48 of the Education Act 1944, will not affect a local authority's general obligation to see that help and advice is available for school pupils with behavioural, emotional or learning problems. The wide range of services embraced under child guidance cannot all be regarded as medical treatment services and while it is envisaged that child guidance staff who can be regarded as providing medical treatment services will transfer to the appropriate health authorities, other staff will not. For those who transfer, the principles set out in HRC(73)25 (Welsh Office Circular WHRC(73)23) will apply.

25. In practice it is thus envisaged that

a. Medical staff, whether at present under contract to or employed by hospital or local health authorities or by local education authorities would transfer (the latter under Section 18(i)(a)(iii) of the Act) to the appropriate health authorities.

b. Psychotherapists (non-medical) who normally work under medical direction would similarly transfer.

c. Clerical and other staff providing supporting services at transferred clinic premises (see paragraph 26 below) would normally also transfer.

The remuneration and other terms and conditions of service of staff so transferred will be protected in accordance with the provisions of Section 19 of the Act. Advice on this is given in HRC(74)2 (Welsh Office Circular WHRC(74)9).

26. Educational psychologists, social workers and any other local authority child guidance staff, other than the above, employed by local authorities outside London will transfer under Section 255 of the Local Government Act 1972 to the appropriate new local authorities. Those employed by local authorities within the Greater London area will remain in the employ-

ment of their existing local authority. While it will be for the local authority to decide in which department social work staff at present employed in the health departments of local authorities should be employed after 1 April, it may be more appropriate for the future for them to be employed, in social services departments, though continuing to be available for child guidance work.

Transfer of premises owned by education authorities

27.   As already indicated in HRC(74)25 (Welsh Office Circular WHRC(74) 24) premises held by local education authorities for child guidance purposes should not in themselves be regarded as premises held for school health purposes. Such premises will therefore remain with education authorities unless they form part of properties whose major use is for school health or other health purposes, and so, under the NHS Reorganisation Act, transfer to the NHS.

Responsibility for existing clinic services in the immediate post-transfer period

28.   In the interim period pending the review by the Joint Consultative Committees referred to in Part 1, paragraph 20, it is recommended that the present arrangements for existing child guidance services should be disturbed as little as possible.

29.   Some immediate organisational and administrative changes will however be required in child guidance services provided by local education authorities as a result of the transfer on 1 April 1974 of the present responsibilities of the principal school medical officer to the specialist in community medicine (child health) on the staff of the area health authority and the fact that some clinics may be within premises transferred to area health authorities.

30.   It is suggested that local education authorities and area health authorities should be responsible for administrative support for clinics, e.g. the provision of clerical staff and general support services, according to whether the clinics are situated in local education authority or area health authority premises but that the precise administrative arrangements should be a matter for local agreement.

31.   Health authorities will be responsible for seeing that medical staff and psychotherapists (non-medical) are provided for child guidance work whether carried on in local authority or area health authority premises. The local authority will be responsible for the provision of educational psychologists and social work staff.

32.   The specialist in community medicine (child health) though having no clinical responsibility will be available to take responsibility for the co-ordinating and organisational functions previously undertaken by the

principal school medical officer in relation to child guidance and will also be available to advise the local education authority on the medical aspects of the service.

To Local Education Authorities
Local Social Services Authorities
Regional Health Authorities
Area Health Authorities
Preserved Boards of Governors
Family Practitioner Committees
Local Health Authorities

References

Ackerman, N. W. (1958) *The Psychodynamics of Family Life*, New York, Basic Books.

Acklaw, J. and Labon, D. (1971) 'School-based therapy: a pilot scheme', *Association of Educational Psychologists Journal and Newsletter*, **2**, 10, 35–9.

Adams, M. (1971) *Mental Retardation and Its Social Dimensions*, Columbia University Press.

Aichhorn, A. (1925; English edition, 1951) *Wayward Youth*, London, Imago.

Ainley, M. T. (1969) 'The Incidence of Maladjustment in a Residential School for the Physically Handicapped', unpublished thesis for Diploma in Special Education, University College of Swansea.

Ainsworth, M. *et al.* (1962) *Deprivation of Maternal Care: A reassessment of its effects*, Geneva, World Health Organisation (Public Health Papers 14).

Alexander, W. P. (1958) *The Alexander Performance Scale*, Windsor, National Foundation for Educational Research.

American Psychological Association (1954) *Technical Recommendations for Psychological Tests and Diagnostic Techniques*, published by the Association.

Ames, L. B. and Learned, J. (1954a) 'Developmental trends in child Kaleidobloc responses', *J. Genet. Psychol.* **84**, 237–70.

Ames, L. B. and Learned, F. (1954b) 'Individual differences in child Kaleidobloc responses', *J. Genet. Pscyhol.* **85**, 3–38.

Ames, L. B., Learned, J., Metraux, R. W. and Walker, R. N. (1952) *Child Rorschach Responses*, New York, Hoeber.

Ames, L. B., Learned, J., Metraux, R. W. and Walker, R. N. (1959) *Adolescent Rorschach Responses*, New York, Hoeber.

Anastasi, A. (1961) *Psychological Testing*, 2nd edn, New York, Macmillan.

Andry, R. G. (1960) *Delinquency and Parental Pathology*, London, Methuen.

Anstey, E. (1966), *Psychological Tests*, London, Nelson.

Applebee, A. N. (1971) 'Research in reading retardation: two critical problems', *J. Child Psychol. Psychiat.* **12**, 2, 91–114.

Arthur, G. (1955) *Arthur Point Scale of Performance Tests, Revised Form II*, Windsor, NFER.

Ascher, M. A. (1970) 'The attainments of children in ESN schools and remedial departments', *Educ. Res.* **12**, 3, 215–19.

Ashcroft, S. C. (1963) 'Blind and partially seeing children', in L. M. Dunn, ed., *Exceptional Children in the Schools*, New York, Holt, Rinehart & Winston.

Association of British Adoption Agencies, *Child Adoption*, quarterly.

Association of Psychiatric Social Workers (1963) *Relationship in Casework*, London, APSW.

Association of Teachers of Maladjusted Children (1967) *Therapeutic Education*, June issue.

Axelrod, S. (1959) *Effects of Early Blindness: performance of blind and sighted children on tactile and auditory tasks*, New York, American Foundation for the Blind.

Bagley, C. (1971) *The Social Psychology of the Child with Epilepsy*, London, Routledge & Kegan Paul.

Bakker, D. J. B. and Satz, P. S., eds. (1970) *Specific Reading Disability*, Rotterdam University Press.

Bandura, A. (1969) *Principles of Behaviour Modification*, New York, Holt, Rinehard & Winston.

Bandura, A. and Walters, R. H. (1963) *Social Learning and Personality Development*, New York, Holt, Rinehart & Winston.

Bannister, D. and Mair, J. M. M. (1968) *The Evaluation of Personal Constructs*, London and New York, Academic Press.

Barclay, J. R. (1971) 'Descriptive, theoretical and behavioural characteristics of subdoctoral school psychologists', *American Psychologist*, **26**, 3, 257–80.

Barnett, M. R. (1955) 'Current problems of the blind', in M. E. Frampton and E. D. Gall, eds., *Special Education for the Exceptional*, Vol. 2, Boston, Peter Sargent.

Bartlett, E. F. (1970) 'Survey of Day Units for the Maladjusted Child', unpublished thesis, Diploma in Special Education, University College of Swansea.

Bateman, B. (1963) *Reading and Psycholinguistic Processes of Partially Seeing Children*, CEC Res. Monogr., Washington, Council for Exceptional Children.

Baumeister, A. A. (1967) 'Learning abilities of the mentally retarded', in A. A. Baumeister, ed., *Appraisal, Education and Rehabilitation*, London, University of London Press.

Bax, M. C. O. and Mckeith, R. M. eds (1963) *Minimal Brain Dysfunction*, Little Club Clinics in Developmental Medicine No. 10, London, Heinemann.

Bayley, N. (1949), 'Consistency and variability in the growth of intelligence from birth to 18 years', *J. Genet. Psychol.* **79**, 165–96.

Bayley, N. (1955) 'On the growth of intelligence', *American Psychologist*, **10**, 805–18.

Becker, W. C., Madsen, C. H., Arnold, C. R. and Thomas, D. R. (1967) 'The contingent use of teacher attention and praise in reducing classroom behaviour problems', *J. Spec. Educ.*, **1**, 287–307.

Belfield, D. J. (1963) 'The Social Adjustment of Most Accepted and Least Accepted Children in Junior Schools', unpublished M. Ed., thesis, University of Manchester.

Bellak, L. and Bellak, S. S. (1950) *The CAT and TAT in Clinical Use*, New York, Grune and Stratton.

Bender, L. (1938) *A visual-motor Gestalt test and its clinical use. Amer. Orthopsychiat. Monogr.* No. 3. (*See also* Koppitz, 1964.)

Bené, E. and Anthony, E. J. (1957) *Manual for the Family Relations Test*, Windsor, NFER.

Bennett, I. (1960) *Delinquent and Neurotic Children: a comparative study*, London, Tavistock.

Bennett, V. D. C. (1970) 'Who is a school psychologist and what does he do?' *Journal of School Psychology*, 8, 3, 166–71.

Benton, A. L. (1963) *The Revised Visual Retention Test*, 3rd edn, New York, Psychological Corp. (distrib. NFER).

Bergès, J. and Lézine, I. (1963) *Imitation of Gestures*, Heinemann for Spastics Society.

Bernstein, B. (1971) *Class, Codes and Control*, Vol. 1. *Theoretical Studies Towards a Sociology of Language*, London, Routledge & Kegan Paul.

Binet, A., *see* Terman and Merrill.

Birch, H. G. and Belmont, L. (1964) 'Auditory-visual integration in normal and retarded readers', *Amer. J. Orthopsychiat.*, 34, 852–61.

Blacker, C. P. (1948) *Neurosis and the Mental Health Services*, Oxford University Press.

Bloom, B. S. (1964) *Stability and Change in Human Characteristics*, New York, Wiley.

Blount, W. R. (1968) 'Concept usage: research with the mentally retarded', *Psychol. Bull.* 69, 281–94.

Blum, G. S. (1949) *The Blacky Pictures: a technique for the exploration of personality dynamics*, New York, Psychological Corp. (distrib. NFER); and in Rabin and Haworth, 1960, ch. 5.

Blyth, W. A. L. (1960) 'The sociometric study of children's groups in English schools', *Brit. J. Educ. Studies*, 8, 2, 127–47.

Boehm, A. E. (1967) *The Boehm Test of Basic Concepts*, New York, Psychological Corp. (distrib. NFER).

Bookbinder, G. E. (1970) 'Variations in reading test norms', *Educational Research*, 12, 2, 99–105.

Bower, E. M. (1969) *Early Identification of Emotionally Handicapped Children in School*, 2nd edn, Springfield, Illinois, Charles C. Thomas.

Bowlby, J. (1952) *Maternal Care and Mental Health*, 2nd edn, Geneva, World Health Organisation, Monograph Series No. 2.

Bowlby, J., Ainsworth, M., Boston, M., and Rosenbluth, D. (1956) 'The effects of mother-child separation: a follow-up study', *Brit. J. Med. Psychol.* 29, 211–47.

Bowyer, L. R. (1970) *The Lowenfeld World Technique: Studies in Personality*, Oxford, Pergamon.

Bowyer, L. R., Marshall, A. and Wedell, K. (1963) 'The relative personality adjustment of severely deaf and partially deaf children', *Brit. J. Educ. Psychol.* 33, 85–7.

Brammer, L. M. and Shostrom, E. L. (1960) *Therapeutic Psychology: Fundamentals of Counseling and Psychotherapy*, Englewood Cliffs, N.J., Prentice-Hall.

Brandon, S. (1960) 'An Epidemiological Study of Maladjustment in Childhood', unpublished MD thesis, University of Durham.

Brenner, N. W. (1967) 'Visuo-motor disability in school children', *Brit. Med. J.*, **4**, 259–62.

Bridgeland, M. (1971) *Pioneer Work with Maladjusted Children*, London, Staples Press.

Bridges, S. A. (1969) *Gifted Children and the Brentwood Experiment*, London, Pitman.

Brieland, D. (1951) 'Speech education for the visually handicapped child', *Int. J. Educ. Blind*, **1**, 9–12.

Brimer, M. A. and Dunn, L. M. (1962) *Manual for the English Picture Vocabulary Test*, Bristol, Education Evaluation Enterprises (distrib. NFER).

British Association of Social Workers (1970) *Confidentiality and A Code of Ethics for Social Work*, Discussion Papers Nos. 1 and 2.

British Association of Social Workers, *Social Work Today*, fortnightly.

British Psychological Society (1962a) *The Teaching of Educational Psychology in Training Colleges*, Report of Joint Working Party of the British Psychological Society and the Association of Teachers in Training Colleges and Departments of Education, London, British Psychological Society.

British Psychological Society (1962b) *The School Psychological Service*, London, BPS.

British Psychological Society (1965) 'Principles governing the employment of psychological tests and clinical instruments', *Bull. Brit. Psychol. Soc.*, **18**, 61, 27–8.

British Psychological Society (1966a) *Notes on the Assessment of Children with Physical Handicaps*, London, BPS.

British Psychological Society (1966b) *Children in Hospitals for the Subnormal: a survey of admissions and educational facilities*, London, BPS.

British Psychological Society (1969) 'Classification of tests and test uses', *Bull. Brit. Psychol. Soc.* **22**, 109–11.

Brittain, M. (1969) 'The WPPSI: a Midland study', *Brit. J. Educ. Psychol.* **39**, 14–17.

Brown, J. A. C. (1961) *Freud and the Post-Freudians*, Harmondsworth, Penguin Books.

Brown, M. (1971) *Introduction to Social Administration in Britain*, rev. edn, London, Hutchinson.

Brown, R. I. and Bookbinder, G. E. (1966) 'Programmed reading for spastics', *Spec. Educ.* **55**, 4, 26–9.

Buell, C. (1950) 'Motor performances of visually handicapped children', *Except. Child.* **17**, 69–72.

Buhler, C., Lumry, G. K. and Carroll, H. (1951) 'World test standardisation studies', *J. Child Psychiat.* **2**, 2–81.

Burgermeister, B. B., Blum, L. H. and Lorge, I. (1959) *The Columbia Mental Maturity Scale*, rev. edn, New York, Harcourt Brace and World.

Burns, R. C. and Kaufman, S. H. (1971) *Kinetic Family Drawings (KFD)*, London, Constable.

Burns, R. C. and Kaufman, S. H. (1972) *Action, Styles and Symbols in kinetic Family Drawings (KFD): an interpretive manual*, New York, Brunner-Mazel.

Buros, O. K. (1972) *The Seventh Mental Measurements Yearbook*, New Jersey, The Gryphon Press.

Burt, C. (1925; 4th edn 1944) *The Young Delinquent*, London, University of London Press.

Burt, C. (1957) *The Causes and Treatment of Backwardness*, 4th edn, London, University of London Press.

Burt, C. (1964) *The School Psychological Service: its history and development*, London, Association of Educational Psychologists.

Burt, C. (1969) 'Psychologists in the education services', *Bull. Brit. Psychol. Soc.* **22**, 1–11.

Burt, C. and Howard, M. (1952) 'The nature and causes of maladjustment among children of school age', *Brit. J. Psychol. Stat.* **5**, 39–60.

Calouste Gulbenkian Foundation (1968) *Community Work and Social Change*, London, Longmans.

Campbell, S. D., Douglas, V. I. and Morgenstern, G. (1971) 'Cognitive styles in hyperactive children and the effects of methylphenidate', *J. Child Psychol. Psychiat.*, **12**, 55–68.

Cantor, G. N. (1958) *An Investigation of Discrimination Learning Ability in Mongoloid and Normal Children of Comparable Mental Age*. Nashville, Tenn., George Peabody College for Teachers.

Carnegie United Kingdom Trust (1964) *Handicapped Children and their Families*, Dunfermline, Carnegie UK Trust.

Carré, I. J. (1961) 'The acute respiratory infections of childhood', *Practitioner*, **187**, 767.

Carroll, H. C. M. (1971) 'The remedial teaching of reading: an evaluation', *University College of Swansea Faculty of Education Journal*, 30–5.

Carroll, J. B. (1964) *Language and Thought*, Englewood Cliffs, N.J., Prentice-Hall.

Cashdan, A. (1968) 'The learning difficulties of subnormal children', in A. B. Boom, ed., *Studies on the Mentally Handicapped Child*, London, Arnold.

Cashdan, A. (1969) 'Handicaps in learning', in J. F. Morris and E. A. Lunzer, *Development in Learning: Contexts of Education*, London, Staples Press.

Cashdan, A. and Pumfrey, P. D. (1969) 'Some effects of the remedial teaching of reading', *Educ. Res.*, **11**, 2, 138–42.

Cashdan, A., Pumphrey, P. D. and Lunzer, E. A. (1971) 'Children receiving remedial teaching in reading', *Educ. Res.* **13**, 2, 98–105.

Cattell, P. (1960) *The Cattell Infant Intelligence Scale*, New York, Psychological Corp. (distrib. NFER).

Cattell, R. B. (1950) *Personality*, New York, McGraw-Hill.

Cattell, R. B. (1964) *Handbook for the Sixteenth Personality Factors Questionnaire*, Champaign, Illinois: Inst. Personality and Ability Testing.

Cattell, R. B. and Cattell, M. D. L. (1960) *The High School Personality Questionnaire*, Champaign, Illinois: Inst. Personality and Ability Testing (distrib. NFER). (*See also* Porter and Cattell, 1963.)

Cattell, R. B., Sealy, A. P. and Sweney, A. B. (1966) 'What can personality and motivation source trait measurements add to the prediction of school attainment?', *Brit. J. Educ. Psychol*, **39**, 109–22.

Central Advisory Council for Education, England (1967) *Children and their Primary Schools* (The Plowden Report), London, HMSO.

Central Advisory Council for Education, Wales (1967) *Primary Education in Wales* (The Gittins Report), London, HMSO.

Chazan, M. (1963) 'Maladjustment, attainment and sociometric status', *University College of Swansea Faculty of Education Journal*, 4–7.

Chazan, M. (1964) 'The incidence and nature of maladjustment among children in schools for the educationally subnormal', *Brit. J. Educ. Psychol.* **34**, 292–304.

Chazan, M. (1965) 'Factors associated with maladjustment in ESN children', *Brit. J. Educ. Psychol.* **35**, 277–85.

Chazan, M. (1967) 'The effects of remedial teaching', *Rem. Educ.* **2**, 4–12.

Chazan, M. (1968) 'Children's emotional development', *Educational Research in Britain*, ed. Butcher, H. J., University of London Press.

Chazan, M. (1969) 'Maladjustment and reading difficulties, I: recent research and experiment', *Rem. Educ.* **4**, 3, 119–23.

Chazan, M. (1970) 'Maladjusted children', in P. Mittler, ed. *The Psychological Assessment of Mental and Physical Handicap*, London, Methuen.

Chazan, M. (1971) 'The role of the educational psychologist in the promotion of community mental health', *Community Dev. J.* **6**, 3, 173–82.

Chazan, M., ed. (1973) *Compensatory Education*, London, Butterworth.

Chazan, M. and Jackson, S. (1971) 'Behaviour problems in the infant school', *J. Child Psychol. Psychiat.* **12**, 191–210.

Child Adoption, see Association of British Adoption Agencies.

Children and Young Persons Act 1969, London, HMSO.

Children in Trouble *see* Home Office (1968).

Clark, A. M. (1972) 'Current issues in the training of psychologists', *Australian Psychologist*, **7**, 2, 90–4.

Clark, M. (1970) *Reading Difficulties in Schools*, Harmondsworth, Penguin Books.

Clarke, A. D. B. (1969) *Recent Advances in the Study of Subnormality*, London, National Association for Mental Health.

Clarke, A. M. and Clarke, A. D. B. (1966) *Mental Deficiency*, 2nd edn, London, Methuen.

Cloward, R. and Ohlin, L. (1961) *Delinquency and Opportunity: a theory of delinquent gangs*, Illinois, Free Press of Glencoe.

Clyne, M. B. (1966) *Absent*, London, Tavistock.

Cockburn, J. M. (1961) 'Psychological and educational aspects', in J. L. Henderson, ed., *Cerebral Palsy in Childhood and Adolescence*, Edinburgh and London, E. and S. Livingstone.

Cohen, A. (1955) *Delinquent Boys: the culture of the gang*, Illinois, Free Press of Glencoe.

Cohen, I. M., ed. (1966) *Family Structure, Dynamics and Therapy*, Washington DC, American Psychiatric Association.

Collins, J. E. (1061) *The Effects of Remedial Education*, Edinburgh, Oliver & Boyd.

Concern, see National Children's Bureau.

Cooper, M. G. (1966) 'School refusal: an inquiry into the part played by school and home', *Educ. Res.* **8**, 3, 223–9.

Cotton, E. and Parnwell, M. (1967) 'From Hungary: the Pető Method', *Spec. Educ.* **56**, 4, 7–11.

Crabb, G. H. (1965) 'An Investigation into the Number Concepts of Children with Cerebral Palsy', unpublished thesis for Diploma in Special Education, University College of Swansea.

Craig, M. and Furst, P. W. (1965) 'What happens after treatment', *Soc. Service Rev.* **39**, 165–71.

Cronbach, L. J. (1966) *Essentials of Psychological Testing*, 2nd edn, New York, Harper & Row.

Cutts, N. E., ed. (1955) *School Psychologists at Mid-Century*, Washington, DC, American Psychological Association.

Dale, D. M. C. (1962) *Applied Audiology*, Springfield, Illinois, C. C. Thomas.

Dale, D. M. C. (1967) *Deaf Children at Home and at School*, London, University of London Press.

Daniels, J. C. and Diack, H. (1958) *The Standard Reading Tests*, London, Chatto & Windus.

Darbyshire, J. O. (1970) 'The changing tune of deafness', *Spec. Educ.* **59**, 1, 26–8.

Davie, R., Butler, N. and Goldstein, H. (1972) *From Birth to Seven*, London, Longman.

Davies, P. and Williams, P. (in press) *Aspects of Early Reading Growth*, Oxford, Blackwell.

Doll, E. A. (1941) 'The essentials of an inclusive concept of mental deficiency', *Amer. J. Ment. Def.* **46**, 2, 214–19.

Doll, E. A. (1953) *The Measurement of Social Competence: a manual for the Vineland Social Maturity Scale*. Minneapolis, Educational Publishing Inc. (distrib. NFER).

Douglas, J. W. B. (1964) *The Home and the School*, London, MacGibbon & Kee.

Douglas, J. W. B., Ross, J. M., Hammond, W. A. and Mulligan, D. G. (1966) 'Delinquency and social class', *Brit. J. Criminology*, **6**, 294–302.

Douglas, J. W. B., Ross, J. M. and Simpson, H. R. (1968) *All our Future*, London, Peter Davies.

Downes, D. M. (1966) *The Delinquent Solution: a study in subcultural theory*, London, Routledge & Kegan Paul.

Dubin, S. S. (1972) 'Obsolescence or lifelong education: a choice for the professional', *American Psychologist*, May 1972, 486–98.

Duncan, J. (1947) *The Education of the Ordinary Child*, London, Nelson.

Dunlap, K. (1932) *Habits, their Making and Unmaking*, New York, Liveright.

Dunn Rankin, P., Schimizu, M. and King, F. J. (1969) 'Reward preference pattern in elementary school children', *International Journal of Education Science*, **3**, 53–62.

Dunsdon, M. I. (1952) *The Educability of Cerebral Palsied Children*, London, Newnes Educational.

Dupont, H., ed. (1969) *Educating Emotionally Disturbed Children*, New York, Holt, Rinehart & Winston.

Durkheim, E. (1939) *The Rules of the Sociological Method*, Illinois, Free Press of Glencoe.

Education and Science, Department of (1962) *The Health of the School Child 1960–61: Report of the Chief Medical Officer*, London, HMSO.

Education and Science, Department of (1964a) *Slow Learners at School*, London, HMSO.

Education and Science, Department of (1964b) *The Health of the School Child 1962–63: Report of the Chief Medical Officer*, London, HMSO.

Education and Science, Department of (1966) *Progress in Reading 1948–1964*, Education Pamphlet No. 50, London, HMSO.

Education and Science, Department of (1967) *Units for Partially Hearing Children*, Education Survey 1, London, HMSO.

Education and Science, Department of (1968a) *Blind and Partially Sighted Children*, Education Survey 4, London, HMSO.

Education and Science, Department of (1968b) *Psychologists in Education Services* (Summerfield Report), London, HMSO.

Education and Science, Department of (1968c) *The Education of Deaf Children*, London, HMSO.

Education and Science, Department of (1969a) *Peripatetic Teachers of the Deaf*, Education Survey 6, London, HMSO.

Education and Science, Department of (1969b) *List of Special Schools for Handicapped Pupils in England and Wales*, List 42, London, HMSO.

Education and Science, Department of (1970a) *Children with Cerebral Palsy*, Education Survey 7, London, HMSO.

Education and Science, Department of (1970b) *The Education (Handicapped Children) Act, 1970*, Circular 15/70, London, HMSO.

Education and Science, Department of (1970c) *Statistics of Education, 1969, Vol. 1—Schools*, London, HMSO.

Education and Science, Department of (1971a) *Diagnostic and Assessment Units*, Education Survey 9, London, HMSO.

Education and Science, Department of (1971b) *The Last to Come in*, Reports on Education, No. 69, London, HMSO.

Education and Science, Department of (1971c) *Slow Learners in Secondary Schools*, London, HMSO.

Education and Science, Department of (1972a) *Children with Specific Reading Difficulties*, London, HMSO.

Education and Science, Department of (1972b) *The Visually Handicapped* (Vernon Report), London, HMSO.

Education and Science, Department of (1972c) *Education: a Framework for Expansion* (Cmnd 5174), London, HMSO.

Education and Science, Department of (1973) Statistics of Education, 1972, vol 2, London, HMSO.

Education, Ministry of (1945) *Handicapped Pupils and School Health Service Regulations*, London, HMSO.

Education, Ministry of (1955) *Report of the Committee on Maladjusted Children* (Underwood Report), London, HMSO.

Education, Ministry of (1959) Circular 347 (with the associated Ministry of Health Hospital Memorandum (59) 23 and Circular 3/59), London, HMSO.

Education, Ministry of (1961) Circular 11/61, London, HMSO.

Education, Ministry of (1963) *Half Our Future* (Newsom Report), London, HMSO.

Eilenberg, M. D. (1961) 'Remand home boys: 1930–1955', *Brit. J. Criminol.* **2**, 111–31.

Eisenberg, L. (1966) 'Reading retardation: psychiatric and sociology aspects', *Pediatrics*, **37**, 352–65.

Eisenberg, L. (1957) 'The course of childhood schizophrenia', *Arch. Neurol. Psychiat.* **78**, 69–83.

Elliott, C. D. (1070) 'Can the memory of subnormal children be improved?', in Mittler, ed. (1970c).

Engeln, R., Knutson, J., Laughy, L. and Garlington, W. (1968) 'Behaviour modification techniques applied to a family unit—a case study', *J. Child Psychol. Psychiat*, **9**, 245–52.

Entwistle, N. J. (1968) 'Academic motivation and school attainment', *Brit. J. Educ. Psychol.*, **38**, 2, 181–8.

European Committee on Crime Problems (1967) *The Effectiveness of Punishment and other Measures of Treatment*, Strasbourg, Council of Europe.

Evans, D. (1956) 'An Experimental Study of a Group of Seriously-maladjusted Educationally Subnormal Children', unpublished MA (Education) Thesis, University of Birmingham.

Evans, K. M. (1962) *Sociometry and Education*, London, Routledge & Kegan Paul.

Evans, R. (1968) 'A Comparison of Methods of Item Analyses', unpublished M.A. (Education) thesis, University of Wales.

Evans, R. (unpublished) *The Swansea Evaluation Profiles: Technical Manual*, London, Blackwell for Schools Council.

Evans, R., Davis, P., Ferguson, N. and Williams, P. (to be published) *Swansea Evaluation Profile (School Entrants)*, London, Schools Council.

Ewing, A. W. G., ed. (1957) *Educational Guidance and the Deaf Child*, University of Manchester Press.

Ewing, A. W. G., ed. (1960) *The Modern Educational Treatment of Deafness*, Washington, D.C., Volta Bureau.

Ewing, I. R. and Ewing, A. W. G. (1958) *New Opportunities for Deaf Children*, Springfield, Ill., C. C. Thomas.

Eysenck, H. J. (1960a) *The Structure of Human Personality*, London, Methuen.

Eysenck, H. J. (1960b) 'The effects of psychotherapy' in Eysenck (1960c).

Eysenck, H. J., ed. (1960c) *Handbook of Abnormal Psychology*, London, Pitman.

Eysenck, H. J. (1964) *Crime and Personality*, London, Routledge & Kegan Paul.

Eysenck, H. J. (1967) *The Biological Basis of Personality*, Springhill, Ill., C. C. Thomas.

Eysenck, H. J. and Rachman, S. (1965) *Causes and Cures of Neurosis*, London, Routledge & Kegan Paul.

Eysenck, S. (1965) *The Junior Eysenck Personality Inventory*, London, University of London Press.

Ferguson, N. (1972) 'The Perceptual, Motor and Language Skills of Infant School Children', unpublished PhD. thesis, University of Wales.

Ferguson, T. (1952) *The Young Delinquent in his Social Setting*, Oxford University Press.

Ferguson, T. and Kerr, A. W. (1960) *Handicapped Youth*, Oxford University Press.

Fiedler, M. F. (1952) *Deaf Children in a Hearing World*, New York, Ronald Press.

Fisch, L. (1960) 'The ascertainment and incidence of deafness among cerebral palsied children', in A. W. G. Ewing (ed.), *The Modern Educational Treatment of Deafness*, Manchester, University of Manchester Press.

Fischer, I. (1968) 'The relevance of behaviour therapy for the understanding and treatment of psychotic children', in P. J. Mittler, ed., *Aspects of Autism*, London, British Psychological Society.

Fisher, B. (1965) 'The Social and Emotional Adjustment of Children with Impaired Hearing Attending Ordinary Classes', unpublished MEd thesis, University of Manchester.

Flanders, N. A. (1970) *Analysing Teaching Behaviour*, New York, Addison-Wesley.

Floyer, E. B. (1955) *A psychological study of a city's cerebral palsied children*, London, British Council for the Welfare of Spastics.

Forder, A., ed. (1969) *Penelope Hall's Social Services of England and Wales*, London, Routledge & Kegan Paul.

Foulkes, S. H. and Anthony, E. J. (1965) *Group Psychotherapy: the Psycho-analytic Approach*, Harmondsworth, Penguin Books.

Francis-Williams, J. (1968) *Rorschach with Children*, Oxford, Pergamon.

Fransella, F. and Gerver, D. (1965) 'Multiple regression equations for predicting reading age from chronological age and WISC Verbal IQ', *Brit. J. Educ. Psychol.* **35**, 86–9.

Friedlander, K. (1947) *Psycho-analytic Approval to Juvenile Delinquency*, London, Kegan Paul.

Frisina, D. R. (1967) 'Hearing disorders', in Haring and Schiefelbusch (1967).

Frostig, M. (1966) *The Marianne Frostig Developmental Test of Visual Perception*, Palo Alto, Calif., Consulting Psychologists Press (distrib. NFER).

Furneaux, B. (1969) *The Special Child*, Harmondsworth, Penguin Books.

Furneaux, W. D. and Gibson, H. B. (1966) *Junior Maudsley Personality Inventory*, London, University of London Press.

Furth, H. (1966) *Thinking Without Language*, New York, The Free Press.

Gallagher, J. J. and Crowder, T. H. (1957) 'Adjustment of gifted children in the regular classroom', *Except. Child.* **33**, 306–12, 317–19.

Gardner, L. (1969) 'Planning for planned dependence', *Spec. Educ.* **58**, 1, 27–30.

Garfield, S. L. (1963) 'Abnormal behaviour and mental deficiency', in N. R. Ellis, ed., *Handbook of Mental Deficiency*, New York, McGraw-Hill.

Garrett, H. E. (1953) *Statistics in Psychology and Education*, London, Longman.

Gaskill, P. (1952) 'The Educational Guidance of School Children with Defective Hearing', unpublished MEd thesis, University of Manchester.

Gaskill, P. (1957) 'Tests of abilities and attainments: pilot experiments in selection and guidance', in Ewing (1957).

Gesell, A. and Amatruda, C. S. (1949) *Developmental Diagnosis: normal and abnormal child development*, 2nd edn, New York, Hoeber.

Gibson, H. (1965) *The Gibson Spiral Maze*, London, University of London Press.

Gittins, J. (1952) *Approved School Boys*, London, HMSO.

Glasser, A. J. and Zimmerman, I. L. (1967) *Clinical Interpretation of the Wechsler Intelligence Scale for Children*, New York, Grune and Stratton.

Glueck, S. and Glueck, E. T. (1950) *Unravelling Juvenile Delinquency*, New York, The Commonwealth Fund.

Glueck, S. and Glueck, E. T. (1962) *Family Environment and Delinquency*, London, Routledge & Kegan Paul.

Glueck, S. and Glueck, E. T. (1964) *Ventures in Criminology*, London, Tavistock.

Goldstein, H. (1956) *Report No. 2 on study projects for trainable mentally handicapped children*, Springfield, Illinois, State Department of Public Instruction.

Goodenough, F. L. (1926) *Measurement of Intelligence by Drawings*, London, Harrap. (*See also* Harris, D. B., 1963.)

Goodenough, F. L. (1950) 'Studies in the psychology of children's drawings II: 1928–1949', *Psychol. Bull.* **47**, 369–433. (*See also* Harris, D. B., 1963.)

Grady, P. A. E. and Daniels, J. C. (1964) *Survey of Incidence of Speech Defect in Children*, University of Nottingham.

Graham, C. (1970) 'The relation between ability and attainment tests', *Association of Educational Psychologists Journal and News Letter*, **2**, 5, 53–9.

Graham, F. J. and Kendall, B. S. (1960) *The Memory for Designs Test*, Missoula, Mont: Psychological Test Specialists (distrib. NFER).

Gray, D. R. (1963) 'The Incidence and Nature of Maladjustment in a Sample of 100 Visually Handicapped Children', unpublished thesis, Diploma in Education of Backward Children, University College of Swansea.

Gray, S. W. (1963) *The Psychologist in the Schools*, New York, Holt, Rinehart & Winston.

Green, J. M. and Herriott, P. (1971) 'Free recall in the severely subnormal', Paper given at Annual Conference of British Psychological Society, Exeter.

Green, L. F. (1966) *Comparative Achievements of ESN Pupils in Ordinary and Special Schools*, unpublished MA thesis, University of London.

Griffiths, R. (1954) *The Abilities of Babies*, London, University of London Press.

Griffiths, R. (1970) *The Abilities of Young Children*, Child Development Research Centre, 53 Staplegrove Road, Taunton, England.

Gulliford, R. (1960) 'Teaching the mother tongue to backward and subnormal pupils', *Educ. Res.* **2**, 2, 82–100.

Gulliford, R. (1969) *Backwardness and Educational Failure*, Slough, NFER.

Gulliford, R. (1971) *Special Educational Needs*, London, Routledge & Kegan Paul.

Gulliksen, H. (1950) *Theory of Mental Tests*, New York, Wiley.

Gunzburg, H. C. (1960) *The Social Rehabilitation of the Subnormal*, London, Baillière.

Gunzburg, H. C. (1968) *Social Competence and Mental Handicap: an Introduction to Social Education*, London, Baillière.

Hall, C. S. and Lindzey, G. (1957) *Theories of Personality*, New York, Wiley.

Halpern, F. (1953) *A Clinical Approach to Children's Rorschach*, New York, Grune and Stratton [and in Rabin and Haworth, 1960, ch. 2].

Halstead, H. (1957) 'Abilities and behaviour of epileptic children', *J. Ment. Sci.* **103**, 28–47.

Hamblin, D. (1972) 'Intervening in the Learning Process II', in *Intervening in the Learning Process*, Units 16 and 17 of 'Personality Growth and Learning', a second level course in Educational Studies. Bletchley, The Open University Press.

Hamilton, P. and Owrid, H. L. (1970) 'Reading and impaired hearing', *Reading*, **4**, 2, 13–18.

Hammer, E. F. (1069) 'The House-Tree-Person drawings as a projective technique with children', in Rabin and Haworth (1960), ch. 14.

Hargreaves, D. (1967) *Social Relations in a Secondary School*, London, Routledge & Kegan Paul.

Hargreaves, D. H. (1972) *Interpersonal Relations and Education*, London, Routledge & Kegan Paul.

Haring, N. G. and Schiefelbusch, R. L. (1967) *Methods in Special Education*, New York, McGraw-Hill.

Harris, A. J. (1947) *Tests of Lateral Dominance*, New York, The Psychological Corp. (distrib. NFER).

Harris, D. B. (1963) *Children's Drawings as a Measure of Intellectual Maturity*, London, Harrap. (*See also Goodenough*, 1926.)

Harris, H. (1949) *Group Approach to Leadership Testing*, London, Routledge & Kegan Paul.

Harrower, M. (1953) *Appraising Personality: the use of psychological terms in the practice of medicine*, London, Routledge & Kegan Paul.

Hartlage, L. C. (1971) 'A look at models for the training of school psychologists', *Psychology in the Schools*, **8**, 4, 304–6.

Hayes, S. F. (1941) *Contributions to a Psychology of Blindness*, New York, American Foundation for the Blind.

Hays, P. (1964) *New Horizons in Psychiatry*, Harmondsworth, Penguin Books.

Health and Social Security, Department of (1972a) *National Health Reorganisation: England; National Health Reorganisation: Wales*, London, HMSO.

Health and Social Security, Department of (1972b) *Intermediate Treatment*, London, HMSO.

Health, Ministry of (1959) *Report of the Working Party on Social Workers in Local Authority Health and Welfare Services* (Younghusband Report), London, HMSO.

Health, Ministry of (1961) Report of the Subcommittee of the Standing Mental Health Advisory Committee of the Central Health Service Council, *The Training of Staff of Training Centres for the Mentally Subnormal* (Scott Report), London, HMSO.

Healy, W. (1915) *The Individual Delinquent*, London, Heinemann.

Hebron, M. (1958) *The Staffordshire Arithmetic Test*, London, Harrap.

Heim, A. (1955) *The AH4 Test*, Windsor, NFER.

Heinicke, C. and Goldman, A. (1960) 'Research on psychotherapy with children: a review and suggestions for further study', *Amer. J. Orthopsychiat*, **30**, 3, 483–493.

Hellings, D. (1964) *Spastic School Leavers*, London, Spastics Society.

Henry, S. (1947) 'Children's audiograms in relation to reading attainment', *J. Genet. Psychol.* **70**, 211–31, **71**, 3–48.

Henry, W. (1956) *The Analysis of Fantasy*, New York, Wiley.

Hewett, F. M. (1967) 'Educational engineering with emotionally disturbed children', *Except. Child.* **33**, 459–67.

Hewitt, L. E. and Jenkins, R. L. (1946) *Fundamental Patterns of Maladjustment: the dynamics of their Origin*, Illinois, Green.

Hibbert, M. (1969) 'ASE reading survey', in *The Child and the Outside World*, London, Association for Special Education.

Hickey, R. (1962) 'Reading ability of cerebral palsied children', *Spec. Educ.* **51**, 2, 18–24.

Himmelweit, H. T. and Petrie, A. (1951) 'The measurement of personality in children', *Brit. J. Educ. Psychol.* **21**, 9–29.

Himmelweit, H. (1963) 'A social psychologist's view of the school psychological service of the future', *Bull. Brit. Psychol. Soc.* **16**, 52, 16–24.

Hindley, C. B. (1965) 'Social class differences in the development of ability in the first five years', in J. Loring, ed., *Teaching the Cerebral Palsied Child*, London, Heinemann for Spastics Society.

Hine, W. D. (1970) 'The abilities of partially hearing children', *Brit. J. Educ. Psychol.* **40**, 171–8.

Hiskey, M. S. (1955) *Nebraska Test of Learning Aptitude* (revised), University of Nebraska.

Hodges, E. F. and Tait, C. D. (1965) 'A follow-up study of potential delinquents', *Amer. J. Psychiat.* **120**, 449–53.

Home Office (1960) *Report of the Committee on Children and Young Persons* (Ingleby Report), London, HMSO.

Home Office (1964) *Report on Children and Young Persons (Scotland)* (Kilbrandon Report), London, HMSO.

Home Office (1965) *The Child, the Family and the Young Offender*, London, HMSO.

Home Office (1967) *Report of the Work of the Children's Department, 1964–66*, London, HMSO.

Home Office (1968a) *Report of the Committee on Local Authority and Allied Personal Social Services* (Cmnd 3703: Seebohm Report), London, HMSO.

Home Office (1968b) *Children in Trouble*, London, HMSO.

Home Office (1970) *Report of the Work of the Children's Department, 1967–69*, London, HMSO.

Home Office (1971) *Criminal Statistics 1970 (England and Wales)*, London, HMSO.

Home Office (1972) *Report of the Departmental Committee on the Adoption of Children* (Cmnd 5107: Houghton Report), London, HMSO.

Home Office and Social Work Services Group, Scotland (1970) *A Guide to Adoption Practice*, London, HMSO.

Honzik, M. P., Macfarlane, J. W. and Allen, L. (1948) 'The stability of mental test performance between two and eighteen years', *J. Exp. Educ.* **17**, 310–24.

Hopkins, T., Bice, H. V. and Colton, K. (1954) *Evaluation and Education of the Cerebral Palsied Child*, Washington, DC, International Council for Exceptional Children.

Horton, T. (1973) *The Reading Standards of Children in Wales*, Windsor, NFER.

Houghton Report, *see* Home Office (1972).

Howells, J. G. and Lickorish, J. R. (1967) *The Family Relations Indicator*, Edinburgh, Oliver & Boyd.

Hulse, W. C. (1952) 'Childhood conflict expressed through family drawings', *J. Proj. Techs.* **16**, 66–79.

Hutt, S. J. (1967) 'Epilepsy and education', in *What is Special Education?*, Middlesex, Association for Special Education.

Illingworth, R. S. (1961) 'The predictive value of developmental tests in the first year, with special reference to the diagnosis of mental subnormality', *J. Child Psychol. Psychiat.*, **2**, 210–15.

Ingleby Report, *see* Home Office (1960).

Ingram, T. T. S. (1965) 'Specific retardation of speech development', *Speech Path. Therapy*, **8**, 3–11.

Ives, L. A. (1967) 'Deafness and the development of intelligence', *Brit. J. Dis. Communic.* **2**, 2, 96–111.

Jackson, L. (1966) *A Test of Family Attitudes*, London, Methuen.

Jackson, N. (1968) 'Employment adjustment of educable mentally handicapped ex-pupils in Scotland', *Amer. J. Ment. Defic.*, **72**, 6, 924–30.

Jackson, S. (1966a) *Special Education in England and Wales*, Oxford University Press.

Jackson, S. (1966b) 'The Growth of Logical Thinking in Normal and Subnormal Children', unpublished MEd. thesis, University of Manchester.

Jackson, S. (1968) *A Teacher's Guide to Tests*, London, Longman.

Jackson, S. (1971) 'The illegal child-minders', *Where?* (Journal of Advisory Centre for Education), Nov. 1971.

Jeffree, D. M. (1971) 'A language teaching programme for a mongol child', *Forward Trends*, **15**, 33–8.

Jeffree, D. M. and Cashdan, A. (1971) 'Severely subnormal children and their parents: an experiment in language improvement', *Brit. J. Educ. Psychol.*, **41**, 2, 184–94.

Jenkins, R. G. and Glickman, S. (1946) 'Common syndromes in child psychiatry: 1. Deviant behaviour traits', *Amer. J. Orthopsychiat.*, **16**, 244–54.

Jensen, A. R. (1972) *Genetics and Education*, London, Methuen.

Johnson, D. J. and Mycklebust, H. R. (1967) *Learning Disabilities*, New York, Grune & Stratton.

Johnson, G. O. (1950) 'A study of the social position of mentally handicapped children in the regular grades', *Amer. J. Ment. Def.*, **55**, 60–89.

Johnson, G. O. and Capobianco, R. J. (1959) 'Physical condition and its effect upon learning in trainable mentally deficient children', *Except. Child.*, **26**, 1, 3–5; 11.

Johnson, G. O. and Kirk, S. A. (1950) 'Are mentally handicapped children segregated in the regular grades?', *J. Except. Child*, **17**, 65–8.

Johnson, J. C. (1962) *Educating Hearing-impaired Children in Ordinary Schools.* University of Manchester Press.

Johnson, O. G. and Bommarito, J. W. (1971) *Tests and Measurements in Child Development: a handbook,* San Francisco, Jossey-Bass.

Jones, A. (1970) *School Counselling in Practice,* London, Ward Lock Educational.

Jones, H. Gwynne (1970) 'Principles of psychological assessment', in Mittler, ed. (1970b), London, Methuen.

Jones, S. (1962) 'The WISC applied to a sample of London primary school children', *Brit. J. Educ. Psychol.* **32**, 119–32.

Kell, J. (1967) 'Partially sighted children', in *What is Special Education?,* Middlesex, Association for Special Education.

Kelly, G. A. (1955) *The Psychology of Personal Constructs,* New York, Norton.

Kendall, D. C. (1957) 'Mental development of young deaf children', in Ewing, ed.

Kephart, N. C. (1960) *The Slow Learner in the Classroom,* Columbus, Ohio, Merrill.

Kershaw, J. D. (1961) *Handicapped Children,* London, Heinemann.

Kettle, D. (1966) *The Partially Sighted School Leaver,* London, Association for the Education of the Partially Sighted.

Kilbrandon Report, *see* Home Office (1964).

Kirk, S. A. (1957) *Public School Provisions for Severely Retarded Children,* Albany, New York State Interdepartmental Health Resources Board.

Kirk, S. A. and Kirk, W. A. (1971) *Psycholinguistic Learning Disabilities—Diagnosis and Remediation,* University of Illinois Press.

Kirk, S. A., McCarthy, J. J. and Kirk, W. D. (1968) *The Illinois Test of Psycholinguistic Abilities,* rev. edn, University of Illinois (distrib. NFER).

Klopfer, B. (ed.) (1956) *Developments in the Rorschach technique,* Vol. 2: *Fields of Application,* New York, Harcourt Brace.

Kodman, F. (1963) in N. R. Ellis, ed., *Handbook of Mental Deficiency,* New York, McGraw-Hill

Koppitz, E. M. (1964) *The Bender Gestalt Test for young children,* New York, Grune & Stratton (distrib. NFER).

Kornitzer, M. (1959) *Adoption,* London, Pitman.

Kounin, J. S. (1943) 'Intellectual development and rigidity', *Child Behaviour and Development,* New York, McGraw-Hill.

Krout, J. (1950) *Symbol Elaboration Test* (SET), Psychol. Monogr. 64, No. 4.

Laing, A. F. (1969) 'Sociometric groupings in ESN adolescents', in *The Child and the Outside World,* Middlesex, Association for Special Education.

Laing, A. F. (1971) 'The construction of an infant school amenities index', *Brit. J. Educ. Psychol.,* **41**, 94–6.

Laing, A. F. and Chazan, M. (1966) 'Sociometric groupings among subnormal children', *Amer. J. Ment. Defic.,* **71**, 1, 73–7.

Lawrence, D. (1971) 'The effects of counselling on retarded readers', *Educ. Res.,* **13**, 2, 119–24.

Ledwith, N. H. (1960) *A Rorschach Study of Child Development,* University of Pittsburgh Press.

Lehner, G. F. J. (1960) 'Negative practice as a psychotherapeutic technique', in Eysenck, ed., *Behaviour Therapy and the Neuroses,* New York, Pergamon Press.

Leissner, A. (1967) *Family Advice Services*, London, Longmans with National Children's Bureau.

Leissner, A. *et al.* (1972) *Advice, Guidance and Assistance*, London, Longmans with National Children's Bureau.

Lenhoff, F. G. (1960) *Exceptional Children*, London, Allen & Unwin.

Levine, E. (1960) *The Psychology of Deafness*, Columbia University Press.

Levitt, E. E. (1957) 'The results of psychotherapy with children: an evaluation', *J. Consult. Psychol.* **21**, 189–96.

Levitt, E. E. (1963) 'Psychotherapy with children: a further evaluation', *Behav. Res. Ther.* **1**, 45–51.

Levy, P. (in press) On the Relation between Test Theory and Psychology, in Kline, P., ed., *New Approaches in Psychological Measurement*, London, Wiley.

Lewis, A. R. J. (1971) 'The Self-concepts of Adolescent ESN Boys', unpublished MSc thesis, University of Bradford.

Lewis, M. M. (1968) *Language and Personality in Deaf Children*, Slough, NFER.

Little, W. R. and Ntsekhe, V. R. (1959) 'Social class background of young offenders from London', *Brit. J. Delin.* **10**, 130–5.

Livingston, J. S. (1958) 'Evaluation of enlarged text forms used with the partially seeing', *Sight-Saving Rev.* **18**, 38–9.

Local Government Act 1972, London, HMSO.

Local Authority Social Services Act 1970, London, HMSO.

Lodge, T. S. (1967) 'Research and research methods', in H. J. Klare and D. Haxby, eds, *Frontiers of Criminology*, Oxford, Pergamon .

Lovell, K. (1966) 'The developmental approach of Jean Piaget', in M. Garrison, ed., *Cognitive Models and Development in Mental Retardation*. Monogr. Suppl. *Amer. J. Ment. Def.* **70**, 4, 80–9.

Lovell, K. and Bradbury, B. (1967) 'The learning of English morphology in ESN special school children', *Amer. J. Ment. Defic.* **71**, 4, 609–15.

Lovell, K. and Gorton, A. (1968) 'Some differences between backward and normal readers of average intelligence', *Brit. J. Educ. Psychol.*, **38**, 3, 240–8.

Lovell, K., Gray, E. A. and Oliver, D. E. (1964) 'A further study of some cognitive and other disabilities in backward readers of average non-verbal reasoning scores', *Brit. J. Educ. Psychol.* **34**, 275–9.

Lovell, K., Shapton, D. and Warren, N. S. (1964) 'A study of some cognitive and other disabilities in backward readers of average intelligence as assessed by a non-verbal test', *Brit. J. Educ. Psychol.* **34**, 58–64.

Lovell, K., White, C. and Whitely, R. (1965) 'Studying backward readers', *Spec. Educ.* **54**, 3, 9–13.

Lovibond, S. H. (1972) 'The qualifications and training of psychologists, 1972–1980: a case for the universities', *Australian Psychologist*, **7**, 2, 95–103.

Lowenfeld, B. (1945) *Braille and Talking Book Reading: A Comparative Study*, New York, American Foundation for the Blind.

Lowenfeld, B. (1963) 'The visually handicapped', *Rev. Educ. Res.*, **33**, 38–41.

Lowenfeld, M. (1950) 'The nature and use of the Lowenfeld World Technique with children and adults', *J. Psychol.* **30**, 325–31.

Lowenfeld, M. (1954) *The Lowenfeld Mosaic Test*, London, Newman Neame. (*See also* Ames and Learned, 1954, re Kaleidoblocs.)

Lowenstein, L. F. (1070) 'A study of the needs of the School Psychological Service in one county, assumed by head teachers', *Bull. Brit. Psychol. Soc.* **23**, 37–9.

Lund, P. (1967) 'New maths for slow learners', *Rem. Educ.*, **2**, 3, 78–81.

Lunzer, E. (1966) *The Manchester Scales of Social Adaptation*, London, NFER.

Luria, A. R. (1961) 'The role of speech in the regulation of normal and abnormal behaviour', in B. Simon and J. Simon, *Educational Psychology in the USSR*, London, Routledge & Kegan Paul.

Lyle, J. G. (1960) 'The effect of an institution environment upon the verbal development of imbecile children: 2, speech and language', *J. Ment. Def. Res.*, **4**, 1–13.

McCarthy, J. J. and Kirk, S. A. (1963) *The Construction, Standardisation and Statistical Characteristics of the Illinois Test of Psycholinguistic Abilities*, University of Illinois.

McCord, W. and McCord, J. (1959) *Origins of Crime*, Columbia University Press.

McDonald, L. (1969) *Social Class and Delinquency*, London, Faber.

McDowall, E. B., ed. (1964) *Teaching the Severely Subnormal*, London, Edward Arnold.

Macfarlane, J. W., Allen, L. and Honzik, M. P. (1954) *A Development Study of the Behaviour Problems of Normal Children between 21 months and 14 years*, University of California Publications on Child Development, Vol. 2, University of California Press.

McFie, J. (1972) 'Factors of the brain', *Bull. Brit. Psychol. Soc.* **25**, 86, 11–14.

McKerracher, D. W. (1967) 'Alleviation of reading difficulties by a simple operant conditioning technique', *J. Child Psychol. Psychiat.* **8**, 51–7.

Maclay, D. (1969) *Treatment for Children: the Work of a Child Guidance Clinic.* London, Allen & Unwin.

Maclay, I. (1967) 'Prognostic factors in child guidance practice', *J. Child Psychol. Psychiat.*, **8**, 51–6.

Maddox, H. (1952) Discussion 'The measurement of personality in children', *Brit. J. Educ. Psychol.* **22**, 205–9.

Maier, I. (1971) 'An operant approach to the modification of hyperkinetic behaviour: a preliminary report', paper given at the Annual Conference of *The British Psychological Society*, Exeter.

Mannheim, H. and Wilkins, L. T. (1955) *Prediction Methods in Relation to Borstal Training*, London, HMSO.

Manning, T. T. and Cates, J. (1972) 'Specialization within psychology', *American Psychologist*, **27**, 462–7.

Marshall, A. (1967) *The Abilities and Attainments of Children Leaving Junior Training Centres*, London, NAMH.

Matthew, G. C. (1963) 'Post-school Social Adaptation of ESN Boys', unpublished MEd. thesis, University of Manchester.

Matza, D. (1964) *Delinquency and Drift*, New York, Wiley.

Mays, J. B. (1954) *Growing Up in the City*, Liverpool University Press.

Mays, J. B. (1970) *Crime and its Treatment*, London, Longmans.

Meacham, M. C. and Wiesen, A. E. (1969) *Changing Classroom Behaviour*, Scranton, International Textbook Co.

Mental Health, monthly, *see* National Association of Mental Health.

Merritt, J. E. (1970) 'The intermediate skills: towards a better understanding of the process of fluent reading', in K. W. Gardner, ed., *Reading Skills: Theory and Practice*, London, Ward Lock Educational.

Merton, R. K. (1957) *Social Theory and Social Structure*, Illinois, Free Press of Glencoe.

Meyer, V. and Chesser, E. S. (1970) *Behaviour Therapy in Clinical Psychiatry*, Harmondsworth, Penguin Books.

Meyerson, L. (1963) 'A psychology of impaired hearing', in W. M. Cruickshank, ed., *Psychology of Exceptional Children and Youth*, 2nd edn, Englewood Cliffs, N.J., Prentice-Hall.

Mhas, O. (1970) *Group Counselling*, New York, Holt, Rinehart & Winston.

Miller, D. (1964) *Growth to Freedom*, London, Tavistock.

Miller, R. V. (1956) 'Social status and socio-empathic differences among mentally superior, mentally typical and mentally retarded children', *Except. Child.*, **23**, 114–19.

Miller, W. B. (1958) 'Lower class culture as a generating milieu of gang delinquency', *J. Social Issues*, **14**, 5–19.

Milner, B. (1954) 'Intellectual function of the temporal lobes', *Psychol. Bull.* **51**, 42–62.

Mischel, W. (1971) *Introduction to Personality*, New York, Holt, Rinehart & Winston.

Mittler, P. J. (1970a) 'Language disorders', in Mittler, ed. (1970b).

Mittler, P. J., ed. (1970b) *The Psychological Assessment of Mental and Physical Handicaps*, London, Methuen.

Mittler, P. J. (1970c) *The Work of the Hester Adrian Research Centre*, Monograph Supplement, *Teaching and Training*, **8**.

Mittler, P. J. (1971) 'Learning deficits in the severely subnormal', paper given at the Annual Conference of the British Psychological Society, Exeter.

Montgomery, G. W. G. (1968) 'A factorial study of communication and ability in deaf school leavers', *Brit. J. Educ. Psychol.* **38**, 27–37.

Moore, E. M. (1971) 'School-based therapy', *Association of Educational Psychologists Journal and Newsletter*, **2**, 8, 18–20.

Moore, T. (1964) 'Realism and fantasy in children's play', *J. Child Psychol. Psychiat.* **5**, 15–36.

Moore, T. (1966) 'Difficulties of the ordinary child in adjusting to primary school', *J. Child Psychol. Psychiat.* **7**, 1, 17–38.

Moore, T. (1967) 'Language and intelligence; a longitudinal study of the first eight years. Part I', *Hum. Dvlpmt*, **10**, 88–106; Part II, **11**, 1–24.

Moore, T. (1973) Letter to Editor, *Bull. Br. Psychol. Soc.* **26**, 90, 81.

Moore, T. and Ucko, L. E. (1961) 'Four to six: constructiveness and conflict in meeting doll play problems', *J. Child Psychol. Psychiat.* **2**, 21–47.

Moran, R. E. (1960) 'Levels of attainment of educable subnormal adolescents', *Brit. J. Educ. Psychol.* **30**, 201–10.

Morris, D. P., Soroker, E. and Burrus, J. (1954) 'Follow-up studies of shy, withdrawn children—evaluation of later adjustment', *Amer. J. Orthopsychiat.* **24**, 743–54.

Morris, H. H., Escoll, P. J. and Wexler, R. (1956) 'Aggressive behaviour-disorders of childhood: a follow-up study', *Amer. J. Psychiat.* **112**, 991–7.

Morris, T. P. (1957) *The Criminal Area*, London, Routledge & Kegan Paul.

Moseley, D. V. (1972a) *Intervening in the Learning Process I* in *Intervening in the Learning Process* Units 16 and 17 of 'Personality Growth and Learning', a second level course in Educational Studies, Bletchley; The Open University Press.

Moseley, D. V. (1972b) 'The English Colour Code programmed reading course', in Reid (1972), chs. 4, 8.

Mulligan, D. G., Douglas, J. W. B., Hammond, W. A. and Tizard, J. (1963) 'Delinquency and symptoms of maladjustment; the findings of a longitudinal study', *Proc. Roy. Soc. Med.*, **56**, 1.

Mundy, L. (1957) 'Therapy with physically and mentally handicapped children in a mental deficiency hospital', *J. Clin. Psychol.* **17**, 3–9.

Murphy, L. J. (1957) 'Tests of abilities and attainments: pupils in schools for the deaf aged six to ten', in Ewing (1957).

Murrell, K. F. H. (1969) 'Specialisation in psychology at undergraduate level', *Bull. Brit. Psychol. Soc.* **22**, 76, 189–92.

Myklebust, R. (1960) *The Psychology of Deafness*, New York, Grune & Stratton.

Naidoo, S. (1971) 'Specific developmental dyslexia', *Brit. J. Educ. Psychol.* **41**, 1, 19–22.

National Association of Mental Health, *Mental Health*, monthly.

National Association of Probation Officers, *Probation*, three times a year.

National Foundation for Educational Research, 2 Jennings Bldgs., Thames Ave., Windsor, Berks. [group and individual tests.]

National Foundation for Educational Research *Test Catalogue* (periodically issued), Windsor, NFER Publishing Co.

National Health Service Reorganisation Act 1973, London, HMSO.

Neale, M. D. (1958) *Analysis of Reading Ability*, London, Macmillan.

National Children's Bureau, *Concern*.

Newsom Report, *see* Education, Ministry of (1963)

Newson, J. and Newson, E. (1968) *Four Years Old in an Urban Community*, London, Allen & Unwin.

Nicholas, D. H. (1968) 'A Study of a Group of Partially Sighted School Leavers—Their Vocational and Social Integration Problems', unpublished thesis for Diploma in Special Education, University College of Swansea.

Nichols, L. A. (1959) 'The catarrhal child', *J. Coll. gen. Pract.* **2**, 43.

Nolan, C. Y. (1959) 'Achievement in arithmetic computation: analysis of school differences and identification of areas of low achievement', *Int. J. Educ. Blind*, **8**, 125–8.

Nuffield, E. (1961) 'Neuro-physiology and behaviour disorders in epileptic children', *J. Ment. Sci.* **107**, 348–58

Nuttall, D. L. (1973) *Principles of Constructing a Measuring Instrument*, in P. Williams and J. Bynner, eds., *Data Collection*, Bletchley, Open University Press.

Nuttall, D. L. and Moore, B. M. (1973) *Practical Aspects of Data Collection*, in Block 3 of Methods of Educational Enquiry, a 3rd Level Course in Educational Studies, Bletchley, The Open University Press.

O'Connor, N. and Hermelin, B. (1963) *Speech and Thought in Severe Subnormality*, Oxford, Pergamon.

O'Connor, N. and Tizard, J. (1956) *The Social Problem of Mental Deficiency*, Oxford, Pergamon.

Ogilvie, E. (1973) *Gifted Children in Primary Schools*. London, Macmillan.

Oliver, J. N. (1966) 'Physical education of ESN children', *Educ. Rev.* **8**, 2, 122–36.

Oppenheim, A. N. (1966) *Questionnaire Design and Attiude Measurement*, London, Heinemann.

Oseretzky, N. (motor proficiency tests) *see* Stott *et al.* (1966).

Osgood, C. E. [re linguistic analysis: *see* Kirk *et al.*].

Osgood, C. E., Suci, G. J. and Tannenbaum, P. H. (1957) *The Measurement of Meaning*, University of Illinois Press.

Oswin, M. (1967) *Behaviour Problems Amongst Children with Cerebral Palsy*, Bristol, John Wright.

Palmai, G., Storey, P. B. and Briscoe, O. (1967) 'Social class and the young offender', *Brit. J. Psychiat.* **113**, 1073–82.

Parker, R. (1966) *Decision in Child Care: a study of prediction in fostering*, London, Allen & Unwin.

Parsloe, P. (1967) *The work of the probation and after-care officer*, Routledge & Kegan Paul.

Pasamanick, B. and Knobloch, H. (1960) 'Brain damage and reproductive casualty', *Amer. J. Orthopsychiat.*, **30**, 298–305.

Patterson, B. R., McNeal, S., Hawkins, N. and Phelps, R. (1967) 'Reprogramming the social environment', *J. Child Psychol. Psychiat.*, **8**, 181–95.

Peaker, G. F. (1967) 'The Regression analysis of the National Survey', Appendix 4 to Vol. 2 of Central Advisory Council for Education, England (1967a), London, HMSO.

Peaker, G. F. (1971) *The Plowden Children Four Years Later*, Slough, NFER.

Petrie, I. R. J. (1962) 'Residential treatment of maladjusted children: a study of some factors related to progress in adjustment', *Brit. J. Educ. Psychol.*, **32**, 29–37.

Pettican, J. (1966) 'Number work at Craig-y-Parc', *Spec. Educ.* **55**, 3, 26.

Phillips, C. J. (1961) 'On comparing scores from tests of attainment with scores from tests of ability to obtain indices of retardation by differences or ratios', unpublished dissertation, University of Birmingham.

Phillips, C. J. (1971) Summerfield and after: 'the training of educational psychologists', *Bull. Br. Psychol. Soc.* **24**, 207–12.

Phillips, C. J. and Bannon, W. J. (1968) 'The Stanford-Binet Form L, Third Revision: a local English study of norms, concurrent validity and social differences', *Brit. J. Educ. Psychol.* **38**, 148–61.

Phillipson, C. M. (1971) 'Juvenile delinquency and the school' in W. G. Carson and P. Wiles, eds., *Crime and Delinquency in Britain*, London, Martin Robertson.

Phillipson, H. (1955) *The Object Relations Technique*, London, Tavistock.

Philp, A. F. and Timms, N. (1957) *The Problem of the Problem Family*, London, Family Service Units.

Pintner, R. (1942) 'Intelligence testing of partially sighted children', *J. Educ. Psychol.* **33**, 265–72.

Plowden Report: *see* Central Advisory Council for Education [England] (1967a).

Polsky, H. W. (1962) *Cottage Six: The Social System of Delinquent Boys in Residential Treatment*, New York, Russell Sage Foundation.

Porter, R. B. and Cattell, R. B. (1968) *The Children's Personality Questionnaire*, Champaign, Illinois: Inst. Personality and Ability Testing (distrib. NFER).

Porteus, S. D. (1952) *The Porteus Maze Test*, London, Harrap.

Power, M. J., Alderson, M. R., Phillipson, C. M., Shoenberg, E. and Morris, J. N. (1967) 'Delinquent Schools?', *New Society*, 19 October 1967, **10**, 264, 542–3.

Pringle, M. L. Kellmer (1964) 'The emotional and social adjustment of blind children', *Educ. Res.* **6**, 2, 129–38.

Pringle, M. L. Kellmer (1970) *Able Misfits*, London, Longman.

Pringle, M. L. Kellmer and Bossio, V. (1958) 'A study of deprived children Pt I: Intellectual, emotional and social development', *Vita Humana*, **1**, 65–92.

Pringle, M. L. Kellmer, Butler, N. R. and Davie, R. (1966) *11,000 Seven-year-olds*, London, Longman.

Pringle, M. L. Kellmer and Edwards, J. B. (1964) 'Some moral concepts and judgements of junior school children', *Brit. J. Soc. Clin. Psychol.* **3**, 196–215.

Pringle, M. L. Kellmer and Pickup, K. T. (1963) 'The reliability and validity of the Goodenough Draw-a-Man Test', *Brit. J. Educ. Psychol.* **33**, 297–306.

Pritchard, D. G. (1963) *Education and the Handicapped, 1760–1960*, London, Routledge & Kegan Paul.

Pritchard, D. G. (1968) 'Education and the handicapped—a historical survey', in A. B. Boom, ed., *Studies on the Mentally Handicapped Child*, London, Edward Arnold.

Probation, *see* National Association of Probation Officers.

Psychological Test Publications Scamps Court, Pillton Street, Barnstaple, Devon. [Test publishers and distributors.]

Pumfrey, P. D. and Elliott, C. E. (1970) 'Play therapy, social adjustment and reading attainment', *Educ. Res.*, **12**, 3, 183–93.

Rabin, A. I. and Haworth, M. R. (1960) *Projective Techniques with Children*, New York, Grune & Stratton.

Rachman, S. (1962) 'Learning theory and child psychology: therapeutic possibilities', *J. Ch. Psychol. Psychiat.* **3**, 149–63.

Rachman, S. (1971) *The Effects of Psychotherapy*, Oxford, Pergamon.

Raven, J. C. (1960–63) *Standard Progressive Matrices and Mill Hill Vocabulary Scale* (revised Manual), 1960; *Advanced Progressive Matrices* (revised, 1962); *Coloured Progressive Matrices and Crichton Vocabulary Scale* (revised Manual, 1963), London, H. K. Lewis.

Ravenette, A. T. (1968) 'Method for Administering the Grid for Children: Three methods of grid analysis', unpublished MSS available from Dr. T. Ravenette, 70 West Ham Lane, London E.15.

Reed, M. (n.d.) Hearing Test Cards. Royal National Institute for the Deaf, 105 Gower Street, London WC1.

Reed, M. (1970) 'Deaf and partially hearing children', in Mittler (1970b).

Rehin, G. F. (1972) 'Child guidance at the end of the road', *Association of Educational Psychologists Journal and Newsletter*, **3**, 2, 71–7.

Reid, J. F. (1972) *Reading: Problems and Practices*, London, Ward Lock.

Renfrew, C. E. (1966) *Articulation Attainment Test*, Oxford, The Churchill Hospital.

Report of the Tripartite Committee, 1972 (Royal College of Psychiatry, Society of Medical Officers of Health and British Medical Association). 'The Mental Health Service, after Unification', pp. 61–3.

Reynell, J. K. (1969) *Reynell Developmental Language Scales.* (*Experimental Edit.*) Slough, NFER.

Reynolds, M. C., Ellis, R. E. and Kiland, J. R. (1953) *A Study of Public School Children with Severe Mental Retardation*, St. Paul, Minnesota State Department of Education.

Richards, C. E. (1971) 'The Employment and Social Adjustment Problems faced by Partially Sighted School Leavers from a Residential School for the Visually Handicapped', unpublished thesis for Diploma in Special Education, University College of Swansea.

Robins, L. N. (1966) *Deviant Children Grown Up*, Baltimore, Williams & Wilkins.

Robins, L. N. and O'Neal, P. (1958) 'Morality, mobility and crime: problem children thirty years later', *Amer. Sociol. Rev.* **23**, 162–71.

Robinson, H. B. and Robinson, N. M. (1965) *The Mentally Retarded Child*, New York, McGraw-Hill.

Rodger, A. (1949) 'A symposium on the selection of pupils for different types of secondary schools—an industrial psychologist's point of view', *Brit. J. Educ. Psychol.* **19**, 154–9.

Roe, M. C. (1965) *Survey into Progress of Maladjusted Pupils*, London, Inner London Education Authority.

Rosenzweig, S. (1945) The picture association method and its application in a study of reactions to frustration. *J. Personality*, **14**, 3–23; and in Rabin and Haworth, 1960, ch. 8.

Rosenzweig, S. (1947) 'Revised Scoring Manual for the Rosenzweig Picture Frustration Study', *J. Psychol.* **24**, 165–208.

Rosenzweig, S. (1948) 'The children's form of the Rosenzweig Picture Frustration Study', *J. Physiol.* **26**, 141–91.

Rothwell, J. W. and Miller, K. M. (1968) *The Rothwell-Miller Interest Blank.* Windsor, NFER.

Rotter, J. B. and Rafferty, J. E. (1950) *The Rotter Incomplete Sentences Blank* (*High School Form*), New York, Psychological Corp. (distrib. NFER).

Royal Medico-Psychological Association, Child Psychiatry Section (1966) 'Report on schools and hostels for maladjusted children', *Brit. J. Psychiat.* **112**, 484, 321–8.

Royal National Institute for the Blind (1965) *Education of Blind Children*, London, RNIB.

Rushton, C. E. and Stockwin, A. E. (1963) 'Changes in Terman-Merrill IQs of educationally subnormal boys', *Brit. J. Educ. Psychol.* **33**, 132–42.

Rutter, M. (1965) 'The influence of organic and emotional factors on the origins, nature and outcome of childhood psychosis', *Develop. Med. Child. Neurol.* **7**, 518–28.

Rutter, M. (1967) 'A children's behaviour questionnaire for completion by teachers: preliminary findings'. *J. Child Psychol. Psychiat.* **8**, 1–11.

Rutter, M. (1972) *Maternal Deprivation Reassessed*, Harmondsworth, Penguin Books.

Rutter, M., Lebovici, S., Eisenberg, L., Sneznevskij, A. V., Sadoun, R., Brooke, E. and Tsung-Yi Lin (1969) 'A tri-axial classification of mental disorders in childhood: an international study', *J. Child Psychol. Psychiat*, **10**, 41–61.

Rutter, M., Yule, W., Tizard, J. and Graham, P. (1967) 'Severe reading retardation: its relationship to maladjustment, epilepsy and neurological disorders', in *What is Special Education?* Middlesex, Association for Special Education.

Rutter, M., Tizard, J. and Whitmore, K., eds. (1970) *Education, Health and Behaviour*, London, Longman.

Saenger, G. (1957) *The Adjustment of Severely Retarded Adults to the Community*. Report to the New York Inter-Departmental Health Resources Board.

Sampson, O. C. (1959) 'The speech and language of 5-year-old children', *Brit. J. Educ. Psychol.* **29**, 217–22,

Sampson, O. C. (1966) 'Reading and adjustment', *Educ. Res.* **8**, 184–90.

Sampson, O. C. (1968) 'The speech development of the severely subnormal', in A. B. Boom, ed., *Studies on the Mentally Handicapped Child*, London, Edward Arnold.

Sampson, O. C. (1969a) 'Remedial education services, Report on an enquiry I: facts and figures', *Rem. Educ.* **4**, 1, 3–8.

Sampson, O. C. (1969b) 'Remedial education services, Report on an enquiry II: views and methods', *Rem. Educ.* **4**, 2, 61–5.

Sampson, O. C. and Pumfrey, P. D. (1970) 'A study of remedial education in the secondary stage of schooling', *Rem. Educ.* **5**, 3/4, 102–11.

Sands, D. E. (1956) 'The psychoses of adolescence', *J. Ment. Sci.* **102**, 308–18.

Sarason, S. B., Davidson, K. S., Lighthall, F. F., Waite, R. R. and Ruebush, B. K. (1960) *Anxiety in Elementary School Children*, New York and London, Wiley.

Savage, R. D. and O'Connor, D. J. (1966) 'The assessment of reading and arithmetic retardation in the school', *Brit. J. Educ. Psychol.* **36**, 317–18.

Schaefer, E. and Bell, R. Q. (1968) 'Development of a parent attitude research instrument', *Child Development*, **29**, 339–61.

Schneidman, E. S. (1960) 'The MAPS test with children', in Rabin and Haworth (1960), ch. 7.

Schonell, F. E. (1956) *Educating Spastic Children*, Edinburgh, Oliver & Boyd.

Schonell, F. J. and Schonell, F. E. (1956) *Diagnostic and Attainment Testing*, Edinburgh, Oliver & Boyd.

Schonell, F. J. and Schonell, F. E. (1957) *Diagnosis and Remedial Teaching in Arithmetic*, Edinburgh, Oliver & Boyd.

Scott Report, *see* Health, Ministry of (1961).

Scott, W. S. (1959) 'Definitions of mental health and illness', in L. Gorlow and W. Katkovsky, eds., *Readings in the Psychology of Adjustment*, New York, McGraw-Hill.

Scottish Education Department (1950) *Pupils Who Are Defective in Vision*, Edinburgh, HMSO.

Sears, R. R., Maccoby, E. E. and Levin, H. (1957) *Patterns of Child Rearing*, New York, Row, Peterson.

Seebohm Report, *see* Home Office (1968a).

Segal, S. (1967) *No Child is Ineducable*, Oxford, Pergamon.

Sen, A. and Clarke, A. M. (1968) 'Some factors affecting distractability in the mental retardate', *Amer. J. Ment. Defic.* **73**, 50–60.

Seth, S. (1972) 'Psychologists in education services: some basic principles of professional training', *Association of Educational Psychologists Journal and Newsletter*, **3**, 2, 4–18.

Shapiro, M. B. (1970) 'Intensive assessment of the single case: an inductive-deductive approach', in Mittler, ed. (1970b).

Shaw, O. L. (1966) *Maladjusted Boys*, London, Allen & Unwin.

Shaw, R. C. and McKay, H. D. (1942) *Juvenile Delinquency and Urban Areas*, University of Chicago Press.

Shearer, E. (1968) 'Physical skills and reading backwardness', *Educ. Res.* **10**, 3, 197–206.

Shepherd, M., Oppenheim, A. N. and Mitchell, S. (1966) 'Childhood behaviour disorders and the child guidance clinic: an epidemiological study', *J. Child Psychol. Psychiat.* **3**, 39–52.

Sheridan, M. D. (1948) *The Child's Hearing for Speech*, London, Methuen.

Sheridan, M. (1968) *The Stycar Hearing Tests*, rev. edn; *The Stycar Vision Tests*, rev. edn, Windsor, NFER.

Slavson, S. R., ed. (1947) *The Practice of Group Therapy*, London, The Pushkin Press.

Snijders, J. T. H. and Snijders-Oomen, N. (1959) *Non-verbal Intelligence Test*, Groningen, J. B. Wolters.

Social Work Today, *see* British Association of Social Workers.

Sommers, V. S. (1944) *The Influence of Parental Attitudes and Social Environment*, New York, American Foundation for the Blind.

Sprott, W. J. H. (1954) *The Social Background of Delinquency*, Nottingham University Press.

Statement by Multidisciplinary Working Party on Future Administration of Child Guidance and Child Psychiatric Services. (B.P.S., Royal College of Psychiatry, B.A.S.W.A.—Mental Health section, Association of Child Psychotherapists.)

Stein, Z. A. and Stores, G. (1965) 'IQ changes in educationally subnormal children at special school', *Brit. J. Educ. Psychol.* **35**, 379–81.

Stein, Z. A. and Susser, M. (1960a) Families of dull children Part II—Identifying family types and subcultures, *J. Ment. Sci.* **106**, 445, 1296–303.

Stein, Z. A. and Susser, M. (1960b) 'Families of dull children Part III—Social selection by family type, *J. Ment. Sci.* **106**, 445, 1304–10.

Stephen, E. and Robertson, J. (1965) 'Normal child development and handi-capped children', in S. G. Howells, ed., *Modern Perspectives in Child Psychiatry*, Edinburgh and London, Oliver & Boyd.

Stott, D. H. (1959) 'Evidence for pre-natal impairment of temperament in mentally retarded children', *Vita Humana*, **2**, 125–48.

Stott, D. H. (1960a) 'Delinquency, maladjustment and unfavourable ecology', *Brit. J. Psychol.*, **51**, 157–70.

Stott, D. H. (1960b) *A Delinquency Prediction Instrument*, London, University of London Press.

Stott, D. H. (1960c) 'Observations on retest discrepancy in mentally subnormal children', *Brit. J. Educ. Psychol.*, **30**, 211–19.

Stott, D. H. (1961) *Third Report of the Glasgow Survey of Boys put on Probation during 1957*, Glasgow, University Press.

Stott, D. H. (1962) 'Evidence for a congenital factor in maladjustment and delinquency', *Amer. J. Psychiat.* **118**, 781–94.

Stott, D. H. (1963a) 'The assessment of mentally handicapped children', *Medical Officer*, **110**, 235–9.

Stott, D. H. (1963b; 3rd edn, 1966a; 4th edn, 1971a) *The Social Adjustment of Children: Manual to the Bristol Social Adjustment Guides*, 2nd edn, London, University of London Press.

Stott, D. H. (1963c) 'How a disturbed pregnancy can harm the child', *New Scientist*, **320**, 13–17.

Stott, D. H. (1966) *Studies of Troublesome Children*, London, Tavistock.

Stott, D. H. (1971) *Learning to Learn: manual for the Flying Start Reading Scheme*, Guelph, Ont., Brook Educ. Pub. Co.

Stott, D. H., Moyes, F. A. and Headridge, S. E. (1966) *Test of Motor Impairment*, Glasgow University Press.

Strauss, A. A. and Kephart, N. C. (1955) *Psychology and education of the brain-injured child II*, New York, Grune and Stratton.

Strauss, A. A. and Lehtinen, C. A. (1947) *The Psychopathology of the Brain-injured Child*, New York, Grune & Stratton.

Stutsman, R. (1931) *Mental Measurement of Preschool Children*, Yonkers-on-Hudson, New York, World Book Co. (Manual for the Merrill-Palmer Test).

Summerfield Report, *see* Department of Education and Science, 1968b

Sumner, R. and Warburton, F. W. (1972) *Achievement in Secondary School*, Slough, NFER.

Sutherland, E. H. (1960, 6th edn, ed. D. R. Cressey) *Principles of Criminology*, New York, Lippincott.

Sutherland, J. D. and Gill, H. S. (1970) *Language and Psychodynamic Appraisal: a Development of the Word Association Method*, London, Tavistock Inst. Human Relations Resch. Pubs.

Tanner, J. M. (1961) *Education and Physical Growth*, London, University of London Press.

Tansley, A. E. (1951) 'The Use of Text Data and Case History Information as Indications for the Educational Treatment of ESN children', unpublished MEd thesis, University of Birmingham.

Tansley, A. E. (1966) 'Studying children "at risk" ', *Spec. Educ.* **55**, 15–18.

Tansley, A. E. and Gulliford, R. (1960) *The Education of Slow Learning Children*, London, Routledge & Kegan Paul.

Taylor, I. G. (1971) 'Recent developments in the education of deaf children', in I. Petrie, ed., *Handicapped Children—Their Potential and Fulfilment*, Cheshire, Joint Council for Education of Handicapped Children.

Taylor, W. W. and Taylor, I. W. (1966) *Services for Handicapped Youth in England and Wales*, New York, International Society for Rehabilitation of the Disabled.

Telford, C. W. and Sawrey, J. M. (1967) *The Exceptional Individual*, Englewood Cliffs, N.J., Prentice-Hall.

Templin, M. (1950) *The Development of Reasoning in Children with Normal and Defective Hearing*, University of Minnesota Press.

Templin, M. C. and Darley, F. L. (1960) *The Templin-Darley Tests of Articulation*, Bureau of Educ. Rsch. and Services, University of Iowa.

Terman, L. M. (1925) *Genetic Studies of Genius I*, Stanford University Press.

Terman, L. M. and Merrill, M. A. (1937) *Measuring intelligence*, London, Harrap.

Terman, L. M. and Merrill, M. A. (1961) *Stanford-Binet Intelligence Scale: Manual for the third revision, Form L-M*, London, Harrap. (Modification for sensory impairment: see BPS, undated.)

The Child, The Family and the Young Offender *see* Home Office (1965).

Thomas, A., Birch, H. G., Chess, C., Hertzig, M. E. and Korn, S. (1963) *Behavioural Individuality in Early Childhood*, New York University Press.

Timms, N. (1962) *Casework in the Child Care Service*, London, Butterworth.

Timms, N. (1964) *Social Casework: principles and practice*, London, Routledge & Kegan Paul.

Tizard J. (1964) *Community Care of the Mentally Handicapped*, Oxford University Press.

Tizard, J. and Grad, J. G. (1961) *The Mentally Handicapped and their Families*, Maudsley Monographs, 7, Oxford University Press.

Trasler, G. B. (1962) *The Explanation of Criminality*, London, Routledge & Kegan Paul.

Trasler, G. B. (1970) 'Delinquency', in H. J. Butcher and H. B. Pont, eds., *Educational Research in Britain 2*, London, University of London Press.

Turner, R. H. (1970) *Family Interaction*, New York, Wiley.

Tyerman, M. J. (1958) 'A research into truancy', *Brit. J. Educ. Psychol.* **28**, 217–25.

Ucko, L. E. and Moore, T. (1963) 'Parental roles as seen by young children in doll play', *Vita Humana* (now *Human Development*), **6**, 213–42.

Ullman, L. and Krasner, L. (1965) *Case Studies in Behaviour Modification*, New York, Holt, Rinehart & Winston.

Underwood Report, *see* Education, Ministry of (1955).

Valett, R. E. (1963) *The Practice of School Psychology: professional problems*, New York, Wiley.

Varma, V., ed. (1973) *Stresses in Children*, London, University of London Press.

Vaughan, T. D. (1970) *Educational and Vocational Guidance Today*, London; Routledge & Kegan Paul.

Vernon Report, *see* Education and Science, Department of (1972b).

Vernon, M. D. (1957) *Backwardness in Reading*, Cambridge University Press.

Vernon, M. D. (1971) *Reading and its Difficulties*, Cambridge University Press.

Vernon, P. E. (1949) *Graded Arithmetic Mathematics Test*, London, University of London Press.

Vernon, P. E., ed. (1957) *Secondary School Selection*, London, Methuen.

Vernon, P. E. (1964) *Personality Assessment: a critical survey*, London, Methuen.

Vernon, P. E. (1960) *Intelligence and Attainment Testing*, London, University of London Press.

Vernon, P. E. (1969a) *Intelligence and Cultural Environment*, London, Methuen.

Vernon, P. E. (1969b) *The Standardisation of a Graded Word Reading Test*, London, University of London Press.

Vincent, P. M. and Wolff, J. (1970) 'A Survey of the Unit for Delicate Children in Swansea', unpublished thesis submitted in part fulfilment of the requirements for the Post-Graduate Diploma in Educational Psychology of the University College of Swansea.

Wagner, E. E. (1969) *The Hand Test: Manual*, Los Angeles, Western Psychological Services.

Wahler, R. G., Winkel, G. H., Peterson, R. E. and Morrison, D. C. (1965) 'Mothers as behaviour therapists for their own children', *Beh. Res. and Therapy*, **3**, 113–24.

Walker, N. (1965) *Crime and Punishment in Britain*, Edinburgh University Press.

Wall, W. D., ed. (1956) *Psychological Services for Schools*, New York University Press (for Unesco).

Warburton, F. W. (1968) 'The Relationship between Personality Factors and Scholastic Attainment', unpublished report, Department of Education, University of Manchester.

Warburton, F. W., Fitzpatrick, T. F., Ward, J. and Ritchie, M. (1970) 'Some problems in the construction of individual intelligence tests', in Mittler, ed. (1970b).

Ward, J. (1971) 'Modification of deviant classroom behaviour', *Brit. J. Educ. Psychol*, **41**, 304–13.

Warren, W. (1965) 'A study of adolescent psychiatric inpatients and the outcome six or more years later. Part I: Clinical histories and hospital findings. Part II: The follow-up study', *J. Child Psychol. Psychiat.* **6**, 1–17, 141–60.

Warren, W. (1971) ' "You can never plan the future by the past": the development of child and adolescent psychiatry in England and Wales', *J. Child Psychol. Psychiat.* **11**, 241–59.

Watson, J. (1970) *The Juvenile Court 1970 Onwards*, London, Shaw & Sons.

Watson, T. J. (1967) *The Education of Hearing-Handicapped Children*, London, University of London Press.

Watts, A. F. (1948) *The Holborn Reading Scale*, London, Harrap.

Weaver, A. F. (1968) 'A Survey of the Treatment of Maladjusted Children within the Educational system in England', unpublished PhD thesis, Oxford University.

Wechsler, D. (1949) *The Wechsler Intelligence Scale for Children* (WISC).

Wechsler, D. (1955) *The Wechsler Adult Intelligence Scale* (WAIS)

Wechsler, D. (1963) *The Wechsler Preschool and Primary Scale of Intelligence* (WPPSI), New York, Psychological Corp.

Wechsler, D. (1971) British amended editions of the above, Windsor, NFER.

Wedell, K. (1972). 'Diagnosing learning difficulties: a sequential strategy', in J. F. Reid (1972), ch. 4.

Wepman, J. M. (1958) *Auditory Discrimination Test*, Chicago, Lang. Resch. Assoc. (distrib. NFER).

Wepman, J. M. and Heine, R. W. (1963) *Concepts of Personality*, Chicago, Aldine.

Werry, J. S. (1972) 'Organic factors in childhood psychopathology', in H. C. Quay and J. S. Werry, eds., *Psychopathological Disorders in Childhood*, New York, Wiley

West, D. J. (1967) *The Young Offender*, Harmondsworth, Penguin Books.

West, D. J. (1969) *Present Conduct and Future Delinquency*, London, Heinemann.

Westman, J. C., Rice, D. L. and Berman, E. (1967) 'Nursery school behaviour and later school adjustment', *Amer. J. Orthopsychiat.* **3**, 7, 4, 725–31.

Whelan, R. J. (1966) 'The relevance of behaviour modification procedures for teachers of emotionally disturbed children', in P. Knobloch, ed., *Intervention Approaches in Educating Emotionally Disturbed Children*, Syracuse University Press.

Wilkins, L. T. (1963) 'Juvenile delinquency—a critical review of research and theory', *Educ. Res.* **5**, 104–19.

Williams, D. J. (1969) 'Maladjustment and reading difficulties 3: Remedial treatment', *Rem. Educ.* **4**, 3, 129–33.

Williams, J. D. (1970) 'Programmed instruction and the difficulties of learning mathematics', *Rem. Educ.* **5**, 3/4, 112–15.

Williams, N. (1961) 'Criteria for Recovery of Maladjusted Children in Residential Schools', unpublished MEd thesis, University of Durham.

Williams, P. (1966) 'Some characteristics of ESN children', *Brit. J. Psychiatry*, **112**, 482, 79–90.

Williams, P. (1970) 'Slow-learning children and educational problems', in Mittler, ed. (1970b).

Williams, P. (1972) 'Assessment Problems in Maladjustment and Learning', Unit 12 of *Personality Growth and Learning*, a second level course published by the Open University Press, Milton Keynes.

Williams, P. (1974) ed., *Behaviour Problems in School*, London, University of London Press.

Willmott, D. (1973) *Principles of Measurement in Data Collection*, P. Williams and J. Bynner eds., Bletchley, Open University Press.

Willmot, P. (1967) *Consumer's Guide to the British Social Services*, Harmondsworth, Penguin Books.

Wills, W. D. (1960) *Throw Away Thy Rod*, London, Gollancz.

Wills, W. D. (1971) *Spare the Child*, Harmondsworth, Penguin Books.

Wilson, H. (1962) *Delinquency and Child Neglect*, London, Allen & Unwin.

Winnicott, D. W. (1964) *The Child, the Family and the Outside World*, London, Penguin.

Winnicott, D. W. (1965) *The Family and Individual Development*, London, Tavistock.

Wiseman, S. and Fitzpatrick, T. F. (1955). *The Devon Interest Blank*, London, Oliver & Boyd.

Wiseman, S. and Wrigley, J. (1959) *The Manchester Reading Comprehension Test (Senior)*, London: University of London Press.

Witkin, H. A. (1960) *Embedded Figures Test*, Palo Alto, California, Consulting Psychologists Press (distrib. NFER).

Witkin, H. A., Dyk, R. B., Faterson, H. F., Goodenough, D. R. and Karp, S. A. (1962) *Psychological Differentiation: Studies in Development*, New York, Wiley.

Wolff, S. (1961) 'Symptomatology and outcome of preschool children with behaviour disorders attending a child guidance clinic', *J. Child Psychol. Psychiat.* **2**, 269–75.

Wolff, S. (1969) *Children under Stress*, London, The Penguin Press.

Wollman, D. C. (1964) 'The attainments in English and Arithmetic of secondary school pupils with impaired hearing', *Brit. J. Educ. Psychol.* **34**, 268–74.

Wolpe, J. (1958) *Psychotherapy by Reciprocal Inhibition*, Stanford University Press.

Wood, D. A. (1960) *Test Construction*, Columbus, Ohio, C. E. Merrill.

Woods, G. E. (1957) *Cerebral Palsy in Childhood*, Bristol, John Wright.

Woodward, W. M. (1955) *Low Intelligence and Delinquency*, London, ISTO.

Woodward, W. M. (1962) 'The application of Piaget's theory to the training of the subnormal', *J. Ment. Subnormality*, 8, 17–25.

Woodward, W. M. (1970) 'The assessment of cognitive processes: Piaget's approach', in Mittler, ed. (1970b).

Woody, R. H. (1969) *Behavioural Problem Children in the Schools*, New York, Appleton-Century-Crofts.

Wootton, B. (1959) *Social Science and Social Pathology*, London, Allen & Unwin.

Worster-Drought, C. (1968) 'Speech disorders in children', *Developm. Med. Child Neurol.* **10**, 427–40.

Wright, H. J. (1972) 'The interpretation of Terman-Merrill scores for British populations', *Occasional Papers* of the Division of Educational and Child Psychology of the British Psychological Society, **1**, 29–35.

Wynn, M. (1972) *Family Policy*, Harmondsworth, Penguin Books.

Yablonsky, L. (1962) *The Violent Gang*, New York, Macmillan.

Young, D. (1964) *Non-Readers' Intelligence Test*, London, University of London Press.

Young, D. and Stirton, M. E. (1971) 'Graded Word Reading Test equivalences and reading ages', *Remedial Education*, **6**, 3, 7–8.

Younghusband, E., Birchall, D., Davie, R. and Pringle, M. L. K., eds. (1970) *Living with Handicap*, London, National Bureau for Cooperation in Child Care.

Yudkin, S. (1967) *0–5: Report on the Care of Pre-School Children*, London, National Society of Children's Nurseries.

Yule, W. (1967) 'Predicting reading ages on Neale's Analysis of Reading Ability', *Brit. J. Educ. Psychol.* **36**, 252–5.

Yule, W. (1969) 'Maladjustment and reading difficulties II: the findings of the Isle of Wight studies', *Rem. Educ.* **4**, 3, 124–8.

Yule, W., Berger, M., Butler, S., Newham, V. and Tizard, J. (1969) 'The WPPSI: an empirical evaluation with a British sample', *Brit. J. Educ. Psychol.* **39**, 1–13.

Yule, W., Lockyer, L. and Noone, A. (1967) 'The reliability and validity of the Goodenough-Harris Drawing Test', *Brit. J. Educ. Psychol.* **37**, 110–11.

Zahran, H. A. S. (1965) 'A study of the personality differences between blind and sighted children', *Brit. J. Educ. Psychol.* **35**, 329–38.

Zazzo, R. (1960) 'Une recherche d'équipe sur la débilité mentale', *Enfance*, **4/5**, 335–64.

Zeaman, D. and House, B. J. (1963) 'The role of attention in retardate discrimination learning', in N. R. Ellis, ed., *Handbook of Mental Deficiency*, New York, McGraw-Hill.

Subject Index

Author Index